# Crossing Centuries

## A Road Trip Through Colonial Africa

BY

# Irene Tinker

*To Martin & Wendy —*

*Great internationalists.*

PORTLAND • OREGON
INKWATERPRESS.COM

www.inkwaterpress.com

ISBN-13 978-1-59299-471-7
ISBN-10 1-59299-471-7

Publisher: Inkwater Press

Printed in the U.S.A.
*All paper is acid free and meets all ANSI standards for archival quality paper.*

1 3 5 7 9 10 8 6 4 2

*To all the many people in Africa who made this trip exciting, informative, and possible; to those who offered assistance and meals and drinks and beds to us; and to my companion on the trip in Africa and through life, I dedicate this book.*

# Backstory

$\mathcal{F}$IFTY YEARS AGO THE WORLD WAS IN THE MIDST OF A CATA-
clysmic change. World War II had undermined the European colonial powers, the countries they had controlled were
in turmoil as nationalism swept the globe. Yet these momentous events were hardly mentioned in my undergraduate
studies at Harvard where my government courses focused
on Europe while political philosophy delved into ancient
Greece. I wanted to experience and understand what was
happening in the world.

Instead of staying in the US for graduate work, I enrolled
in the fall of 1951 at the London School of Economics with
its diverse student body, many from the colonies. Listening
to their discussions and debates, I was chagrined at my lack
of knowledge about their countries and histories. I quickly
learned to ask questions, then listen.

One incident stands out. On a chill November evening

a group of us were sitting around the glowing fireplace in student digs at Oxford. The young woman next to me on the couch sighed, saying how a fire reminded her of home, in Nairobi. Now, in sixth grade I had drawn a map of Africa on a wooden slate, and colored in the countries with flour paste. I remembered drawing the line for the equator right through Kenya and imagining the country filled with the hot jungles so vividly projected in Tarzan movies. I couldn't image why you would need a fire to warm yourself in the jungle, but by then I was smart enough not to say anything. Instead, I went to the library and looked up Nairobi – elevation over five thousand feet.

London was a great place to broaden my worldview. The city was still filled with bomb sites, rationing continued, but the National Health Plan had been passed and as a student I was eligible. Debates about this centerpiece of Labour legislation escalated when the government called for election in February 1950. Winston Churchill, who lost in the July 1945 elections, hoped for a comeback. Those elections were a stunning loss for Churchill, but the country was weary of war and did not support his desire to hold onto the British Empire. Rather the English were searching for greater equity at home and abroad. Independence for India was promoted by the Labour government while Churchill famously said that he had not won the war to lose the empire. Already my fellow students from independent India lectured me about their new Constitution and the coming elections. Having immersed myself in the British elections in 1950, I decided to investigate how British institutions were being adapted to India and spent the next year studying its history and culture and figuring out how to get there.

My thousand dollar grant, which had provided support for two years in London as well as train travel in Europe, was nearly exhausted. Happily my application for a travel grant for another thousand was successful. Airplane travel was not yet common and quite expensive; I had taken a boat to London but I decided to go overland to India. My notice on the LSE bulletin board brought two others into this adventure. We agreed to share the cost of the Ford Anglia which I had bought from a couple working for the Marshall Plan in Paris for fifteen hundred dollars. The car had an international license plate which facilitated our travels. In return for articles describing the journey which were published in the Ford magazine, the Ford Company had their mechanics do a thorough check up of the car. They also provided a repair kit and arranged for a second check up in Jordan.

That journey was a fine preparation for the Africa trip, though not nearly as challenging. My articles focused on the road and the car more than the political turmoil though which we drove, but I continued to ask questions of everyone, and listen. Nationalism was high in Iran, so we decided to fly an American flag on our English car. Along the route we bunked with fellow students from LSE, stayed in student hostels and pilgrim inns, and even camped out in empty houses of diplomats.

The desert tracks in Afghanistan seemed remote, but were much more traveled than those we encountered in Africa. In Kabul we were lucky to have one room for the three of us since the hotel was crowded with Pathans who were sleeping on chairs and floors outside our room. They were celebrating independence from British control and demanding that a new state of Paktunistan be carved out of Pakistan and Afghanistan. One turbaned sheikh demanded that we smuggle some guns across the border. Realizing the danger of doing smuggling and worried that the Pathan might threaten us, we sneaked out of the hotel in early morning while he slept.

The mountains on either side of the dirt road leading to the border were lined with stone forts, and men with guns. Our relief at reaching the Pakistan customs station was immense: the smartly dressed officer welcomed us as classical music from the BBC filled the air.

Once in New Delhi, my companions took the train to Bombay and a boat to London, leaving me to sell the car and repay each their five hundred dollar investment. I was shocked to learn that the international license meant that no taxes had been paid on the car since the owner had diplomatic status. At the time, India had 100% tax on automobiles, pricing our tiny car out of the market. Searching for diplomat to buy it tax-free, I met a young Foreign Service officer, Millidge Walker, who, after a brief courtship, bought out my companions as my bride price. Our wedding was held in New Delhi on 2 February 1952; we have been married for fifty-eight years.

Although I affiliated with Delhi School of Economics, I soon found that newspaper reporters were by far the best source of information on the upcoming elections. I had obtained press credentials from a London magazine that allowed me to attend briefings by the Election Commission and debates in the Indian Parliament. Concerned about the vast numbers of illiterate voters, the commission introduced many innovations that have since been widely copied such as the use of symbols for candidates and making all voters with indelible ink.

During the elections, I traveled throughout the country interviewing government officials, politicians, and voters. Because the actual dates of voting were staggered to allow experienced election officials to supervise several states, I could write up once state study before moving to another state. Several of these case studies were immediately published in London because so little information was available. I realized that political observations were as saleable as travel articles.

After the elections I interviewed members of all the various parties including a Sunday morning interview with Prime Minister Jawaharlal Nehru. The workings of parliament intrigued me: the religious and ethnic diversity of members had to be considered in all policy debates. Historically over ten groups had had separate seats filled by voters from separate lists. Muslims had their own list separating them from the general electoral rolls. Having separate seats exacerbated the tensions between Hindus and Muslims, instead of encouraging compromise, and were instrumental in the Partition of the country which created a separate Pakistan. The Indian Constitution abolished all separate seats. I began to wonder whether other British colonies were still giving separate representation to different groups or were trying to create a national identity in countries not yet independent.

So when it was time to pack up my notes and return to London, I reiterated my desire to drive back to London through Africa. That way I could also observe how other colonial powers had influenced the countries they controlled. I arranged to write commentaries on the Indian communities in East Africa for the English language newspaper, the Calcutta *Statesman*. Then I contacted a literary agent in New York City about publishing a *New Yorker* style travel/commentary book on our travels.

Since Mil had decided to resign from the Foreign Service and return to graduate school, we planned on spending five or six months on the trip. For the resignation to be accepted, he had to return to Washington for de-briefing. We were astounded when he was told that he would not be paid for our travel until he appeared! Thus a major constraint for our road trip was our available cash. Also I needed to be in London for my final academic year while I completed my doctoral dissertation.

The first thing we did in preparation for the trip was to prepay for a car to be picked up in Mombasa, Kenya. Of course we would have preferred a Land Rover because of its rugged reputation, but we could not afford one and so settled on an Austin A40. It was not an ideal choice, but it was all we could afford and dealer was willing to ship it to Mombasa. The second thing was to reserve a passage on the ferry across the English Channel. In the days before the Chunnel linking England and France, it was necessary to reserve and pay for the ferry months in advance. Our date for the ferry was 22 June 1953. After paying these costs and for the boat from Bombay to Mombasa, I made a budget for our remaining cash and decided that we had to keep our daily costs to ten dollars a day.

We packed all our winter clothes and my research notes for London, sent household goods to Mil's mother in New York. While Mil finished his work, I wrote letters to everyone we knew or had been given introductions to along the way. I collected information about roads and routes, and poured over the newspapers for articles about the Mau Mau in Kenya and the unrest in the Belgian Congo and Ethiopia. I read history books about pygmies and Arab slavers, about European countries contesting power in Africa. None of this prepared me for the realities of our road trip.

We had planned to leave New Delhi the end of November to allow us time to visit the palaces and temples of southern India. The night before we were to depart Mil came down with a raging fever. For a week the doctors were baffled. Mil was isolated; even his eating utensils had to be kept separate. Only when his eyes took on a yellow cast was he diagnosed with jaundice though the cause was uncertain. The fever left him exhausted; weeks of bed rest were prescribed. We discussed the Africa trip with the doctor. He believed that whatever had caused the jaundice was cured; what Mil had to do while he regained his strength was to rest often and drink lots of glucose.

Finally, a year after we married, we embarked for Africa. Throughout the trip I kept copious notes and wrote several articles for the *Statesman*. Trying to write a book in the midst of travel proved very difficult. Much of the manuscript published here was written in the year after we reached London. My agent thought she found a publisher, but their interest in my serious travel book was overshadowed by the romantic tale of the affair between its author and the Prince of Morocco. Ironically, two years later, I was asked to review this light-hearted tale for the *San Francisco Chronicle* while I was working as a researcher at the University of California Berkeley where Mil was enrolled for his doctoral studies.

And so the manuscript languished though I utilized the information about colonial Africa in college courses I taught over the years. The political commentary became dated. My academic publications pushed this adventure to the background. Now, over fifty years later, the book has become an historical document, a glimpse of the time when most of Africa was still controlled by European powers. Nationalism was emerging among the educated but many people lived as they had for centuries. For the reader, **Crossing Centuries** provides background to the origins of the many political struggles and civil wars that have wracked the region.

# Crossing Centuries

A Road Trip Through Colonial Africa

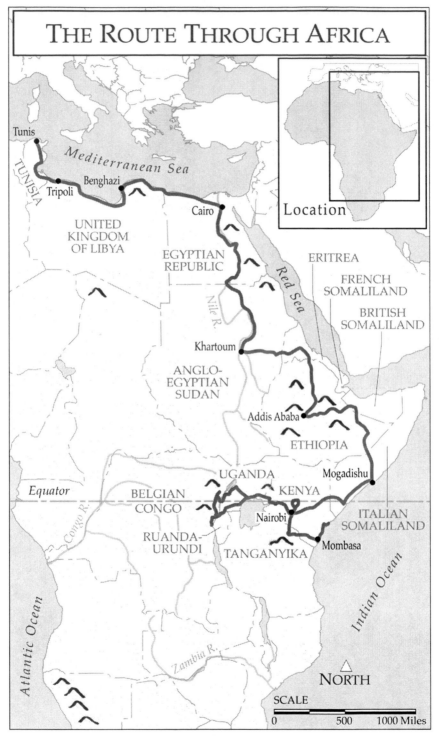

Map of the route

# Part I

Unrest in Colonial East Africa

CHAPTER 1

# Getting to Africa

THE FIRST IDEA OF THE TRIP HOME CAME ON THE TRIP OUT, FOR what goes must come! I'd driven out to India through the Middle East, which is another story. But it had taught me where places are, not only on a map, but in what sort of surroundings. I learned that two hundred miles are not always merely two hundred miles, that it may be five hours or ten hours or two days away. And this you do not learn from a map. You taste the dust, broil during long days across desert and steppe, sleep in strange often dirty places, get ill from the food, go weeks without a proper bath – are generally exposed to all the things that keep some people coming home but make others, like me, confirmed travelers. For in all this you learn, and grow, and meet people, and begin to understand.

Perhaps in a slower world, in the romantic age, I would

5

have sailed by clipper around the world or taken a camel caravan to Samarkand. But I was born in the wrong century, of the wrong parents. I had no inheritance to feather my bed, but I had learned how to obtain grants for graduate study, first in London and then in India where I would gather material for my doctoral dissertation. Go by boat and miss all the countries in between? No, I said to myself, go by car at less cost and with oh so much more understanding. And so I did.

India's first national election after its independence was scheduled for 1952; its government's decision to allow all illiterates to vote was viewed skeptically around the world. I planned to study the electoral process and politics. New Delhi in August radiated heat; the British sent wives and children to the hill stations, a practiced continued by most foreigners in those pre-air conditioned days. As one of few young women in the capital, I was invited to receptions most evenings and met a tall blond single man who worked at the American Embassy, Millidge Walker. Born in Shanghai, Mil had been trained as a Japanese interpreter in World War II, and had studied political science. We found we had much to talk about.

Also at these receptions I met both foreign correspondents and Indian reporters who wrote for the English language newspapers. It was quickly apparent that these Indian journalists had the best grasp of Indian politics and understood the preparations for the election. Several began to tutor me in the intricacies of party politics as I absorbed the culture and government of the country. The Electoral Commission staggered voting dates around the country so that their members could supervise the actual elections around the country. This arrangement was a great help for my research as I was able to observe actual voting in five different parts of the country.

One of the first states to vote was tiny Himachal Pradesh,

situated in the foothills the Himalayas bordering on Tibet. Since snow would block passes and tracks well into the summer, the elections were held in November 1951. Would the citizens, less than five percent of whom were literate, bother to walk five or ten miles to put a piece of paper in one of the boxes, each with a party symbol on the front? I went as far up the India-Tibet Road as was possible in a motor vehicle to try to find out what the mountain peasant understood about this strange process called voting.

They voted in Narkanda on Thanksgiving. Thanksgiving is also a holiday in all American Embassies. So Mil offered to come up to Narkanda and drive me back to my base at the YMCA in New Delhi. After early morning observation at a polling booth, we climbed up a hill above a narrow dirt track where the road had turned into a donkey trail. We carried our sandwiches there away form the political turmoil in the village of Kotgarh below in the valley, and sat on the cushion of pine needles. The light flickered through to our rock table, turning our minds away from the immediate. Elections, today-tomorrow-yesterday, seemed trivial in the face of the ageless Himalayas. We sat in awe of mystery and majesty, holding hands and letting the endless universe envelope us. The raw power of nature seemed to fuse our hearts as it fate were speaking. Such deep stirrings cannot be put into words, but I understood that this wonderful man did not challenge my fierce independence, but complemented it. Together where could we not go, what could we not do? Hushed, staggered by our revelation, almost frightened by our joy, we sat mesmerized.

A temple gong brought us back to the day. Words and plans and kisses tumbled out. We began to list all the places we wanted to see, together. "Ceylon and Kulu," Mil began, "and I'd like to show you the school I went to in Shanghai."

"Kalimpong, Manipur, Nepal!" I added. "And when we drive home, it must be through Africa."

As we drove back to the plains we planned our wedding to take place after I had observed the elections in four more states. For our honeymoon, after the elections were almost over, we went back to the hills, to those brooding silent snow-capped Himalayas. Our lodge was actually in a district where the people had not yet voted; but all I saw of this election were the party symbols on every store and tree.

In the year that followed we went to Kulu and to Kalimpong; we haven't been to Ceylon or Shanghai, not yet. And we began to plan our trip home via Africa. At first we thought of driving all the way, that is along the Indian Ocean through Pakistan and Iran, across Saudi Arabia to the Red Sea and on into Egypt. Geographically this is possible; politically it is not. The intransigence on both sides of the Israeli-Arab conflict meant that driving from Jordan to Egypt across the Sinai Peninsula was impossible. So you'd still have to take a boat somewhere.

Dismissing this, we next looked into boats from India to Africa. A cargo that tramped between Colombo and Cape Town every three months did not sound promising but there was a regular fortnightly service between Bombay and the east coast of Africa. This seemed the best choice and we made our reservations for departure in January 1953 and ordered an automobile sent out from London to Mombasa. With reservations on a ferry across the English Channel the end of June, we would have six months to explore African and its politics. When Mil's illness postponed our departure to Mombasa by a month, we knew we might have to shorten our route, but how we did not know.

The Automobile Association in London collected information on out-of-the-way travel. They'd issued mimeographed routing schedules for the Middle East trip out, so I wrote them about Africa. Back came a four hundred page book called "Trans-African Highways." How tame, I thought, to have adventure so nicely bound up. The book gave details of two routes from East Africa to Europe. They recommended putting your car on a Nile steamer from Uganda to Luxor, then driving north to Cairo and east across the top of the continent. A second route took the traveler east through central Africa, then north across the Sahara. The state of roads through central Africa was uncertain, and "motorists must be prepared to encounter heavy drift sand, water courses, many of which have steep banks and are difficult to negotiate, marshes and rivers."

Once you reached Niger, you then had to cross the Sahara on a route controlled by a French Societe which had exclusive right to run transport over them. During the winter months, the Societe even provided an air-conditioned bus service in addition to the regular bus and truck traffic. From May to November, however, the routes are left to the winds and the sun. If the roads to Niger were not too bad, we might just make it.

How else could we go? The upper right hand corner of the African touring map was entirely blank. There was not even a ferocious lion chewing the words "Hic Leones." With such drawings did the Roman cartographers conceal their ignorance. Were there no roads in this so called "Horn of Africa?" Surely we could drive to Addis Ababa? We would try to find out about routes from Kenya north through Ethiopia's mountain barriers.

The only map of the Horn of Africa that we could find in New Delhi was a continental map in an old sixth grade geography book. I searched for books about Ethiopia, finally finding one that described a mule-back journey through the

9

country in the early thirties. So at last I took myself over to the Ethiopian Legation to inquire after the state of roads in their country. The Ethiopian First Secretary was charming, his frizzy-haired children were absolute dolls. The visit produced little help on routing but it increased our determination to visit this remote Kingdom, if we possibly could.

We knew no more about the state of the roads on the day we sighted Africa. Despite this airborne century, we were headed for unknown lands. I was almost pleased at our lack of route information. Ahead was Africa, its many countries ready to throw off their colonial masters and emerge as independent nations. We came, not to conquer but to learn.

THE NINE DAYS ON board the boat from Bombay to Africa had really been an extension of our stay in India. Somehow I had never realized how many Indians had become pioneers in Africa, fanning out among the African tribes as traders or settling down to run a jungle corner store. Yet our ship to Africa carried not a single African, few Europeans, and thousands of Indians, some going to Africa for the first time, others returning home after a visit to the home country to see relatives or to marry.

When we first got on board I thought most of the Indians were seeing off friends. Many did stream off before the gangplank was drawn. But many more stayed, jamming the rails, tossing coconuts overboard for luck and cheering on the ragged little boys who swam out from the quay to collect them. As the ship picked up speed, the decks cleared quickly, for even in February there is a chill wind on the Indian Ocean. We followed the crowd below, assuming that they, like we, were looking for tea to warm them.

Yet there were hardly a dozen people in the large dining room. Only three of the fifteen or so family-sized tables were even set. We soon discovered the reason. The dining room served European food exclusively; of the three hundred odd second class passengers there were only nineteen who would eat this sort of food. In fact, it was not too long ago that the British India Steamship Company simply refused to let Europeans travel anything but first class; any other class was considered beneath their dignity. Besides us, the only "Europeans", were an Australian couple with their six-month old baby. The other "European" diners were either Goans – and therefore Christians – or "modern" Indians who no longer observed the dietary restrictions of their religions. The orthodox Hindus or Muslims in all classes were expected to contract for their food from either the Hindu or Muslim catering services which were installed on a lower deck. No one was supposed to cook her own food on board, but many deck passengers did. Behind the lifeboats or hidden back of luggage piles, primuses – those pressure kerosene stoves campers use the world around – were going all day long while the Indian women made their curries and chappatis.

The European diners had set meal hours; but the Indian food, borne from the hold on copper trays, seemed to appear in a continuous stream from dawn to midnight. Curious, I had gone wandering one day down through the airless dormitories of the "inter" class and out into the fourth deck down from the hatch deck. Here, as on the three decks above and several more beneath, deck passengers had spread their belongings, set up their charpoys (Indian rope beds with four "char" legs) and were lounging happily. Actually,

Deck passenger preparing a meal under a life boat

a few bunks for the deck passengers lined the wall, but it was dark in these shelves and most passengers seemed to prefer the open areas.

In the center of the boat were the two kitchens; the Hindu one had the most customers and served both a vegetarian and a non-vegetarian meal. It was hardly eleven o'clock when I was down there; yet already the brass trays were lined up along the floor way up to the front hatch well and on each the cooks were placing a variety of small dishes of rice, curried vegetable and curds. The vegetarian dinner time was at hand. This explained the constant procession of trays to the cabin above, for the Muslims tended to juggle their mealtime to fit in between the two Hindu servings. Muslims must have fresh meat, and up on the rear deck behind yet another kitchen for the use of the Goan stewards were the goat pens. Even in the mild weather of the Indian Ocean some of the animals got seasick. They were a pathetic sight, bleating mournfully and continuously.

Down among the piles of trunks and people I met the ship's doctor. The overworked young man had to tend, willy-nilly, the twelve hundred deck passengers, and still be on call for the other three classes. The ship had halted in mid-ocean about four days out to bury a ten month old baby who died of pneumonia. The doctor said there is hardly a voyage in which one person does not die. Usually it is a child since a mother never brings her child to the doctor unless it is literally deathly sick. These cases are unfortunate, but expected. What the doctor really fears is an outbreak of any contagious disease. Every person is inspected by a nurse before embarking; but the doctor is kept busy nonetheless.

The top deck is the most desirable 'camping" spot for deck passengers – at least in the dry seasons. Our cabin faced the fore deck and through our port hole we could see the intimate life of families: children being fed, girls braiding each other's hair, Sikh men drying their equally long hair in the sun, washing being pounded and dried. I was intrigued, and spent hours watching them. At last I decided I'd have to photograph them. It is often difficult to take pictures of Indians for some of them fear that the camera will capture their soul. Then, they believe, that as long as a copy of their photograph exists, their ghost will be condemned to roam without peace. On the other hand, I found that Oriental men often dismiss women as unimportant, whatever they are doing. So I went photographing alone.

On the rear deck, under a striped canopy, an impressive old Sikh was lounging on his charpoy with as much aplomb as if he were under a tree in his own village. Yet on all sides washing fluttered, people chattered, and babies screamed. What a wonderful pose! But he instantly moved as I aimed, then with courtly grace invited me to tea! Later I took a picture of his four infant daughters, with and without their father. But he never regained that unperturbed gaze. I couldn't but wonder what Persian love poems he was repeating to himself. How else could he have been so detached from the melee?

This Sikh, like most of the men on board, spoke enough English so that we could carry on a conversation. The women, on the other hand, seldom knew more than a few words in English or in Hindi. Most of the Indians in Africa came originally from the arid plains north or east of Bombay and spoke Gujarati. Elementary students were taught in the local language. The boys might continue to secondary school and learn English; the girls were lucky to get to school at all. So I exchanged nods with the women, and little else. In any case they were much too busy to talk as they tended their flocks of children, seeing that one or another did not slip over the rails.

As in overcrowded India, the only difficulty we had on board was in finding a quiet place to read. We soon discovered that the crew's catwalk outside the first class staterooms was just wide enough for a chair. Here we read the voyage away, on one side in the morning, on the other in the afternoon. Occasionally a mate would stop to talk, wondering why we were traveling second class; surely we couldn't be that broke! When we mentioned the long journey back to London, he would shake his head and log us as crazy Americans.

For nine days, time was practically suspended. Like the boat, my mind floated back and fourth from India to Africa and back. What exactly was I doing here? Why were we headed for Africa? Mesmerized, I drifted back across the centuries. I was an Indian princess sailing on the monsoon winds toward the kingdom of one of Sinbad's Arab princes. I was the heroine of "The Desert Song," or Katherine Hepburn in "The African Queen." One moment I was lumping along on camelback, in the next I was shooting an elephant, or something romantic.

Crossing the India Ocean
on the S.S. Karanja

But except for Hollywood, the twentieth century is not a romantic century. It is a practical one of economic development, of road building, or political advance, a century of airplanes and automobiles not of camels and walking safaris. And an American is the most unromantic of all. If you look at my picture, you can compare my skirt and blouse and my short cropped hair with the curls and hooped skirts of a hundred years ago. I looked the part all right for a twentieth century adventure, a car trip through colonial Africa.

THE SHIP STOLE UP to Africa under cover of night, then stopped to wait for clear light. The quiet woke me, and I rushed on deck trying eagerly to read shape into the twinkling lights on shore. As the sun rose like a moon from the mist, all pale pinks and blues, it caught the jewels on the Indian women turning the solid shadows into sparkling images, etching color into the saris. The ship was still India – romantic India, but Africa was in sight. As if to underline the difference, the sun suddenly broke through its haze, and bathed the world in a stark, unflattering glare.

On that signal, the motors of the S.S. Karanja started again. Softly the boat divided the turquoise sea. Palm fringed shores reached out on all sides to encircle us. An Arab dhow, under full sail, cut across our wake and headed out to Zanzibar.

We were closer now, heading straight for the gleaming beaches which ring the island of Mombasa. Over to the right the dhow harbor crowded whitewashed walls leaving no space for ships our size. Ahead the iron silhouette of a sunken freighter, twisted into almost artistic proportions, seemed to warn the pilot of the folly of our course. Then, at the last breathless moment, we spun sharply to port into Kilindini – the deep harbor. The old-century look vanished as cranes and ships became visible. The harbor was whirring about its task, every berth filled. So we dropped anchor and waited our turn to dock. So near and yet so far.

Customs men, immigration officials, a port doctor came aboard; in leisurely fashion they passed out forms and stamped passports. I was intrigued by one paper that we had to sign; in it we were made to promise not to export any ivory, hippopotamus teeth or rhinoceros horns without proper certificates. I promptly demanded the reason for this regulation, but the customs man just laughed. It was only later that someone told me there was an avid market for hippo teeth and rhino horn in India for use as aphrodisiacs! We did not sample either one and so cannot vouch for their properties.

Still we did not dock. Lunch was served; groggy with the heat and lack of sleep we went to our cabins and lay dripping on the bunks. Hours later a Polish freighter began to move, opening up a slot. At last, sometime after five, our crew threw lines over and tied our ship to Africa.

Red fezzes and white nightgowns, that's what the natives seemed to wear. Blue-clad policemen, in British style shorts and knee socks, tried to keep order as hordes of porters swarmed towards the boat to meet the advance guard of departing deck passengers. All mingled in disorganized array. The dusk fell quickly; in it the mass of people rushing to and fro seemed to undulate like the waves. That sea was not inviting; I had visions of the two of us clinging to our baggage, being crashed about by those waves like flotsam. No, better to wait til the storm subsided.

Nor were sure how to proceed. Somewhere on Mombasa Island our car was supposed to be waiting. In India we'd written London to ship a car to us in Mombasa; a Land Rover was simply too expensive. By return mail, as if it were the most normal thing in the world, we received a note telling us a gray-green Austin A40 had been duly shipped and would we please send them $1439.20.

We did. Now we could only hope the car had arrived. We

had planned to find the car, and drive back to the wharf for our belongings. We were carrying so many odd bits of stuff: a suitcase here, a tote bag there. Easy to pack for car traveling, but the devil any other way. Besides, we had no hotel reservations, and all the papers were full of news of the Mau Mau rebellion in the Highlands, and how the wives and children were all fleeing the interior for the coast.

As we stood, debating what to do, the mass of people thinned, and almost miraculously the dock became deserted. Just then the red-haired mate walked by and seeing us still on board asked, "Isn't it Mombasa you're getting off at?"

I smiled at his Indian-ism. We'd had drinks with him and knew he hadn't been home to England for two years. It's a long time to wait for the six months leave. We asked what happened to the people, and he explained the curfew. It wasn't exactly a law, but it was wiser for the Africans to avoid the white part of town at night. With this Emergency on, every African was suspect so the porters had all disappeared. He guessed we'd just have to spend another night on the boat; Africa would simply have to wait a day.

Or so we thought. But after dinner the deserted quay, under moonshine, looked so calm and inviting we couldn't resist a walk on African soil. We meant only to stroll on the wharf; but the gates were wide open even though piles of unclaimed baggage lay along the dock. It hardly seemed possible that there might be an Emergency here in Kenya!

Prompted by the serenity, we followed the path beyond the gates. There was a sweet cool fragrance to the air; the palms waved shyly at the moon. I felt a surge of delight and pirouetted down the path, dancing with my shadow. Africa at last!

The path along the road widened into a sidewalk; the road became a boulevard, functional concrete buildings replaced the dark lot on either side. Several shops had brilliantly lit window displays, and other Europeans besides us were strolling. It could have been a small city anywhere; but its smugness somehow brought Texas to mind, or perhaps Australia. Certainly the town was not Africa, or even England, not along the main street.

Most of the shops are Indian-owned, but the clothes displayed were for the European customer. Indian, Arab, and African shops in the bazaar would sell goods at cheaper prices if you could bargain well. The bazaar was perched on the edge of the dhow harbor, on the opposite side of the island from Kilindini harbor where our boat lay. At the Anglican Church, just short of the bazaar, we turned back; it was over a mile back to the boat and we were already tired. Nor had we found the Austin agency. We questioned a young lad who was window-shopping with his mother.

"Do you know where the Shell petrol station is?" We said we didn't.

"I'll show you," he replied, "if you'll walk back to the hotel with us." It seemed he and his mother were down from Moshi in Tanganyika, for a week's vacation.

They'd driven down in a Land Rover – the English version of a Jeep. "It's the only kind to drive around East Africa," he volunteered. "In the mud you've just got to have four wheel drive, and all the roads are mud when the raining season starts. The Austin agency's there. You weren't planning to use the Austin much outside towns, were you?"

We admitted we were.

"Well, good luck" he said skeptically. "At least you can get through to Moshi during the Rains. We don't have any of this Mau Mau there. Africans still remember how the Germans used to beat them up, so they're grateful to have us English run the country. We don't have a color bar, either. Indians own most of the sisal plantations and turn a good profit. And the Africans around Mt. Kilamanjaro were taught how to raise coffee long ago. Real prosperous, now, they are. Yes, do see how things are in Tanganyika."

# CHAPTER 2

# Exploring Mombasa

*M*OMBASA WAS BACK IN AFRICA IN THE MORNING. NATIVES, banished in the night, swarmed everywhere. At least six of them began fighting over our baggage, trying to grab a piece and so establish his claim. Only with screaming did we stop them from tearing my tote bag in half. Mil picked out the quietest two and shooed the others off. Exaggerating the motion, I wrote down their numbers and counted the baggage. They counted, too, twenty-one pieces! We all nodded, and they gathered up the first load.

Customs didn't open for an hour, so we ate our breakfast and then went hunting on the quayside for our huge wooden crate of canned food. There it was with one side bashed in, looking bigger than ever. Why it must be half the size of the Austin, I thought with horror. How will we ever get all that

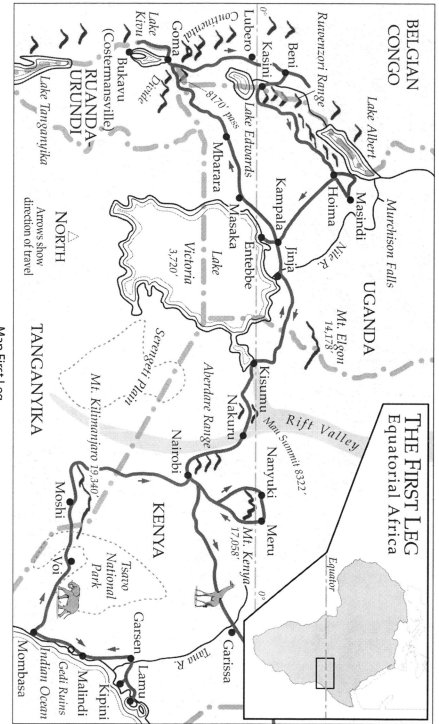

Map First Leg

staff into the car? I felt kind of foolish, wondering why I had bought and brought so much.

Back in New Delhi, Africa had sounded both remote and uncivilized. Even in India canned food was all imported, and expensive. But at the Embassy Commissary you could buy American cans, and I'd gone rather wild, I guess. The trouble was, I had had two months to brood about it. For the night before our original date of departure Mil had come down with jaundice. Everything had been packed and shipped; we'd given up our apartment, gone to a score of fare-thee-well parties. So there wasn't much to do but nurse my husband, and plan the trip. Mil needed glucose; I bought a dozen cans. Fruit juice was good for jaundice patients; another dozen. The day we left, in desperation, I gave much away. Yet there was the crate, bulging!

I refused to think about it. The rest of our stuff was problem enough at the moment. Our mound of belongings seemed to amuse the customs officer. Without opening a thing he absent-mindedly chalked the four suitcases, two overnight bags, two tin trunks, two briefcases, my zip leather notebook, typewriter, camera case, tool box, plaid tote bag, Mil's junk and pipe bag, a green sack full of books, two sleeping rolls, a plastic bag of coats, and the wooden crate which was still outside on the quay. Then leaving the night-gowned porter as chief protector and guardian of the lot, we hurried out of the dock area in search of our car.

Just beyond the railroad crossing we found the Austin agency; we'd passed it in the night because it was also the Jaguar agency and the show windows were displaying that sleek sports car. We asked politely if they had an Austin here that we had ordered so we could drive it back to London.

"Oh, yes, your auto is here all right." said the agent non-chalantly, as if every day people arrived from India to pick up cars to drive to Europe. Maybe they do. "We were wondering what happened to you," he added; then, in Italian, he addressed his assistant who promptly went out to the garage. Moments later he drove up to the plate glass show window in a gray-green Austin A-40 with British license plates.

It was as easy as that. Nobody asked to see anything. We got in while the agent took us for a trial spin and then offered us a lemonade as we discussed the car. I was super-critical. The clutch seemed to stick, the brakes squealed. Really, I guess, I was worried. It's easy enough to talk about driving through Africa, and plan the trip on an atlas. An army tank could obviously get through anywhere with or without roads. But could this ordinary little Austin? It was a fine car for the well-paved rolling English countryside, but for African mud? I remembered the English boy's words about four wheel drive. So many times, later, we futilely wished that we were driving something more rugged, with high ground clearance and four wheel drive. The simple fact was that we couldn't afford anything larger, or anything that used more gasoline per mile. Our budget was tight, with no lee-way. It was this Austin, or nothing.

After all, I tried to console myself, it _is_ larger than "Sahib" was. "Sahib" was the old-style Ford Anglia – that baby English version of a Model A American Ford – that I' d driven out to India.

"Honey," I said, interrupting Mil and the agent who were deep in discussion of things to do to fit this ordinary Austin for the rugged trip ahead. "Honey, before anything, we've got to have a name for the car."

It was such a little car, we'd have to mother it carefully if it were going to see us through. "Bublee," I shouted, triumphant. 'Bublee's a pet name for children in India," I explained to the agent.

He retorted with a laugh; "This your bambino? Ha-ha. It had better be stronger than you, or you never drive to London." Seeing my frown, he added, "If you drive to Mogadishu, I think you make it. Me, I come from Italian Somaliland, near Mogadishu. Everybody's leaving Somaliland; won't be no Italians left in ten years when them natives take over. We leave when we can."

We pressed him about the road. My geography of Africa still was not very good, but I did know that Mogadishu was in the Horn of Africa somewhere. That would mean we'd be driving east again, back toward India. It seemed a long way around. We planned to drive straight north from Kenya, heading for Addis Ababa, if there was a road, that is.

"Roads? No roads go north from Kenya. It's all desert. Straight north in Ethiopia it's all mountains; you'd never get to Addis that way. But Somaliland is pretty flat. In the war that's the way everything went back and forth. So now there's sort of a trail. I came here by boat, but my brother – the one living in Tanganyika – he drove his lorry down. He sent his wife and kids down by boat, and they came before he did. Were we ever worried! The lorry got stuck in the mud by a swamp; took him a week to get it out. They all have rifles, and they love to shoot for fun. We were just teaching them to behave when the war started. Now they are worse than before."

"And if we get to Mogadishu, what then?" I asked. What good would it do to be in Mogadishu, I wondered, it sounds like the end of the world.

"Don't know," he grinned. "We Italians planned a real highway from Mogadishu to Addis after we conquered Abyssinia. But the war, she stopped all of that. Ask the British in Nairobi. They occupied the Horn, you know, and pushed us Italians out in 1942."

As for Bublee, the agent wasn't much help either. He had lots of suggestions, but no spare parts, not even a roof rack. There was a big Austin agency in Nairobi, we could get everything there. But with all our luggage, we'd never get to Nairobi without a rack. Eventually he found us an old Jaguar rack and had his mechanic fit it onto Bublee. It didn't look too secure, but the agent assured us it would hold. I suppose he didn't realize how much weight we were going to put on it.

We finished our lemonade, and drove off, in reality as much unprepared for the trip as was Bublee. It's probably just as well. If we'd known what we were getting into we might never have gone!

WE BOOKED INTO A hotel in the center of town and then started looking for truck or jeep to hire so we could get that horrible old crate off the quay. I certainly didn't want to unpack it where it was. No trucks-for-hire were listed in the phone book, and the Austin agent hadn't known of any. For lack of a better place to ask, Mil suggested we check with the American consulate. In no time at all we were on our way back to the dock in a jeep driven by a young Kenyan employee of the consulate, Colin MacLeod.

Fluent in Swahili, Colin quickly took charge of the situation. Ordering the porters about with that assumed superiority which we soon learned was typical of all whites in Africa, Colin had the crate loaded in no time. The twenty-one pieces fitted easily around it. An Arab retainer waited til Colin had gone in to check with the customs official, then advanced indignantly on me, demanding baksheesh for watching the luggage.

"You didn't watch it," I retorted angrily, "that porter did."

"He's my porter. So I watch."

I didn't believe him. He'd interfered with our porters in

25

the morning trying to substitute his own. I would have none of him. But he persisted, pestering first Mil, then me. His voice rose, in ugly cadences. It was obvious he was used to browbeating the innocent, or a tourist, though in all honesty we were both. But we were far from wealthy. I was for ignoring him, but Mil wanted him to shut up and paid him ten shillings he demanded, thinking it will cover the porter too. $1.40 is too much for mere baksheesh. But this is what it turned out to be, for he melted away leaving the porters to press their own demands! I was furious. For in the family I'm bookkeeper and budgeter. On a ten-dollar-a-day budget, tips of that size can wreak havoc. Suddenly I was glad of all those cans of food, of all the "free meals" to help balance the budget.

Colin deposited me and our personal luggage at the hotel while he and Mil took the big things over to a Consulate garage where they could stay until we figured out what we were going to do with them.

Our room was with a single window that looked out across the verandah into an empty lot which was rapidly, and noisily, being built upon. It was hot, and I groped automatically for the fan switch; overhead fans are everywhere in India. But there was none here. Somewhere I'd read that once Bombay's climate was considered so "mild" that fans were considered unnecessary; whether today the weather is hotter or the people weaker I don't know, but there are millions of fans in Bombay now. I wondered when Mombasa would admit the usefulness of these air machines.

Along one side of the room were two marble-topped wash stands complete with jug and basin; running water was confined to the annex in back where the showers and toilets were. This was an old hotel by Kenya standards, nearly as old as the colony itself. Like most of the hotels, the price included meals. In town there was hardly another place to eat, except in hotels: only one tea room and a new American-style soda fountain.

The dining room was a dreary irregular space just behind the palm-and-wicker-chaired terrace where locals – Europeans only – drank their tea or sun-downer. The waiters were all Africans dressed in the typical East African servant costume: a sort of elongated white shirt belted with a gay colored sash, bare feet, and white skull cap. Most of the waiters seemed happy enough, but the one that usually served us looked continually as though he would die of suppressed laughter. When we sat late he'd begin to sing half aloud, his grin almost engulfing his chocolate face. He looked particularly amused when he would bring us a morning paper, for two shillings. After watching him a couple of days we figured out his joke: he resold the same paper four or five times, banking on the fact that its sparse news would be devoured along with the large, dull breakfast, and left behind. He was happy we were usually among the last people in for breakfast; we kept the paper! But he'd made some 500 % profit by then anyhow!

He thought it wonderful that we caught him, and even better when he saw we didn't mind, wouldn't make him get a clean paper. So he was happy to talk, in a drawled pidgin English. When we asked what tribe he was, he replied, "Me, Ahmed, me Swahili." By then we realized that most of the natives in Mombasa claimed to be Swahili. It was rather like saying, "Me loyal," because the Swahili are people of the coastal areas who were apparently unaffected by the highlands troubles. Their language, a mixture of Bantu and Arabic, is the <u>lingua franca</u> of East Central Africa and we were trying to learn a little of it. We always tried to sit where Ahmed could wait on us. We preferred him over any other "boy." This term is applied indiscriminately to servants all throughout Africa, an impersonal term which would be all right if it didn't somehow convey contempt. Yet it was hard to know what else to use, or even to know whether the Africans themselves actually disliked the term. Were we just being overly sensitive? After all, Mil commented, he had grown up in Shanghai using the same form of address.

Anyhow, on the last day of our stay Ahmed admitted to us that he was really a Kikuyu, but that if he said so to the hotel manager, he'd be fired. Terrorism hadn't reached Mombasa yet, but rumor had, and no one was hiring Kikuyu. Yet later, after we had met many Kikuyu in Nairobi I was sure that Ahmed had not been one. It's so strange, once you think about it, that most Europeans (and I include Americans) lump all Africans together. Books I was reading described the various tribes and their varied ethnic background; but it was some time before I became aware of the distinctive variations in physic or skin color, and could tell a Swahili from a Kikuyu, easily pick out the Somali.

I don't know why the waiter claimed to be a Kikuyu. To frighten us, or to give us a thrill? The paper Ahmed brought us every day was full of news of the Emergency, declared in 1952 when British troops were brought in to fight the Mau Mau. Lurid stories of Mau Mau atrocities against both whites and loyal Kikuyu, details about counter measures, and implementation of the law drafting young Europeans into the Kenyan National Guard filled the pages. Colin was expecting to be drafted any day. Meanwhile he continued working at the Consulate, work which included among other things the teaching of American-style square dances to the local population. This is an admirable way of spreading good will; indeed similar attempts in Nairobi have also been a great success. Yet it seemed strange that only Europeans were taught to dance. Colin took us with him one night, across the harbor to the Navy post. The British there were bored, and grateful for the diversion. But how much more did the Africans need friendship and guidance? Square dances in their new civic center would have been a heartwarming gesture.

DHOWS, IDENTICAL WITH THOSE which brought the earlier Arab settlers, sail in and out of Mombasa harbor constantly. But the large migration follows the monsoon. These winds blow from north-north-east from December until February, then obligingly shift to south-south-west during the months between April and September. So we were in Mombasa when, so to speak, the fleet was in. Arabs and some Persians from Arabia and all the ports on the Arabian Sea sail the African coast selling rugs, trading spices, and – they tell us – hashish and other narcotics. Or they smuggle out ivory, hippo teeth, and rhino horn.

We often stood watching the dhows jostle each other, shaded by the rocket-like tower of the white adobe mosque. At first the tower looked more like one to mark a fortification than a religious meeting place, but as we approached the

Dhow harbor, Mombasa

29

harbor steps we passed the open entrance to the courtyard where men were sitting, shoes off, gossiping. By the door, where the shoes were stacked, was the fountain for ablutions, and beyond the men you could just make out in the gloom the entrance to the mosque proper.

Below us men were loading large burlap sacks onto row boats with much noise and confusion but little action. Finally one, then another, made its way through the maze of boats, bumping into a few as if in sport, misjudging one contact and colliding head-on. As their raucous shouts died away you could hear over the subdued hum of conversation children reciting memorized lessons in a near-by school.

Looking around at the Arabs, the Africans, the Indians, sitting thoughtfully on the steps or bartering for bags of mysterious sizes, or devouring bananas in between heated arguments, I wondered what sort of people met the Greek sailor whose first century record of the East African ports is the earliest written account of the monsoon trade in what was called the Erythraean Sea. In his guide "Periplus" he records that many of the various native chieftains had been under some sort of Arab suzerainty for years, and that Arab captains who sailed the coast knew the local native dialect and frequently married local girls. Even then, he writes, slaves were the most important item of trade. It was the prolonged effort to stop this slave trading that finally brought the British to the coast.

PEOPLE SAY THAT THE dhows ride so choppily that even the most seasoned skipper will frequently become seasick. In the harbor the water hardly rippled as the slanting rays of an afternoon sun skipped across them. It looked like a good day to find out. The taxi-boat we hailed was far rockier from the deliberate movements of the grinning pilot than from the waves; but the dhows, as we coasted between them, pitched decidedly. Various sailor-passengers clambered into our "taxi" as we sneaked between the dhows; several were bound for a celebration on one boat from which rhythmic chanting pulsed across the water. "Marriage," said our pilot wisely.

By now we were on the outer circle of the dhows; the last Arab passenger caught the rope ladder of the dhow. If we wanted to see inside, or rather the topside, of a dhow, it was now or never. How did one ask to come aboard in Arabic? My mere presence in the boat was amusing enough to cause half the crew to lean over and exchange banter with the pilot of our skiff.

"Me, dhow?" I gestured, trying to stand up. Arabs may lack chivalry to their own women, but not to me. Hands steadied the ladder to the boat; arms helped me over the solid wooden rail and supported me over the first lurches of the dhow. It seemed horribly small for the number of people on board. And so unsteady. Their risk of accident is so great, I was told, that no company would insure them or their cargoes, for they sail without radio and often without compass.

The fore deck was piled with rope, burlap bags, lounging sailors. Around the forward mast and all its rigging cables hung a canvas lean-to under which the sailors slept, at least in port. I wondered what was below and was about to ask when one gawking sailor motioned me aft. Here, under the overhanging half deck the captain awaited. The entire semicircular room was carpeted inches deep, with "Persian" rugs; these weren't simply for comfort for they're an important trade article. Nor did the captain forget his merchant's role.

"Jambo, Memsahib," he nodded. "Pana Kitu hapa..." he began eagerly, disarranging the pile of rugs where he'd been sitting, spreading them about so we could examine them.

As I reached for my Swahili phrase book a deep voice

translated. "You want see rugs? Don't must buy, jus' look." It was the young sailor who'd come out in the same taxi-boat. He motioned for me to sit down on the soft rugs. I craned my neck to talk to him, for no one else sat down. He was not a sailor after all, but a clerk in a rug store in the bazaar. Before I could question him further he had waved Mil away. "Captain wants you, memsahib, meet captain memsahib," he proclaimed grandly.

In the corner of the enclosure I noticed a black curtain and from here the Captain led a rotund woman. "Salaam alaicum?" I greeted her, but she shyly hid her face. "Dhow, Arabia?" I questioned the Captain. "Naam..." I knew that meant "yes" in Swahili. A pause. "You, little bwana?" I asked, rocking the heavy air. When I looked up again, she had disappeared behind the veil. "Chai" offered the Captain. That's one word that is similar almost the world over; but it was late for tea and the "taxi" was still waiting below. As we pushed off, with many salaams, we passed the stern of the dhow where the age-old sanitary installation protruded: an outhouse really out in the elements!

I though of the poor shy wife.

CHAPTER 3

# The Liwali and the coastal Muslims

MANY ARABS, OVER THE CENTURIES, HAVE LOOKED OUT FROM their dhows over Mombasa's lush tropical coastline, contrasted verdant land with the barren deserts of their homelands, and stayed. When the first European to visit Mombasa, Vasco da Gama, sailed into the harbor in 1498, Mombasa was one of several flourishing East African Arab towns along the east coast of Africa, all semi-independent, but with ties to the kingdom of Oman, in Arabia.

For two and a half centuries after da Gama's visit, the Portuguese claimed the coastal cities as their colonies, trying to maintain garrisons in the towns and exact tribute from the rulers. The interest of Portugal in East Africa was less in trading slaves and ivory than in using the ports as supply stations for their ships sailing to the fabulous Indies, principally

Goa. Proud Mombasa continually resisted the Portuguese; in consequence the town was sacked and burned three times before the Portuguese finally built a fort on the island to guard the harbor and port. Only with the help of the Iman of Oman were the conquerors finally expelled. Today, only a reconstructed Fort Jesus and some eight thousand Goans who live in Mombasa recall Portugal's dreams of Empire.

For yet another hundred years the Arab towns gloried in their isolation, prospering on slave trade during a period when slavery was becoming repugnant to the Western world. In 1822, the British rulers of the sea began to blockade the coast, seizing slave ships. The Iman of Oman, pressured by the British to outlaw the slave trade in his dominions, moved his capital from Muscat to Zanzibar where he could hold tighter rein on the East African cities. Yet the slave trade continued. Finally, determined to stop this infamous traffic but also unwilling to allow the Germans to infringe on their sphere of influence, the British established the Protectorate of the Mombasa coast in 1905.

The British continue to pay the Sultan of Zanzibar £16,000 a year – some $44,000. – rent for the Protectorate, which is a goodly sum to pay for a strip of land only ten miles deep and about a hundred fifty miles long. But the Protectorate includes all the major port cities; Kenya Colony wouldn't amount to much if its only access to the sea were across some sand dunes.

The Sultan of Zanzibar, as technical ruler of the Protectorate, maintains a representative in Mombasa to look after the welfare of his Arab subjects. This representative, called Liwali – the governor – had his headquarters just across from the British administrative offices. Built on an age-old Arab pattern, the building was cool and airy, a pleasant contrast to the heavy heat outside. I had walked from the hotel with neither hat nor sunshade, and I felt a little dizzy. "Mad dogs and Englishmen," I thought: which am I? But then, it was only eleven o'clock, not quite "the mid-day sun."

On the benches along the wide corridors sat both Arabs and Africans, all male. For a moment they ceased their chatter, regarding me curiously. When I asked to see the Liwali I sensed a certain puzzlement and guessed these male-oriented Muslims were speculating on whether the Liwali would waste his time on a mere woman, unveiled at that. But he did.

I had listed all manner of detailed questions I wanted to bring up with the Liwali, but after my corridor reception the first thing I wanted to ask was about the status of women. From behind his huge and cluttered desk the Liwali rose courteously, European fashion, as I entered. The corner of the room behind him was shadowy, giving his white clothes an almost ghostly cast. The white <u>kofia</u> or skull cap is the typical Arab headdress along the coast; Liwali's kofia was perhaps more ornate than most. He wore a flowing white shirt, so flowing that it was practically a smock. It reached below his knees so that you couldn't see much of the white pajama-pants which nearly concealed his pointed slippers. In addition, most incongruously, he wore a European style white coat over his shirt. This East-West mix-up of clothing is frequent in India, but for some reason Liwali was the only man I met in Africa who attempted to combine two traditions of dress. I was sure this spoke well for his basic moderation.

"Welcome," said Liwali, "Salaam alaicum."

"Alaicum salaam," I replied, exhausting my Arabic. "It is kind of you to see me for I know the lowly position of women in Arab lands. You are the Sultan's representative. Does he encourage women to remain in purdah?"

"You ask about Arab women?" Liwali commented,

smiling ever so slightly over his mere suggestion of a moustache. "They are man's most valuable possession; and must be protected from the gaze of other men. This is our religion and our custom. But it is expensive to maintain a wife in complete purdah. When we had slaves to do the work it was easy; now our community is one of the poorest in Mombasa. So more and more women are coming out from behind the veil. It is also too expensive for a man to have more than one wife at a time, though most men have several during a lifetime. It's a funny thing, but many of the Swahilis are more insistent on observing purdah than are the Arabs."

"Are all Swahili Muslim?" I asked.

"Technically, no. The word 'Swahili' comes from the Arabic word 'sahil' meaning 'coast.' Most of the coast natives were once slaves and usually they adopted the religion of their masters. They have become so Arabized that perhaps 95% of them observe purdah. Yet the government does not recognize them as Arabs. In fact, only this year did our Central Arab Association win the right for mixed Arab-Africans to vote. Now any male who can trace his lineage to an Arab father is considered a legal Arab and can vote for the one elected Arab member of the Legislative Council. Most of these legal Arabs belong to the 'twelve tribes' of coast natives who were never enslaved. A lot of Swahili are more Arab in their customs than Arabs themselves."

As the Liwali spoke in his polished English I was captivated by the charming lilt to his voice; it was almost as if he were singing. I was familiar with the tune: in India the British introduced legislative councils as early as 1892 and gradually increased the number of elected Indians who were elected by communal lists. This dangerous divisive approach was now being used in Kenya. The Legislative Council was composed of 21 elected members: 14 Europeans, 6 Asians, and one Arab. Another Arab and 6 Africans were appointed. Government officials brought the total to 54. No wonder the majority Africans were fighting for independence!

Suddenly, the Liwali cleared his throat, and continued in a higher pitch, more in a monotone. "We Arabs once ruled this country. Today we have only two Arab members in the Legislative Council of fifty-four members. And we are so poor that only fifty Arabs earn enough to pay income tax. But the Ismailis – you know, the followers of Aga Khan, they are becoming a wealthy group. And there are so many Swahili." His voice trailed off, but I followed his thought: Muslim solidarity. If all the Indian and African and Arab Muslims worked together they could all have more stature in Kenya's plural society than any of them had at the time. Unfortunately race was the basic line of division among Kenyan Muslims.

Next day we drove round to the back of Mombasa Island to see an example of growing Muslim co-operation in the educational system. Across the street from each other, the

Muslim Technical School, Mombasa

37

new Arab Secondary School and the even newer Muslim Technical School gleam at each other. Both buildings are versions of new-Arab architecture often lightly referred to as "horizontal marzipan." The pink-tinting of the Arab School, as opposed to the traditional white of the Technical School, did make the decorations look edible!

It was Friday morning, but school was in session as was evident from the pile of bikes outside the Technical School. It is obvious who runs the country: Mombasa observes Sunday as a holiday though, of course, Friday is the Muslim Holy Day.

The Arab School, as the plaque on the entrance arch proclaimed, was opened by H.H. Seyyid Sir Khalifa Bin Harub, GCMG, GBE, Sultan of Zanzibar, on the 16th of March, 1950. Its one hundred fifty male students were required to prove Arab descent through the male line in order to attend. Most of the boys lived at the school for the phenomenally low cost of one hundred shillings a term; that's fourteen dollars! Even so there are not too many Arab families that can afford to send a son to school for three terms at $42 a year. Day students paid about seven dollars a year. But day students were not encouraged, since much of the training of the boys was done in the dormitories. Based on the English public-school pattern, the boys must do such un-Arab duties as making one's own bed, sweeping the floor. Centuries of acclimatization in a slave economy had shaped their attitudes toward such menial tasks. Indeed throughout Asia there is a very strong prejudice against working with your hands. But the boys seemed to learn quickly, for the bare dormitories were smartly done up, a blanket folded on the end of each bed, belongings carefully put away in a locker.

Mr. Ricketts, the trim young English headmaster who had taught in a British public school and been five years in the RAF, did not look like one to indulge the Arab boy's notions of leisure. "They learn to pitch in," he smiles, "don't seem to mind at all. They take it as part of their character training, which it is. But the trouble is they wouldn't dream of doing any work in their home, nor even insist that their homes are clean. If only the women were educated a little, then these old customs would be more easily overcome."

Ah, I thought, an argument for women's education I hadn't heard before. But I was to hear it reiterated over and over throughout Africa: the women are the conservative, the retarding force. A boy must look up to his mother; a wife must obey her mother-in-law. In this way are traditions enforced. If you can teach the young women, perhaps when they are head woman of the house, things will begin to change.

Mr. Ricketts led us through the patio and back past the modern classrooms into the verdant garden. It looked decades old; but tropical growth is rapid. If only schools could grow as rapidly...

"There wasn't any need to have an Arab secondary school before the war," Mr. Ricketts was going on, "not enough Arab children were of sufficient standard. Unless we lower the standard, and I want to see it raised, I don't see how we can stay a strictly Arab school even now. I think in a few years this secondary school will have to become all-Muslim to justify the expenditure. It's one of the newest, best-equipped schools in the country; the staff is all English except one Indian. Still, the Arabs on the whole aren't keen to join with the Indian Muslims. Mostly it's pride. They can hardly even speak Arabic, only their local dialects. Yet they want us to teach everything in pure Arabic. It wouldn't be of much use to them except for "face;" it would make the boy who's only part Arab feel more Arab than the pure but uneducated one. But we must teach them English. After all, this is Kenya!"

We stood in the shade of a palm tree watching the

all-Muslim Technical School pupils swarm out of class. In moments the road was a moving carpet of bikes as the boys, wearing neat white shirts with the school emblems sewn on and long white pants or khaki shorts, streamed back into town. Most of these boys are Indian, generally Ismailis, but only Muslims may attend. The school was built by the Aga Khan for his community, and was originally to be the first college of a university. But here again came the question of qualified students. There is already one university for all of East Africa in Uganda, so instead of a liberal arts school this badly needed technical school was set up, presently at the high school level. Its well designed workshops were built for post-secondary school training and in a few years it will undoubtedly reach that standard.

Of all the Muslims in East Africa, the Ismailis are the most Westernized. Their women seldom observe purdah, and many wear Western dress. Still I'm told that when the then-Princess Rita Hayworth and Ali Khan visited Mombasa in 1950, Rita was rather coolly accepted. The only comment I heard about her directly was from some boys who showed us around the Technical School. The boys were from Zanzibar where the stigma of working with one's hands has begun to rub off. They were telling us how lucky they were to be in the school since many more Zanzibar boys want to come than the quota allows.

"The coast quota is hard to fill," they said, "the Mombasa Arabs think it's wrong to work for a living; we think they're old-fashioned!"

They stopped before a heavy wooden slatted chair, intricately carved.

"That's a typical old Arab chair from Lamu," one said with pride. "We show it to everybody."

I started to sit in it, but changed my mind; it's hourglass

shape didn't look very comfortable. It was just as well, for the boys were giggling now. "Rita Hayworth got stuck in that chair. She has a very big bottom!"

CHAPTER 4

# Driving Kenya's coast to Lamu

COLIN ARRIVED BREATHLESSLY AT OUR HOTEL FOR A SUNDOWNER one evening. "I've got my notice to go fight those damned Qukes," he shouted, plunking himself exhaustedly into a chair, and slowly subsiding into his usual young-gentlemanly manner. "What I mean," he repeated softly, "is that I have to report in Nairobi in two weeks for the draft to fight the Kikuyu. I may never have the chance again, let's drive to Lamu tomorrow."

"Don't be so grim," I teased, "and have a drink."

"Oh, I don't mean that I shall be killed. It's just you can't get through on the Lamu Road except a couple months of the year. And after the Emergency I'll probably go to college in England or in South Africa, and I may never be in Mombasa when the road's dry."

And so it was decided. We had just joined the Royal East African Automobile Association and were studying the maps in their Road Book of East Africa and reading its many cautionary instructions about "motoring in Africa." Mil was anxious to see something of treacherous roads before we initiated Bublee; he was glad to have old-Kenya-hand tutelage. The Lamu Road, Colin assured us, would be the worst we'd hit in Kenya, and good practice for anything anywhere.

Ever since the big bluff man in the tourist office had glowed so about the untouched Arab Island of Lamu my romantic streak had insisted upon going. My practical side counseled that breaking in Bublee on such a road might literally break her. Now Colin would show us how to navigate the wastes with his parents' seasoned, heavy (compared to our Austin) Standard. Colin knew most of Kenya well, having grown up on a Highland farm. Only recently had his parents moved to Mombasa, turning over their farm to Colin's sister and brother-in-law; the Highland altitude had troubled his mother's heart. But Colin had not wished to drive those two hundred plus treacherous miles to Lamu alone. For all of us, it seemed like a delightful prelude to adventure.

The road was excellent as it led northward along the coast away from the modern port. A few sisal plantations, both European and Indian owned, bordered the route in between the prehistoric baobab trees – those grey-green improbables, all trunk, huge trunk, with withered branches – like children's arms on a giant's torso, which bring forth white water lily blossoms.

"They say," explained Colin, "that the baobab bark is so soft, people hollow them out to live in, like caves. I've never seen it, though."

On trips we'd taken in India, Mil and I had alternated driving with navigating. Now he was apprentice-driving; but for me there was no navigation to do; there was absolutely no choice of roads to take. So trying to be useful I looked up sisal in our pet reference book: Fitzgerald's Economic Geography of Africa. "Sisal," it says "was imported from the Yucatan in 1893," I reported to the front seat. "It's used for making rope and twine and is the most successful commercial plant along this littoral."

My researching was interrupted by yells; we were at the Mtwapa ferry. A single cable stretched across the watercourse, propped high at each shore and hung from barrels in the center. A wooden barge, two car lengths long, was beached at the far shore when we drove up, but already the shout had taken effect and men were fast appearing from all sides. Each wore khaki shorts and a once-white shirt in more or less disrepair. A few of them had battered straw hats jammed onto their close cropped heads. Forming a line along the cable which ran through pulleys at each end of the barge, they began to pull...and chant. Instead of going hand-over-hand on the wet cable, each man held fast, walking the cable toward the rear pulley, then catwalking to the front of the line. As the barge neared our shore they stopped pulling and broke into jazzy hand-clapping.

Cable ferry at Mtwapa

We could see a faint "PWD" stenciled on their shirts. A hangover from India just like the use of "memsahib," it means "Public Works Department." I suppose this should not have surprised us, for the general pattern of administration in Kenya was copied from India; even some staff was borrowed from India's civil service when the Protectorate and Colony were first established.

Colin followed a truck onto the barge, the men stood poised. Their leader shoved us off with a pole while the men tugged, lazily; then he sounded a conch shell for pitch and began improvising a call.

"Bwana and memsahib" called the conch man.

"Zum, Zum," responded the men, pulling mightily.

"Taking a safari."

"Zu-um, Zum."

"From Mombasa...to Malindi...in a Standard."

The chant was in Swahili, of course; Colin translated. As the pulling became easier, the chant grew louder. The men, as they swung from back to front of the line, clapped their hands in rhythm, shimmying as though the barge were a dance hall.

All this delight was for their pleasure; the ferries were free. Yet at every ferry stop, early morning or at dusk, the gaiety which accompanied the cable-crew's exertions was as spontaneous and warm.

The road beyond the ferry was rougher, and the car threw up clouds of red dust which drifted into the back seat giving an interesting color to my complexion. As we were to discover, most "made-up" roads in Kenya were rolled gravel which threw up a fine smoke screen all through the dry season. Worse, this type of road developed corrugation the day after it was smoothed. You have your choice of riding the bumps, and hoping there are no sudden holes; or going slowly and hitting every one. Usually you do this alternatively; either way both you and the car are exhausted.

Well beyond a second ferry, and off to the right in the jungly tangle that festoons the sea, lay the ruins of the old Arab city of Gedi. Little archeological work has been done in Africa, and some experts believe that many such cities could be found scattered along the coast. Since Indian and Arab traders probably knew of the monsoon winds centuries before they were mentioned in the "Periplus," such excavation might reveal amazing facts.

Gedi, however, can be traced back only to the thirteenth century. Copper and white Ming vases, Celedon plate, intricate pottery, all fix the date for the experts. A selection of this finds are displayed in the cool museum; we surveyed them more than carefully, the temperature was so refreshing!

Paths lead off into the bush, rather like a maze. Here and there a wall, an arch, a small mosque, modestly catch the filtered light; the bush is heavy all about. We photographed the Sheikh's palace and the "dhow" house – so named for the carving over the doorway – and got lost trying to find the car again. Our exhaustion called for refreshments. Sinbad's Bar, a lean-to near the museum, was equipped for such tourist necessities; the turbaned owner produced cold cokes from a battered kerosene refrigerator. We were obviously still within the borders of civilization!

Fortified by our archeological venture we decided to follow a sign to the fabled Blue Lagoon where Sinbad the Sailor once swam. On and on the jungle track wound, past several unmarked road forks. With the sea just beyond the dunes we figured we couldn't go far wrong. Colin was driving as we suddenly emerged from the mangrove shrubland into the midst of a Girama village. We plowed on directly through the village toward the dunes and the blue lagoon we could see beyond. But cars are not made for climbing sand piles; after a certain slippery skid, our action ceased.

The women at the well continued drawing water, their ballerina skirts of bark cloth unaltered by Westernization, but their gourd vessels, for the most part, had been exchanged for the less picturesque kerosene tins. I wandered over to them, camera over my shoulder, candy in hand. In such cases I used a Rolliecord; few natives realize that you are taking a photograph if you put nothing in your eye!

"Jambo, rafiki", I called in my best Swahili. They giggled and kept on dipping water. One little boy in a graying lungi – that sort of male sarong tied at the waist – was adventurous enough to smile, delighted at the candy. But his brother, clad solely in a wire necklace, ran crying away.

Meanwhile Mil and Colin were unsuccessfully trying to recruit the local man power which had materialized, from their siestas, no doubt. A bit of Kenya-lore was impressed

Girama women drawing water near the Blue Lagoon

upon us here. Colin didn't even try to push the car out himself; after all, he insisted, that's what natives are for.

But the impropriety didn't worry Mil or me. While Colin bargained in Swahili – these men knew about as much Swahili as we did – we tried to dig out the wheels and put palms under them. But by now Colin had arranged to pay each man 25 East African cents for a push. There are one hundred cents in a shilling; 14 American cents equal a shilling. So the total labor costs reached all of $.42!

Once more the native rhythms of the country burst out as the leader organized the push.

" gRombay," he sang.

" Hunh" answered the men, shoving.

" gRombay, hunh, gRombay, hunh...," we all joined in.

" nGuva," yelled Colin in an obbligato. "Strength."

Out of the sand pile the car spurted; the men almost lifted the car around back the way we'd come. Hands stuck out to receive the shillings; "baksheesh...baksheesh" they laughed, not seeming to expect any, but trying their luck all the same. None of the sullen demanding so typical in Asia. Cigarettes and candy were gratefully received.


BACK ON THE MAIN road, we reached Malindi in no time. Ahead the sun glanced off the wide beaches, danced with the smooth rollers. Out a mile or so other white caps set off the blue of the sea where a coral reef protects Kenya's favorite bathing beach from sharks and other unpleasantness.

The road skirted a small bazaar, passed a few *dukas* – those Indian-run general stores that have appeared in almost every Kenyan village – and continued along the shore. A gleaming white Arab palace basked grandly in the sun; only as we were upon it did an inconspicuous sign "hotel" destroy the illusion that some Arab princes still abound.

We chose a hotel that looked a little less prepossessing, less expensive, and raced for the beach. A chill wind had perked up, for it was tea time already, but the water was warm and soothing. We would have to wait for our tan.

Our waiter here, too, was the gay type, and foxy. The five and six course meals usually fill me to bursting before I am half through, though after days of living out of cans, I have been known to devour seconds of everything. But in Malindi I was well fed, and often skipped dessert. This delighted the waiter. Whether he didn't like the other courses, or didn't have time to gulp them down, I don't know. Ah, but dessert! He'd bring three orders in gaily, ignoring my previous refusal. And lo, when Colin and Mil were finished, their empty plates joined a third on the tray which the cheshire-grinning waiter bore away.

During the day Malindi offers golden swimming, adventures too, if you go in for goggling. But the beaches were strangely empty.

"Off-season," said the manager.

I couldn't imagine why. The weather couldn't have been better.

"It's so hot here now," he continued. "Nairobi people wait to come down in the cool season, when it's muggy up in the hills. They're used to cool climate, and can't stand the heat."

From Malindi the road to Lamu turned inland through desolate bush to meet the muddy Tana River at a crossable point. Actually the road pointed straight north; it was the coast that arched out to the west forming a bay marked on the map with an amazing name: Formosa Bay.

The road was gently hilly, and I thought Colin was playing roller-coaster when he stopped abruptly at one crest. Looking like stuffed puppets, a string elephants were crossing the road only a crest away. Wise to animal ways, Colin waited some time before starting again, just to be sure no strays from the herd were loitering in the scrub. For if you tangled with an elephant, he could crush the car. Here on all sides the bush grew just about elephant height, the thorns, if climbable, would give no protection. The road was narrow, hardly more than a car width; you certainly couldn't turn around fast enough to outrun a mad beast.

After this we saw nothing at all, man or animal, though piles of elephant dung added obstacles to an already difficult run, until we came to the Tana River. Once more, to gay chanting, we were pulled across on the ferry. This barge was only one car size – the traffic here hardy required a larger one – and the "crew" was more ragged, less precise. The river is one of the few bush rivers that reaches the ocean still raging with water, for the bush is thirsty. The Tana not only makes it to the sea, but carries tons of highland topsoil with it. Underneath its red murky waters lurk crocodiles; along its wild banks all manner of jungle life drink and wander.

The map in our Road Book labels the area "UNINHAB-ITED BUSH." An area more desolate, more forbidding, is hard to imagine. For centuries the tsetse fly kingdom has proved more of a barrier than deserts or swamps. Neither man nor his domesticated beast can withstand the ravages of this enemy. And so the bush remains untouched. The road to Lamu skirts this desolation, retreats at once toward Witu on the coast. Little did we anticipate our own bout with the bush, for then we did not know that our only route north to Ethiopia lay across the heart of this wild nothingness.

If the bush was frightening – pressing in on the track, threatening to reclaim this puny effort of civilization – the driving was more so. The back seat became more unstable than a dingy in a blow; and I was getting seasick! The road had stopped at the ferry: the track we following had never been planned; it just grew. If three trucks chose the same path, that was route. Where the ground was rocky the ruts were troughs in which Bublee would have drowned; even the Standard floundered. Colin kept one wheel atop the center rut, the other running the jungle edge. Thorns and creepers popped through the open window to view these intruders. No sooner had I shifted and steadied myself on the other side than, plop, we were into the trough and up the other side.

Or the sand would take over. Colin would see it ahead and race across hole and trough, zagging drunkenly through the sand trap like a novice golfer on the 18th hole.

Surely, I breathed, this must be worse than any road we'll see. Bublee is so small, and our luggage so heavy! Actually, this drive was a useful preview; but unlike a movie preview, it was not the most exciting part of the show, only an inkling of it!

Miles followed miles...many more than the map said, many more than the Standard showed, for how do maps or meters know the effort of distance? They measure only in one dimension. American concepts of distance, of time, go awry in this continent. They are no more related than is the local skyscraping ostrich to the Empire State. A mere 143 miles and several centuries later the track stopped abruptly at the edge of a mangrove swamp.

A BATTERED LAND ROVER was parked in the sand; beyond, at a rickety pier, a strange-looking boat was tying up. A youngish Englishman hopped lithely from boat to pier to shore.

"That was well timed," he grinned, after nodding recognition. "There's no regular service, you know." Then, obviously intent upon some business, he made for his Rover and departed.

One of the four crewmen from the boat was standing respectfully by, waiting for some sign from us. He took the loose end of his white shirt and brushed the sweat from his forehead; then rearranged his white <u>kofia</u>, grinning. The minute Colin opened the boot he sprang to his side and bore off our suitcases with the air of a salesman who's just closed a deal.

Standing guard in the boat was the "captain," replete with red fez and a white bush shirt buttoned only at the top; underneath it flowed a lungi, lapping at his scuffs. He was not really guarding the boat; his joy and his pride was the old truck engine mounted in the center of the craft, complete with its old radiator head! He ignored us as we slid past this monument to the rough plank seats in the stern where sailcloth was stretched horizontally for shade, but the man at the tiller tucked his bare feet under to make room for us. The porter tossed the bags to the pusher-offer and clambered aboard himself.

With a wrenching chug the engine responded to the captain's touch, and we headed out away from the mangrove shores to open water, west toward the low-lying islands. At first all three looked desolate. The farther island, Patta, had once been even more prosperous than Lamu. But that city and its sultan gambled wrongly in the game of war; today there is little but drifting sand, so thoroughly was Patta destroyed.

The engine, under the maternal care of the captain, was constantly sucking water as if this, rather than petrol, made it go. So intent was I on his mannerisms that I hardly noticed we cleared a sandy point and were heading in to dock. A string of imposing two story buildings faced the waterfront, each with a covered balcony built out over the colonnade front. The white-washed walls glowed in the lengthening sun; a Union Jack flying above the marzipan decor of the fort, set back from the sea in the center of the town, played red and blue with the light.

Palms ringed the houses, and as we drew closer we could see huts scattered among the trees. Two piers jutted out from the sea wall, each from a three story building. I pointed to the one toward which we were heading. "Customs House" intoned the captain at my query; he was relaxed now, his engine had made another trip.

But the man at the tiller was frantic, as we coasted in, yelling guttural pizzicatos to men whose boats we were grazing past. These were fishing boats, small versions of the dhow. Several, full triangular sails glinting gold and crimson, were just now homing for the night. At the other pier a lone steamboat was tied, its heavy smokestack looking clumsy next to the sailboats, but its trim proclaiming reliability. The boat and house suggested local aristocracy.

"Not a sultan's house," laughed Colin, cutting short my plans to call on His Highness' harem. "It's the D.C.'s residence."

Seldom, in India, did the District Commissioner live in such palace-like houses; later I found they didn't normally in Kenya either. I suppose they felt they had to impress the local Arabs; or maybe this old Arab palace was the only available house.

A crew of uniformed Africans was loading the D.C.'s boat. Looking closer we saw two horizontal strips on their loose blouses. They were prisoners all right, but they couldn't have been very dangerous ones, we reasoned, for the *askaris* guarding them held their rifles casually, chatting with their charges.

The porter with our bags disappeared into one of the two story Arab houses just beyond the D.C 's. We followed him through the carved wooden door into gloom. In the light at the top of the stairs stood a figure – patch over his eye, ear cocked to help his hearing. You couldn't have asked for a better-cast pirate! Rotund Mr. Petley, owner of Lamu's only hotel, boomed out to us to come up. We were just in time for tea!

The open balcony was obviously the town's social center on a Sunday afternoon. The Reverend Cheese, an estimable octogenarian, sat wistfully staring out across the water.

"He's probably translating to himself," said Petley kindly. "He's working on putting some Biblical texts into Somali. It's his life."

Petley's words brought a benign smile to the Reverend's lips.

"Sit down, my child," he modulated, without a sign of surprise at our project which Colin was loudly outlining to Petley. "Did you say Ethiopia?" asked the Reverend, leaning forward, memory in his eyes. "If you have time, you must stop at Kismayu. Such a charming town, it's just up the coast, a few days on the dhow. Oh, you are driving. The sea is easier, but you cannot sail a boat to Addis Ababa! Let me give you some friends to look up in Addis."

To him these places were as well known as Brooklyn to a New Yorker. To him, it was natural that we should wish to see them, and if we drove where he would take a boat, well, that was the younger generation.

Petley, on the other hand, probed into our modus transportante. He wanted to be sure we knew what we were getting into. He'd seen too many dilettantes in his day, people coming to Africa for the excitement and not willing to work, and wasting their time and money and health trying to farm and going home broken in body and spirit. Worse were the fools who wouldn't take quinine and died.

"They said it'd hurt them. They're dead. I took a carload of pills and am whole and hearty," chortled Petley.

Thoughtlessly I questioned, not very loudly, "But doesn't it hurt you?"

"It makes you deaf," whispered Colin.

Petley had lived and farmed down near the Tana. He loved the country too much to leave, and when he grew old he'd retired to Lamu. The hotel was almost an after-thought, to hear him tell it. A service, sort of, a pub for the officers, a room for the occasional visitors. "Why I almost feel guilty making money having fun!" he would say, and conjured up images of his previous okie-like existence which seemed a bit too austere to be true.

Lamu's third permanent European was a different vintage entirely. Willowy and straight as a dhow's mast, tanned almost to Arab brown, ex-Indian Army Major Anson completed the trio of the island's "unofficials"; no wonder guests at the hotel were more than mere customers!

An island that had never seen cars; a town with only three resident Europeans! The feel of real exploration, of story-book adventure, came back. For a few days we had escaped the century. I guessed this was what drew the Major to the island. Living all his life in the tropics, a member of the ruling class in a primitive society, he had acquired that easy patronizing attitude, an assured top-man-on-the-totem-pole bearing so characteristic of the white elder brother. Why should he adjust, at an age far more advanced than his trim gentility would suggest, to the demands of equality from younger upstart brown brothers? Why should he melt into nonentity in London when in Lamu he could be distinct? Puttering around an English country garden would have broken him; here he caught youth from adventure, spent half the year riding dhows to Mombasa, the Seychelles, Zanzibar.

Here was a man without a country; the land he loved had been taken away from him--and given back to younger Indian brothers. He was glad when the shortage of administrators during the war gave retired men a chance to be active again. As a temporary D.C. in East Africa he had found something of his old milieu once more. Again retired, he had set up his home among these Arab-Africans, to write, and think, and live his nineteenth century life to its end.

Major Anson invited us to orange squash with him the next day; his rooms, in an Arab house, were sparse as his own figure. The only rugs – sacrilege to Arabs though it was – were skins of an Indian tiger and a cheetah, reminders of the glory days in India. Yet Major Anson did not only live in the past. Pictures of his daughter, his mother, himself in the Poona Rifles, were almost eclipsed by a stark white-on-black sketch of a marketplace done by an obscure Somali artist.

THE MAJOR WAS OUR tireless guide. It amused him to see the town he knew so well through our eyes. We'd meet him by the Arab fort whose round tower still served as a prison. Beneath the aristocratic mango tree before the fort was usually one soapbox orator or another, watched casually by a native policeman, black legs below khaki shorts luminous against the white dress of the crowd. Under the arcades of the buildings, in the alleys, anywhere in the shade, the marketing went on.

Leading us down twisting alley-paths between the high outer walls of the Arab houses, the Major would stop before a favorite doorway. Many of the houses retained their old intricately carved doorframes and decorated doors: true arabesque art famed along this coast for its decorative, but functional chairs, chests, and doors. Since these articles brought good prices from the Europeans, and the Arabs without

Mil standing before a traditional Lamu carved door with DDT scrawled on it

their slaves were quite poor, those in Lamu, as in Zanzibar and Mombasa, sold artifacts to the tourist. Petley offered us a "bargain," a large double door for only $150. "All Americans who come, buy doors," he stated grandly.

That was all Bublee needed, I thought, a deck! And when we got home we'd have a door, if no house to go with it.

Most of the doors had chalk marks on them; it was some time before we would discover one that was readable. It said: "DDT 29-10-52" All over the country, as we drove, we saw similar legends painted on huts, chalked on the mud walls. Nonetheless we took our anti-malarial pills every Sunday...a painless ounce of prevention.

Often, in the narrow ways, houses converged overhead, family joining family. More room for the captive women – two courtyards instead of one. Some women still spend most of their lives inside the stone-mud walls. But the wives of more "modern" men are allowed to go out swathed in shapeless yardage. In the evening, women in white *chador* hovered like frightened birds at the far end of the waterfront; during

Swahili woman peering out of the entrance to her mud and wattle house

the day these figures were shadows running before the sun. Foreigners, even female, were strange and mysterious things to be avoided at all cost. Several times I got lost in the maze, pursuing a white phantom.

The Swahili women kept the custom of purdah less rigidly. Indeed, as all fashion, it varied with social standing. Lamu city began at the waterfront and extended up the hill behind. As you climbed the winding paths the tight Arab town thinned to individual houses, and then to mud huts; Arab blood gave way to African, and the white chador turned to a black shawl which, at the top of the hill, was wound as a turban, or forgotten. The gay printed calico – mostly imported from Lancaster, was much more fun to wear, and to be seen in.

In the cool air on the hill summit these women worked with their men weaving mats from palms leaves, pounding grain, or putting up supports for a new home. They stared at the camera, flattered that a memsahib would care to take their picture. A covey of little girls posed endlessly. One charmer, all of eight, must have been Somali, for her arms and legs were thin and supple. She struck such a cheese-cake pose that the Major was moved to pontificate on the troubles caused by such beautiful Somali women, who form, it seems, most of East Africa' s street-walking population.

Up on the hill, too, was a simple little chapel to which, perhaps, the unveiled women belonged. Its mud-mortar walls still gleamed from the annual Christmas whitewash.

"The nativity plays," explained the Major, "are the high-point of local worship. Sometimes an English preacher on vacation conducts, but regular services are held by a native minister."

Inside, rows of wooden benches marched toward a wooden platform on which was an ordinary kitchen table and chair. The floor was well swept – not an easy chore with the shifting sands on the wind – and fresh flowers were in glasses on the table. A thick cross, painted on the front wall, was the focal point; on either side eight-pointed stars in brilliant colors proved the native adaptation of the faith; this was no longer a foreign religion, a temperate flower half withering in tropical heat. Here Christianity had become as native as the flame trees, and as hardy.

Halfway down the hill was a fairly new square concrete block building, the hospital. Here was a legitimate meeting place for the shrouded women, the only place in the town where women gathered in daylight to gossip.

Everywhere else were men. Men sat drowsily along the seawall; men gossiped in the shade of the massive round tower of the old fort. Men bought coffee

Arab boy with his coffee pot
set on a charcoal warmer

from the Arab boy with his tin pot set on a portable charcoal warmer and drank it sitting on the shop steps. Men smoked the local version of a hubble-bubble – a long pipe smoked with live coals on tobacco leaves, but without the "bubble" or water part. At the vegetable booths, barefooted men in "nightgowns" jostled their neighbors in vivid printed lungis or in khaki pants. Turbans, kofia, fezzes, or loose Arab wrappings topped their costumes like whipped cream or a cherry on chocolate-mocha ice cream.

The hatless men you could spot as Indians. There were enough of them on the island to support a separate school, in the Gujarati language, and a Sports Club. A Goan, incongruously the owner of the "Pakistan food shop," proudly showed us around the Club's volley ball, badminton, and tennis courts. Da Costa's father had first come to Lamu to work in the customs and had brought his son along for company. But da Costa went back to Goa, where his mother still lives, for his higher education before he, too, joined the customs service.

"But these new Ingleesh men," he fluttered, "they are a new type. They are not kindly, not thoughtful, like before. I did not like that they treated me so, and I quit. Perhaps I sell my shop and go to Mombasa."

Da Costa was probably lonely, being the only Goan on the island. His closest friends were the town's two Parsees. He played tennis with some young Indians in the customs service, and occasionally with European officials. He knew them all and frequently had a beer with them at Petley's pub.

For da Costa, old Lamu was British Lamu; he was disturbed at the impending change. For us, old Lamu was Arab Lamu; picturesque and secretive. But my twentieth century blood to the fore...I was for a change, in a hurry. "Women of Lamu, unite," I kept thinking, "You have nothing to lose but your veils."

THE BEFORE-DINNER BEER WAS almost a ritual among the town's bachelor officials: the customs, forestry, prison and PWD officers. Like the Major, they generally ate their meals at Petley's rather than bothering to cater at their quarters. Sometimes the D.C. and his wife dropped by; but he was off on tour while we were in Lamu.

These young officers, unlike the D.C. and most of the senior men in the administration, were Kenya born and bred. Perhaps their background explains da Costa's complaint against the new men. Englishmen might display reserve, might govern their actions toward the "lesser breeds" with distance and paternalism, but always with civility. These young men betrayed the arrogance and disdain of people who must constantly assure themselves of their superiority.

The forestry man extolled the advantages of his job which keeps him in Lamu only six months of the year, giving him another six months respite in the metropolis of Mombasa during the Rains. He came to Lamu only to supervise the cutting and marketing of the mangrove trees, leaving to the natives the planting of new shoots. The waterfront was crowded with stacks of drying wood, cut in all shapes and sizes, ready for dhows to pick up,

For the P.W.D. officer, Lamu was the point of civilization, his weekend haven. He spent his weeks in the bush supervising telegraph and ferry "crews" or construction gangs on any number of projects. Right now he was setting up a scheme for improving the Mombasa road. Those prisoners we'd seen the day we arrived were to be put to work.

These prisoners were the nightmare of the prison official. He was a young boy with an adolescent complexion, fresh from Nairobi. The prisoners were the first lot of suspected Mau-Mau to be sent to Lamu,

"Tomorrow I have to take them over there. Me, alone

with them damn Qukes. God knows what they'll start. They butcher us, up country, cut out our guts. The last one, they got him in his bath. The water was still warm from his entrails when they found him...Petley, another drink!"

He coddled the drink, ignoring all efforts to distract him. Colin urged a game of darts. Petley brought out a box of junk and old jewelry, not really hoping to sell – for by now he'd decided we weren't quite as gullible as most tourists – but for laughs. A harem belt, carved medallions chained together, had for a clasp two large semi-circles modeled like an Amazon's brassiere. Petley wore it as such, but the youngster who tomorrow would swagger among the prisoners as an invincible "bwana" did not even look.

Suddenly he grimaced, and staring at the beer as though it were human blood, took on a deathly mien. "Another, they chucked his leg in a corner, cut off his head and left it staring from his platter at his body, the bloody devils. But I won't give 'em a chance," he growled to himself, wiping a tear from his bloodshot eyes. "My guns'll all be loaded," he shouted, swaggering, then running toward the door.

If he hadn't gotten sick, I would have. But his talk was not just drunken exaggeration. Crazed Mau Mau had done this, and more, up country, where we were going next.


IT WAS STILL DUSKY when we got up the morning we were to leave. The neo-Victorian coverings on the bed table lost some of their dowdiness in the half-light. Maybe they really were Victorian, like the washstands. This room (I think there were only two guest-rooms in the hotel) had beds in every possible position so that getting out of bed itself was something of an expedition, especially when groggy as I invariably am at such waking hours.

Mil was already off to have a shower. So far I had

contented myself with a sponge bath; one look at the dark little room where the punched bucket hung had not been encouraging. But I needed it this morning. Even the dribbling water might help. In the end, however, it was more work than it was worth. The shower being a man's preserve, I had to recruit a door-keeper as well as a water carrier. Servants, too, are sleepy in the morning.

Of course, Lamu had no plumbing. Jubes – deep open gutters – trickled through the main streets. They must have been flushed out with sea water, for no telling odors rose from them as they do most everywhere in the Middle East. Nor were they used alternately as water pipes, a dangerous custom I had observed even in such a "modern" town as Teheran. So the water carrier had to be sent to the well, if Petley's reserve fell short. There was, however, one bit of modernization at the hotel: chemical toilets had replaced the traditional commodes.

Though it was early when we left, the prison officer and his Mau Mau had departed before us and had docked down the coast from our car. We knew, as we slithered back toward Witu, that over in the tangle somewhere he was controlling his fright with harsh orders. No murders of officers were reported, so his dissembling must have been convincing.

We had almost as nerve-wracking a crisis of our own: we had run out of matches. Even had we been Boy Scouts there weren't two sticks to rub together; all was reed grass, and sand. I was getting seasick again and was trying to doze when the car jerked with particular violence and Colin let out an unaccustomed "Damn!"

In the sand behind us stretched a snake which we'd hit despite Colin's efforts to avoid it. "That," said Colin, his voice still agitated, "is a puff adder." I still didn't understand his tension. "Never run over a poisonous snake – and that is one of the most deadly. They're tricky things. Sometimes they curl around the wheel and joy ride...and bite when you get out of the car. You're dead ten minutes after one of those fangs hits you."

I looked back at the snake; its pale brown coloring blended into the sand and only its darker criss-crosses showed its four foot length.

"But it's dead" I said, comfortably, just as it seemed to skate off into the bush.

"They're tough all right," retorted Colin, grimly. "I remember a friend of mine had an old car. Jack thought he was funny, running over snakes. The only way you kill them is to skid over them on a hard road. He'd try, but sometimes he'd miss. One day during the rains he tried killing one, but the earth must have been too soft. Anyhow, suddenly, there the snake was, slithering up the brake pedal. Jack climbed up on the seat, still steering, til the car stopped by itself. We had to wait hours in the rain til the thing got tired of the car and came out into the open for battle."

Involuntarily we all glanced at the brake pedal.

"Never run over snakes," repeated Colin decisively as we started again.

I needed a cigarette more than ever now! I wasn't the only one. At the Witu fork there was a shack along the road with a sign that said "petrol." In additions, they sold matches, Eveready batteries, and tins of butter or herrings or Cadbury's chocolate biscuits! What cconomic sccpagc, down to this palm covered hut!

" Merikani," voiced the owner, as I poked around.

"Yes" I answered, surprised that he should know we weren't English; more surprised when he produced bolts of gaudy calico cloth for me to look at.

"Merikani, merikani," he said, caressing the printed material; heartbroken when I shook my head and left.

Later I found that indomitable Boston merchants in their schooners were the first European traders to come to Zanzibar with printed calico. Though the British soon outsold our traders, the name stuck. Some distant ancestor of mine, maybe, saw a Zanzibar much like the Lamu we'd just left. The thought was so pleasing that I walked right into a puddle without seeing it. Colin had just finished pouring water into and around the over-heated radiator.

"Cotton soil!" observed Colin, helping me out of the goo. "The slightest moisture and it's like glue. Nasty stuff." A mild statement, we found later to our sorrow. For most of the soil under the "uninhabited bush" was this black curse. To be out on it during the Rains is to court disaster; and nobody knows exactly when the Rains will begin.

By the time we reached the Garsen ferry over the Tana, the Standard was erupting again. We drove onto the raft and immediately both Colin and Mil began to dip up the murky water to cool the car. As usual, Mil had his extra glasses in his sport shirt pocket: the dark ones for outside, the clear glass ones for indoors. The crew pushed off from the sticky bank with a jerk; Mil leaned out to keep hold of the bucket on a rope – and his clear glasses plopped into the river.

Without thinking, both he and Colin stripped to shorts and dove. The crew pulled the raft back to shore, but my Swahili offer of shillings brought no response from them. A few naked youngsters who had been bathing near the edge of the raft walked in a little deeper, but none of them would go in all the way.

Strange, I thought.

Then I remembered the crocodiles. "The Tana's lousy with them," someone had said.

But Colin and Mil splashed on, momentarily. Suddenly Mil gave a startled look and raced back for the shore; and Colin pulled himself hurriedly back onto the raft. Something rough and scaly had touched them both.

Cursing his stupidity, but in no mood to try diving again, Mil pulled on his tee shirt and pants without drying himself at all. Still, across the river, we stopped at the town of Garsen – all two houses of it – and reported the loss to the local District Officer.

For weeks Mil went around, a la Hollywood, in a dark glasses haze. In Nairobi our loss insurance company wrote them off without a thought and paid for replacement. But, incredibly, eight months later, a package arrived in London from Mombasa. In it were Mil's glasses, not even scratched! Not a word of explanation. Did they wash up? How could they, from the gluey bottom? Did the river recede after the Rains? But it was at the low point when they were lost. Did someone shoot a crocodile and find, instead of a pearl, Mil's glasses?

CHAPTER 5

# Building a Railroad, with Indian Labor

WANDERING IN THE MOMBASA BAZAAR WAS DULL AFTER LAMU. The people – Arabs, Indians, Africans – all seemed to have diluted their own traditions with bits of westernization. A hat, sun glasses, a western shirt. These may have made their own life more comfortable, but they destroyed something of the picturesque.

The streets were wider, with none of those weird enticing alleys. The high whitewashed walls of Arab and Indian homes were unrelieved with decoration; the few wooden gateways were pale imitations of a perished art. The old glory of the city had been impaled on the Portuguese sword; the new wealth of the port, though only across the island, had not flowed into this market where only basic foods and the simplest jewelry were for sale. Without doubt the bazaar was more humble than it had been over three centuries before when the Portuguese, emissaries from a curious Europe, first sailed into the harbor. At that time, with the slave trade flourishing, Mombasa had been a prosperous town. But her wealth could not compare with that of India. So first the Portuguese, then the French and British, had sailed passed East Africa and on to the famed and fabulous land of the Maharajahs and Nawabs. In the contests for Kingdoms that followed, Portugal was soon out-challenged, left holding on to her African and Indian port cities with the tenacity of a child determinedly proud of the booby prize.

The East African Arabs were faster at dislodging the Portuguese than the Indians have been. Even today a man from Goa travels with a Portuguese passport; the centuries of contact between Portuguese and Indian has resulted in Goans who are generally Catholics and almost certainly of mixed ancestry. The British, rulers of the Indian Ocean, among others, did not begrudge the Portuguese their Indian enclave of Goa. But they needed the Arabs as friends against the French and therefore helped them regain the East African ports. That was all the British wanted in Africa; people not unfriendly, not too strong. They were not interested in the hot unhealthy continent for themselves – not, at least, until the Germans and French began to claim parts of Africa – not until the institution of slavery became repugnant to the British people, whose consciences, stung by the realization of the wealth this invidious trade had brought their own country, demanded penitence.

During the nineteenth century, then, money and missionaries began to pour into Africa. Expeditions sent to suppress slave trading explored as they went, and soon in the blank areas of the unknown continent rivers and mountains replaced the fiercely-drawn lions. One of the more famous explorers, H.M. Stanley, journeyed around Africa's largest lake, Lake Victoria, some years after he had found Dr. Livingstone in the nearby wilds of Ujiji on Lake Tanganyika. Here on the northern end of the lake live the Buganda tribe, one of the most advanced in all dark Africa. Anxious to bring Western civilization to this remarkable tribe, Stanley urged missionaries to penetrate to this remote part of the continent and proselytize the people.

So successful were the missionaries, English Protestants and French Catholics, that soon large congregations were formed. The "zeal of converts" had real meaning in this tropical land, and within a decade Catholics, encouraged by the French, and the Church of Englanders, undoubtedly cheered on by some Englishmen, were struggling for control of the Buganda kingdom. The German missionaries and the local Muslims all entered the fray and the country exploded into a full scale civil war. Several Englishmen were killed, and the London public clamored for the British Government to restore peace. True to the policy of *laissez faire* then in ascendancy in England, it had not been the government but a private trading company, the British East African Company, which had up to that time been protecting British interests in East Africa. But a renewed pride in the glory of an Empire was sweeping London. So for the glory of the flag and the lives of the missionaries, the British Government in 1893 declared a Protectorate over the land of the Buganda.

To reach this interior kingdom from the coast at Zanzibar was still a matter of months. Wars or rebellions were not heard about for many valuable weeks; the slave trade flourished in the back bush. Obviously, a railroad would have to be built, and in 1895 work was begun.

Almost immediately the railroad was nicknamed the "lunatic line." Jibes were made about the 600 miles of rusting steel stretching from no place into nothingness. Critics guaranteed that the venture would fail. The obstacles were unnerving, from the escarpments of the Rift Valley to the man-eating tigers of the bush. A classic book about the railroad is Col. Patterson's "The Maneaters of Tsavo" which tells how two enormous tigers struck terror into the railroad gangs. For nine months they preyed upon the railroad camps, eating several Englishmen, twenty-eight Indians, and uncounted Africans, stopping all work entirely for three weeks. Until Patterson shot these nine-foot giants, the coolies believed them to be spirits of two dead local chiefs, angry at the railroad trespassing on their lands.

Building the railroad was back breaking work. The Africans, happy in their self-sufficient culture, did not need money and would not work on the railroad. So most of the laborers were Indians imported from the West coast of India. Of the 32,000 indentured Indians who came to work on the railroad, nearly 7,000 remained in East Africa when we were there. Their descendants are a complicating factor in Kenya's bitter race problem, and one which particularly interested us, fresh from India.

The Indian press had been filled with righteous wrath at the failure of East African Indians to identify themselves with the Africans' claims against the colonial government. Recalling India's recent struggle for independence, Jawaharlal Nehru himself repeatedly urged support for what he considered the legitimate and peaceful aspirations of the Africans. But the Indian settler is no more amenable to advice from New Delhi than the English settler to London's repeated suggestions. "We have our own battle to fight," declared C. H. Patel, a Mombasa lawyer and member of the town council, when I asked him about the Indian settler's views.

I was sitting in his tiny square office, clean and uncluttered in frugal Indian custom. But Mr. Patel's white clothes, indistinguishable against the whitewashed wall, were Western. The movement of his hands, darting like puppets in a shadow play, added emphasis to his words which poured forth with turn and cadence, but not accent, of India.

"For we are still only second class people here. I cannot take tea with you at a hotel. Yet believe me, some are Indian owned! Only to one can I come. That owner, an Ismaili, begged venerated Aga Khan to stop and take an ice at his hotel some years ago. But Aga Khan refused this hospitality asking for why he should enter this hour when next hour his followers would be excluded from hotel? So owner promised never again to discriminate against Indians. But he is only one."

I started to ask a question, frowning, but his sudden gesture held the quiet a moment. Then he continued.

" You wonder why we are staying if we are only second class? We are East Africans! This is our America, we come to improve ourselves. We Indians are a community of petty traders and clerks; only a very few are very wealthy. We are living here one, two generations, but already we are losing the cultural ties of India. Already I am feeling foreign there, yet I am living here only since 1935. It is true some men are going to their village for a wife, but in twenty years, even family ties will be finished."

"We wish to stay here, for we are happy. Here it is cleaner than India, our standard of living is higher. So we are not really minding these new immigration restrictions," he added candidly. "If too many new Indians are coming, the living standard goes down."

He sipped his tea reflectively, slipping his toes out of his sandals, and back. "Really the immigration restrictions are as good as not," he repeated deliberately, "yet Kenya Indian Congress has officially condemned these restrictions for discriminating against us Indians, but welcoming Europeans. The Muslims, now, they admit where their own interest lies. They are openly for restrictions."

Muslim-Hindu rivalry. This sounded familiar; this feeling created Pakistan, has kept armed tension between the children of British withdrawal, Pakistan and India. What were their relations here? I queried.

"In Mombasa we are getting on fine; for nine years we are having uncontested seats for the Municipal Board. All Indians vote together for seven seats; we have gentleman's agreement that four seats will be Muslim, three Hindu. But for Legislative council seats – we call it Legco – government made separate electoral rolls now so that one Hindu and one Muslim represent us coast Indians."

The term "Legco" slipped easily off Mr. Patel's tongue as though everyone should know about it. Of course I knew that it was the central legislative assembly, but the number of members changes so often, it seems, that it was hard to keep up. So-called *official* members are colonial administrators; the *unofficial* members are all elected on communal rolls, with Europeans electing Europeans, Arabs electing Arabs, Hindus electing Hindus, and so on. At that time the Africans could only indirectly say who would represent them. All this compartmentalizing tends to make each race or group think only of itself, and so adds to racial tensions.

"Schools, too, are compartmentalized, which is not good." Mr. Patel leaned forward earnestly. "Our children go to Government schools; in primary levels Gujerati is used, but later English. Some Muslims come to these schools or maybe they go to an Urdu primary school. Ismailis have their own Ismaili schools. So many schools are expensive. Even the youngest must pay fees of twelve shillings a month.

This does not seem high, yet many cannot afford it. This is one of our greatest problems, to educate our community."

"We are having many faults," he confessed, "but mostly they are due to lack of education. Every European will tell you that the Indians are bad citizens because they do not pay their taxes. You have heard this?"

I admitted I had, many times.

"Have you ever tried sneaking something through customs?" he demanded sharply. Before I could reflect long enough to feel guilty he rushed on, "With you it is a game. Why then do the English not think it as game to dodge taxes? Many Indians ask this because they have no sense of civic responsibility. If one lacks education, if one is not well off, then there is no time for worrying about roads and sewers."

When I asked about the attitudes of his community toward the Africans, Mr. Patel stressed that the Indians believed in non-violence to achieve their goals, so naturally they were repelled by Mau Mau. "In any case, we are too busy to help support the African demands, even if we wanted to. But you know," he said quietly as we stood by the door, "color has a natural repulsion; we feel it, so we know the European feels it. But with education this prejudice should go."

I was surprised at his honesty. Most Indians deny having a color prejudice. Yet I knew that in India a girl's beauty was often judged by the lightness, the "wheatish color," of her skin. While American girls acquire a suntan, the Indian girls stay out of the sun. It may only be a question of fad and fashion, but I think in India the feeling went deeper.

"How can we support the African's demands?" Mr. Patel demanded. "Common suffrage just won't do, not til they also learn civic responsibility." Then with that typically Indian shrug of the head, he said resignedly, "But I cannot say this openly. Still we must find a better formula, perhaps educational qualification. In a hundred years, maybe, all of us will be assimilated. Then we shall be having no more worries."

# CHAPTER 6

# Mombasa Africans

*I*N THE EVENING LIGHT I PASSED A FEW INDIANS IN THE ALLEY outside Mr. Patel's office. Further along, the main street was alive with strolling Europeans. Yet this is Africa, I reminded myself. What of the Africans? Kenya is their country, and the aims of the British government, at least as stated in 1923, recognize the preeminence of African interests. Next day I walked into the office of the Municipal Officer for African Affairs, Mr. E. C. Eggins, and asked him what the government was doing in Mombasa for the Africans.

"Have you seen our housing schemes?" Mr. Eggins asked eagerly, not waiting for me to finish identifying myself. "We are making real progress with the housing, and other things too. Don't let this Mau Mau fool you. The Africans are not the problem here; they will learn self-government, all right.

The difficulty is what to do with the minorities, how..., what safeguards... But you came to ask about the Africans."

With that Mr. Eggins was already striding out of the door, still talking, his emphatic gestures injecting a bit of African volubility into his British civil servant's calm. He was a tall man, good-looking in a dark, almost American way, yet charmingly English. As we walked from the cool of the thick walls into the sun he described the different tribes represented in Mombasa.

"The tribes are distinct in temperament, outlook, – yes, even feel. You will understand the difference after you have been here awhile. There are some 220 tribes in all of Kenya, so naturally the Africans themselves are conscious of differences. Between some tribes there is bitter rivalry. Mau Mau won't spread far as long as it represents the aspirations of one tribe only. We've had no trouble here in Mombasa with the eruption of nativism." His face screwed with distaste. "There have been other cults before, you know, mystical perversions, I suppose you might say. The group that received most publicity before this Mau Mau was one in Tanganyika back in 1905, called Maji-Maji. Their leader told them that European bullets would run to water. They soon learned differently!"

The brilliant flat light of a tropic afternoon bore down upon us. In this environment strong passions and violence became credible, almost expected...if you ever get out of the shade. For the shadow is seductive, the merest patch beckons you to sit, and catch the quiet puffs of air. The Kikuyu, more than any other tribe, has been out in the sun. It was an ardent Kikuyu organizer, Chege Kebachia, who led the Mombasa dock strike in 1947. Mau Mau, too, is a Kikuyu invention.

"The Kikuyu are clever," mused Eggins, following my thoughts. "But they must have outside help from somewhere

The Africans are simply not sufficiently educated nor are they emotionally stable enough for such sustained action."

THE DRIVE TO THE housing schemes was itself instructive, up the wide European streets to pick up husband-photographer Mil, twisting through the snaky alleys of the Arab quarter. The road changed from paved to dirt; the white-washed houses gave way to huts in all shades of brown and white. At the poorest section we turned up over the curb and drove into the dusty village, not green but brown.

To one side, under a huge tree, a corrugated tin closet enclosing a water spigot served as the village well. Most of the water-fetchers, all men in this Muslim village, gossiped in the shade, their kerosene tin containers sometimes serving as a doodle-drum to give emphasis to tales or laughter. Some of these men were professional water carriers, for this was the only tap in the area. Mostly they wore undershirts and shorts, perhaps a ragged shirt; but their turbans, though faded, were neatly tied. When Mil took their picture their teeth grinned whiter than the soiled whitewashed huts in the background.

"The municipality put in the water pipes free, but we lack the funds for free water," Eggins said apologetically, as we walked past the mud-and-wattle huts. "The man by the water tap collects 1 cent a debbie – which is about four gallons or one kerosene tin."

The huts were jammed together, eighty of them in the first plot. The lanes between were hard-packed earth wherever the sun penetrated; but in the shade the slopped water made them sticky mud paths. There were no drains to carry off either water or sewage; the only sanitation system in the "village" consisted of buckets. All this is admittedly sub-standard and had been allowed only as a temporary measure. That was before the war.

"We are moving these people to our other developments as quickly as possible." Mr. Eggins continued. "We want to tear down this whole area, but we must, of course, provide alternate housing. Til then, we control the Asian owners of these huts by rent ceilings; a house cost seven shillings a month. This is less than the legally required housing allowance given the lowest paid employee. Though the conditions are not good, they are better than in the reserves. Few that come to town want to go back. They are generally grateful for whatever the government does for them, not like the tribes in the highlands. But then, here there is no problem of land. Many Mombasa Africans are descendants of freed slaves and have no memory of a reserve and would hate to go back farming. Make no mistake," he urged us, stopping his walk for emphasis, "the tribes are different here on the Coast."

Gesturing toward a group of smiling women sitting on a door step, Mr. Eggins remarked that his department hoped to curb prostitution once the area was razed. Right now it is a lucrative trade. Obviously no municipal housing would be provided for them and lack of headquarters might persuade them to return to their homes. Every day the government gets request from the families of these young women to send them home so they can be married!

At that moment a little girl splattered across the path in front of us chasing some chickens in the mud. A woman in the hut behind grinned broadly, and waved to me. "Jambo rafiki," I greeted her, "Hello, friend," and poked my head into the hut. It was undefined blackness; the friendly native herself blended into the blackness. Not a ray of light entered except by the door, and my eyes, accustomed to the glaring sun, could make out nothing.

"You will see," said Mr. Eggins over my shoulder, "that women are the most conservative force throughout Africa.

They want to do things as their mothers did. In the villages they like their huts air tight. They stuff up every crack so that the smoke and smells hover near the roof." Smelling what he meant, I retreated. "You'll find the same thing in the new experimental houses we have built. So we must send inspectors around to see whether that the air vents have not been clogged with rags. Let us have a look at them."

These new houses, high on the leeward bluff of the island, are set back from the main road by a grassy play area. Across the macadam road European bungalows enjoyed the same breeze and lovely view of beach and inlet.

The central green, the road, and the yards of the houses were clean and neat. "The municipality employs a maintenance staff for the grounds," commented Eggins, in response to our questions. "All families who move in must promise to keep the property and houses clean as well as pay rent. Lapse of either can mean eviction."

Set among tall palms and short heavy shade trees on either side of the circular road were four two-story white-washed apartment buildings with bright red tile roofs. Most apartments had their green shutters closed against the sun. But still, in the open backyards, children were playing.

We called at several doors before we found a woman at home. She had been scrubbing the bare concrete floor of one of the three bedrooms. The living room was furnished with mats, and nothing more. In the kitchen two segrees–portable charcoal braziers – were still warm. All was austere and clean, including the bathroom with its "bomb sight" or seat-less toilet. The windows were shuttered and closed, but the permanent vents in the bathroom were wide open.

Much better adapted to the needs and economics of the African than the more European apartment, were the houses based on traditional Swahili huts. They were square houses with four equal rooms off a central passage which ran from the entrance to a courtyard in the rear. Here was a lavatory and shower, and cooking space for the four small families who lived in the house. The partition of the rooms did not reach the roof, for the Swahilis apparently love to shout at each other over the walls.

These experimental houses were being rented at a market level rather than being subsidized. The apartments cost 56 shillings, about $7.50 a month, while one room in the bungalow ran about $4.40 a month. This is too high in relation to the African's income, which starts at the $7.64 a month minimum wage and rises only very slowly. But as Mr.Eggins explained, their aim is to rent the houses to companies, such as the three story apartments belonging to the East African Breweries, who subsidize the cost to their employees.

The Government itself subsidizes housing for its own employees in a separate location. For $1.15 per month, which is the added housing allowance for employees making less than 100 shillings per month, pleasant row apartments are provided. Mr. Eggins piloted us beyond the more humble apartment, through a "middle-class" apartment dripping antimacassars and crocheted spreads, and on to the "wealthy" household of Mr. Banks. An assistant deputy making perhaps $1500 a year, he has no income tax to pay. His free house was furnished with solid respectable tables and chairs; only the bed was exuberantly ornate. Yet even here, permanent non-closeable vents were built into the bathroom walls.

This housing was for municipal employees; the central government did even better by its employees, with fancy "refinements" such as glass louvered windows and electric lights. These houses backed on a soccer field on the far side of which stood a municipal nursery school. With most of the education for Africans in the hands of government-subsidized missionary schools, this is indeed an innovation. The uniformed children were just drinking their free milk as we walked by their very modern school.

But most impressive of the municipality's amenities for its African population was the spick-and span African Social Center which was so up-to-date and European that it took some time before the Africans would use it. Now its cinema, its dances and volley ball games, its beer and coke bar, form the center of African life in Mombasa. So fine are its accommodations that Asian as well as African groups meet in the lecture room.

The clock tower over this red brick and white plaster building is the only part of the center that is the worse for wear, despite warnings by more conservative Europeans about the African habits. "They do not know how to treat good things," they would say, or "everything will be stolen." Yet nothing of value has been stolen, while the Center's rooms are in inspection-shine. Credit for this goes equally to the users of the Center, mostly African, and to the staff and manager – all of whom are African. The clock itself was harmed when it was dropped accidentally by workmen repairing the roof.

By the colonnaded entrance gaudy posters advertised the movie: Bob Baker in Ghost Riders. Large glass doors led to the library where for ten cents a year Africans may borrow English and Swahili books. The chairs around the heavy table were each donated by an African group. "Aiyar's Social Club" read one plaque, "Kikuyu Barber's Association," said another. "These aren't trade unions," Mr. Eggins reminded us. "It is the policy of the government to foster unions; but here the time is not yet ripe. Unfortunately the one union which does make an attempt at existing is no example; so much dues go in, so much advance goes out into the pockets of the chairman and the secretary. But," he paused, searching for the right words to convey in understated English his hope to an effusive American, " but in this as in our other goals, we shall succeed in the future."

The cafeteria was airy and light, with glass French doors opening on to a luxuriant garden. The moment we entered with Mr. Eggins several Africans came over to greet him. At his suggestion they immediately began explaining to us the workings of the Native Trust Fund which pays all the operating costs of the Center. Most of the money in the fund comes from the sale of beer to Africans. For the same reasons – real and imagined – that we Americans restricted the sale of intoxicating liquor to American Indians, so the British limit liquor to Africans. To satisfy demand and simultaneously to control consumption, there are only three beer-pubs in Mombasa where an African may be served. They sell the cheap and safe toddy-palm beer known as "tembo," but only two bottles a day to any one customer. All profits from these pubs are put into the Native Trust Fund; and there are lots of profits, grinned one African, for after all, Africans like their beer!

The Africans talked freely before Mr. Eggins, mutually agreeing that there was more give and take between rule and ruled along the coast than upcountry. "You will see," they said sadly. Yet strangely in the presence of authority, or in its absence, the Mombasa Africans had little to say about the great problem of the savage Mau Mau. It was difficult to believe that they did not have any opinions on the subject; so we assumed that they were just being careful.

We returned again and again to the Africa Center. Here at last was something of Africa, not the picturesque and primitive continent that the tourist folders rave about, but the emerging, hard, real, confused Africa. It is the Mombasa African's coffee house; here men meet, and ideas grow. We, too, sat at round tables drinking coke or orangeade and talking with them. Theoretically anyone of any race can use the Center; but except for our guide for the first visit, Mr. Eggins, we never saw another non-African there. Nor another woman.

Without the presence of Mr. Eggins our table mates opened up a bit more. Still, the words 'Mau Mau' and 'Kikuyu' were repeated and linked until they were nearly interchangeable, we began to sense the aloofness of these coastal Africans to those upcountry. This Mau Mau fight was between the Kikuyu and the European. It hardly concerned Mombasa Africans any more than did the conflict between Somalis and Italians in Somaliland, which is about as close, or between the Arabs and French in Morocco, which is a continent away. Behind this aloofness was jealousy and mistrust of the Kikuyu, for they are the best educated and the wealthiest of all Kenya's tribes.

"They no like marry outside Kikuyu tribe," said one.

"They ask for big dowry for Kikuyu women, so big many Kikuyu take no wife!" added another slyly.

"But they have real grievances," rejoined a third. "Of all tribes, they suffer most, the whites took their land. So naturally are more aggressive."

"You know," laughed a rotund and aging man, "we are lazy people here. Coast weather is bad weather. We don't bother so much about anything." Everyone nodded in agreement.

All the Africans at our table conversed in English – some in polished cadences, some in pidgin. Still any knowledge of the language marked them as the small number of educated leaders of their community. Nearly all of them had learned English at missionary schools, and they retained a high regard for the missionaries, in vivid contrast to the bitterness toward the missions we would encounter upcountry.

"After all," said Mr. Banks, "many of our grandparents

were slaves. The missionaries founded towns for freed slaves, and really helped them."

One of the most vocal of our "Round Table" set was Mr. F. J. Khamisi. Unlike all the other Africans we met he had been educated not only in missionary schools but also in an Arab school. But he was a Christian and had actually studied for the ministry. His error was to read the Bible too well and take to heart the preaching of Jesus when He said "Love your neighbor." Khamisi believed that when the preacher spoke of everyone's being of equal worth before the Lord, he meant just that.

"Now the settlers claim to be Christian," Khamisi pointed out, "yet they obviously do not practice the Bible. At first I thought, well, maybe the settlers are simply poor Christians. But when the ministers and teachers kept up the color bar even among the candidates for the ministry, this was too much of a contradiction. I left."

For a time Khamisi worked in Nairobi as an editor of the government supported newspaper "Baraza." It was started during World War II to counter wild rumors about an Italian invasion from Ethiopia and give an accurate picture of the war effort to the Africans. Khamisi was free enough from government control to publish what he wished. That is until he ran a picture of an African lawyer in England with his white wife; Khamisi was then retired.

For two years after this he was a member of the Nairobi Town Council. All the while he put out a weekly newspaper on his own, editing and printing it himself. He ran a secretarial service on the side. On top of all this he had time to become the first general secretary of the Kenya African Union and editor of their official organ called "African Voice".

"KAU," Khamisi said, pronouncing the initials of the Kenya African Union as one word, "was set up to help the first African member of the Legco, Mr. Mathu, bring to government the grievances of his people. Africans from all tribes belonged, at least at first, when I was general secretary."

He paused, and cocked his head to watch me jot down notes in my journal which I had lying, inconspicuously I hoped, on my lap. I looked up a bit embarrassed.

"But I am a newspaperman," Khamisi said smiling at my fluster. "I too take notes."

"You said KAU used to have members from all tribes?" Mil questioned, getting us back on the subject.

"Yes," replied Khamisi, "until Jomo Kenyatta returned from his studies in England and Russia. He's a Kikuyu, and all the Kikuyu were impressed by his fresh ideas and wanted him as general secretary. Of course I didn't oppose him, for he is a strong man. Whatever he will do, he will do it well."

Perhaps six months later Khamisi returned to the coast. Why? "I am a coastal man. I like it here. And I couldn't stay in KAU, for it was now Kikuyu. I am not knowing Kenyatta's views and perhaps I am not agreeing with some of his methods. But I believe Kenyatta is not involved with Mau Mau. Surely the British will hold a fair trial and so he must be acquitted."

The trial of Jomo Kenyatta, accused of being the mastermind behind Mau Mau, was still going on while we were in Kenya. No two people projected the same outcome, and I am sure if you talked to them after the verdict that no two of them would agree about the final results of the trial.

Once, when our "Round Table" was expanding beyond the tete-a-tete to a mass discussion, I threw out a question about the Indians. The replies were surprisingly violent.

"I hate them" spat one. "They squeeze us out of middle man jobs."

"They're after our blood" shrieked a little man at the edge of the circle.

"Those Indians on the Municipal Council help us less than the Europeans. They're only on our side if there is bacon in it," contributed a calmer voice.

Grinned another, "In India, they are fine, but not here. Just like Englishmen are fine in London, but not the settlers here. Immigrants are second class people."

Out of all this came the feeling that the government and to some, the missionaries, were the African's knights tilting against both the Indians and the European settlers. Faith was still high. The benevolent administration was just what they wanted. But this was on the coast.

As we prepared to drive inland, I thought about the years of struggle for independence in India. Could Europeans and Indians ever fit into a free African country?

# CHAPTER 7

# The road trip begins

T HE EUROPEANS WHO SAT ON OUR HOTEL'S LONG PORCH HAVING tea in the afternoon wanted the British troops to stay. Over the clink of the teapot and the swish of spoons, you could hear favorite theories of the "treat 'em rough" school directed at the Mau Mau and the same condemnation of Indians that we had heard from the Africans. These wicker-chair experts disliked just about everyone in Kenya, except themselves of course. But they retained special hate toward those "journalists who fly in for a few days and tell us how to run our colony."

The backwash of such conversation was enough to drive me to our room where I was working on my first article for the Calcutta *Statesman*. The heat usually turned such a retreat into siesta, even at tea time. Particularly the day we finally undertook the dreaded job of unpacking all the tins of food and Mil's glucose in our wooden crate. Out in the vacant lot we surrounded Bubble with our equipment and wondered how such a little car would carry all that and the two of us as well. Hot and grimy, Mil fitted jerry cans, sleeping rolls, trunks, jigsaw-like onto the roof rack while I pretended great energy by transferring tin cans from one box to another and wishing fervently the whole crate had fallen overboard. It was hopeless!

Tire chains, tools, and tracks (wire mesh for putting under tires in sand), the primus cooking stove, and food all had to go into the diminutive "boot" (the English and more appropriate name for the "trunk," somehow less refined, more utilitarian!) We had a tin trunk in which we'd stowed thermos bottles and the like on the ocean crossing. I now filled it with cans that were duplicates, triplicates, quadruplets. Then one of each went into cardboard box: corned beef, Spam, stew, packaged soups and bouillon cubes, sardines, liver pate, butter, fruits, vegetables. I remember buying these, selecting for the small size can rather than for content. Now to my horror we seemed sentenced to live on beets and fruit cocktail.

Filled, the tin trunk was too heavy to lift. Even if we got it in once, it would have to come out only too frequently since in the boot the tin trunk would sit on top of the spare tire which was inconveniently stored on the floor with no protecting shelf. So out came all the cans again. This time we began packing them loose. The grapefruit juice fitted into a ledge in the back of the boot, the little milk cans just slid down a space between exposed braces. Canned brown bread, baked beans, soup, all merry-go-around the tire. Then the tin trunk, now lighter with boxes of cookies, tins of Saltines, and some odds and ends of clothes and rags to keep the glass jars of jam, mustard, pickles and olives from smashing.

On top of the tin trunk went the stove, and a box of various cans for immediate use. Another reserve box of food went on the roof while a box of lunch spreads, instant coffee and jars for half-used food went into the back seat. Aye, we were well supplied! As if this were still the lost continent, as if we were a brave safari packing in all our food for the months we would explore the blank parts of the continent where the cartographers painted "hic leones"...

I was daydreaming again, and getting a sun-burned face from the glowing tropical sun. Mad dogs and American women go out without their hats. I made a mental note to buy a sunshade, pushing myself back into the twentieth century. Really, surveying all our food, I felt rather foolish. Mombasa stores had plenty of cans though their contents were more limited, and the large size of most of them might not have fitted so compactly into the boot! I vowed never to let my super-budgeting get the better of me again, little aware at how fast two people can eat through a pile of cans – as long as they have the help of a can-opener.

After a shower and a siesta and smears of cream on my red burnt nose, the anticipation of the Trip began to grow. We had yet to pack our personal suitcases and pile them in the back seat. Our warmer clothes, spare towels, maps and books for the second half of the safari were already packed into a second tin trunk and tied securely on the roof of the car.

Each of us had two suitcases. Mine were weekenders; Mil's were larger and usually crammed with assorted feminine articles that just would not go into my own. Besides these we each had a canvas overnight bag with our toilet articles, bathrobes, pajamas and slippers, and a sweater for the cool wind. Suitcases, cameras, books, notebooks, two thermos bottles (the quart one for coffee, the gallon one for water), the first aid kit, our raincoats, a pillow and a camp stool – all were assigned a place in the back seat. But fitting them in was a breeze compared to that mountain of cans!

On our last night in Mombasa our administration friends feted us in very unBritish fashion: the music of the African continent had invaded their composure. Each guest was assigned an "instrument," like pupils in kindergarten! Mil, not the most musical of husbands, became expert on the triangle, then tried the paper-on-the-comb. At first I whacked at a wooden block but was promoted to a piccolo. Still the only recognizable music came from the host and his guitar. A rollicking evening, undimmed by any bright-and-early getaway plans. We knew that our final packing, the last checking of the car, would take hours. And the animals in Tsavo Park through which the Nairobi Road passed, showed themselves only in the early morning. Our plan was to drive to the park the first night, a mere 94 miles away.

It was late when we finally got into bed. The moon was full into our window, the air soft and tropical. Had I not been exhausted from last minute packing I should have daydreamed once more; instead I fell asleep, fitfully, climbing tin mountains growing with cans instead of trees. The moon lit the weird scene enough so that I could feel shadows pursuing me. A black hand was reaching out...

Suddenly I was awake, bolt upright in the bed. Mil was high-jumping right out the window onto the veranda. But I wasn't asleep now. My notebook which had been on the table by the window was askew on the floor, our glasses were knocked on the bed. When my hand stopped shaking I put mine on. Only then did I notice that Mil's keys and wallet lay full in the moonlight, asking to be stolen! The party had been too gay!

But where was Mil? All the tales of Mau Mau we'd laughed at, or shrugged off, came crowding into my receptive mind. How foolishly courageous to run after a thief and into a gang! Despite my gonging heart I pulled myself up, hid the wallet in the bedclothes, and thrust my head out the door. Growing bolder I slipped down the corridor – no husband – and along the veranda – still no husband. Shouts from below. A policeman's whistle.

Mil finally reappeared from chasing the intruder, a splinter in his bare foot his only battle wound. Luckily the thief had been alone.

CLOUDS WERE HEAVY IN the sky as we jammed the rest of our belongings into Bublee; the air was close and muggy but not quite heavy enough to rain. February, on the rain chart, is supposed to be rainless in Mombasa and Nairobi; but the Kilimanjaro area, toward which we were heading, lists two to five inches of rain for that month. Obviously some rain cloud didn't know its geography and had crossed the boundary line. Later we found, as a matter of record, that few clouds did in fact follow either map or rain chart. Only in Uganda, where it rains all year round, did cloud and chart agree. Elsewhere, as we drove over dirt roads, we would always watch the clouds apprehensively, and hope they'd looked at the chart. Too often they had not.

Colin marveled at our packing, insisted upon taking us to lunch at the town's sole soda bar, and waved us off from the calm coast into the erupting interior. On the coast Colin, too, was calm, a 90% English and 10% colonial young man with a natural shy stutter that takes many Oxford and Cambridge students years to perfect. So completely did his gentle sweetness prevail that I felt I hardly knew him, upcountry, when he reversed to 90% colonial. The power of the terror had only just brushed us: the prison officer at Lamu, the thief at our hotel. But a touch can communicate disease; we were lucky, our resistance was strong.

AS WE CROSSED THE low bridge from Mombasa Island to the mainland the sun gathered up the clouds and hurried them south. Back from the coast the palm belt ringed the mangrove swamps, then gave way to bush. A few villagers clustered along the road; huts made from mangrove spares interlaced with mud and coral filler were roofed with palm. Here and there a whitewashed hut glared in the sun; a few were even decorated with blue wash outlining the door or splashed on walls in a geometric design.

Our progress was slow for we were not only favoring the new engine but the whole car, it was so heavily loaded. We were gaining altitude rapidly; almost at once the tropical vegetation thinned into endless savanna. Thorn, aloe, acacia trees cleared the undistinguished bush only by inches. Three-fifths of the colony is as barren, or worse. The coastal strip is like a coral reef isolated on each side by an expanse of wilderness. The sea laps out to Zanzibar, bush flows all around the island peaks of Kilimanjaro and Kenya. Caught between these massive peaks, which rise from thorny tangle to year-round snows, is the Aberdare Range, backbone of the highlands. On this island of mile-high land, comprising only one-fifth of the Kenya Colony, live the European settlers and the Kikuyu and the Masai.

But on the wastes almost no one lives. Caravans took thirteen days to march across this arid steppe! For once I was glad of our century!

We hugged the left side of the road, trying to avoid the clouds of dust kicked up by an occasional passing car. Here, as in India, the English rule of driving on the left side of the road has been adopted. But Bublee, being an export model designed for the US, had a right hand drive. It meant that which of us was driving could only see the edge of the road, and usually stayed there; the occasional "overtaking," to use the British word, required cooperation from whoever was the navigator. Happily this seldom happened, for the cars were few and we were usually the slowest. Loaded as we were we dared not try the bump-riding technique, since the potholes, even on the main Mombasa-Nairobi road, were all too frequent. Like most of the "made up" roads in this part of Africa, the route was surfaced with ground granite; "water-bound macadam" the technicians call it.

Without warning, almost from a clear sky, rain began to fall in heavy, outsized drops. Across the Irish bridges, dry just moments before, rushed miniature torrents. I wondered vaguely about the name...surely "Scotch" would be more appropriate, since it's a way of saving money by dipping the road to let the water course over the road instead of building a bridge that might be washed out in the next downpour. The way this short storm had set the streamlets gushing, I understood why the railroad, which we glimpsed occasionally, often rose majestically, almost mystically, several feet above the plain.

Bublee took several smallish Irish bridges unconcernedly, so we raced through a larger one without thinking – and the engine died on the far edge. Water had splashed on the spark plugs, but in a few moments it dried. Wiser now, we slowed down as we approached the next stream. This one coursed through a gully, concentrating its depth. It looked ominous; on the far side a car drew up and waited. So we did the same. Honking assuredly, a Land Rover sped up behind us, paused long enough to shift into four wheel drive, and plowed on. Envious, we followed suit – and got stuck in the middle! Off with shoes and socks, roll up pant legs, we both pushed and shoved to get Bublee out of the water, and back on the side we'd started from. I waded across, plotting the route, and Mil drove slowly into the roaring bridge-dip. Too slowly; water got into the exhaust pipe and the engine died again. The third time, neither too fast nor too slow, we made it. This was lesson one. Soon we learned to stuff rags around the spark plugs, remove the fan belt to cut down splashing, drive speedily through, and expect the engine to die – on the far side. A bit of hand-drying of the sparks and we would be off again. For in the desert-bush where the smallest rain-storm produces a flash flood, real bridges are a foolish luxury except over all-weather streams. We soon acclimatized our-selves, and indeed became so blasé about crossing un-bridged rivers that we nearly crossed into disaster. But that was much later, in Ethiopia..

The rain storm also gave us lesson two; how to tack a car on mud. It's not unlike skidding over ice, except there is more drag so that the flick of the wheel must come just a little slower, as if you were leaning into the wind a second before coming about. Here the slick road was merely leveled ground, built up here and there to keep an even surface – and this one of the major roads in the Colony! On the map it is a thick red line. The road to Lamu is a solid but thin line. What sort of a road was the dashed line, we wondered, that led to Mzima Springs where we were planning to go. Actu-ally we found little correlation between the lines on the map and the roads on the ground. Often the dashed roads were smoother because it takes frequent traffic to corrugate them. As often, the solid roads were sand traps or mud holes or bush tracks. Few of any kind were all-weather roads. Driving just anywhere was something of an adventure, for if the roads did not play tricks on you, and the weather obeyed the charts, then there were always the animals to mess things up.

But we were still novices on African roads that first day. The shakes from the corrugations jarred like a dentist's drill. Odd noises on the roof, groans from the boot, knock-knock-knock by the window. Periodically we would stop and inspect – tires, oil, water, baggage. We were chiding ourselves for our timidity when, skur – runch! Crash, Bang!

The car wrenched to the side, sounding like an earthquake.

Shaken, we jumped from the car. The roof rack teetered at a rakish angle. The trunks, boxes, sleeping rolls and cans were still tied securely on to it. But one of the clamps had shorn off.

"Ye gods," I exploded. "A dud. 200 shillings worth. How long do you suppose it was sitting around in that garage, rusting?"

But Mil was too busy to answer. He was bracing the rack to keep it from sliding off. Re-packing this time was really a puzzle. Miraculously the back seat expanded and everything fit, but it broke my heart to jam hard square corners of the tin trunk into the soft tan foam seats. We covered the tan finish with old rags; but the battle gray paint scarred the back of the front seats so indelibly that the marks are still there. Tan was a silly color to have in any case. We thought we'd ordered dark brown. If all green Austin's have tan insides, nobody had told us.

Mil roped the empty rack criss-cross onto the car leaving only one door free to open. How funny Bublee looked all bound up! But we were not in any light-hearted mood and when a huge American car bore up behind us, loudly honking, we only scowled harder. And then roared with laughter. The horn had stuck. The driver, a rotund Indian, clambered out some distance beyond us, and leaving his servant to stop the noise, waddled back toward us apologetically.

"You wish to sending messages to Nairobi? I must be arriving by nine tonight." A slight exaggeration, for it was already late afternoon.

I explained that we were foreigners and knew no one in the city.

"Americans!" he guessed. "Why you have English car?" he asked disdainfully. "You must be bringing here American car; you make much money on it. I never buy such little cars. So slow! Why you have rack that doesn't fit? That is why it falls off, isn't it? You must be watching what you buy in this country. Why you are not fastening the rope to the door handle? You have broken piece to solder on?" He spoke all this pompously, offering nothing but advice. Still he had stopped, and I thanked him for it.

"Well, I was forced to" he shrugged, and departed.

All this in 42 miles!

At mile 47 tarmac began, and we sailed into Voi, passed the hotel, and put up at the railroad Dak bungalow. In India "dak" means "post." Spaced along all main routes, these bungalows provide simple, clean accommodation for all comers. But the word there has come to mean any government-run stopping place where you furnish your own bedding. Some serve food, some do not; and almost none have plumbing. If you took a shower, it was Indian style, dipping from a bucket; there were oblong tin tubs for a bath.

This Dak bungalow was in the super class: a tub with running water, a flush latrine. The dinner, too, though typically British, was above average: a flavorless soup, nondescript fried fish, roast mutton with browned potatoes and the inevitable cabbage cooked like mush, gelatin drowned in custard, and bitter coffee. We were quickly to bed, in proper beds not sleeping bags, to rise with the animals in the morning.

OUR DAYS IN TSAVO National Park were pure joy. The road to Madanda Rock was not on the map at all, but it was well-packed rust-red earth and fairly smooth. As the light came into the bush, there was movement on all sides. A herd of grazing zebra started, and scattered, not from us, but from a sleek large Oryx-antelope with straight swept horns. Their movement seemed infectious; from all sides darted gazelle with curved horns, long necked gerenuk, baby-sized dik-dik, looking like Disney creations! All sizes, all colors of buck, a striped-pants type in most abundance. Birds gathered like blossoms on the dull gray-green trees, then darted off again. Ugly warthogs skittered across the road, a mongoose darted behind a pile of elephant dung.

The park had been a reserve only since 1948, so the animals still take flight when they hear the motors chug. We sat quietly for a time, watching from the car, and secretly thanking the tse-tse fly for preserving this scene. Without its ravages to man and his cattle, it is inconceivable that such a large area would have been set aside for a game reserve. No one wanted the land but the wild animals, and it was theirs, completely.

After driving past the abundant game, it seemed a bit strange to park by Madanda Rock, leave the car, and climb cement steps set on the huge outcropping. I confess I looked about carefully before I stepped out and watched for snakes as I climbed; I was very much a tenderfoot. In most game parks the one rule is to remain in the auto. There you are safe from all but the wildest elephant or rampaging rhino.

On the flattened top of the rock was a lean-to, shade for the tourist and shelter for the native guard. From the

Mil and the guard watching
elephants at Madanda Rock

welcome shade of the hut we could see all corners of the shallow pool which lay some twenty feet below. It was a grandstand seat, though the players are oblivious of the audience. Only if the wind blows hard down from the rock can they smell, though not see or touch, any interlopers. Three sides of the pool are rimmed with greenery – not lush, but soft relief from the grayish thorn wastes beyond. A perfect scene! I had seen it before, in movies of ivory hunters!

On the stage, when we arrived, were storks, standing like clay statues, immovable throughout the drama. Hogs darted about like impatient children at a circus. A lone wild buffalo sauntered up, looked haughtily at the unseen spectators, and departed.

"Elephants, come?" I begged the guard.

"Elephant, before, come. Now all gone. No elephant, then more come," he said expressively in English after giving up on my Swahili. At length I gathered that only one herd will water at a time; if a second one comes, the herd will wait in the bush for the other to depart. Sure enough, a lead elephant poked his trunk into the clearing, and seeing nothing, trumpeted. From all sides swarmed the beasts – thirty or more of them – so large compared to Indian elephants, so wild and virile and tusked.

"This side Africa, elephant teeth more better," explained the guard, pointing to his own white incisors. Later I found his pidgin was accurate; tusks are indeed but outsized teeth! And East African ivory is the most highly priced variety, being whiter and more easily carved than that from West Africa.

One elephant family, well-trained, came right up to the footlights to play, dousing each other with the cool red mud, and tossing water so high that I swear I could feel the spray. For by now we were out along the edge of the rock, oblivious of the sun in our delight.

The bush, in the heat of the day, is as deserted as Wall Street on Sunday. Not an animal was in sight as we drove on to Mtito Andei and cut back toward Mzima Springs on the slopes of mighty, but misty, Kilimanjaro. A busload of boat passengers from Mombasa on a three day junket of parks were gossiping loudly in the spring's parking lot. Certain they had scared off the hippo with their squeals, we took off to a distant spring with our lunch which we had forgotten to eat in the excitement. In a shallow pool we waded, and relaxed. The ferns and water palms hung narcissus-like above the mirror water; idyllic Africa.

Somewhat commercialized, the main springs had little viewing piers built out over the marshy edges of the springs. But these did not clear the foliage, so we found a log which jutted out from the bank. As we balanced precariously, a huge old hippo came up to snoop around. Across the pool junior was having a bit of a time grabbing leaves from an overhanging bush for his supper.

Down by the river we looked for rhino, not really sure whether we wanted to see them or not. The guidebook notes that it can see only about 35 yards and its hearing is not good. But it can smell! At close quarters in bushy country the rhino is dangerous. But only baboons came to plague us, jaywalking all over the road; once more, in the shadows of day, the buck and zebra were out. Unexpectedly, gawking over the thorns, was a giraffe, grinning welcome.

Moonlight accomplished what the sun could not do, and drew out exotic Kilimanjaro from veils of mist. "Kilim" means "mountain", "N'jaro", "high, shining"; it was exciting to see the mountain portraying her name, rising from near sea level conical, to two jutting, glistening peaks. From the veranda of the lodge we thought we could hear the animals – surely a few lions among them – doing obeisance to her majesty. For a moment, my daydreams were real.

# CHAPTER 8

# Tanganyika: a quiet country in the midst of turmoil

*I*T WAS IMPOSSIBLE TO TELL EXACTLY WHEN WE ENTERED TANG-anyika. There were no signs, no border posts, no guards. The road skirted east of majestic Kilimanjaro, both of her peaks modestly decked with clouds. Once out of the game reserve the varied bush was replaced by the drab green-brown of sisal cactus planted in long rows in the dull crumbly earth. Vividly I remembered making a flour-and-water paste map of Africa...was it in sixth grade? But Tanganyika had been pink, not olive brown. So much of Africa had been pink, the traditional color for British possessions. I had sent away for some information on a class project in that geography class. Months later during vacation a thick government report arrived. I don't think I ever read it through. But what a smell! On the inside cover was stamped this explanation: this book has been sprayed for termites, but still the book was riddled with their holes. What a wild country, I thought then!

But once here it looked quite peaceful. Politically it was more peaceful than any of its British neighbors. To the south both Nyasaland and Northern Rhodesia were maneuvering unhappily within the new Central African Federation. To the north the part of Kenya we had just come through was simply nervous, but the part of Kenya into which we were going was seething with resentment and fear. To the northeast, Uganda was fearful of future, and building up to a constitutional crisis. Tanganyika seemed peaceful indeed.

Undoubtedly one reason for the peace was its land policy. In Kenya the highlands were rapidly settled by "whites" as soon as the railroad was completed. By 1930 over 30,000 Europeans, a majority from South Africa, occupied the most fertile land in the country. Africans, who had roamed the area for centuries, were pushed into reserves. These settlers greatly complicated the political scene in Kenya. By contrast, in Tanganyika, many of the endless sisal plantations were Indian-owned. Further on, nearer Moshi, Africans own much of the best coffee land. In Kenya, Indians cannot own land except in the Sultan's coastlands or in special areas in the cities. In Tanganyika there are no such restrictions, and the large Indian population of the coastal towns has fanned out into the semi-highlands which they have farmed with much profit to themselves and to the country. Most of these Indian planters acquired their lands after World War I when the German colonizers were deported by the new British administration after they took over the colony under the Mandate system of the League of Nations.

As British and South African settlers replaced the departing Germans, they agitated for union with Kenya in order to obtain the special status which was accorded to

Kenya whites. But the administration, backed by the international treaty and strengthened by visiting international commissions, withstood the settlers' pressures, more or less. Instead of allowing white settlers to buy the lands around Kilimanjaro occupied by the Wachagga tribe, the administration encouraged the tribe to cultivate coffee themselves. In Kenya, for many years, the white coffee growers were able to keep Africans from growing any coffee at all, since coffee cultivation put the Africans in direct competition with the white plantation owners. To maintain the quality of the coffee crop, and to help the 12,000 African planters market their coffee, the Wachagga formed the Kilimanjaro Native Co-operative Union under the aegis, persuasion, insistence, and encouragement of remarkable Mr. A.L.G. Bennett, long time agriculture officer in the Tanganyika civil service. As a result, the Wachagga is one of the most prosperous tribes in East Africa.

Most settlers continue to favor a United East Africa, similar to the newly created Central African Federation. But the merest mention of a union upsets the Africans who see it only as a way of perpetuating white-man's rule. The East African High Commission, begun after the war, has only limited powers over such things as customs, transport, communications, postage and currency. It is not likely to acquire any further powers, due to the frequent review of conditions in the country by the United Nations Trusteeship Council which replaced the old Mandate committee. The UN Trusteeship Council had recently censured the British for failing to provide a time-table for self-government in Tanganyika although the administration was moving quickly toward this goal, much faster than, say, in neighboring Ruanda and Burundi, Trust territories held by the Belgians. By proposing a Legislative Council for Tanganyika with equal numbers of representatives from the three communities – European, Indian, African

– the British have greatly annoyed the white Tanganyika settlers and rudely shocked the white settlers in Kenya. This parity does not reflect the population ratios of the communities of course, but considering the lack of African rights in the neighboring countries, giving Africans equal representation with Europeans and Indians is quite revolutionary. This formula: 9-9-9, has become an African password.

How to elect the members of the legislature had not been decided. The administration did not want to set up separate electorates. Under this system Africans would vote only for an African candidate, Europeans only for a European, Asians only for an Asian. It is easy to see how this system leads to extremism rather than compromise, for a candidate appeals only to the narrow interests of his group instead of to the broad national interests. This certainly happened in India where separate electorates for Muslims and Hindus greatly increased hostility between these communities which have continued even after the creation of the separate Muslim state of Pakistan. Until a new system for elections is agreed upon, completed, the members of the Tanganyika legislature continue to be appointed.


WE COULD SEE AN approaching car miles away; the dust cloud which trails all vehicles on gravel roads is visible long before the automobile or truck. Being a little car, we usually pulled way over to the side of the road, and wound up the windows til the car and its dust cloud had passed. But one truck, with an even larger dust cloud than usual, was dragging a tree behind it.

"Whatever for?" I asked Mil. But he didn't know. Only later when we passed another truck, this time pulling an iron road scraper, did we realize that the dragged tree was road maintenance! It pushed the gravel from the humps and corrugations back into the valleys again, until another car passes. I remember in Iran seeing peasants sweeping the road. Tanganyika's use of trucks and trees is not just a sign of modernization, for in the native reserves are many unemployed who could, if they would, maintain the road. But then the Africans have never been eager to work as coolies or farm laborers for the whites. Why should they? This is one of the questions behind much of East Africa's history. The immigrant Europeans wanted to set up plantations, or small factories, or railroads. For this they wanted labor, as cheap as possible. Africans were everywhere; but they would not work. On their farms the Africans grew enough food to live on; they were happy, what else did they need?

This attitude infuriated the settlers. In the reserve they saw the young warrior class lazing about. Pax Britannica had robbed them of their traditional role as defenders of their villages but they considered manual work demeaning, a woman's chore. So they lounged and gossiped and no doubt some learned the evils of drunkenness. Meanwhile the settlers fumed, then finally prevailed upon the administration to force the Africans to work. A head tax was levied, payable only in cash. At last the African had to work, for at least a few months of a year. No wonder, though, that the labor was unreliable.

After 1919, when labor was extremely short, district officers in Kenya were ordered to impress natives for compulsory labor on public works, a practice sometimes also used for work on European farms. Forced labor was not allowed in Tanganyika, but even there wages were kept pitifully low, and the head tax levied, to keep the African at work. Before the last war, in some areas a Kenya African paid over half his cash wage as tax; yet an income tax on settlers was begun only in 1936.

Things improved after World War II. Africans are not

forced to work, and in Mombasa the tax on Africans comes to a mere 3% of the minimum guaranteed wage. I multiplied on a corner of my notebook, figures skraggling with the bumps.

"Imagine," I signed to Mil, "imagine paying only $3.22 a year in taxes."

"Imagine the income," he growled back. And I scribbled some more.

"Minimum monthly wage in Mombasa: $7.84 plus housing or a housing allowance. My flat-mate in London made 6 pounds a week as a typist; with my room rent her income would be, let's see, about $50 a month. That's still over six times as much as the African makes."

"What are you muttering?" Mil demanded.

"Only that the Africans pay sounds like more if you compare it to English incomes rather than American. After all, costs of living are lower here."

"How about Indian pay?" Mil interrupted. "Remember that sweepers in New Delhi got only fifty rupees a month. What's that, about $10?"

Suddenly I felt very wealthy. I'd been budgeting – taking our total bank account, subtracting a kitty to save for London, then dividing the rest by the number of days we expected to be enroute. It came to $10 a day, all in all. We'd have to skimp, for a large car repair would eat up many days' allotments.

But still, ten dollars was a sweeper's monthly income.

At first, in India, I had been annoyed that my protestations at being an "impecunious student" weren't treated very seriously. After all, they suggested, I had enough money to come all the way to India. Whether a traveler spent only a few dollars a day as I did, or bought hundred dollar ivory chess sets as others did, all were rich to most Indians. And we were rich to the Africans – no matter how poor we felt.

IN THIS MOOD, WE drove into Moshi. Low enough on the mountainside to look tropical, Moshi had a transplanted air about it, as if it were not certain that its European character would survive the life in the tropics. The hotel we chose had green sheets on the beds, obviously new. Yet the pace seemed tired. It was a small town hotel which did not really cater to tourists despite its listing in the brochure of East African Hotels which noted that "usual sports" were available. As far as I could see, this meant only that there were darts in the pub. Un-athletically seated on a bar stool, we were served heavy English beer by the chic redheaded wife of the manager. Questions directed at her were soon being answered by other bar-stool perchers who were a variety of European types: Greek, Polish, Italian, as well as British. We had asked about the Ground-nut Scheme started in Tanganyika just after the war by an England still badly in need of fats.

"Ground-nuts. Of course they won't grow," scoffed a portly, sandy-haired man. His accent was obviously British but his khaki pants and open shirt belied that old cliché that the Englishman of the tropics dresses for dinner. "Your countrymen call them peanuts, don't they? Government tried to grow 'em in the south; never bothered to run tests, just threw the nuts, and money in. The rain didn't rain and the soil blew away, and the bush refused to be cleared. I could've told 'em. But no, they went ahead. All we've got to show are rusting machines and some beat-up lorries."

"Come, Jock, some of the land is being used now," teased the bar-maid.

"Little you know about farming, lass," he grinned at her. "But more'n the natives, I'll wager. They sit around and let their women work, won't earn a decent wage from us. The Germans had the right idea; the natives understand force...a whipping now and then just to show who's who."

He gestured graphically, almost upsetting his gin. "Used to give 'em twenty-five lashes with a hippo hide whip, just for talking back. Now, if they steal, maybe they go to prison – where they get better food and clothes than in the reserve. They think it's fun. If only the bloody Government would leave us alone. All they do is send us Commissions – from the UN, from the Colonial Office, from Parliament. Always they take the side of the damned natives. Do they want us here or not?"

Jock turned his complaints toward more receptive ears. The redhead leaned across the bar to let Mil light her cigarette.

"That crazy man," she giggled, tossing her curls toward Jock who was now dangerously tossing darts at the wall around the bull's-eye. "Listen to him talk. The new ones are the worst. He's only been here a couple years. Guess he's not the Bwana he thought he'd be. Got to work hard for your living here." And she was off to serve another customer.

The marketplace in Moshi was brilliant with printed calico hung out on clothes lines for sale. African women, their faded calicos tucked into short sarongs or sewn into shapeless dresses, slowed their swinging gait as they passed the bright cloth on their way to the vegetable stalls. None of them bothered to glance at the snowy peak of Kilimanjaro floating on its cloudbank just above the trees. But I could hardly stop looking at the mountain, or photographing it. Only when the clouds closed over the view did I finally turn to the business at hand, buying tomatoes and cucumbers for our roadside lunch.

As I hovered uneasily over the purchase, wondering whether Africans overpriced things in order to bargain, or whether they named the real price, a memsahib bounced her Land Rover right up to the raised vegetable platform and with peremptory commands began filling up the car with a

Moshi market below a cloud-covered Mt Kilimanjaro

month's provision. Once again I felt the inadequacies of my egalitarian up-bringing. She could order the natives about so easily, with assurance rather than arrogance. I was fascinated at the way the vegetable sellers vied to serve her, arguing down their prices with hardly a word from her. Relations seemed cordial, she was obviously kind – the manor lady to her serfs.

KILIMANJARO FLOATED IN AND out of her mists as we sped on newly laid tarmac toward Arusha. The thrill of her snow-covered eminence only increased with each glimpse, and we stopped a dozen times for photographs. Playing with the telephoto lens Mil took the same shot twice. The regular lens shows a straw thatched *shamba* set into its banana fields, the mountain in the distance; the other, distorted, had Kiliman-jaro so immediately in the background that it seemed the owner of the *shamba* could have cooled his tea with snow. Yet this is how it seemed, as if Kilimanjaro brooded, watching,

109

all pervasive. It was hard not to believe in a god of the mountain, as the natives apparently do.

Its prescience followed us most of the day as we skirted back toward Kenya. The watered greenery of the Wachagga lands thinned, and the grey-green haze of the thorn wastes stretched endlessly. Animals instead of people darted across the road. We ate our lunch under the stares of two curious giraffes. They stood so close and so still, their Mortimer Snerd-ish expressions a bright spot in the dull bush, that they made a perfect target for our camera, and would have for a gun if we had one. Not until I learned they are protected animals – it is an offense to shoot them – did I understand how they had survived.

As I peeled the cucumber a fly settled lazily on my arm. I stopped to watch it closely. The guidebook said that you could tell a tsetse fly by the way it folded its wings on top of each other. Four-fifths of Tanganyika is affected by this dread insect, and I was curious. For some reason I thought that unless there were infected people around for the fly to bite before it bit you, there was no danger of sleeping sickness from the tsetse. So I let him wander up my arm, sniff the cucumber, and fly off. As we drove on, though, I read that a tsetse fly can bite animals and then give humans sleeping sickness. I felt slightly ill, even though I was certain it had not bitten me. For some days, whenever I felt lazy, Mil would tease that I was only getting sleeping sickness!

At the border the paved road stopped, and we bumped back into Kenya. Sun haze shielded the mountains and water mirage dampened the road. Bush endlessly, broken only by the road, and by the telegraph lines which were strung on iron poles so that the termites wouldn't eat them. Dust, clouds of it, everywhere, fine and red and clinging, kicked up by herds of bony cattle. The altitude was lower, the weather hotter, our tempers shorter. Out of nowhere a bulbous little mosque appeared, its four white towers at the corners glinting in the sharp sunlight. Just beyond it was a squat building which proclaimed itself clearly as "Sayed Omar's Store."

I wanted to stop, but we were still arguing over the possibility as we bumped past it. Mil had filled all the jerry cans with gasoline, and now he thought we should use them up and so lighten the load on poor Bublee. So on we went, coughing with the dry dust. Bublee began to cough too, and die. It seemed awfully hot to bother about filling the gas tank from the jerry cans. And lo, ahead was yet another "Sayed Omar's Store," this time without a mosque. Nothing would do but that we should push the car into the gas pump! I was furious, but dared not show my anger in front of all the people. For in the shade of Omar's store a cluster of cattle herders was gossiping, their cattle straggling across the road and fields untended. They watched us idly as I shoved from one side, Mil from the other, one hand through the window on the steering wheel. As we pushed the car off the road, a rotund little man came out of the store and made a gesture of helping us. While he filled the tank I walked over toward the herders to take their pictures, but as I approached they retreated further into the shadows. I still could see that their hair, braided into short pigtails, was yellow-red, as if they had rolled their heads in the dust and asked the attendant what it was. "No, not dust," he chuckled, "ochre. Them say pretty for hair, them Masai. Also put ochre on head, get no..." and with this he graphically scratched his balding head. No bugs, I supposed he meant. Local type DDT!

We again turned to stare at the Masai. These famed and untamed nomads, to believe most writers on East Africa, are straight out of the unspoiled Golden Age. The Masai were taller, leaner than any Africans we had yet seen; they towered over the little Swahili who was filling up our water tins. As several herders drove their cattle past us along the road it became apparent to us that their flapping serape-like blanket, thrown casually over both shoulders or draped under one arm, was their only clothing. Beads and bracelets plus earrings, hung from rope-like plunging earlobes, completed the masculine finery. They carried long spears, though some looked so frail they seemed more of a gesture than a weapon. Two Masai were dueling with each other behind the petrol pump, their right ear lobes tucked up and out of the way of their spears. It was thrilling to watch, even in play. But other Masai, aping Western ways, stood hiding both finery and dignity beneath beat-up army overcoats.

In most African tribes, certain duties are assigned to different age groups. Among the Masai the young men, called *moran*, must live a Spartan life to make them into sturdy, skillful warriors. These tightly trained bands of *moran* had terrorized the tribes of the plains ever since they had migrated southwards from the Upper Nile sometime in the eighteenth century. While the *moran* may not marry and are forced to live apart from their families in one communal hut, it is part of the tradition that the unmarried girls of the tribe visit them. As a result practically everyone in the tribe has syphilis. This disease, combined with their being pushed onto poor land by the immigrant Europeans, has contributed to the decline of the tribe.

Yet they do not wish to change their ways. Cattle are their wealth; they hoard them, seldom buying anything except a wife or two, or a spear. More, cattle are literally the tribe's life blood, for the Masai, scorning the wildlife which surrounds them, live primarily on milk and blood, only occasionally chewing beef or mutton. Blood-letting does not kill the animal; and so the herds multiply. The British have stopped the tribal wars and checked many cattle diseases; and so the herds multiply even more. Today some hundred thousand Masai keep over a million cattle and probably two million goats and sheep! Two herders with some forty-five cattle roam over every square mile of the reserve. If they were free today, as they once were, to roam up and down the Rift Valley – now the center of Kenya's "white highlands" – the situation might not be so serious. But the Kenya-Uganda railroad cut the Masai's pasture land in two. Then the new settlers, fearing that their cattle would catch all the diseases which the Masai's cattle had, forced evacuation of the Masai from the land north of the railroad and gave them in return a "reserve" land on the Kenya-Tanganyika border where the weather is so dry that one-third of the "reserve" is too arid for cattle grazing. So now the Masai wander over drier, poorer land with more and more cattle. Yet, secure in their pride and superiority, they do not rail at the white man nor join the Mau Mau. As they grinned at us as we were checking the tire pressure and tightening the rope holding the roof rack which was already marring the paint, we felt they somehow pitied us. It was a strange sensation.

Off we went, in our own little dust storm, somewhat refreshed, and awfully glad we did not have to fill the gas tank under the blazing sun. We had hardly finished congratulating ourselves for running out of gas in front of a pump when Bublee began to pull suspiciously to the right. A flat tire.

First we had to untie the ropes that held the roof rack on; then we had to unload the boot to get at the spare tire. Then we had to figure out how to use the jack. Once you know how, the side-jacking system on these little cars is a cinch; but we had blithely assumed as much, without ever trying it out! And now we didn't know how. Mil found the open pipe under the edge of the car by the front door, but it took some poking to figure out that the seat comes off, and the rug up, and the rubber plug out so that the handle of the jack can come up through the floor. The rain and dust had clogged the insert area of the pipe and knocking it out under blazing sun didn't help our tempers any, particularly since by now we again had a silent and disdainful audience of Masai herders. We could imagine them giggling later around their campfires over the silly plight of these mechanized whites!

But at last, with the tire changed, Bublee was again loaded and bandaged. Both of us could use some glucose, I thought, as I mixed for the first time what soon became our African cocktail: sun hot grapefruit juice near-crystal-line with glucose powder. We needed the energy, physically and mentally. We had lost nearly an hour on the tire change and this meant approaching the troubled highlands at night. Dark falls early and suddenly near the equator; imagination grows more vivid in the night.

It was black and moody as we neared Nairobi. There should have been a moon, but instead, the clouds decided to drizzle. At every bump, the tied-on roof rack teetered, the lights blinked. But tension over the car had long since given in to that dread thought of Mau Mau. Was the terror real? Where were the check points along the road? Ahead the sky glowed, dull red, blood red. Raiders? Only a dump, but ominous.

Tense, we drove quietly, carefully, into the brightly lit center of town and stopped at the first hotel we saw. Oblivious of my wet and dirty jeans the Swiss receptionist greeted me eagerly. "Yes we still have rooms in the annex. Ah, but the hotel is so crowded these days, so many farmers in from their farms to relax in town, that I'm afraid we have run out of pillowcases, if you don't mind." The lobby was indeed crush-full of chattering groups, all Europeans. Beyond, in the dining room, a three piece orchestra jazzed restrained English tunes. It was all so gay – after the gloom outside town – and so normal, except for the large plain sign over the desk: PLEASE LEAVE FIREARMS AND AMMUNITION IN THE HOTEL SAFE. Seeing my glance the Swiss girl commented pointedly, "You know there's a seventy-five pound fine if you lose your revolver." Yet despite the sign, several men wore pistols conspicuously draped around their waists, which joggled as they danced. Tanganyika seemed a long way away.

CHAPTER 9

# Nairobi: Divided City

*N*AIROBI WAS CALM, THOSE FIRST FEW WEEKS WE WERE THERE, too calm. You could feel it, like a dense fog, enshrouding, and liable to be blown away at a moment's notice. Police cordons drawn tightly around white Nairobi ostensibly made it one of the safest cities in the world. That first tiring night we left our car, half packed, out all night in the street. The jerry cans and food boxes on the roof would have become the passers-by for the untying. But nothing was touched, a fact which made us careless, to our deep regret, our first night in Kampala.

White Nairobi extends up the hill away from the river and the swampy flat lands where the railhead camp had first brought Europeans to this mile-high plain. At the foot of the hill the houses are varied, well planted, comfortable-looking but unpretentious. The newer look-alike composition brick houses higher up the hill resemble a middle class suburb anywhere; a few are less nondescript with colored plaster, pink or green. All the houses have heavy criss-cross webbing on the window, less severe than the old fashioned bars on windows along the coast; but they serve the same purpose: to keep out the thieves. We wondered at our luck at having nothing stolen from our car –I've had packages taken from a locked car in the middle of New York City.

The fancier houses over in the Indian section had bars on the windows, too, hiding some of the rococo decoration which Indians love. Many of the wealthiest people in East Africa are Indians; but there are many poor ones too, huddled in mud and petrol-tin huts along the river bank. The Indian slums merge into the African slums; the mud is as deep and the huts as crowded, the only difference is the slightly darker complexion, the kink of the hair, of the children playing in the street. In contrast to this filth and dreariness a model township sits showily some distance out of the main part of town. Later we went for an intimate and revolting tour of African housing. But in the beginning we only looked, and pondered at a city so divided, so demarcated within itself. It was easy to drive from one area to another, but to meet people in all groups was more difficult. As white Americans we were classed as "Europeans". That gave us station, position, and was supposed to restrict us socially.

But there was a growing fourth group of people in Nairobi; the foreign press. Although we belonged only to the lowest echelons of this group, we made our entrance into it gratefully and as quickly as possible. This gave us entree and the ability to move around to appraise this polyglot capital, and we didn't like what we saw.

On the surface life seemed to go on as usual, almost. The

tourist bureaus and the souvenir stores complained that the Emergency was ruining their business; but the foreign press, at least the more affluent of them, probably made up for the loss, safari-ing for Mau Mau as well as for animals. My hairdresser was a German woman who had literally worked her way around the world with her finger tips. "You don't need to know Italian to set an Italian's hair, pet, you know," she explained as she cut. But, well, she'd been in Nairobi over a year and though the geographic climate was pleasant, the mental climate was not; she thought she would mosey along.

There were Africans on the streets in the day time, but many fewer than seemed to have been normal in pre-Emergency times. All Africans had to carry identification cards giving the place of their employment; this was a European imposed regulation And Africans were told not to ride on buses, or smoke in public, or drink English beer; these were Mau Mau regulations – and broken by very few Africans indeed. For all of the terrorism against Europeans, a primordial, ghastly terrorism, only nine European civilians had been murdered by the Mau Mau when we were there. The final tally was a mere twenty-three civilians murdered, twenty-five soldiers and police killed in the line of duty. Hardly a good day's automobile toll of dead in the United States. Nor were many Asians killed though many were robbed, one suspects by ordinary thieves under cover of more sinister forces.

It is the Kikuyu themselves against whom the Mau Mau has wreaked the most continuous vengeance. Mau Mau wanted, demanded, the solid backing of their own tribe. Those Kikuyu who co-operated with the British government – even worse those Kikuyu who were members of the Home Guard – were looked upon as traitors. One Chief was murdered, for Chiefs of tribes were a British innovation in East Africa and so were considered members of the civil administration. Here and there Home Guards and "loyal" Kikuyu were murdered. Then came the Lari Massacre.

We were returning from Uganda and it was already late at night. The moon, though only in its early quarter, shown clear light on the road, and on the police checkpoints. The police were tired, and perfunctory, hardly looking into the car once a white face peered into their flashlight beam. We knew our way to the hotel, and turned in without a second thought about the becalmed capital.

Yet as we had driven by, almost within shouting distance of the road, a massacre was being brutally carried out that blew away the calmness of the capital. Trouble exploded all through the town. The settlement attacked was one of the so-called "loyal" Kikuyu. The terrorists waited until the men and youth of the settlement were away patrolling another area. Only then did the "brave" Mau Mau swarm upon the houses, slashing and torturing the women and children. We heard about the horrors only too graphically the next afternoon. It was tea time and we were sitting in the noisy brown lounge of the hotel speculating over the truth of the grim reports in the local newspaper, debating whether to go out to Lari or not. Alt, a hard-boiled professional Swiss freelance photographer was slouched in the far corner. Seeing us, he wandered over in a daze, upsetting the milk pitcher as he came.

"Been out to Lari?" he asked, pouring himself into a chair. For a moment he looked as though he had passed out, pale. Suddenly he put his hands before him his face as though protecting himself. Then he shook himself all over, and screamed at the waiter to bring him a drink, fast. Looking through us, he began talking softly, almost incoherently. He looked hypnotized.

"Awful, I keep seeing the arms and legs piled up, like firewood. The bandits-terrorists-bastards,...they burned the huts and slashed the women and children as they jumped out. Foxes catching rabbits. But it's not for food, or for any reason. Sadistic revenge. Dead woman, her unborn kid cut out from her belly. Don't go to see it, its an everlasting nightmare."

For several days he was like that, drunk more on thoughts than liquor though he had plenty of that too. Later he said: "If it hit me that way, imagine what it did to the Kikuyu. It was Mau Mau killing its own. Mind now, this is the turning point. Those Africans have something worse to hate than the Whites." And he was right.

The Lari massacre showed the Mau Mau for the terrorists that they were. Before that most of the Kikuyu sympathized with the Mau Mau, though they might not like its methods, just because it was for Africans and anti-White. Besides, Mau Mau carried out reprisals on those who refused to cooperate, who would not agree to take the horrid oaths – old tribal oaths robbed of any traditional meaning but terrible enough to frighten many a Kikuyu. Still, a group that could mutilate one Kikuyu settlement might do it to another. Resistance to Mau Mau stiffened, particularly as the power of the administration became strong enough to protect "loyal" Kikuyu.

Suddenly, as a mass movement, Mau Mau was dead; it became clear that they could not base a country on one tribe alone. Their appeal had been a horribly clever conglomeration of tribal rites and superstitions combined with modern ideas of political organization and nationalism. And in some ways it succeeded. The world, and especially Great Britain, became very much aware of Kenya and its White Highlands; the settlers would not walk off with the country when no one was looking. More money and energy was allocated in land development. The Emergency gave the administration power to make the changes it has long wished to do. Resettlement of Kikuyu farmers introduced village life to these formerly scattered people. Consolidation of land made larger crops possible; the tendency toward individual ownership of land instead of communal ownership meant that more care was taken against the constant erosion, more interest was given to fertilizing.

Did the terror of Mau Mau help or hurt the African's position in the long run? The settlers argued that the uprising proved how backward and incapable of ruling themselves the Africans are. But the organizational ability displayed by the Mau Mau and their ingenuity in valuing firearms suggested to me that given legitimate outlets for their energies, such Africans could advance rapidly to self-government. Undoubtedly, though, the fears generated by the Mau Mau widened the distances between black and brown and white making much more difficult any real advance toward a truly multiracial government. Racial tensions had certainly increased.

We felt them. Walking along the streets we began to look over our shoulder, eye doorways, jump when the room servant glided quietly into our hotel room. It was if, every day, the violin strings were drawn tighter. The sound grated more and more on your nerves. Surely it must break.

One was no longer a person, one was merely a color. My white skin pushed me into the elite, the aristocracy, of Kenya; it also might push me into a *panga,* those huge and deadly knives the Africans use. Group protectiveness, and fear. How else to explain the settlers' views? They were incredible.

"Come now," coaxed a Lord's son over the fifth course at lunch, "you Americans did it to the Red Indians, the Australians did it to the aborigines, why can't we get rid of those Africans who won't play the game our way? Would you put Sitting Bull in the White House? Why you don't have a single one in your Congress, and we've six bloody Africans in the Legco? And what about your Africans? Nigger in the White House? You'd fight another civil war."

I couldn't think of the right answers. I felt like a black kettle with little right to complain to the pot. "But the sheer numbers," I stammered, "won't the Africans keep fighting on and on?"

"The future as I see it," said this titled not-so-young man, settling into a visionary pose, "is Africa as a white continent. All Europe will go to the Communists...France, Italy, Spain. Maybe England, too. The American war machine needs Africa's raw materials; your businessmen are already over here in numbers. America will come in, with no nonsense, to protect their investments. East Africa will unite with Central Africa... it'll all be run as the last outpost of Western civilization, and if the Africans don't like it, they can leave or be shot."

I couldn't finish my dessert.


OUT AT THE MUTHAIGA Country Club, haunt of the European settlers, I heard much the same theory, but others, too. "Separate the White Highlands off and give it self-government, the administration can run the African reserves," said an old Scots farmer. In a quiet corner one young Englishman dared suggest, "Let's go by Cecil Rhodes' old motto, 'Equal rights to all civilized men', let the educated, the **well** educated, vote. It will quiet the Africans."

Michell Blundell, leader of the settlers less reactionary wing, a member of the Legislative Council and later a member of the multi-racial Executive Council, preached a vapid paternalism which was nonetheless considered radical by many settlers. Over lunch he talked well, too well, in fact. Calculated to please. Too much a politician to inspire trust among the non-Europeans, yet perhaps the most "liberal" elected European member of the Legco. His reactionary opponents still live in the nineteenth century. Blundell is only a few decades behind the times. But he was, after all, under pressure. Guards protect him wherever he goes. At his home in the countryside his young daughter, who loved to ride, could not be let out of sight. Perhaps if you grew up in Kenya "knowing" your superiority to the Africans, and felt the fear even we visitors were experiencing, perhaps to be anything but reactionary took courage.

One such courageous man is Richard Vasey who was attacked as "socialistic" because, as an elected member of the Legco, he was firmly behind the administration's plan for a multi-racial government. His support had made his re-election unlikely so the government offered him the post of Treasurer in the ministry which made him an "official" member of Legco, unelected but with full voting rights..

A few Whites were even more openly pro-African. One we met was a not-too-recent immigrant. He had been threatened with deportation for his subversive activity-meeting and sympathizing with Africans and was forced to be more circumspect in his attitudes. But these men are so few.

It is the fear. What else could have so altered Colin? Shy sweet Colin left Mombasa only a few weeks earlier because he had been drafted into the Army. He came to the hotel for drinks one evening with a young couple, apprehensive lest we give him away for being too soft. Almost before introductions were finished he jutted out: "It's so easy to criticize us, you don't live here".

The girl nodded approvingly.

"Beating is all they understand. It's the new fellows, the kind ones who are soft with their natives, it's these who've been murdered," Colin said.. "That Dr. Meiklejohn, the female doctor, she treated patients free," argued the muscular young man.

"The guy they cut up, slowly," he continued, using his hands too descriptively, "cut off his head and put it on the table facing his body, he ran a store at no profit for his labourers and others."

Colin, feeling left out, rejoined, "Those Boars from South Africa over by Nyanza, they haven't been touched. They know how to discipline them natives."

Tension mounted. These three young Kenyans argued more and more irrationally as it became clear they had found in us the dangerous belief in equality. When all other arguments failed, Colin would return to his piece de resistance. "It's the Communists behind it." Somehow he felt that all Americans so feared that ideology that the mere suggestion of it would make any solution fair. Nor was it only from Colin that we heard this reasoning. Communism had no connection whatever with the problems of Kenya. But the Kenyans already knew the value of deflecting arguments by creating a bogeyman. In this, at least, they were living in present times.

CHAPTER 10

# Kenya Indians: sitting on a fence

OTHER COMMUNITIES IN NAIROBI WERE ALMOST SHOCKINGLY up to date. In the center of town the rather pretty onion-on-a-stick Indian type mosque was not only decorated with traditional Arabic writing, it also had written, boldly over the elaborate entrance, the immortal words: **None to be worshiped but Allah, Muhammad is his Prophet.** The strange thing is that, unlike mosques just about everywhere else, these words were written in English.

Nor was the mosque the only modern thing about many of the Nairobi Muslims. Most of the influential ones were members of the Ismaili sect. The Aga Khan had helped them build their schools in Nairobi as well as in Mombasa. The children in these schools, both boys and girls, study in English; their mothers go about the streets in European dress, never in purdah. In all ways this community has identified itself with the Europeans, politically and socially. The gayest party we went to in Nairobi was at the home of Ismailis. Drinks flowed freely despite strictures in the Koran about alcoholic beverages; African servants were ever-present with refills. Real Iranian caviar was piled high on crystal serving dishes; I confess I concentrated my attentions on it until dragged away by my embarrassed husband. Ham was among the meats on the buffet table, though the Koran forbids the eating of pork in any form. No wonder the spiritual leader of this Islamic sect can remain a horse-racing fan and still be revered. He has helped liberate his community from age-old restrictions and long suffering poverty. What matters if he and his son display their wealth ostentatiously?

The debonair host of the party was the owner of one of Nairobi's European hotels. I asked him if he allowed non-Europeans in the hotel's night club. "Ah, I must allow them in, but unless they are my friends the tables are always all reserved," he answered honestly. Then after a moment he continued, a little defensively I thought, "It happens everywhere. The hotel next to my coast house outside Mombasa refused to sell me beer. They were afraid they'd lose European business by serving me." He laughed as though it was a joke, but his eyes were solemn.

"You know," whispered another guest as the host wandered off, "he was so furious at the Mombasa hotel that he sold his house! Yet he does the same thing in Nairobi. He'd be more English than the settlers if they'd only accept him."

The Ismailis have chosen sides in Kenya, but the rest of the Indians are not so sure. In fact the more hysterical of the European settlers spread the rumor that the government of India was really behind the Mau Mau. According to these rumor mongers, the Indians wanted the Whites and

Blacks to kill each other off; then the Browns would take over. "Ya know," hissed one crotchety old settler to me in the office of the rabid Electors' Union – unkindly called the settlers' tribal H.Q. "Ya know, Kenya is to the Indians what America is to the Europeans. A place for overflow population. Only we beat 'em to it. Haw haw. Some Colonial Office bastard tried to give the country to 'em once. Another time those fools in London tried to make our Kenya the promised land of the Jews. But the Jews turned it down; they'd rather fight Arabs than Africans." He rocked with laughter at his own joke, then said to the whole office in his high pitched country accent, "We wouldn't let any of 'em have it then and we won't let any of 'em have it now."

This story of supposed Indian designs on Kenya was given a push by one of those "mealy-mouthed inside dope sheets" that had been circulating around England as well as Kenya. This broadsheet named the Indian High Commissioner's Office, though not the High Commissioner himself, as the guilty agency. The office of the High Commissioner is down in the Indian commercial part of town, further toward the river from the European center, but within a hot walk. It is so inconspicuous a place, being on the second floor above shops, that I circled the block several times before I saw the small sign pointing up the steps. Squatting on the terrace, where a cool wind circulated from the patio below, were the ever present *chaprassis* – messengers – so typical of Indian offices. The rooms, all with cross ventilation, had high ceilings more necessary on the Indian plains than here in the cool high atmosphere.

The actual office of the High Commissioner, Apa B. Pant, was uncluttered and modern, more London than New Delhi. And so, in many ways, was the handsome, thin-faced Mr. Pant. Dressed in an immaculate, London-cut white suit, his

accent a soft cultured Cambridge English, he spoke so pater-
nalistically about the people of East Africa and all their foi-
bles that it was hard not to imagine him as an English colonial officer talking about "the natives." For however earnestly
Mr. Pant talked about the need to teach to all the races of
the countries the meaning of the new century in which races
are equal and multi-racial societies accepted, he still talked
as a ruler from above, as a Brahmin. Mr. Pant was indeed
a Brahmin, and his father was the ruler of a small princely
state in India until 1947. This royal background combined
with the best of British training gave Pant an assured manner
that must have riled many Europeans who, often with much
less education, lower class accents, and no lineage, would
attempt to maintain their "natural" superiority to him on
racial grounds.

To spread his message of the future multi-racial society,
Pant traveled widely over East and Central Africa. In order to
avoid problems of hotels, Pant took with him a large entourage
so that he could stay at government rest houses in between
towns, and at homes of friends in towns. One time he whooshed
through Uganda at the head of an eleven car cavalcade with
such pomp that many natives, thinking their Kabaka – or king
– was passing, fell worshipfully to the ground.

Wherever he went, Pant would tell Africans, Europeans,
and Indians, that Africa must become a multiracial society.
But he emphasized that this society must come about by an
evolutionary, not a revolutionary, process. To achieve such a
society, without violence like Mau Mau and without perse-
cution of Africans as in South Africa, **that** was Africa's challenge; one day it will be Africa's greatness.

Few people in any of the racial groups liked his message, and everywhere there were mutterings against an official of the Government of India interfering with what was

an African problem. Most Kenya Europeans explode at the thought of a multiracial society which, to them, did not mean races living amicably side by side but intermarriage. Feeling themselves as on a small raft in a big black and brown sea, the Kenya Europeans felt they could maintain their identity only by staying on top. To stay on top they must either command leadership by helping the mass of the people, or must demand – if not enforce – leadership on the basis of their "inherent" superiority. Few Kenya Europeans with whom we talked were willing to try the first alternative. Most stayed apart from Africans or Indians, basing their claim for position not on acts but on color.

I suspected that perhaps the reason so many Europeans disliked Mr. Pant was his very superiority since it belied theirs. Even those who admitted their admiration of his idealism would be the first to reiterate that Kenya Indians were not like Pant, that they were strictly commercial men taking a penny where they could. "All East African Indians with talent go home to India," the Europeans would repeat over and over. "Those here are second rate."

The Africans seemed to share something of this view, for most of them drew a clear distinction between Indians in Kenya and the Indian government in India. As a result they liked and respected Pant, both for himself and as the representative of the Prime Minister of India, Jawaharlal Nehru. Most African leaders looked to Nehru as an influential friend in international relations. African students studied in India; African politicians visited India. But the single greatest gesture of friendship, according to most Africans, was India's sending to Kenya a lawyer to help in the defense of Jomo Kenyatta. Further, this Indian, Diwan Chaman Lal, was a close associate of Prime Minister Jawaharlal Nehru, a Member of the Indian Parliament, and had been Indian

Ambassador to Turkey. That personally he might not have been the best lawyer India had to offer made little difference to the Africans. It was the idea that mattered; and they lionized the Diwan. Said one earnest youth to me, "It just proves that all Indians are not simply interested only in pounds, shillings, and pence."

Yet it seemed obvious that money was a major concern of most local Indians. Pant himself made this point so emphatically to me that his carefully combed dark wavy hair bobbed down onto his thin aristocratic forehead. "The Indians here are business men par excellence," he said. "They will, perforce, adjust. They will accept a multiracial society as long as it allows them to do business. Already businessmen have contributed to the fund to set up a Gandhi Memorial College here in Nairobi. It will be open to all races."

The Indians, on the whole, were neither pleased by Pant's declarations of a multiracial future nor happy over the appearance of Diwan Chaman Lal. Mostly they did not criticize Pant very loudly. I remember meeting a group of Indian commercial leaders in a cluttered office above the shops along one of Nairobi's main commercial streets. I'd walked over from the hotel and had gone back and forth along the street for several minutes, missing the dark doorway between two rather glittery clothing stores. At last, in desperation over missing my appointment and in frustration at being so blind, I went into one of the stores. The clerk bowed almost as a servant when I mentioned his employers' name. With utmost politeness he quickly led me up long uneven steps to a small office which seemed cave-like after the brilliance of the morning sun outside. As my eyes focused I made out a slim figure, wizened by age and privation, sitting before a roll top desk nearly buried in files and papers, and looking more like a character from Dickens than anything else I'd ever seen.

I sat down on a chair that tilted precariously even under my not too heavy weight and watched, fascinated, as the old Indian tied papers together with red string. What a contrast, this old-fashioned filing system, with the neon and chrome in the store below! His son, Romesh, a much heavier man of a mere fifty summers, appeared and, in answer to my question, at once began to discuss the Diwan. "The Diwan did not much impress people here, you see. They are expecting a seasoned statesman who will be considering the Indians' responsibility to all communities. But no, you see, he justifies the Mau Mau, only condemning the methods they use. No, you see, we are feeling there was something not healthy about Chaman Lal." With each "you see" Romesh leaned forward, spreading his broad hands out as though I were to read his palms.

"It is a pity Chaman Lal wasn't more fair minded," interjected a tall thin man who had just entered. "The British sent out Mr. Pritt, and whatever his politics he has done a tremendous service for British liberalism and the British system of law. He has restored the Africans' confidence in the English and their sense of duty."

When I asked them about High Commissioner Pant, they hesitated. Finally Jivan, the tall man, got up from his perch on the desk and began to pace half out in the hall. In English-English rather than Indian-English, he began to explain. "You might say that there are three Indian views here in East Africa. On the one side are most Muslims – what are they, about forty percent of us Indians? – and the few Parsees and most Goans, and some Hindus, too. They act and think like the Europeans, and say the Africans are unfit for any position above his present one, and that the

Government is right in suppressing them. On the other side are mostly young Indians who are revolutionaries and think that the Mau Mau is justified, even in its extremism. But they are a small group, and can do little." He stopped pacing and turned towards me. "And in the middle are most of us Hindus, including Pant."

And it is indeed true that most of the Hindus are in the middle, sitting on the fence. But that isn't quite what Jivan meant. For he went on to say that the Hindus are represented in the Legco by the Kenya Indian Congress which, in theory, supports Pant and Nehru in their sympathy for the aspirations of self-government by the Africans.

"But I am just now thinking," said the old man for the first time, "that India is having no right to be telling us what to do. For many years I am working and living here. I am East African, not Indian."

"They do not like us, you see," said the rotund son, sadly. "Some Europeans are trying to copy South Africa and are stirring up African riots against us; they even hired natives to boycott our shops, you know. Government has passed tight immigration laws; they said they had to, you see." Romesh paused, looking at his palms, "the settlers screamed that we were swamping them by our high birthrate. It is twice as high as either that of the Europeans or of the Africans. So Government passed the law."

I remembered one settler's comment on this: "They're like rats, they breed so fast." There was obviously no love lost between these two immigrant groups. But what of the relations between the Indians and the Africans?

"The Indian is a protection to the African, a buffer," answered Jivan obliquely. "If there was not a substantial Indian settlement, the reaction of the Government to this Mau Mau would have been more crushing. But Indians live everywhere, and see everything, and we have an efficient grapevine. So our journalists recorded the truth, and the world learned what was really happening here. And we have helped the African. Jomo Kenyatta; he has two Kenya Indians defending him besides Chaman Lal. And back in 1933 the Indians began to demand that Africans be made members of the Legco. Without the Indians and their *dukas* – general stores, I suppose you would say – the African would not have learned about the modern world so fast." Jivan paused, and then added the keystone: "You see we want to cooperate with the Africans, and be their business organ."

"But," Jivan continued after a moment, making a gesture with his hand, a questioning gesture, yet one of acceptance. "Still they do not like us."

It is true, most Africans did not like, or trust, the Indians at all. Even those Indians who had long before gotten down off the fence and were openly, often actively, pro-African. Even these Indians did not seem to be completely trusted by the African leaders. But then, I am not sure these Kenya African leaders trusted anybody, even each other. Hate was rampant in Kenya then.

Jiwan was wrong to call these pro-African Indians "revolutionaries." Rather they were genuinely and thoroughly humanistic; they were pro-African because the Africans were on the bottom of the pile. They were also realists. Since they loved Kenya and wished to go on living there, it followed that they agreed with Pant and Nehru that the future of Kenya must be multiracial.

Such a liberal humanist is J.M. Desai whose spacious home is open to all races. English lawyers in Kenya to defend Africans, journalists from everywhere, members of the British Parliament, politicians from West Africa, Indians, Africans – we met them all at the Desai's. Had a settler come, I am sure that the Desai's hospitality would have been as gracious as to anyone else. For Mr. Desai constantly said, "I take no interest in politics; but I believe in brotherhood with other communities."

Yet brotherhood was suspect in Nairobi, and anyone visiting Desai's home was considered a bit subversive by the watching police. It was not long after our first meal at his house that we began to realize we were frequently being tailed. At first I admit I was rather flattered to be considered of such importance. Indeed, in hysterical Nairobi, the thought of an armed guard was almost reassuring.

But police surveillance was extremely annoying to the permanent residents. It became rather a game with them to elude their trailers. As a result I met many of the Indian and African leaders in odd rooms or in a "neutral" home. It all seemed a bit over dramatic and very un-English. Perhaps this cloak and dagger business was a reaction of the English to the tropics.

Particularly, visiting the homes of Africans was a <u>sub rosa</u> thing. What a circuitous route we took the night we went to a buffet dinner where the then president of the Kenya African Union, F. W. Odede, ate his last free meal. Later that night, or rather early the next morning, Odede was arrested. He remained in jail, untried, long after we left Kenya. The British, so scrupulous about the rights of the individual at home, did not dare repeat the fiasco of the Kenyatta trial. In legal terms the Government of Kenya had almost no case at all against either Kenyatta or Odede. But the belief was general among settlers and the administration that both men, indeed the whole Kenya African Union, were connected with the dreaded Mau Mau. Thus, the Government felt that it simply could not allow these men to remain at large.

Kenyatta, whose trial was then in progress, was a forceful

leader, a revered hero, clever, demonic, and tyrannical. The court found Jomo Kenyatta guilty of organizing the Mau Mau, but no one was sure. Someone must have started the oath ceremonies; but it was the widespread discontent and more than a few leaders, that gave Mau Mau its strength. Soon malcontents of all sorts joined the ranks and whatever central leadership the movement had soon lost control. Isolated guerillas led by "generals" committed more and more atrocities. As these guerillas were driven high into the mountain forests by the crack British forces, most Africans were relieved that peace had come again. And with peace, reforms. The Mau Mau forced London and the world to revise their slow planning for independence and made sure that the settlers would not quietly take over the country as happened in the Rhodesia. So most Africans are not really sorry about Mau Mau; and until rouge elements turned on their own, they did not entirely condemn it. As the leading force for independence, most Africans sympathized with Mau Mau, even those most opposed to joining it.

Then why should Odede be arrested for taking the African side in a fundamental split between black and white? True, he was president of the Kenya African Union, but in this he was largely a figurehead. Because of the Mau Mau, it was essential that a non-Kikuyu be president, and Odede is a member of the Luo Tribe. He is an affable man, well-built and well-spoken, but somewhat bookish. As we were introduced – Mil and I were the only Europeans at the dinner – Odede looked us up and down, made up his mind that we were friends and talked openly and genially. I couldn't have been more astonished to read the next day of Odede's arrest. For though he was obviously a sincere and dedicated African, this ex-school master is simply not the leader type.

Of a very different cast was W. W. W. Awori, a dapper

crocodile-skin trader from the shores of Lake Victoria. The crocodile trade is a lucrative one, as Awori's clothes and car testified; but trading takes skill at bluffing, at keeping a poker face. While Awori was gay and animated, answering our questions and generally helpful, I still do not know what cards he held in his hand. Presumably the Government does not know either; for Awori was never arrested and for several years continued to represent Africans in the Legco as a nominated member. Perhaps even the Africans were unsure of his intentions for he was defeated when, for the first time, Africans elected their own members to the Legco in 1957.

When dinner was eventually served, most of the dishes were Indian or Arab; and I soon learned why. All the neighbors had helped prepared the food; and in fact we were in an Indian neighborhood, not in an African section of town. Although theoretically we could have gone into the African reserve at night, in practice neither we nor Indians would have been invited or welcomed there. How, I demanded, was it possible for an African to live here in the Indian section? "Ah," smiled a wizened old Arab version of Peter Lorre, "all Indians sublet their homes. More money." That seemed a bit of an exaggeration, but it was the only explanation anyone would give me. I promptly wandered about the compound. Four apartments shared one patio, and in all the other houses were Indians. Still, the flow of food, and then of dirty dishes, moved from one apartment to the next, as if this buffet dinner were a village fete.

I think our host must have borrowed all the chairs from the neighbors, too. The living room was lined with the straight-backed wooden variety, looking rather like a teenagers dance class. All other furniture was removed, if indeed there had been any other. Around the room on the chairs sat many wallflowers, mostly men – both Africans and Indian.

Some sat for hours, hardly talking, looking rather frightened. I, too, was seated on one side but a constant flow of the more articulate came over to interrogate this female intruder. Once or twice I tried moving about, but it was like walking on stage – even the wallflowers noticed me. Only when I escaped into the kitchen with the other women did the scrutiny cease. But though the women in the kitchen were pleasant enough, none knew more than a dozen English words; so after a few minutes I returned to my hard chair once more.

I was rescued by Diwan Chaman Lal who had just arrived, breathless. This debonair politician, whom we had last met in India at a night club surrounded by a bevy of gorgeous Indian women, seemed somewhat out of place in the stilted, crowded room. After surveying the room in a glance, nodding to a few, he beckoned to Mil and me. Drawing us aside into a tiny bedroom, he went out and returned with Odede and Awori. Then in a hushed tone that would have done justice to a Hollywood version of a conspiracy, he read to us bits of a letter which Jomo Kenyatta had just written to Jawaharlal Nehru and given to him to deliver. It was exactly the sort of letter one would have expected: thanking Nehru for his sympathy with the Africans and for sending Chaman Lal to act as his defense lawyer. The letter continued, in surprisingly thoughtful and moderate language, to condemn the way his own trial was being handled. In fact it was not a sensational letter, even when played, as the Diwan was doing, for all its emotional charge.

Seeing we were unimpressed, the Diwan leaned over and whispered, "When I leave I'm going to try to take Murumbi back with me!"

Now, that did surprise me. Joseph Murumbi was the general secretary of the Kenya African Union, and in many ways the most capable of those members not in jail. Further, the

Africans all delighted in that fact that he was part Masai. They used this fact as additional proof that the Kenya African Union was not only an organization of Kikuyu. Murumbi is tall and good looking, calm in his arguments and full of facts and figures. While I had been sitting on the hard chair Mil had spent an hour discussing the land problem with Murumbi. His very reasonableness had become a political handicap; the Europeans found him the easiest African to negotiate with. Their support was dangerous. But his going off to India, I felt sure, would spell the end of his promising Kenya career.

Although Murumbi's mother had been a Masai, his father was Goan and a Catholic. Young Joseph had been raise in Goa and had worked for the British Army in Somaliland during World War II. He had met his tall, slender, beautiful wife, who was part Somali and part Italian and who was also a devoted Catholic, in Mogadishu. Only since the war had the couple lived in Kenya. With the dearth of talented and educated Africans, Joseph's religion and race were overlooked, if not forgotten. But running off to India at a time when Kenya Africans were so hard pressed might be interpreted by some as running out. Certainly, once Murumbi was out of the country, he would have trouble getting back in again, for his citizenship was in question.

But Diwan Chaman Lal did convince Murumbi to go with him to India. Murumbi toured that country, and then England, appealing for funds for the African cause. But gradually his name stopped appearing the papers. I wondered if he would ever go back.

CHAPTER 11

# Land: Africans versus the settlers

*L* AND, AS MURUMBI HAD SAID, IS THE BIG PROBLEM IN KENYA. When the whites came the government cordoned off areas for whites only and put the African farmers into reserves. But the reserves couldn't hold all the Africans as the tribes grew. So they spilled over onto settler land, as squatters, becoming a bit like indentured serfs, working for the feudal lord in return for land to farm. In some countries such serfdom had been a benevolent system. The lord provided security, helped in marriages and on feast days, perhaps even aided the sick. But that was centuries ago. Somehow, today the system doesn't seem right no matter how paternal it is. And when there is some truth, however illusive, that the land does not really belong to the lord but was stolen from the serf, well, there is bound to be trouble.

When the first white explorers at last braved the treacherous wastes inland from the coast and ventured into the highlands, the areas around Nairobi were thick with Africans of a tribe called Kikuyu. But when the first wave of railroad surveyors plotted the line of the rail-bed, the land near Nairobi was deserted. Famine, wars, and disease had devastated the Kikuyu, driven the survivors back to their ancestral homes near Mt. Kenya. Whose land was Nairobi? The Kikuyu had conquered another less civilized tribe, the Wanderobo, before they themselves had settled in the area. Centuries before, the whole Kikuyu tribe, like other Bantu tribes, had migrated from further north. Wherever they lived, all conquered land was held communally by the whole Kikuyu tribe although the use of land was given to individuals. The British administration claims that when the railroad and the settlers came to Kenya, all Kikuyu living in the area were compensated for their lands; the British also insist that at that time most of the land was vacant. The Kikuyu, for their part, insist that no individual had the right to alienate tribal land and all sales are therefore invalid. Besides, the whole area belonged to the tribe whether they were actually farming it at the time.

Whatever the history, today the African reserves are extremely overcrowded. Squatters have been sent back to the reserves, for during Mau Mau most white settlers feared having any Kikuyu on their grounds. In Nairobi, streets were fenced off so that squatters in transit could be kept behind barbed wire. Sometimes Mau Mau suspects were herded into these enclosures. But often they were squatters who had been told to leave what many regarded as their homes – where they'd been born and wed and had expected to die. Now they were added to the already burgeoning reserves while their farms on white land lay fallow or were taken over by members of other tribes.

I wanted to see the reserves, and talked a young British agriculture official into showing me around. I was surprised the reserves didn't look crowded, not from the road. Kevan explained this is partly because Kikuyu do not live in villages, but prefer to build their *shamba,* or hut, right on the land. Each *shamba* has a patch of banana plants growing near it, beyond come the fields of maize. He went off on a detailed explanation of the crops, the types, diseases, seasons, etc., and of the administration's efforts to improve agriculture. Most of it was technical, but I remember his saying that an African family needed seven acres of land for mere subsistence living if they farmed the old way. With improved methods only five acres were needed.

"What would happen," I asked, "if you gave every family five acres? Is there enough in the reserve?"

Kevan gave a hopeless laugh, and answered disparagingly, "Of course not." I hoped he would suggest a way out of this maze, as a Royal Commission did later by saying that white land should be open to all who could pay the price. But he was silent.

Then after a moment he began describing the efforts the government was making to introduce erosion controls. "The soil is really young, as soils go; it hasn't weathered enough centuries. Cut off the forest cover and the bit of good top soil washes right away. Frightful problem. So many of the settlers have found their land is only good for herds."

"Is that why so many Africans say settlers do not farm all their land, because it is so poor?" I asked him. Murumbi had pressed this point that there was unused land in the highlands, as proof that more land was allotted to the whites than they could use.

"No. There is some farm land not in use. Only whites can farm in the highlands. But making a living from farming is not easy. Not too many whites are willing to work that hard. Those settlers with big cars and fancy houses that you see in the Clubs usually have money from outside. They live here because taxes are low and because they can't stand how egalitarian England is today. They really lived it up before the Emergency."

We stopped at one *shamba* and got out to look around. Only an old man and two young children were in the clearing. The old man looked frightened and could hardly answer Kevan's schoolbook Swahili. Nor did the smell encourage us to stay. "No sanitation," muttered Kevan. "That's one thing the Emergency is good for. The government has started resettling squatters on newly cleared land; but they are insisting that the Africans live in villages where electricity and sanitation can be introduced."

"You know," he continued, thoughtfully, "this Emergency is really helping us help the Africans. It gives us special powers to make Africans do things for their own good, like terracing against erosion, that years of persuading wouldn't do. And it has given us power against the settlers so that we can help the African. Like clearing new lands."

He was off again, describing the process of clearing lands. "First you get rid of the tsetse fly, then..."

I wasn't listening. Here was an earnest man, a technician imbued with his science. Political questions bored him; for they could not be answered by laboratory experimentation. Anything to do with the soil or plants got him excited. Yet the real problem, which he readily admitted, was that the Africans were suspicious of government motives and would only make changes under pressure. So, I said, feeling I had won the point, politics are at the root of everything.

"One thing the Kikuyu do better than we do," he retorted, getting even, "they know how to handle their women! See all the women over there in the fields. They do all the work, and the men sit around and gossip! It makes our job harder, trying to get women to improve their methods. Generally they are less educated and much more conservative than the men. Besides they belong to the men, and won't do anything unless told to. And the men are away in town earning money."

"I thought you said the men sat and gossiped," I said, interrupting him.

"Well, they used to. Some still do, only now they say it isn't gossip but philosophy. That makes them politicians! But most men have to earn money to pay the head tax. Levying that tax was the only way to get the Africans to work for the whites. The men used to work only long enough to make tax money and then come back to the farm. Only now the reserve is so crowded that many Africans even move their families into town, and live jammed up in bachelor quarters. Conditions are much worse in town, and so are politics."

I decided I must see the African "location," and got a young and eager Kikuyu member of the Kenya African Union to take me around the next Sunday. Sunday, so that the men would be at home and so that my guide, Oni, could take off from his own job. Without Oni as escort, entering an African area would have been foolish as well as dangerous with tensions as high as they were then. Only days later the Nairobi police began arresting Mau Mau suspects living in the town. In many houses weapons were recovered, hidden in food baskets or in dirty laundry. In one foul shanty mutilated bodies were found buried in the ground, obvious Mau Mau victims.

The most typical of the housing provided for Africans before the last war are long brick buildings with prison-cell like rooms backing on each other. Each room has a window over the door, but no light and no water. Water from a pump across the way was free, and toilets were down the way.

Africans were sitting everywhere, on the ground, on beds, on the door step. We went up to one young man and asked him what he did in Nairobi. He stood up as we approached and looked hostilely at me. But a word from Oni and he began chattering happily. He was a messenger in a government office and earned 45 shillings a month, about six and half dollars. He owned his own bike, he announced proudly, and pointed inside. I went into the gloom, and at first all I could see was the small charcoal brazier sitting inside the door.

"Up" said Oni, "Look up."

Hung from the ceiling, and surrounded by bedding and clothes, was the bike. It was his prize possession and had to be kept inside for fear of robbery. At night he and his two wives and his bike all slept behind a lock door in the stuffy cubicle. And for this he paid ninety-one American cents a month. All in all, he seemed pleased with his "home;" he knew that if he chose to leave there was a long waiting list for his room.

"Oni," I said, "I want to talk to the women. How can two wives live together in such tiny space?" But Oni just shrugged, and walked away. Politics were his avocation; he was not about to waste his time delving into the private life of a messenger's wives!

The post-war housing was much more comfortable and more expensive even though it was still highly subsidized: a good value for the money. But rent was about the only thing that was cheap. A government clerk and his wife lived in one of the newest African housing units; he said that his half of a white-washed duplex cost him 32 shillings a month ($ 4.48).

But the bus ride into town cost fifteen shillings a month. In contrast, the Catholic mission school outside town where he sends his two daughters charges only 45 shillings each a year. All these expenses come out of his salary of 200 shillings a month.

The house itself had two rooms plus a kitchen with running water. There were wide windows front and back, but those in the back had been carefully boarded up while the front windows had heavy shutters on them. I pointed to the windows which were heavily screened and asked if this were not enough protection against insects and animals. The clerk smiled, "but screens do not keep out the thieves."

On the whole, I was favorably impressed with the housing that Oni had showed me. If he had been a government official instead of an active member of the Kenya African Union, I would have assumed that I had been shown the best. As we drove back toward town, Oni began to lecture me. "Now you see, government takes our labor and gives us this. I have to live in one room with my wife and two children."

"Wouldn't you have lived on one *shamba* in the reserve?" I asked tentatively.

"You don't understand," Oni exploded. "**They** came here, we didn't want them. **They** build big houses and force us to serve them. Our labor has made them what they are. **They** owe us everything." He intoned each "**they**" with all the hate he could.

He subsided a bit. "You'll see. Government builds houses too slowly. Stop, stop here," he shouted suddenly.

We were in front of a row of tumble down shops, and as we got out of the car I could see that the shop owners were Asians. Curious to see what they were selling I walked off without locking the car door.

"Come back Irene,' Oni screamed at me, "you must

always lock the door. They will steal the seats right off the floor." This time I was not sure whom he meant by "**they**."

After I had locked the door, Oni led me along a muddy path behind the shops and across a field. Here, hidden by mud walls, was a weird collection of shacks, hardly more than frames with tin-can roofs. They had no floors and no toilets other than the fields. The whole place was dank and nauseating. It reeked of filth and squalor.

Pleased at my obvious reaction, Oni continued his lecture. "This, this is 20 shillings a room. Owned by those thieving Arabs out there in their shops. Illegal, of course. But where else can these Africans go? If they complain to government about the rent, government will burn this down. But if they have no place to live, government won't let them stay in Nairobi. They die if they go to reserve. So they pay rent, half of their wages, maybe. They can't afford it, so they find money, if they can."

With that, Oni, gave me a big wink, and twisted his hand in front of him as if he were locking a door.


THE FOLLOWING SUNDAY I was again driving through the African section of Nairobi. At the very outskirts of town I located a certain petrol pump, as I had been instructed, and pulled off the road to wait. Some ten minutes later a carefully dressed young Africans rode up on a bike, looked the car over very carefully, stopped at the car window and asked politely, " You wish my help, memsahib American?"

"I wish to visit the Reserve, " I replied on cue.

Without another word the Africans wheeled his bike over to the station and pushed it inside, shouted something in Kikuyu to the attendant who was lounging by the door, and returned to the car.

"I show you where you buy nice carvings" he said in a

very loud voice for the benefit of anyone around, and then got into the front seat next to me.

He didn't speak again until we were into the Reserve. Then he seemed to brighten and began, in a very limited English, to describe the plants and the cultivation, interspersing his monologue with such casual directions that I frequently had to back up or go around several blocks. The roads became farm tracks, then bumpy, dusty paths. Several times I was convinced we passed the same corner twice, but as I was about to complain I looked up at the guide. A huge grin spread over his face, admitting to me that he was purposely confusing any sense of direction I might have had.

"You see, you need a guide," he added slyly. "You want meet man no want meet you." He paused, then directed me: "I get down here,. Wait until you finish. House you want first good house down that straight road."

He got out, and I wondered whether I had really been on a useless chase. But there ahead was a proper stone house set back from the dirt road and surrounded by a small lawn. As I stopped the car an *askari* appeared from behind the thickets and demanded my business in a sharp tone, "What you want?"

"I wish to see Mr. Mathu," I said. "Is he home?"

"Wait," he commanded. "I go."

I stood in the shade. As I waited I noticed that the house was clear of bushes although the jungle surrounded the edges of the lot. I had not heard of any Mau Mau attacks on Mathu, but he might have been a logical choice since he did not make any secret of his opposition to the movement. As one of the then African members of the Legco, and in fact the first African ever to sit in that chamber back in 1944, Eliud Mathu has been for many years an articulate and respected leader of the Africans. But as a moderate, his steady voice was often lost amid the screams of the extremists. Many of the KAU members sniggered when I asked of Mathu; others said he was a good man, only too conservative. But none would take me to meet him.

I wanted to meet an African leader of different persuasion than all those I had already met. So I asked everyone I met if they knew how I could reach him.

One sympathetic Indian explained that at present Mathu was avoiding foreign correspondents. I was flattered at the inclusion. "Many Africans like Mathu," he said, "but if he were portrayed in the foreign press as a strong leader against Mau Mau, then someone might decide he must be eliminated. He is not idle, however. He is helping to organize the resistance groups to Mau Mau out in the Reserve. But he is not all for the Government. When Emergency Powers Order came up in the Legco, he voted against it. Oh, the settlers were furious, denouncing him as typical untrustworthy African. But, you see, this is helping him now. All Africans know he is not a Government man."

Still no one would help me find Mathu.

That is, not until I mentioned my problem to the Political Officer of the American Consulate in Nairobi. Mr. Phillips had just finished telling me about how pleased he was that the New Stanley, the leading hotel in Nairobi, had at last agreed to put up an official American Negro visitor. It was the first time the color bar had been let down this far.

It had not been even occurred to me to ask Phillips for help until he began to talk about another visitor expected shortly. John Gunther was traveling working on the latest book in his series of social and political commentary with the title *Inside Africa*. Phillips had been asked to arrange a series of interviews for Gunther at his hotel. He was to meet everyone of importance, go off for a weekend with one of the settlers, then drive into the danger zone area with some army people. Altogether Gunther would spend only a week to ten days in Kenya, he would leave with the "inside" story due in large part to the extraordinary assistance from Phillips. It was clear that Phillips was very much aware of the problems in the colony and knew most of the principal actors on the local scene.

Yet after Gunther's whirlwind visit I heard many Africans and Indians complaining about Gunther's technique. "He gives you half an hour. It's like being on trial. How can you explain everything in so short a time? Still, if you do not meet him, he will not mention you in his news reports or else he will believe lies others tell about you."

So most persons who were asked to meet with the famous reporter, kept their tryst. I admit I was jealous of the ease of his operation: scheduled interviews taken down in shorthand or on tape, all the right people met, the correct places seen, Kenya all tied and wrapped up after ten days.

"Will Gunther see Mathu?" I asked Phillips.

"No, not now," Phillips replied. "Gunther may be back later. But right now Mathu won't come into Nairobi."

"But will Mathu see people out in the Reserve?" I asked hopefully.

"I don't know," he answered, " but I'll try to find out for you."

To my delight Phillips did finally contact Mathu through the "bush telegraph" originating with a young office boy in the Consulate. I was told to come, that the office boy would arrange for a friend to act as my guide. I was not to ask any questions of the guide, but merely to give the boy ten shillings after I got back to Nairobi.

Standing in the shade by the stone house I began to wonder at the wisdom of my coming to the Reserve alone.

The guide had vanished; but he knew my purse held at least ten shillings. Oni's words about stealing came back to me in sudden force. I looked around uneasily at the empty compound and moved out from the thickets, into the sun.

Just then a woman came out of the house, smiled shyly at me, said "Good morning" softly, and walked right on past me into the road.

The sun was hot. My curiosity conquered my trepidation and I walked up to the house. It too seemed deserted. Annoyed, I sat down on the raised porch and wondered what to do. I was still staring moodily around when a hefty African with a round pleasant face came up from behind the house. The *askari*, I noticed, was trailing him at a distance.

"Welcome, friend," Mathu greeted me, "I am sorry that I was away from my house when you arrived. Please do come into my humble home." He was puffing slightly. Wherever he had been, at a meeting or at a hiding place, he had come from some distance away.

Mathu led the way into a book-lined room fitted comfortably with overstuffed chairs. He took a chair near the fireplace, and relaxed utterly into the cushions. He did not look like a man who feared for his life. Perhaps I had misread the symptoms.

"I am glad to see you here," he began. "You are a student from London? But you are not English? It is time other lands knew of our troubles." He shook his head sadly. "And how would you deal with these troubles?" I asked.

"First," he said, arching a short stubby finger in front of his face, "first we must have reforms, short terms reforms, to restore the faith of the African in the government. The obvious social services – education, hospitals, recreational facilities, housing – all must improved and increased. Wages must go up; and we must be given five acres for each farmer, with some guarantee of tenure."

"But these things will solve nothing really," I objected.

"I said those are short term objectives. Without <u>faith</u>," he said the word softly, caressingly, "without <u>faith </u>the Africans will do nothing; and without Africans the government can do nothing constructive. Remember that faith is what counts."

He paused as the *askari* brought in some lemonade and for awhile we sipped in silence while Mathu caught his breath.

"But what of the land problem?" I asked, eager to see how his view might differ from Murumbi's.

"That is a long term problem," Mathu said thoughtfully. "But Government must begin by clearing as much as they can of the Crown Land, bringing in irrigation and ridding it of tsetse fly. They have already started doing this near Thika; they must do much more."

"Now, in the Highlands," he began carefully, "Government must take over unused land and absentee landlords must be forced to sell. But those settlers who farm, we don't want them to leave. They can help our country if they wish." His voice dropped, "But they are so very selfish now."

"And foolish," I suggested. "They do not know their own future interests."

He nodded agreement.

"But the Government is trying to help, isn't it? More than the settlers?" I asked, certain in my own mind that there was a distinction in these two white "tribes."

Mathu straightened up slightly and asked rather cynically, "Is there any difference? They are one and the same thing. The settlers are running the country. They aren't sincere when they condemn Government. They control the country: the settlers have more say than civil servants." He stopped, then added, slowly, "But on the attitude towards home rule, there is an exception. It is true that without the Colonial Office we'd be nowhere, our country would be a big jail with the bars removed."

Mathu relaxed again into the cushions sighing. Suddenly he leaned forward, sitting on the edge of the chair, and spoke earnestly, his words carrying out beyond me into the yard as if I were in the first row of a large crowd. "My own point of view – it may differ from other Africans – is of a society in which <u>all</u> communities live together in as amicable a way as possible. No one community, especially when it is only a small minority, should dominate everyone else and make others..." hesitating, looking for the exact word, "well, not slaves, but as some _thing_ which doesn't really exist...just because they have no respect for human elements."

All the bitterness was there toward the settlers; all the suspicion toward the Indians. "They only exploit us." Yet Mathu at this very dangerous time could advocate peace between the communities, and coexistence. An African statesman indeed.

CHAPTER 12

# Monkey Robe: honoring Kenyatta's English lawyer

T HE HERO OF NAIROBI, OF AFRICAN NAIROBI THAT IS, WAS, Jomo Kenyatta. The whole city avidly followed his trial; when Jomo Kenyatta's English lawyer, D. N. Pritt, was in town, the Africans lionized him. I noticed that whenever Pritt was in the company, the reserve color bar which the Africans built up of wariness and suspicion seemed utterly to disappear. Pritt was wholeheartedly the African's friend, and if <u>we</u> were with Pritt, why, we must be on their side too. Pritt himself, however, was much on guard against us, and always chose his words carefully when we talked.

One night, after a gathering a Murumbi's house, Awori got out his flashy car to drive Pritt and us back to the hotel. As soon as the car doors shut making the interior car light go off, out from the night shadows came at least a dozen men, big men. The car was surrounded; I felt they could bodily lift us and the automobile on their shoulders. But instead, they gleefully stuck their heads in through the open windows, mumbling – almost humming – praise of Pritt and of Kenyatta and of the new Africa. One rather sharp-suited young man grabbed my hand and begged, "Sister, will you wish us good luck?" Pritt was signing autographs; the eager hands shoved the books at us too. Others hands reached for mine. "Fight for us, sister," one breathed, "fight for us and we will fight for you."

All this emotion, with undercurrents I didn't comprehend. I felt distinctly uncomfortable, like a skeptic at a Christian revivalist meeting, committing myself to something beyond my knowledge. I think I shrank a little inside, wondering.

But Pritt thrived on the adulation, you could almost see him glow. When we got back to the hotel he suggested a nightcap of tea, being too keyed up to go immediately to bed. He showed us a letter from some Kikuyu women addressed to Pritt's wife hailing her husband's defense and asking for her sympathy. It was good, I thought, for at least one press story in London.

The hotel "boys" nearly fell over themselves waiting on Pritt. I noticed that our own stock went up considerably among the various servants as a result of that tea. And their service improved a hundred percent.

The servants' attention was particularly useful the next afternoon. We had invited two Indians to have tea with us at the hotel. This was our gesture at breaking the color bar – that invidious divisioning of peoples by skin alone that breeds hate so easily. The hotel's Indian owner would be annoyed at having Indians in the lounge, we knew. But we hoped he would want to avoid a scene at all cost. As for the settlers living in the hotel, we didn't talk much with them anymore. They had judged us by the company we kept. The other guests, mostly newsmen, we knew were on our side. So as long as the servants waited on us we were sure all would be well.

It had seemed like such a trivial thing at first, this tea. I had issued a general invitation to a group of Indians and Africans who were standing about in the office of the Kenya Indian Congress. They had been eagerly answering my questions, and the invitation was a simple desire to repay them. As I knew of no restaurants in Nairobi, it seemed logical to invite them to the hotel. But I hadn't really thought through the implications, and was a bit surprised at the hedging replies.

Why, if I wanted tea, they would make some right there. Besides, they would have to brush up to go to the hotel for tea, and it would be too late.

"But you are as neat as we are," I protested.

"Ah, but you are white," said one softly. I had almost forgotten how rigid this classification was. All at once I burst with anger at the restrictions, and also at the unwillingness of these young leaders to break tradition.

"But I have asked you to tea. You complain about color bars, yet you make them yourselves if you refuse to come to tea at the hotel. There is no law against it, you have nothing to lose."

One African gestured impatiently, "You don't <u>know.</u> The police would watch us afterwards so carefully."

"But they watch you already, for coming here," I chided, "and that is more political than having tea."

"But less explosive. If I took tea with you," and he spread his black fingers across my wrist to emphasize the color difference, "it would threaten the whole social structure of white Kenya – not just the color bar. It's like starting a social revolution. <u>That</u> the settlers could not allow."

155

I suddenly realized what he meant. The crudest of the settlers questions, fears, always touched on this: white woman, black man. Dimly, too, I realized that these Africans and Indians had helped me all out of proportion to my deserts and that they had done so because I was a woman, and trusted them. Europeans aided me out of courtesy, or novelty, as the young and eager wandering American. But the response of these non-Europeans was deeper, more complicated. European men often met with them, and some had treated them as equals. But the memsahibs, they were characterized – caricatured – as shrews, always screaming at Africans as if every one of them were a personal servant.

Indians used to say that it was the *memsahibs* that lost India for England. The complete separation of the races for social purposes began as soon as white women settled in India in any numbers. The Indians always blamed the exclusiveness of the European society – in all its own various levels – on the women. But I wonder what part the husbands played in this separation, husbands who could mingle, even sleep, with the "lesser breeds" but who perversely demanded purity in their women, purity even from contact. It was thus in Kenya. Always it was the men who demanded, "Would you like your daughter to marry an African?"

So the white woman becomes a symbol of true equality. No wonder that African and Indian students in London flock to date a white woman, any white woman. Often marry her. And all too often these young men from respected backgrounds in their own culture choose women whose only qualification is the color of their skin.

Now, for the first time in Africa, my being a female became a problem. For it added an explosive ingredient to a defiant tea party. This realization made me stubbornly more determined.

"Perhaps we could go to the United Kenya Club," Pinto suggested as a way out. This was the interracial club, self-conscious, unnatural, but a beginning.

I was adamant.

At last it was agreed that two of the Indians, Pinto and Sharda, would come to tea the next afternoon. None of the Africans would accept – being far wiser in European tribal lore than I was.

Precisely at four Pinto arrived, spickly turned out, his smile masking any apprehension. He joined us casually, and immediately several servants descended upon us, anxious to help. Pinto jiggled his tea cup nervously as we talked. But the crowd in the lounge was apparently unconcerned at his presence. A few people stared, but no one moved, or made ostentatious references.

Pinto is a Goan, small and intense, and very concerned over the future of Indians in Kenya. Frankly admitting the distrust prevailing between the three races, he hoped that the actions of some Indians like Chaman Lal and Pant and the Indian lawyers on the Legal Aid Committee would show the Africans that they did have friends among the Indians. "We have to live with them, after all," Pinto said, emotion and excitement bordering his words with a suppressed hiss. "Yet most Indians know nothing about Africans, how they live, or think, or act. Caste shuts them up into their social cubbyhole from which they see the world as pounds and shillings. If only they had a strong leader."

It was strange hearing him talk of the country as an outsider would, without identifying with any racial group. I wondered if this were because he was a Goan and simply thought of Indians as Hindus or Muslims while seeing Goans as a group apart. But occasionally Pinto would mention men he felt had transcended race, who treated all races equally, and who, if Kenya were lucky, would lead the country in the future. It was in this elite that Pinto hoped we would place him. Certainly the Government placed him in this "dangerous" category, for it later arrested him on charges of conspiracy with Mau Mau. When this news was published I felt guilty, wondering whether his audacity at coming to tea had marked him just as the African had warned it might.

Sharda, perhaps wisely, phoned about four-thirty to apologize for being tied up and so unable to come to tea. This surprised me a little, for Sharda was a daring man. As an editor of an Indian Press he had dared to print Swahili pamphlets for Africans. As a result his paper had been banned and he was left without a livelihood. Of course it is possible that Sharda was simply detained with business, but I doubt it. We knew he was being watched and decided he probably felt that a tea party was not worth a run-in with the police. A gesture, but what would it accomplish? With our privileged shade of skin, we risked nothing. The tea party, we concluded sadly, was a useless defiance.

Later, in Uganda, where a policy of equality in public places was being determinedly supported by the colonial Government, I was delighted to see several neatly dressed Africans order drinks in the hotel lounge. But the lesson of this was clear: it was not the defiance, but the Government's attitude, that made the difference. Social ills do not change without pressure, whether in the American South or in Kenya.

PRITT KNEW THIS, OF course. His whole technique at the Kenyatta trial had been to play for the foreign press. But it wasn't only world sympathy or understanding that he wanted; it was the pressure of public opinion in Britain on the Colonial Office. The letters to the *Times* and *Manchester*

*Guardian*, the articles and controversies in all types of British periodicals, the Parliamentary Delegation to East Africa, the Royal Commission to study land in Kenya – all showed the efficacy of this approach. Kenya is still a colony despite efforts by the settlers to achieve home rule. Clearly British public opinion was in reality more important to the Colonial Office that white opinion in Kenya. The settlers had recognized this by starting a Voice of Kenya outlet in London to present their views. But their "white man's burden" outlook was a minority view in England at that time. As long as liberal opinion was informed about Kenya, the Colonial Office would be pressured to introduce equality and freedom in the Colony.

Pritt played for this audience. The Africans were immediately aware of the value of his voice as they were of support from Indian Prime Minister Nehru or Fenner Brockway. Brockway was a British Labour Party MP who was instrumental in founding the Congress of Peoples Against Imperialism, an international group which aimed at independence for all colonies. He had for years agitated in London for greater awareness of the African's problems. In recognition of his aid the Africans had made him an honorary chief. Now they proposed to honor Pritt in this manner.

The small auditorium was already crowded when we arrived, everyone milling about all over the stage, the wings, the floor. Several reporters were there already, including a couple of Europeans, one of whom we recognized as a police officer though he was not in uniform. Also in the group was a young well-dressed African, Tom Mboya, who was a member of the Nairobi City Council. He acted as our guide and mentor for the rest of the day, introducing us to everyone, interpreting the ceremony, commenting on the personalities. His manner was charming, his opinions candid. "Violence defeats its own ends. We can win more, faster, working within the rules of the British colonial game. Like India." His words were prophetic since Mboya was elected as the representative from Nairobi when the Africans were first given the right to vote in 1957. Emerging as the leader of the eight Africans elected on the communal roll, Mboya was quite proficient in agitating within the rules of the game. Very much aware of the importance of public opinion in England, Tom Mboya often wrote articles for London periodicals. He recognized that London was not prepared to risk her relations with the various colored members of the Commonwealth for a few thousand discontented white settlers in Kenya who had not yet learned what century they live in.

In this nationalist gathering, I was amused to find that refreshments were all foreign: American Coke, English tea and cakes, Indian sweets. Not until we reached the Arab countries on our journey to London were we offered local native food to eat. Was it simply that the Africans prefer the taste of these foreign concoctions? Does their courtesy to guests make them over-cautious of our tastes? Or is food, too, part of their ambivalence toward the modern world, that love-hate relationship which produces an inferior feeling toward traditional culture and values, making a consistent outlook difficult. As a reaction, some Africans take over the new culture perhaps too completely, like Eliud Mathu. Others, like Jomo Kenyatta, emphasize the hate, and revert to a tradition which, because of its contacts with the new is no longer as self-sufficient a philosophy that it once was.

Here before us a so-called traditional ceremony was beginning. An anthropologist would have been quick to point out the completely ersatz flavor. Much more appropriate than reviving old customs, this ceremony was a gesture of gratitude. Using traditional symbols made the honor more understandable to the Africans than the presentation of a medal or cup would have been. The ceremony was thus a synthesis of old and new that proved so difficult to achieve on more basic issues.

Odede was shouting for order, his voice hardly carrying above the hubbub of the audience which was almost entirely African, though a few fezes or turbans marked an Arab or Indian. Slowly, most of the chattering crowd sat down, women in the cooler seats on the stage. The audience quieted as they were caught up in the flow of words the speakers poured forth. Odede and Awori, both Luo, spoke in Swahili; several local men spoke in Kikuyu which Mboya, a Luo himself, did not translate for us. As the pitch of praise spiraled, the women on the stage were almost dancing in their excitement. Once again the room pulsated with murmurs, coordinated now, a Greek chorus to the speaker's monologue. As Pritt walked forward the crowd let out a deafening roar of delight. From then on we could only watch the actual ceremony, for the chorus hummed even louder as Odede handed to Pritt the symbols of the chieftainship. First came a basket, woven from fibers gathered all over Kenya; next was an oxtail which the Kikuyu use to keep off flies. The Luo had carved a stool which is for them a symbol of authority; and this was presented to Pritt. Then finally, with a great flourish, Odede enclosed Pritt in a lovely long haired white and black cape: a rare Colobus monkey robe.

These symbols of honor were also to be sent to Nehru while his emissary, Chaman Lal, was given an elephant-headed walking stick. But all eyes stayed on Pritt, savior of the day, as he was cheered out of the hall and along the streets. Color was forgotten, for Africans had faith in this man in the monkey robe. Elusive word, faith, yet so important for the future of the continent.

CHAPTER 13

# Seeking our route and testing our car

I T WAS TIME TO MOVE ON TO LONDON. I HAD FINISHED MY interviews, written my articles about Kenya, and convinced one of the Indian lawyers who was leaving for Calcutta to take the articles and photos directly to the *Statesman* offices. What a relief to know that my work would be on the editor's desk within a week.

The question was: which route to take? Our Road Book of East Africa sketched several routes besides the easy one: taking a ferry down the Nile from Uganda to Cairo. One went north to Ethiopia; a second went northeast toward Somaliland, and a third went west through Uganda to the Belgian Congo. Notations like "uninhabited bush," "dense forest, "or "thick bush" filled blank areas on many pages. And even these sparse maps stopped at the borders of East Africa. So we asked for advice of everyone we met.

"Driving around Kenya is bad enough," many said. At the US Embassy, where we went to collect our letters, no one had driven further than Uganda. Most US citizens used the Embassy as a post office; the consulate was happy to hold letters because that was one way to keep track of itinerant Americans. We also used the Embassy as a bank. Because Mil still carried a diplomatic passport, he was able to cash personal checks there, saving us from carrying American Express checks or large amounts of cash.

I had asked around town whether anyone had heard about Chuck Trieschmann who had sent me a Christmas card in New Delhi with a Nairobi return address. I had no idea who this mysterious man was, but near the end of our stay in Nairobi, he turned up at our hotel, told by Embassy staff that I was in town. Chuck was from Evanston, Illinois, had graduated from Stanford, and knew my Radcliffe College classmate Carol Jones. It was one of those small world stories: Carol knew I had gone to London to study. When Chuck decided to drive around Europe he has asked how to contact me. Carol gave him my father's phone number who told him I was in New Delhi.

CHUCK NEVER DID GET to London, but after driving up to the Arctic Circle through Norway, he decided he wanted to get warm and had headed for Tangier. After three months in that exotic city he pushed south, following the west coast of Africa and taking ferries where roads didn't exist. After Liberia and Nigeria, he headed into Belgian Congo, then drove through Uganda to Nairobi and planned to keep going on to South Africa. This fellow, mid thirties I guessed, had a bland round face, pleasant, but revealing none of the character surely necessary to drive all this way alone. We were reassured that he was driving a Hillman, a car even smaller than Bublee. The route he took proved there were roads west across the continent, but we decided that his leisurely pace and roundabout journey was impractical for us. He had no information about desert routes north through Algeria.

Another possible route was north through areas of Kenya marked "arid lava strewn country" to Ethiopia. A good road to Marsabit continued straight north to the border less that 150 mile north from Nairobi. Late one evening as we were sitting at the hotel bar talking over our options: whether we should go north, or drive into Congo and see what information we could gather about the desert road through French West Africa, a young English couple strode in looking haggard and ready for a drink. "Thought we would never make it to Nairobi," exclaimed the man, downing a pint in a few gulps. His wife continued: "We broke the axle on our Volkswagen when we ran off a mountain road just over the border in Mega, Ethiopia. Guess it was weakened by all the horrid tracks in between Addis Ababa and Mega. William hitched back to Addis to get a replacement and I was stuck in this village guarding the car. Took over two months to get a replacement." Listening to their tales of woe, we crossed off that route. We could not afford two months waiting in a middle of nowhere.

We had two deadlines: time and money. When we ordered Bublee, I also made a reservation for 22 June 1953 on the car ferry which crosses the English Channel from Calais to Dover. Miss the date and your might wait for months until someone failed to show. We could not afford the time or money if that happened. I had to register with the London School of Economics for my final terms so that I could complete my dissertation and get my doctorate. Mil had to return to the US in order to receive his compensation for travel, money we would need for our year in London.

MONEY WAS THE OTHER constraint. Our budget was ten dollars a day. So to keep track, we wrote down every expenditure in a school exercise booklet. In East Africa, currency was shilling and cents: 1 shilling was worth 14 American cents. A hat and shoes for me at 6 shillings was less than one dollar. Mil bought a bush shirt with button down pockets so he wouldn't lose another pair of glasses. I totaled all these living expenditures to date and was relieved to find that we were within budget on hotels, food, and personal things including some wood carvings as well as 95s for Mil's glasses to replace those the crocodile swallowed. Even an anti-snake-bit kit and film for the camera fit within our ten dollars a day. So did petrol which was averaging about 50 cents for an imperial gallon.

So I was a shocked when I added up everything we had spent and found that we were averaging nearly fifteen dollars a day. Bublee was the major culprit. Fees for insurance, a license plate from Great Britain, and a Carnet de Passage – which allows owners to drive through different countries without paying an import tax – were high. Outfitting the car for the bush was even more expensive: we followed the advice in the Road Book of East Africa which was filled with cautionary tales about the hazards of driving in Africa.

> First of all, the following maxim should never be forgotten: *Better to be late than to be dead.* Apart from rough roads, swampy patches, blind corners turning precipices, well know bridges suddenly non-existent, you may have to content with herds of cattle, sheep or camel and the indolent or even non-cooperative drovers and, or course, roaming game from a mouse to a score of very large elephants or bad tempered rhino"

Their advice about driving through streams flooding the

roads proved useful many times in our journey: "wade across to check the depth, remove the fan belt, protect the electrical wiring from splashing with sacking, block the exhaust pipe." We bought everything they recommended: two jerry cans, tool box, tire patch, tins of oil and brake fluid, spare tire, tracks and a shovel to get the car out of sand or mud. Much of this stuff fit onto our new roof rack which we covered with a tarp and tied down with rope.

Once we were beyond areas where Europeans have settled with their frequent hotels, we planned to camp out at night, sleeping in the car. Mil ordered a mattress that fit into the bottom cavity of the car once we removed the sliding bucket seats and pushed the rear seat up. We packed sheets and light blankets in the bed roll we brought from India, but needed new pillows. Altogether, the bed was quite comfy. Because of the heat we would want the windows open, Mil also bought a mosquito net; we experimented with draping the net from ties to keep it off our bodies. To cook we bought a primus stove, tin plates, cups, and utensils. These things for the trip stretched out budget. Clearly we would have to economize for the rest of the trip!

ANOTHER ITEM WE PACKED was an old 38 revolver that Mil's father had given him. I have never fired a gun and was not in favor of having one at all, but since Mil had served in the army during World War II, he knew how to fire it and decided it would be wise to have it along. In Nairobi he had it cleaned, and bought ammunition for it.

Our experience trekking on the slopes of Mt. Kenya scared me enough to agree. We had driven out from Nairobi to visit Roy Spendlove whom I had met in London where he was studying at LSE for the colonial service exam. He had been posted as District Commissioner in Meru, north of Nairobi. Mil was anxious to test out the auto repairs and I wanted to see the White Highlands, so we accepted his invitation to visit. We chose to circle Mt. Kenya and headed first to Nanyuki.

The road was "bituminized" or hard surfaced as far as Thika, then gravel to Nanyuki. The valley was a treeless plain covered with farms owned by Europeans using modern equipment. Huddling near the road were huts for the African workers. Cows grazed everywhere. Carts pulled by four, six, even eight oxen bit into the gravel; pickup trucks bounced along the ridges. Crowds of women and young girls, heavy earrings weighting their earlobes, walked along the edge of the road. All leaned forward, straining under monstrous loads slung from forehead thongs. The constant weight injures the pelvis, often causing difficult childbirth; women near hospitals often have Caesarean sections as a result.

After Fort Hall, the forest closed in with many ridges and valleys, fine hiding ground for the Mau Mau. The weather went from overcast; to rain, to enough sun to see flitting views of Mt. Kenya between the clouds. A jagged peak, rugged and masculine, it reminded me to the Grand Tetons in Wyoming. Above the dense forest of trees and bamboo I could glimpse brilliant green grasslands. Ahead the Aberdare range loomed like two breasts on mother earth. Beyond Nyeri the European farms gave way to the reserve which was dotted with small plots. Towns consisted of a petrol tank, a rambling general store, and a few Indian *dukas*. Nanyuki was larger, the main road lined with trees and a parking lane before the shops.

THE KENYAN AFRICAN RESERVE was much in evidence all along the road. There were frequent check points, prison camps, and trucks filled with soldiers. Near Nanyuki a ruddy Scotsman in an army truck hailed us. "We have an ammunition scare," he said, "some of our soldiers selling supplies to the Mau Mau." He was sent out to check the rumor but had left some papers at the check point. "Would you take a man with you to Nanyuki to fetch them?" he asked in his lilting accent. Without waiting for a reply, an African soldier climbed into the front seat with his Sten gun. Since we were not carrying all our gear, there was room for me in the back seat. I asked the soldier where he was from. He replied, speaking fluent English with a north England accent, that he had been in the army for 12 years and was from Nyanza Province on Lake Victoria. He told us to turn up a dirt track which led to a clearing where several trucks were parked. When the soldier explained what he needed, the white soldiers laughed, and explained to us that their major was absent minded. Still laughing, one of them took off in a truck to take the soldier back with the papers.

As we skirted the northern side of Mt. Kenya beyond Nanyuki, the road deteriorated; parallel dry tracks on either side of the "all-weather road" were smoother, but full of big holes. The Northern Frontier District spread out to the north. To save time, we munched cheese and fruit in the car as we drove, taking turns driving every hour. Finally the road turned south toward Meru. Like Nanyuki, Meru lies almost on the equator; yet the air was almost chilly since both towns are over five thousand feet.

We located the DC's bungalow just as the light was beginning to fade. What a relief! All the military activity had put me on edge. Roy was standing outside to welcome us, a tall thin man with reddish blond hair looking very English and quite at home. He seemed delighted to see us and so did his dog Caesar, a small terrier, which bounded out to the car wagging his tail. It must be a lonely posting, especially for a bachelor with only a dog for company.

"You look tired," he said. "You need something to drink. Beer or whiskey?" His servant appeared with the drinks and some cheese sticks. Sipping whiskey before the fire, my tension eased and I relaxed as Roy began to talk about his posting to Meru. "Land has been in contention for years, not only between the settlers and the Africans, but between tribes. I read in a 1937 Meru District Report that the Kikuyu's were fostering 'land consciousness' which made the Meru fear the Kikuyu wanted to take over their land. That DC wrote that all attempts to convert 'land consciousness' to land conservation among all the tribes had been a failure. They treat the forest as granted by their ancestors and see no need for reforestation or changes in their agricultural practices. Soil erosion is a growing problem, so the government offers cash, food, and seeds to farmers if they terrace their land, do contour planting, and experiment with interplanting legumes between rows of maize."

"You sound like an agricultural extension officer," I teased. "I am the government out here. I have to be interested in everything that happens," he responded indignantly. "For example, the army has been rounding up cattle in areas where the Mau Mau are operating in order to obtain information about the thugs. Right now there must be nearly fifty heads grazing on the golf course. The owners are given 14 days to supply us with information. After that the cows are walked about 50 miles to an abattoir for slaughter; their meat is tinned and sold with the proceeds going to the Emergency Fund. Of course, there are no informers. They would be killed the next day."

Over dinner Roy talked about education. "Those early

DC's were wise," Roy commented. "One wrote that 'every academic success is a tribal failure.' What he meant is that going to school means that the boy is separated from his tribal age-based cohort. He is not initiated into tribal lore and so is lost to the tribe forever." Roy paused, then continued "Perhaps the fact that all education is run by the missionaries who try to convert the students is even a more direct attack on tribal tradition."

"No government schools?" I questioned. "Not for Africans," Roy responded. "Meru has three mission schools with about 4,600 students. Not many when you consider that the total population of children is over 86,000. Government does provide grant-in-aid to the Indian school which has only 52 students. We also run a government hospital in addition to those run by the missions. I'll drive you around tomorrow to see the missions and the hospital."

Next morning Roy drove us over back roads to the missions; I noted that almost all the students were boys. "Girls help their mothers grow the food," Roy told me. "And when they are married, the husband must give her family cows and beer. So girls are worth too much to allow them to study."

After lunch at his bungalow, Roy suggested we visit at a reforestation project and exercise his dog. The cool of the forest was welcome after a short walk under the tropical sun. Up we hiked, through bamboo groves interspersed among the trees, til we came to a meadow. New trees had been planted on one side, and were fenced against roaming cattle or wild animals. On the far side of the meadow, the ground dropped precipitously. Roy called to us to come to the edge. "See that camp on the ridge? Those are Mau Mau thugs." They could see us staring, but the jagged escarpments on either side of the valley kept them from being a threat. So I stood and watched them cook over an open fire.

WHEN I TURNED TO walk back to the bungalow, I realized Roy had disappeared. "He's chasing Caesar who was running after a chipmunk," Mil explained. "I'm sure he will be back soon." We waited and waited, as the shadows deepened on the meadow, but Roy did not return. Finally we began to descend through the bamboo and trees. Neither of us had been watching the path closely since we had been chatting with Roy as he showed us medicinal herbs and unusual trees growing along the way. I was getting chilled, and scared, as we tried one path, then another. I kept imaging running into a Mau Mau camp. At last the forest thinned and we could see the bungalow below.

Roy was reading, a tea cup by his side. "I wondered where you were," he said pleasantly. "I was sure you could find your way back. Caesar ran to the far side of the forest so I came back on a different path." I was both upset and furious, sure he had left us as a prank. I retreated to our bedroom and washed up very slowly. Mil and Roy were having a drink when I returned, and I readily accepted a whiskey. I needed it.

I held my tongue til after dinner as we were sipping brandy before the fire. "Roy, don't you worry about running into Mau Mau when you hike up the mountain?" I asked. "Oh no," he replied, "and you needn't have been either. Those thugs on the mountain are intent on harming those who are taking away their power. They hate the settlers for farming the land that they themselves left fallow for years. They hate the loyal Kikuyu whose chiefs we created because they undercut the power of traditional chiefs. And they hate the missionaries who are educating their daughters and training them to be nurses. Traditionally men control their women, paying a bride price for young women who then must farm for their husband and bear him children. Losing control of women was the last straw, I suppose. How else explain the barbarous attacks at several missions against the young girls who are not circumcised: these thugs cut out their genitals with *pangas* and killing them in the process."

No wonder so few girls were in the mission schools, I thought. "But how can such a backward-looking ideology become the basis for independence?" I asked. "It's one thing to seek mythical and real heroes from the past to stir nationalism, as they did in India. But their leaders, even Gandhi, were educated and politically astute."

"OF COURSE," REPLIED ROY. "This nativism is precisely why Kenya is not ready for independence. The Meru have refused to have small pox vaccinations since they were started in 1923 because a few had a reaction to the vaccine. They refuse to understand science; instead they resort to magic when they are sick. Independence will have to wait until more Kenyans are educated"

He seemed so disdainful of the Africans that I started arguing with everything he said, devouring his Cadbury chocolate-covered biscuits, and generally being an obnoxious guest. Mil finally intervened with his more diplomatic comments, suggesting that we needed to retire so we could leave early for our return to Nairobi so that we could get our brakes adjusted before we set off for London.

CHAPTER 14

# Uganda: three towns — three cultures

W HAT A RELIEF TO FOCUS ON TRIVIAL THINGS: HOW TO PACK clothes to keep out the red dust; how to squeeze all the new gear into the already loaded car – deciding which things we wouldn't need right away and could be packed on the roof, which to go into the boot, and which we might need in a hurry, like the snake bite kit. The night before we headed to Uganda I wrapped all my clothes in towels or cotton bags. Mil put his ties and a good shirt in my small weekender bag to keep them flat, as his main bag was a rucksack. We each had an overnight bag with towel, soap, cosmetics, pajamas, and a change of clothes. I usually put my Rollie in mine to protect it from the dust.

Packing the car was even more of a challenge than in Mombasa. On the roof was a tin trunk and two jerry cans of petrol; water bags hung from the roof rack and blocked the right back seat car door and window, the one facing traffic. By now we had gotten used to driving on the left side of the road with the steering wheel on the right side, but we had to be careful in loading the backseat to be sure that the driver could see out of the rear view mirror.

All the packing and re-packing took most of the morning, so it was nearly noon when we finally drove out of Nairobi and headed west on a paved road up through wooded hills and nurseries of Aberdare range. Near the summit, a stiff breeze was blowing off an invisible Mt. Kenya and gusted against Bublee's tall silhouette causing Mil to slalom down the road. The tarmac disintegrated into washboard gravel as the road wound down to the level brown floor of the Rift Valley. We paused to eat our lunch where we could see the marvelous pink flamingos standing on one leg, their hooked beaks plunged into the blue-green algae that flourish in the alkaline waters of Lake Nakuru. When startled, the birds took off looking as if a pink carpet was being pulled from the blue lake.

It was mid afternoon already, and we were hungry; we ate ham sandwiches made with bread and fresh butter we appropriated from our breakfast. We also had cheese, pears, and chocolate biscuits from the market. To celebrate our first day traveling west, we opened jars of pickles and olives from our cache of food we had brought from India. We weren't roughing it yet.

The weather was warm, distinctly warm, and still windy. The low hills were wooded, but acacia trees dominated the valley floor. The road began to climb up the escarpment on the west side of the valley floor to the Mau summit at 8322 feet, according to the map, about 3000 feet higher than Nairobi. The tarmac road turned northwest but we took the route west toward Kampala on washboard corrugated earth which recent rain had given a slippery surface. Most autos we saw were understandably Land Rovers. To add to the mess, road construction meant detours onto the parallel cart trails thick with dust. An approaching car, billowing dust, turned across the road just in front of us looking every bit like a boat in heavy seas.

Night falls suddenly at the equator, so before the sun set we checked into a hotel in Londiani. The parking lot was full and the pub was crowded. A couple was playing ping-pong in the spacious lounge before a warming fireplace. But by the time we had checked in, the place bar was nearly empty: no chance to talk to the locals. The woman manager, in a short wool skirt, kept munching nuts, as she showed us rooms with inner spring mattresses, running hot water, and our own fireplace. "The hotel has its generator for lights and hot water," she explained. "All the troubles have lessened the night trade, but we have more people coming in for drinks and food. I think they want company."

We dug out our woolen sweaters before we sat down to eat the best dinner we'd had since Bombay! Mil beat me at ping-pong 2 to 1 before we returned to our room to luxuriate in the warm water and soft beds. Morning tea was served in the room; I crawled back in bed with my cup and read a novel while Mil slept. Breakfast was lavish, so we packed some of the food for lunch.

Out of Londiani, the road was hellish. It was my turn to drive: 1½ hours on corrugated gravel. I kept wondering whether you should drive fast and ride the top of the bumps or slow down to sink into each indentation. I alternated techniques but either way awful and cause a cacophony of noise both from the car and its contents. The road was so dusty there was no point in closing windows because the red sand puffed up from floor. Mil took over the driving as the road wound down from the escarpment. Driving took extra concentration because the second gear was sticking. Hunks of dried mud kept falling off the car as we bumped along. "Maybe Bublee has diarrhea!" Mil joked.

As the road improved with a crushed stone finish, so did the feel of the place. More and more people were walking along the road. The men were quite friendly, saluting us with their hand held in front of their forehead or calling out "jambo." Most of the natives were wearing western dress: short or long pants for men and knee length skirts on women. Huts were round and made of sticks slathered with mud or of corrugated iron probably taken from the railroad supplies. The thatched roofs reached over the walls to provide a sort of terrace. Most had a single door and no windows – for warmth, I supposed since we were still some 5000 feet above sea level.

As the road descended toward Lake Victoria, the weather became warmer and we began to see sisal growing and cattle grazing. Bikes were everywhere, one ridden by on real dude fellow in white coat, shorts, pink tie. Near Kisumu, where the railroad ended in 1905, I tried to take a photo of a Chief in full regalia, but he ducked behind a car as spectators laughed at both of us. Large birds with heads and goiters in fiery red perched on acacia trees.

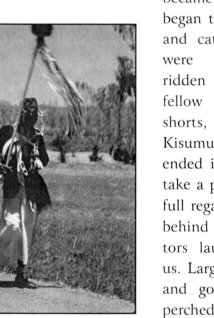

Chief in full regalia near Kisumu

Mil and Bublee near Lake Victoria

Red bottle-brush plants and trees with red blooms lightened our mood. Already we felt as if we were in another country. Indeed, I found out later that most of the area west of the escarpment had originally been part of the Uganda Protectorate. The British annexed it to Kenya when the railroad was being built in order to have the entire system under one jurisdiction.

Soon we could see Lake Victoria – at least a gulf of that huge expanse of water, the second largest freshwater lake in the world after Lake Superior. In town, drivers were washing off the red dust from their cars and themselves. The glistening water looked tempting, but we only paused briefly before driving past the small market area with its very modern new Aga Khan school and on toward the Uganda border.

Driving inland across a flat plain, we found the road crowded with people walking to and from the market. Women carried all manner of things on their heads: banana bunches, pots, sugar cane; they also had children tied to their backs or a chicken tucked under one arm. Men, walking behind bunches of women, were dressed in bush shirts, shorts, hats; the only thing they seemed to carry was a walking stick which could easily double to prod their women folk. Passing cars was difficult with all the people, so when I wanted to stop to take a picture looking back at the Nandi Escarpment, Mil refused: he had just passed a truck.

Rectangular houses lined the road, all with windows. Everywhere uniformed children were walking to schools, most with signs referring to the mission supporting them. A bunch of boys starred at us when we stopped for a quick lunch. As we neared the permanent market in Kakamega, the road became clogged with buses piled high with bikes and crowded with women, some smoking long thin stemmed pipes. Only one was dressed in traditional finery: six inch bead strings hanging from her ears.

Outside town we stopped to fill the tank from a jerry can and noticed that the petrol gauge wasn't working; we would just have to guess when Bublee needed a refill. Using the stop to relieve ourselves among the bushes, we were a bit embarrassed when one of the few white drivers we encountered on the road all day stopped to ask if we were all right. Most other cars were driven by Indians or Africans, adding to the distinct change in atmosphere we had felt since Londiani.

The border between Kenya and Uganda was just as relaxed. We simply signed our name in a book. A rabies control officer ignored us. Nothing more. As we drove on, we noticed a sign saying the border was 4000 feet above sea level. And that petrol was cheaper! Women's dress had changed to long skirts, while more men were wearing long flowing Arab gowns. We passed a nun driving her own car, several mosques, and more schools. Both houses and stores sported corrugated tin roofs. As we neared Jinja we saw more

Men fishing on the rocks that give Jinja its
name at the start of the Nile River

European style houses with plastered walls. Clearly this area
was prosperous.

The British were building a dam where Lake Victoria emp-
ties into the Nile; it was due to be in operation within a year.
The construction had brought many whites and Indians to the
town both to work on the dam and to set up factories once
the power came on line. The Ripon Falls would be covered
once the dam was complete, but we could still see the rocks
that gave Jinja –rock – its name, and see the water spill over
the many channels as it began its long journey north. The raw
energy of the water reflected the frontier nature of the town.
Soon it would become the industrial center of Uganda.

Indians outnumbered whites in the town; many streets
bore names like Kutch or Nizam, and most shops had Indian
names. The hotel, however, was European, and expensive. Its
manager had come out from England only the year before,
but was already planning to leave. Over a drink he told us
why: "I don't like the Africans. I don't like the Indians. But
the Europeans are the worst of the lot. Hypocrites, all of
them. No future for Europeans here, and its all the whites'
fault. They won't let the natives in their clubs. In Mbale, a

London-trained doctor treats everyone and is married to a white girl, but was blackballed from club. No wonder the educated Africans become politicians and then pass laws restricting immigration."

"What about here in the hotel?" I ask. He replied: "I wouldn't like Africans in the hotel bar, though can't legally throw them out. If they were here, whites wouldn't come." "And Indians?" I prompt. "Well, there are more Indians than whites in Jinja."

Next morning, we filled all the jerry cans with cheap petrol. Doing so meant we had to unload the roof rack, a task we didn't have to do as long as we were staying at hotels with an all night guards and enclosed parking. Repositioning the cans on the roof led to repacking most everything and swearing at each other in frustration. Mil's suitcase and some tins in boxes went on the roof along with the bed rolls and the tire. Still not satisfactory. Mil tied and retied the cords holding the tarp, and I grew impatient. Must be a better way of doing it. So silly we should fight over the delay caused by the loading problems, especially on my birthday.

We made up most of the delay by speeding along the amazingly smooth dual highway all the way to Kampala. Nearer the town, the road expanded to four runways: two for through traffic and two for all the local traffic including bicycles pedaled by men in shorts, and often carrying wife and baby balanced on the back. The road to Entebbe, capital of the Uganda Protectorate, was equally smooth and we quickly drove the 21 miles to the town. African huts along the road reflected the local prosperity; they had windows and doors and some had plaster walls and tile roofs. We hoped to learn more about the economy of the region by talking to Protectorate administrators.

Entebbe Mayor A.N. Maini was the most knowledgeable

of those we met. He was born in Nairobi and had graduated from London School of Economics. The fact that an Indian could be the mayor underscored the difference between Kenya and Uganda. The mayor explained: "The Municipal Council was set up in 1949 with all appointed members, a mix of communities: Europeans and Indians each five, four Africans, a Goan, plus officials. We have not only avoided the Kenya trouble, but a better type of person stands for nomination because there are no communal splits. When Uganda adopts elections, I hope for a common electoral roll not separate rolls for each community. If this happens, the Europeans won't contest. If you admit to communal rolls, where do you stop? Some tension exists between Hindus and Muslims but, as home ties become more distant, their focus is here in Uganda."

"What about the Africans?" I ask. Mayor Maini continued: "Over the centuries, the Bantu farmers moved into this area while the nomadic Nilotic herders came from the north; unlike Kenya, or Ruanda-urundi, they melded together in the area around Lake Victoria. Eventually several feudal kingdoms emerged, fighting each other for the best land. When the protectorate was set up, Buganda was the largest kingdom so the British negotiated only with the Kabaka. He bargained hard for freehold rights to their land. As the British rule expanded to include the other three kingdoms, and then the rest of the country, they decreed that all land was crown land to be held in trust for the tribes. Freehold rights gave much power to the Buganda, so even today, if Europeans or Indians or the government wish to build a house or factory, they have to pay rent. Sort of reverse discrimination," he laughed.

A British officer, who had been listening, chimed in: "The Kabaka was wily, indeed. He insisted on the exclusive use his language, Luganda, within the Protectorate and secured the right to collect taxes in all the area under British rule. Tax collectors created such enmity between the Buganda and the rest of the country that it continues today, long after this practice was abandoned. The Kabaka also decreed that the proper dress in his realm was the *kanzu*, a long shirt that had been traditionally made out of barkcloth until the Arabs introduced cotton. You can tell the *kanzu* from the Arab dress because of its maroon markings down the front. Women also had to wear long skirts called *gomesi*. You can tell where a woman is from by the length of her skirt."

The Mayor seemed eager to return to his focus on economics. "The area around Lake Victoria was ideal for growing cotton and the British textile mills provided a ready market," the mayor said, gesturing at the map. "The Buganda chiefs with their freehold estates and commoners to work the land responded to the British demand, and became quite wealthy. After World War I the colonial government limited the amount of obligatory labor the chiefs could demand so most chiefs sold the land they could not farm alone to their tenants, creating a class of well off peasant farmers. Since the government guarantees the price of cotton, local farmers won't grow vegetables: they must be imported from Kenya by rail!"

The Mayor continued to illustrate the advantages of a protectorate, which is controlled from London, versus a colony. He noted that once the Kenya government opened the "white highlands" to Europeans, the whites have dominated both the economy and the politics of that country. In Uganda the government promoted cotton for the Africans, but allowed the Indians and British to control cotton ginning. After the war, the African farmers formed a union and began to agitate against price controls for the right to set up cotton gins. The union also organized coffee growers whose production was also regulated by the government. In 1949 the union was banned by the conservative governor after riots in Kampala.

In 1952, a new reformist governor, Sir Andrew Cohen, was appointed to prepare the country for independence. Responding to the African demands, he proposed that cooperatives should be formed to run cotton gins and he set up programs to train Africans to improve their coffee and cotton crops. His proposal to set up a national legislative council which would include African representatives elected from all districts in the country was being opposed by all the feudal chiefs, especially the Kabaka, who continued to demand a dominant role for the Buganda. "The Kabaka is like a second rate Indian prince, a playboy. For example, the Kabaka congratulated the Lukinko, that's the nominated council for the Buganda province, for jailing a journalist who had written that Buganda Prime Minister a "weak man." After all, he said, dishonoring an official was against African custom. How does the government appeal that? It's just mischief. Of course the central government has final say, but it is a bit of a problem."

"The young educated Ugandans do not want a continuation of feudal rule and are busy forming political parties favoring a united country as Uganda moves toward independence," he asserted. To me, this planned transition seemed like a compressed version of India: feudal kingdoms wanting federation and political parties demanding central control. For all the careful planning in India, the Partition of land between India and Pakistan precipitated the slaughter of many as Hindus and Muslims fled across the Western border. I wondered whether the optimistic words of Mayor Maini would be a reflection of a future Uganda.

Entebbe itself reflected many colonial towns in India with its government housing set among trees and gardens. Even the hotel was spread out along the lake to catch the breezes. I wandered around the polished floors without my sandals. The second night I had a bump on my foot that I thought must be an infected splinter. But one of the room boys looked at it and was horrified. "You have a worm. It will get into your blood and eat your heart," he moaned. "You must let me cut it out." I was frightened, and let him probe the lump and pull out a worm. I have no idea what kind of worm, or whether it would eat at my heart. But I never went barefoot in Africa again.

As Mil drove back toward Kampala, I told him how the town got its name, according to our guide book. The Kabaka of Buganda used to hunt impala in the forests in the area that locals referred to the hills as the place the Kabaka hunted impala, or "Ka -empala." At the time when British explorers first arrived in the 1860s, seeking the source of the Nile, Buganda was the largest of four major feudal kingdoms in the region. The British government was not interested in setting up a colony, so they licensed the Imperial British East Africa Company to control commercial activities in the area. European missionaries soon followed and a rivalry arose between the British Protestants and the French Roman Catholics, each building a church on one of Kampala's hills. In 1892 a civil war erupted between the converts which the Company could not control. So in 1894 the British government declared a protectorate over Buganda which they gradually extended to include the other kingdoms and neighboring tribes.

"Reminds me of India," I say. "Trading companies lose control forcing the reluctant British Parliament to take over the country or lose face. Kenya is like British India where

Kabaka's old palace constructed of traditional materials
and now used as tombs for the royal family

English run the place; Uganda seems like the princely states which ran their own affairs."

Princes are much more difficult to interview than engineers or civil servants: they are permanent rulers with no need to talk to or please the public. The closest we came to the Kabaka was visiting his palace, a two story expansive building with little charm, located on one of the higher of the town's low hills. In contrast, the nearby traditional Luganda round structures of bamboo, reeds, and wood were elegant. Their thatched roofs reached the ground in the rear, protecting the rooms from the sun. At the entrance, the angled roof shaded the door and provided space to sit in the shade outside the walls. Once the multi-room palaces of the Kabaka, they were used as their tombs.

We were told to get permission from the Prime Minister to visit or photograph the palace or the tombs, but when we went to his house, we were told he was away on a long trip. Yet when we showed up at the palace, the askari's only concern was how much would we pay. He started asking for 15 shillings, went down to 5 shillings; I offered three. Two young man overheard the exchange and started calling the askari a "bad man" for being so expensive. No one seemed worried that we didn't have any permission.

On the top of another hill we found the remains of the old fort erected by the East Africa Company. It was now just a grassy mound where a family of Indians was picnic-ing. Nearby, a flag pole marked the spot where the first British flag was raised. The two churches that started the war– Church of England and Roman Catholic – are still in use, secure on their own hills

On yet another hill was Makerere College, set among brightly flowering trees and bushes. The British rector was eager to show us around, explaining that the institution was founded in 1922 a result of pressure by missionaries who wanted a secondary education available in Uganda for the many students graduating from their schools. Originally designed to train Africans in technical skills , the college had expanded its offerings to include medicine, teacher training, agriculture, and veterinary science. The rector proudly told us that in 1950, Makerere became a college affiliated with University College in London. He boasted that "Makerere is the largest college in all of southern Africa and attracts students from all the British territories. The present student body has only fifteen women out of 380. We are pleased that the first woman to study medicine has just graduated. Despite the need for men trained in agriculture, most preferred prestige degrees as doctors or lawyers." "Just like India," I told him.

Knowing that the Kabaka had decreed bananas as the only proper food worth eating, I asked the rector about food provided students living in the dormitories. "We do feed them bananas," he laughed, "but also bread, rice, and sweet potatoes. Students also have fresh fruit, vegetables, and meat daily and even two egg meals a week." The students certainly seemed well fed and greeted us in careful English as we walked back to our car.

The government offices were at the base of the old fort hill near our hotel and the sports club. We sought out Perry Stone, the officer charged with keeping tract of Buganda affairs for the Protectorate, to tell us about issues in the kingdom. "Currently the Lukiko has 86 members with 40 elected indirectly by parish councils and another 20 selected among the chiefs. Such a system reinforces feudal rule and is now being challenged by young educated Luganda who want at least some members elected directly. All provinces but one now have some sort of provincial council with a mix of elected and appointed members, but the demand for change has been growing since the government banned the Uganda African Farmers Union in 1949. The union demand for their own elected representatives frightened the Kabaka. Now he is not only resisting any change in the Lukiko, he has proclaimed the right of Buganda to leave the Uganda Protectorate and become a separate state."

Stone introduced us to Ignatius Musazi, former leader of the banned Uganda African Farmers Union, who had just formed the Uganda National Congress. Musazi envisioned a national party working for independence, one that would be open to all tribes and races because "I do not believe in domination of one race by another." Yet later, when I asked about the other union demands for more open pricing and greater ownership of cotton gins by Africans, he complained that the majority of Indians are only interested in money and not independence, and so "say nothing." Nor was Musazi happy with the proposed reforms of the cotton industry, complaining that "the government didn't know what it was doing when it bought the least efficient cotton gins and continued subsidizing them. The government is only interested in a stable economy, not morals."

Musazi's goal of forming a multi-communal party seemed idealistic, especially when compared to the parties in Kenya. A local paper criticized his shift from organizing African farmers to forming a national party as opportunistic. A journalist told me that he thought Musazi's approach was a clever way to organize Africans without being banned once more. Whatever his reasoning, Musazi's effort was a challenge to the Kabaka.

As I BEGAN TO write up my notes on Uganda, I kept reflecting on how the three towns we visited each presented a distinct aspect of the country. Entebbe is a colonial capital, but once independence happens, the British influence, unencumbered by white settlers, will diminish. Jinja displayed the power of Indian traders who would certainly benefit from the growth of industry once the dam was complete. Their entrepreneurial skills could benefit an new country. Mayor Maini told us that many Indian businessmen were partnering with Africans, but Musazi's statements about Indians signaled deep resentment. Kampala is an African town, poised to become the capital of a new country if Uganda holds together. I did not think the British would allow Buganda to become a separate state. But how would a federation work in face of the historic antagonism from the other tribes against the Buganda supremacy? How long would the chiefs continue to wield power?

CHAPTER 15

# Ruanda-urundi: seeds for future conflict

WHILE MIL SAW TO CAR REPAIRS, I BEGAN TO WRITE THE BOOK
I had promised my agent in New York now that my
articles for the Calcutta *Statesman* had been finished. I had
run out of carbon paper, I had to mail the manuscript as I
went along. The day before we to leave for Belgian Congo,
I put the first chapters into an addressed manila envelope
ready to take to the post office after we finished a final
interview at the government offices. However, Perry Stone
invited us to join him for a drink at the Bamboo Grove Club,
a colonial club that restricted membership to whites. In New
Delhi such exclusive clubs welcomed Indians immediately
after independence and I am sure the same will happen in
Kampala. So I did not feel too guilty enjoying a dance by the
pool. But of course the post office had closed by the time we
returned to the hotel.

Kampala was so quiet and relaxed after Nairobi that we had gotten rather lax about security and left the car in front of the hotel, ready to pack and leave the next day. I was devastated when we went out in the morning to find the door jimmied open and the manila envelope missing. Even worse, the glove compartment had been emptied and the carnet was missing along with my address book, maps, and extra ammunition for Mil's gun. I could presumably rewrite the chapters, and locate the addresses. Good riddance, I thought, about the bullets. But how could we continue our trip without the passport for Bublee?

Mil dropped me at the government offices while he took the car in to repair the damage. I chased down Perry as he was on the way to a meeting. He didn't know of any place to get the carnet reissued closer than Nairobi. Seeing that I was close to tears, Perry took me to see his superior, District Commissioner Spencer. DC Spencer had served in the British Army in East Africa during the war; everyone called him Major. He reassured me that since most local cars did not need a carnet anyhow, an official looking document showing that we owned the car would be sufficient to get us into the Congo; we'd have to go back to Nairobi for another carnet, though. The Major said he would need the engine number as well as the license number to complete this document, so Mil would have to bring the car to the office.

Grateful, I walked back to the hotel to tell them we would be staying another day. I then started writing letters to find addresses for later in our trip; I was sure that we could find the plantation of the brother of the Belgian Ambassador to India without an actual address. After all, both Ambassador de San and I had written him that we would visit. I refused to think about all the work I'd put into my missing manuscript; at least I still had my notebooks. When Mil came back with the door fixed, I sent him off to buy some new maps and get our substitute carnet.

Mil returned to the hotel with Major Spencer who was interested in our impressions of Kenya. The Major had been all over East Africa during the war and did not like what he had seen of British colonial policy. He supported the Labour Party during the 1945 elections which had defeated Winston Churchill who was opposed independence for India proclaiming that he did not win the war to lose the British Empire. Back in England, the Major joined the Colonial Service to help bring independence to the East African colonies. He was impatient with the white settlers in Kenya who thought independence meant the whites would rule. "Don't they see what is happening in Asia?" he asked. "We have already left India, Ceylon, and Burma, and are working our way out of Malaya. The Dutch have left Java and are holding on to scraps of the Indies. And the French are fighting a losing war in Indochina. Do they think the British army will come to their support? What a mistake it was to sell them land in the highlands, anyhow, just to pay for the railroad."

Some of his anger was no doubt directed at the Kabaka who was not willing to let his power slip away as the princes had in India. Still the analogy wasn't quite correct because the most industrialized part of India had had an elected parliament for a decade before independence. In contrast, most of Uganda was still dominated by tribal chiefs. Major Spencer was not concerned. "Uganda's a small country with a well-educated core of administrators and teachers who chafe under the Kabaka's feudal antics."

"Enough about Uganda," the Major prompted after a reflective silence. "Tell me how you plan to drive to London. You know that East Africa is hemmed in on the west by the jungle and on the north by the mountains. Don't recommend either. In any case, you have to go back to Nairobi for the carnet. That leaves the desert route to Moghadishu. During the war, my company took over Italian Somaliland, so I know it is possible to get that far. The Italians had built roads from there into Ethiopia but we did not repair them during the war."

I was sipping a Pimms Cup, that strange British concoction of spicy gin and lemonade decorated with cucumber and lemon. The Major's knowledge of the area fascinated me. "You say the road to Moghadishu is a flat track of sand?" I ask. "But you must go before the April rains or you'll get stuck in the mud." he cautioned.

"Tell me about Ruanda-urundi and Belgian Congo," I begged.

"The road to Lake Kivu goes though a corner of Ruanda. You'll find the country much the same as when Stanley first explored it. The feudal Tutsi chiefs still treat the commoners like serfs. Although the Germans claimed the area they saw no economic possibilities there and left it alone. They did cast an eye on Buganda and tried to compete with us here by getting the Kabaka to sign a treaty with them. It was just mischief. Later they agreed to withdraw in exchange for a tiny British island in the North Sea which they actually used during World War I. Little good it did them. After they lost the war, the Belgians took Ruanda-urundi and we got Tanganika."

Another round of drinks later, the Major continued. "The Belgians had their hands full, just taking over from King Leopold. He was a thoroughly nasty man. Only cared about making money. He beat the natives, forced them to collect rubber in the jungle; virtual slaves. Finally the Belgian government was compelled take over in 1908. Ever read Joseph Conrad's *Heart of Darkness*? The Belgians still want to make money, so they have almost no health care and limit education to technical skills of use to the copper industry, for example. One native was trained as a priest and sent to study in Belgium; but the government won't let him return, might stir up trouble. Some people think that this is the way to treat the natives. I think they are asking for trouble."

VERY EARLY THE NEXT morning, we finally drove southwest out of Kampala, across the equator and toward the mountains that formed the continental divide. The prosperity of the Buganda was evident in the tile roofs climbing the hills as the road steadily gained altitude. The dress was clearly Luganda: voluminous gowns on the women and men with skirts, usually white, but I saw one in pink! Perhaps the maroon markings bled into the cloth. Masaka was perched on a hill and the road barely touched the market. This might be the last opportunity to mail my last batch of letters re-requesting addresses I had lost to the thieves. But the steep and narrow tracks up the hill were intimidating, so I asked a policeman if he would mail them for me; he most politely agreed.

Even the main road was bumpy but having a left hand drive meant we could look out to the rough edges of the road and miss some of the worst holes, sometimes. Red earth blew into the car; Mil's blonde hair began to look as if he had rinsed it with henna! He needs a hat. I usually tie a scarf around my hair, though the red does not show so much on my dark brown hair. Tall red ant hills were as frequent as trees. Suddenly the road dipped into a swamp. Thousands of vultures were circling, spreading ominous clouds over the trees. Eerie!

We had planned to spend the night in Mbarara, at the rest house there. But it was full, so we continued, leaving the kingdom of Buganda. Now the women no longer wore voluminous skirts but rather a variety of short skirts. Every man and woman seemed to smoke pipes. The modern buses we had chased from Kampala stopped in Mbarara. The topography changed from tropical to green turf hills, reminding me of the treeless moors in Scotland. We found a clay quarry just off the road where we camped. The primus had sprung a leak and had to be pumped constantly, using so much fuel that we had just enough to heat water. The canvas water bags dripped water. At least the mattress fit, and removing the front seats so we could stretch out was not as much a problem as I had thought it might be.

Next morning we left the site about nine: we never seem to leave any earlier. The weather was chilly; everything was green and damp. The women walking along the road had capes over their short cotton dresses, often sheltering babies on their backs. Some of the boys were wearing sheepskins, inside out, and nothing else. Houses were of mud with thatch roofs and no windows; some had roofs made with reed that formed steps, pagoda like.

At the Kabale market, the most fashionable women decorated the back of their sheep skins with beads in strings

Mil shaves after our first night car-camping

and edged the leather with rings of wire or even pop bottle tops! Some beauties displayed ankles laden with 200 or so large wire bracelets. One side of the market was lined with corrugated iron stalls; in one a man was sewing clothes, in another a man was

Sheepskins, decorated with beads, ward off the chill in Kabale

repairing bicycles. A man on bike came over to the car, selling gaudy calico squares. Maize, potatoes, pulses, and goats were for sale, but no bananas: too cold for the palms to survive. I tried to by some potatoes which looked fine, but I couldn't make the women understand that I only wanted a few, not a bushel. So all I got were pictures.

Walking up the main street we found a general store run, of course, by Indians. I was able to buy a couple potatoes and some crackers. Looking for the baskets which locals were using, I finally found them in a shop attached to local government offices up the hill by the District Commissioner's house which was set in a pleasant green space.

We checked into the town's only hotel: too cold to camp out and hungering for a last huge meal before entering the Congo with its high prices. Often hotel food, which comes with the price of the room, is just so-so, but that night I ate every course: soup, a British grill of liver, potato, and tomato; omelets with mushrooms, cold meat and salad; sweet custard, cheese, and fruit. I even tried a tree tomato. Papyrus was used as paneling inside the hotel and imitated the pagoda style roof on some huts. I talked to a party from Leopoldville driving around in a truck who confirmed that Congo was expensive. A young English couple was delighted to be out of the heat of Kampala where the husband worked for the Barclay Bank. I was cold and could have used some warmer weather.

Next morning we continued our climb toward the volcanoes which divide the African continent not only east and west but north and south. In Uganda, the rivers drain into Lake Victoria, then meander north as the Nile runs through swamps and deserts. To the west of the mountains and the continental divide, the rivers flow into the Congo River. The Rift Valley cradles a string of lakes along the divide: water from Lakes Edward and Albert flows into the Nile, water from Kivu and Tanganyika, the two most southerly lakes, flows south before circling west and becoming a major source of the Congo.

The views were fantastic as we drove over an 8170 foot pass. The map showed four volcanoes over 14500 feet. We passed through bamboo forests then dropped down into a lush green valley with sparsely wooded hills. Occasionally we spotted herds of cattle with huge semi-circular horns. We stop so I could take colored photos of the waves of hills looking over Lake Bunyonye. Landscape photos seldom really capture the depth or texture of such scenery, but I had to try.

Further into the valley was the Ugandan customs post, located where the road splits with the main route going directly into Congo and our more southerly road heading through Ruanda-urundi to Lake Kivu. The customs official stamped our passports but thought we might have trouble with Belgians since we were not only missing the carnet but, as he noted, our three month visa for the Belgian Congo had expired. When we had gotten the visa in New Delhi on November 29, we did not expect to spend so many weeks in Kenya and so had forgotten to check the date!

Either we get in, or we don't, I thought, as we headed

toward Ruhengiri. At the border, we stopped at the douane post with a guard whose English was obviously limited. He looked at our documents, then put down our name as "Millidge," entered the license number as the engine number, and for no reason noted our destination as "Baggage." As we drove off, his son smiled "au revoir" to us. At Ruhengiri we stopped at a second douane post where a more official looking douanier filled out two long forms that included an entry for the visa. "Hum..," he said under his breath, counting the months on his fingers, but he said nothing. As for the car, we only had to pay 10 francs for a paper on which he also wrote the number on our cameras. "Bon jour, et bon voyage," he smiled.

We drove into a lush valley, cupped between mountains that directed the water flow south. The land was gently rolling; huts and small farms covered the hills with crops running up to top. The road itself was lined with columns of trees that seemed to come right out of the French countryside. Tree roots made the ride very bumpy. We have to remember to stay on the right side of the road – it had been a long time since we had driven ala droit. People were everywhere, and everywhere they saluted "Jambo, Madame" doffing their hats or raising their hands. One chap lifted his basket to lift his hand, another offered a barrel. They were wearing cloth sarongs tied at the waist though some women had secured them above their breasts. The unmarried women had patterns shaved into their very short hair; once they marry, they shave the fuzz all off and let it grow naturally in tight corkscrews. I saw one woman whose hair formed a six inch halo about her head.

Looking for a place to camp without becoming a local sideshow, we turned down a side road that led past a gorgeous garden – hydrangeas all blue, roses on trellises – surrounding a compact brick house. Smog from the chimney hung caught in the trees. "Surely this can't be Africa," I said to Mil. A lady who looked completely English was observing our approach as she picked roses and politely told us that American Mission was down the road. The douanier had mentioned a mission when we asked about a place to stay the night if we couldn't find a place to camp.

Further along, on the left, we saw a sign: Rwankeri, Seventh Day Adventist Church. Perhaps we could camp on their grounds. It is worth a try, at least. We followed the sign toward the home of the "Directoire;" damp bricks made a moss covered path through a trellis, past hydrangeas, to a small bungalow. No one was there but two pleasant natives emerged from behind the house. Between pidgin French and Swahili we gathered "Bwana there gone; mademoiselle there but no one home but cat; madame there home." With some trepidation we walked up to madame's house. A plain, sober looking woman with a baby in her arms welcomed us.

We ask about camping on their grounds. "Of course," she smiled, "but that house is empty, so why not sleep there?" In no time we were inside her house, recounting Mil's missionary roots in Japan and China, and being asked to eat a lunch leftovers. Cold. They don't even so much as cook on their Sabbath - Saturday. The diapers lay in the bathtub...no work on Sabbath. "The boys are off...it's our Sabbath. No hot water. What a mess is Sunday morning after Sabbath."

Sabbath was also the time for visiting. The mission's Swedish nurse, Miss Larsen, brought over her guests, missionaries from a station down the valley who had previously worked at Rwankeri. Like our hostess, Mrs. Evarts, the visiting Bradburys were from South Africa and had driven up from Pretoria when they first arrived. They often drove around Lake Kivu or into East Africa, but they didn't know

anyone who had tried to drive north through the Congo...
The South Africans brought their superior racial attitudes
with them. I could only wonder how they could convert the
natives who would then be saved and go to heaven just as the
missionaries would, yet treat them so unequally in this life.

Mr. Evarts was away inspecting "outschools" which taught
the scriptures as well as technical education. Remembering
that the Congo forbade non Catholic missionaries, I asked if
the Ruanda-urundi government made it difficult for them.
Speaking in accented English, Mrs. Bradbury reminded
me that the Germans were the first to claim the valley; like
Uganda, they allowed both Protestants and Catholics to open
schools for the natives. "When the Belgians took over after
the First World War, they were too busy trying to control the
Congo to interfere much here. You know that King Leopold
was only forced to turn over his private colony to the Belgian
government in 1908. Colonialism was new to them so they
tried to run that vast area from Europe. Impossible!"

Mr. Bradbury joined in. "Now they are trying to take
more control. For example, we have so many people in this
area that there are periodic shortages of food; the Belgian
government sets up barriers against the speculators and
moves their own food in. It also tries to convince families to
move via free transport to free lands in Congo. The natives
are not too willing. They remember tales about slave labor
under Leopold."

Our dinner was served on a small table in the living area
since the dining table was filled with the missionaries. We
ate a meal of bread already spread with creamy peanut butter
and syrup, cold fried eggs, and milk. I couldn't figure out
what the rest ate, if at all, besides coffee, which we weren't
offered. It was only eight o'clock their time, but we had lost
an hour and were tired, so we politely retired to the empty

house armed with a pressure light and some blankets. We'd refused Mrs. Evart's offer of sheets and towels and spread our own bedding on a welcoming double bed.

Up at seven, we took a quick, cold, sponge bath: too early for the boys to heat water, I was told. But the stove was hot and Mrs. Evarts fed us a huge waffle breakfast. "As you drive toward Goma," Mrs. Evarts told us, "you will see the large house belonging to a seven foot tall Tutsi chief. The Belgians use the Tutsi to keep the Hutu farmers in check." After serving us more waffles, she continued: "When we travel in the Congo, we always stay at a Gite, a resthouse where you do your own cooking and use your own bedding. Quite inexpensive. You must stay in the one at Lake Kivu with its view of the water." After thanking her for her hospitality and information and with our thermos filled with milk, we left for Kivu.

CHAPTER 16

# Belgian Congo: Complacent Colonialism

*A* S WE DROVE TOWARD THE CONGO I RECALLED IMAGES OF
Tarzan swinging through the trees on loops of vines.
What we saw was quite different: rolling savannah and a lake
4,790 feet above sea level; not a steamy jungle with huge
spiders and wild animals!

In the Belgian Congo, we had been invited to visit the
plantation owned by Maurice de San, brother of Louis de
San who was the Belgian Charge d'affaires in New Delhi in
1952. I was anxious to hear what a resident thought about
the way colonialism was practiced here. The several British
civil servants who mentioned the Congo during interviews in
Kenya and Uganda strongly disagreed with what they considered to be the Belgian's heavy-handed policies to control
the natives and limit their education.

201

Our immediate problem was to find de San's plantation. His letter explaining how to drive to his home was among the papers stolen in Kampala, but I remembered that the road took off from Lake Kivu. Mil and I were discussing the best way to find him when, suddenly, around a bend, the lake was visible, clear and still. We had driven past the Ruanda-urundi border and into Goma before realizing it or deciding what to do.

Goma's main street was spread with rough gravel and had telephone poles running down its center. The stores, perhaps ten, were in various stages of construction, adding to the dust. A restaurant next to the cinema had placed tables on its long verandah. We stopped to drink wonderful café filtre and talk with a handsome white haired Italian who was touring on this motorcycle and had driven from Mogadishu. Ah, another person who assured us that we could drive that way in our little car.

The restaurant owner thought that a de San sister lived nearby and suggested we ask in the hotel in Kisenyi because the owner's wife spoke English. So we drove back the few miles into Ruanda where we were told that Madame de Broqueville, nee de San, had moved from town to the lake. Following her directions, we drove down a single lane "beating" road – one where a native pounds a warning to oncoming cars that they must wait til you pass. Finally a lane led to a small stone bungalow set near the shore in a grove of trees.

Hearing our arrival, Madame appeared at the door, hastily dressed in a strapless black cotton dress. As I explained our reason for coming, she offered us an aperitif: either the bitter Amar Picon or a sweet grenadine. Very French, I thought, but a bit early in the day. Then I remembered that the major meal of the day was probably served midday. Besides the drink, she gave us her brother's address in the hills. When I admired the house with its huge fireplace and a view of the lake, she told us that she had designed it and was supervising its still unfinished construction. As we chatted, a tall man with straight black hair joined us and was introduced simply as Michael. Evidently husband and oldest son were in Belgium and her daughter was studying in Nairobi. Only the youngest son was with her, and he was swimming with friends from town. When we offered Michael a ride into town, Madame replied "He stays here." Again, so French: she seemed fairly young and I guessed the husband was old, perhaps a marriage of convenience.

We drove back to Goma and followed the road around the lake. For a short distance we could see houses fronting the lake, some delightfully modern, others heavy with Flemish roofs. When we tried to find a road leading to the lake so that we could enjoy the view as we ate cheese and fruit, we kept ending up at private homes, all unoccupied, apparently without even servants to protect them. As the road turned northwest to skirt an inlet, we encountered black humpy lava that signs proclaimed had flowed across the road in 1948. Next came signs for a 1938 lava flow which has ferns growing on it on the edge of the road; its sign showed a map of the lake narrowed by the ash and mud flow. Scrub trees had taken root in the 1912 flow and had enclosed a small lake which was green from algae and scum. It was a stark reminder that volcanic activity is frequent in the area, even bubbling up in the lake, according to local myth.

Beyond the lava flows, the dusty country road was only somewhat less bumpy as it twisted and turned on its way toward Costermansville at the other end of the lake. Apparently a proclamation has changed the name of the town back to the older native Bukavu, but our map still showed the route to C'ville. As I drove along, I was baffled to see all the natives get off the road and bow their heads as we passed. I looked back thinking some high official must be close behind us. But no, just us in our casual clothes, driving a dusty little car. Apparently our white skin was enough to prompt this obeisance. No joyous salutations as in Uganda, no stares as in Kenya, no salutes as in Ruanda. Just bows, a sign of how the Belgians has instilled "respect."

After 2 hours driving so slowly on the twisty road that we had covered only seventy miles, we finally spied the Gite at Nyamukubi. Rain was beginning to fall so we were anxious to get inside, but the guard had no key to the bungalow and spoke no French. All he could do is gesture toward the town. I asked for help from several well dressed locals walking along the road. "Je suis l'etranger" said the man in a dark green shirt, tie, white hat and pants. As we were about the drag the askari with us to find the key, he pointed toward a man in local calico dress waving the key in front of him. Just in time, as it began to pour. We were let into a spotlessly clean bungalow with 3 rooms plus bath. The room with fireplace, shelves, table and chairs, overlooked the lake, and here we dumped our stuff. The dining room also had shelves and table, but the bedroom only shelves. The bath was a tub of concrete, a sort of slab with a hollow. The outhouse was a clean smelling pit. We dined lightly, heating a few tins on the primus. We still had not recovered from the huge breakfast. The rain had stopped, so we disassembled the car bed and put the mattress on top of suitcases and car cushions in the bedroom. The arrangement gave us more room than sleeping in the car and was stable enough to make love.

In the morning, the lake was lovely, still, pale pinks and light greens. Breakfast was easy with the primus working again. We piled the "bed" back in the car, checked the tires, and made one last trip to the john. We paid the guard 25 francs since we could find no list of rates anywhere. He seemed pleased.

Back through the lava flows – I was able to see more of the devastation with Mil driving – then north to "Les Mokotos," four lakes up in the hills. At a Burungi "village" – three huts and a store – we branched right and drove through part of Parc Albert, over volcano cinders, out of the parc, and, after one wrong try, toward the de San's Lubaga Plantation. We could not phone as almost no one has phones in this part of the country.

As we drove up the path, we nearly ran into a Studebaker pick-up. Everyone seemed to have these trucks. Ahead we could see a low bungalow built with black volcanic rock; the steep roof was dark tile. The door of the house was open and we could see into a dining room. But no one was about so I called "Bon jour." A man with light yellow hair, dressed in shorts and knee socks, handsome still but with too much tummy, came to the door. "Je cherche pour Monsieur Maurice de San," I say in my best French accent. "Je sais," was all I heard before I started to explain, in English, our loss of letters and to apologize for not telling them when we would arrive. In moments we were inside the spacious living room being warmly welcomed by his wife and two young sons. The room was dominated by a fireplace alcove, rounded and raised, with benches on the sides, and similarly arched windows framing a view of Les Mokotos. "This area is an extension," de San explained, "we started with only two rooms: one for dining where we slept and a bedroom for the boys. Gradually we built a master bedroom, a study, and this room on the ground floor and a guest room upstairs." The bathroom had running hot & cold water with a cement bathtub and an enamel washbowl. Across the open hall between kitchen and dining rooms was the lavatory which I happily used. It was very clean, but spiders instantly wove again the web I had broken by shutting the door.

Almost immediately we sat down for lunch, joined by another guest, the Belgian Agent *Sanitaire* who would be inspecting native workers for yaws. After lunch, we followed Maurice and the agent to watch the inspection of workers who had lined up with their shirts off. Nearby were de San's new coffee plants, tea bushes, and eucalyptus groves. The drying sheds were off to the side; at one bench workers were making very small tea packets to sell to the natives, who only buy a little tea at a time.

Later we drove higher up to the pyrethrum fields; from here we had a lovely view of the two active volcanoes which had spilled the lava we saw near Lake Kivu. Every half hour we could hear blanks being fired in an attempt to scare elephants from the parc. The sound ricocheted off the hills, day and night. We stop at the fields of strawberries and artichokes to pick some for dinner. How luscious. By contrast, the meat was like

Belgian Agent Sanitaire inspecting
African workers for yaws

shoe leather. Maurice explained that only the natives sell it in this area.

After supper, we sat around the fire listening to Maurice talk about his life in Congo. He had come out before the war as a surveyor, driving from Mombasa as most settlers did. When the Germans occupied Belgium in 1940 and the king cooperated with the Nazis, the Congo stayed loyal to the government in exile in London. So Maurice stayed on in the Congo, working for the government until five years ago when he bought this plantation. But running it had not been easy. "Finding reliable natives is increasingly difficult. Workers come and go and many who appear only work in the morning, so we pay by piece. Our workers are not from this area and definitely have a superior attitude toward locals who were food for the neighboring tribes til whites came!" His cook and one house servant had been with him for many years. A modest number, I thought, compared to Kenya or India.

I asked Maurice whether he agreed with people I'd met in Uganda who admired the Belgian colonial policy. Instead of a direct reply, he talked about the questionable practices of the various Belgian Societies which had bought up government land, promising to improve it with roads and services, but most didn't. De San himself had helped put in a road for the "Simca" group, big exploiters whom the government had only recently tried to control. "That's why some Congo-ites are wealthy," he said grimly. "These Societies also ignored regulations meant to improve conditions for the natives who were badly treated when King Leopold controlled the country. People at home do not have much interest in the colony. They think limited education will allow very gradual change. But the Congolese troops who fought in the Abyssinia campaign are challenging the old system, striking at the Katanga mines, and even staging a revolt. Now the United Nations is pressing for democratic reforms. But no one listens, here or at home." So Maurice, tres gentile, did not expect to hand the plantation to his sons. "Trouble will come."

Breakfast was cheese and salami accompanied by advice about local roads and places to visit while in the country. I helped his wife finish the ironing before saying goodbye to family. We drove back to Goma and headed north; the road skirted Parc Albert at first, then turned into its midst where we saw an elephant only yards off the road. High up in the trees were multicolored birds with monkeylike tails that opened as fantails when they fly.

Ruindi Camp was set in a clearing of the forest. For one night we decided to live as tourists, at tourist prices. Guests were housed in individual native type huts with heavy grass roofs over mud and wattle sides; the floor was black volcanic rock set into cement. It was cool inside, but a bit damp and dark despite the four windows. A tree next to the hut was covered with upside-down yellow birds building hanging nests that were round like a ball. In the lavatory two brilliant lizards were crawling, each about a foot long, with blue heads, red necks, with yellow green bodies and purple tails. Amazing!

As the sun set, we walked a few yards beyond the camp hedge to hear hippo in the river, elephant trumpeting, and see buck bound across the grassy hill. Birds kept chattering. So immersed were we in the smell and sights and sound that we felt part of the park, not just observers. Later I wished we'd stayed another day to see more game, but 250 Francs each per day seemed too much for one more night of luxury: 500 francs was equal to our daily budget without including costs for petrol or car repairs.

As dark enveloped the forest, we walked to the main lodge for dinner. A sign at the entrance explained that this magnificent park was established in 1925 as the continent's first national park. A nagging thought crept into my mind – did the Belgians care more for animals than natives?

A fascinating part of our stay was observing the other guests. A Dutch couple, middle-aged, was on their way to South Africa. The husband, a geologist, had gone to Leopoldville for a month's work; she met him in Stanleyville, where they hired a car and were driving to Lake Tanganyika where a ferry would take them to Northern Rhodesia.

One lone old maid from Paoli, Penn, who signed the register as F.A. Orr to hide her status, came to the restaurant twice, once to ask when dinner would be served and once to eat. When she arrived the first time, I said hello: in my jeans I thought she'd know I was an American, but she fled. At dinner she did manage a horsey smile. What brought such a timid woman to the wilds of Africa? But she was not interested in talking.

A French family driving a Citroen came late to dinner: two sons, a small girl, and maman. They only talked to Madame, the restaurant supervisor, who sat on the terrace, feet up, reading a French novel. Plump, and a bit haughty I felt, perhaps because I did not say "bon jour" and shake her hand. The French speakers all did so, including the sixtyish man accompanied by his much younger wife dressed in short balloon shorts.

Early the next morning, we drove north along the plain, marveling at the herds of wild buffalo, elephant, and many kinds of buck. Strange flamingo-like birds settled on the road and I honked to make them fly until Mil, worried it might arouse the buffalo, asked me to stop. Large signs warned "the route lacet." It certainly did, up and up 1000 feet in 12 miles. At each turn, the herds of animals receded, then vanished as we drove into the fog of low clouds drifting across the mountain tops. Then rain, pouring down. It was like driving through tears. Then the motor cut out. Something was too wet. Out in the rain went Mil, in raincoat and his new corduroy checked hat. We later discovered we had both paid for, making it a $6 hat – a lot for our $10/day budget.

Eventually Mil got the car started; the rain lessened and finally stopped. We were in a heavily populated area near Lubero. People looked different. Men, did not shave their heads but let the hair grow several inches long. Most wore only a loin cloth, but women covered themselves from the waist and threw a cloth over their shoulders, often on top of a fancy ruffled blouse. The area seemed prosperous: cultivation reached up to the hill tops, as in Ruanda. A plantation village on a distant hilltop looked like a primitive drawing. Perhaps the cannibals, who ate the people near Kivu, didn't come this far or perhaps these people fought back.

We passed several dispensaries, many missions, gites, and several lovely European homes. Road "separators" had elephant grass planted between lanes, and shelters shielded the walking natives from the sun. Outside Butembo, several signs advertised "Ford Service" and "Hotel Oasis." Beni's streets around the administrative center were lined with fat palm trees. Round the corner, the typical commercial center was dusty, the square lined with two hotels and several shops with a continuous covered verandah. Can this be Africa? It is sometimes so hard to correct one's many preconceptions.

We pressed on over the continental divide which defines the river basins: Congo to the west, Nile to the east. We were back in Africa! Road gangs in black pullovers with yellow lining both armholes and neck, a yellow star on the front, worked repairing the road. We continued through the Ituri forest to Oysha, looking for the United Protestant medical mission run by Doctor Bekker and his wife, from Pennsylvania. Maurice de San had met them when he was prospecting for a mining company and had made alcohol for them out of native liquor for the clinic when their supply ran low. Maurice admired their work and suggested we visit them.

By now it was late afternoon and Doctor was teaching his native staff. Mrs. Bekker was pleased to have visitors and happy to talk about her years in the Congo. The two of them had come to the Congo in 1930, via Nairobi, Kampala, and the lakes. She spoke about the increasing restlessness among natives, how they had once spoken of the wisdom of the white man, and now they were only annoyed at not being white and not attaining while civilization immediately. Also she felt a nastiness replacing their sweet simple souls. "Father," when he came, thought this change was not so pronounced. He was very mid-western in speech though from Pennsylvania, and preoccupied. We stayed for a quick supper, but he had white patients down from a plantation and left quickly.

We asked for a Gite but, because it was some distance away, we decided to try the guest house across the road since it was 8 pm already. Bad choice: a dumpy place, like a run-down drive in. A mulatto maid showed us to a room. The wash stand held two bowls of water to wash in, but neither a slop bucket nor more wash water. The commode smelled; we spied centipedes on the floor and bed bugs in the straw double mattress. We spread DDT everywhere and crawled under the mosquito netting. So to bed to see if bed bugs bite. Well, don't think they did, but unseen mosquitoes got to my ankles while I wrote up my travel notes. "Let's see how well Diaprin works," I thought.

Mrs. Bekker had invited us back for breakfast and talk. Despite the growing sullenness of some natives, she thought that the Belgian government was doing a good job and that

British were "too soft on natives." But she scoffed at the idea that the Belgians thought all American missionaries were American spies who want to take over the Congo! Unlike their experiences, she said that all doctors and teachers now had to attend a one year course in Belgium prior to their coming out. I comment: "probably for standardization and for propagation of correct ideas."

While we were eating, the doctor was interrupted several times by patients. He came back after one consultation to tell us the mountains were clear and rushed us out to see the Ruwenzori range before the clouds descended again. As we marveled at the view of "The Mountains of the Moon," he told us about the Mission's leper colony and its new approach for treating the disease. "Leprosy is not as easily transmitted as people used to think," he said. "So, although we do separate the huts of the natives who are contagious from those that are not, we let their children eat with them but provide another hut where they sleep. All our lepers are allowed to move freely, and some are even cured!" I recalled all those stories I'd read as a child about gallant doctors sailing to leper colonies on remote islands to sacrifice their lives! Doctor Bekker presented a much more hopeful view.

Before we retraced our route south toward Beni, Mrs. Bekker told us how to find the pygmies. She said that the villagers along the road are short, but are not pygmies. Each village along the road has their own group of pygmies who live back in the forest and kill meat for them in exchange for plantains and vegetables. Recently, after the reserve areas were established in the forest, more game has drifted away, depriving the pygmies of their meat so they welcome tourists. All we had to do is stop along the road at the village and ask "Bambuti, eeko wapi." Mbuti is the name of the hunters-gathers in Ituri forest, and "ba" means people, she explained.

Wondering how to proceed, we saw the Belgian officer mustering his road gang. He laughed when I asked about bambuti but turned to question the men. One was chief of his village and offered to send for his pygmies. But that meant waiting. Besides, I wanted to go into the forest. So he directed us to a collection of huts that was his village and asked a sharp looking native in a red shirt and green-grey hat to guide us. This guide, who knew perhaps ten words in French, felt very full of himself as he directed us to drive through the village and stop at the far end in a sea of children. One boy was designated to guard our car by the guide in a manner of a prince offering a gift. An older boy carrying a bow and arrows was selected to accompany us. The toy arrows seemed good perhaps for birds, but he was replete with enough BO to scare anyone. Two other boys came along as forward and rear guards.

The forest was dense bush and tall trees, the path narrow, the air humid. "This is the forest primeval..." kept repeating itself in my head, remembering the Longworth poem I'd memorized in school.

I was dripping wet by the time we reached a cluster of small leaf huts in a clearing. The tiny chief came forward to shake our hands. He wore torn shorts; most of the men and women only wore cloth tied around their waists with a panel of cloth in front. As ornament, most women wore beads and had cuts and scars circling their necks. One had a piece of wood stuck into her chin. All the "clothes" were the shade of the people – dirty brown-black. "See dance?" asked the guide. I nodded. The men and boys began to move rhythmically in a circle, several tooting one note pipes of different pitches. Their drum was a large piece of bark which they hit with sticks. Really like very young children. They were not at all shy, but happily posed for pictures.

Deep in the rainforest the pigmies dance to one-note reed pipes and drum

The chief asked for 150 francs, then 100, but seemed satisfied with 50. I was annoyed at having to bargain; I could never tell if I was giving too much or too little. Compared to them, we were rich, but we had little money and a long way to go. As we came out, I saw two more cars parked to visit pygmies. Being a sideshow provides a good income now that game is scarcer and it cuts down the stealing that Mrs. Bekker complained about.

All the volunteer guards held out hands. I tried two cigarettes each. One refused so I gave him a franc. He feigned annoyance, but laughed as we pulled away, as they all had laughed when Mil tried jumping rope that some girls were turning. Some way down the road we stopped to change into dry clothes.

On the drive to Beni, I personally felt the whites' need to control when a Belgian pointed a double-barreled shot gun out of his window at me to prevent me from passing his truck.

The planter we talked with over coffee in Beni had no such need. He loved the work and the climate: "eternal spring" he called it, but complained at the expense: he could live in Kampala for three days what he paid for one in the Congo.

After Beni, we took the route southeast toward border at Kasini in order to pass south the Ruwenzori Mountains before circling north on the Uganda side of the range. As we drove, the mountains came out, slowly, from behind their veil of clouds but the mist and humidity enveloped everything and made the road surface yucky. As we were crossing the Semiliki River on a ferry, the boys pulling the barge pointed out a hippo not one hundred feet away and threw stones to urge it to move out the way. Further on we stopped overlooking the river and saw mama hippo and two babies playing on an island. Brilliant birds played among the trees and many antelope grazed on the hills, but we saw no other game. Signs pointed to another tourist hotel at Muwanga and we passed several guests from the Ruindi Camp driving back to Beni.

The hills were growing higher and ground damper. I was driving. A truck ahead backed out of the way so I could pass; only as I saw the black goo up the hill did I realize it was stuck. Shifting down into second, I plow past and get three-quarters up the hill before the car shuddered to a stop. Desperately I switched to first and raced the engine: no movement. Mil was annoyed because I got stuck and that he had to get out to push. The truck people helped, for cigarettes, and eventually I slithered the car to the top of the hill. Mil walked up, caked with mud. I hold the water bag to wash him off, and we continued awhile til I got stuck again, by crossing sides at his suggestion. So I suggested he try driving, and he did for awhile, unsuccessfully. But he didn't want me to push and get dirty so I drove while he, barefooted, pushed us out yet again. So I kept going up the hill to the Customs house, careening through several quite bad mucks.

Free of the bad roads, we thought. Mil rinsed off again. It was two already and we had had no lunch so we ate some bread and cheese. Yet even at that hour we had trouble rousing anyone at the Belgian customs. Finally a tall thin man, unshaved, appeared, obviously hung over, and opened the office. Inside, were a Flemish couple, middle-aged and fat, drinking wine and finishing their meal. The husband stamped the passports; the thin man seemed to be only a visitor. Must be lonely out here for the Belgians, I thought.

This lethargy was quite a contrast with our reception at the Uganda customs post which was just over the hill. The Uganda officer, a native dressed in a clean uniform, greeted us with a smile and stamped our papers with dispatch. What a relief to be back in Uganda where education had produced a competent native who was happy living in this remote area, unlike the disgruntled Belgian officer.

CHAPTER 17

# Alternative views of Uganda's future

OF COURSE WE GOT STUCK ONLY SLIGHTLY UP THE HILL FROM the Uganda customs post. Mil pushed us out, then washed his feet for the third time. But he was no longer grumpy; we were both just glad to be past the border with our substitute carnet. Driving again, I saw a long black hill ahead and was defeated before I began and got only half way up. With the help of four boys to push, the car slithered and slid and did three half turns before talking off on a careening mad drive ahead to harder soil. More cigarettes, and barefoot walking for poor husband...and more spongy soil for miles.

Lake Edwards shone ahead as we were enveloped by swarm after swarm of grasshoppers. In the middle of the road, ugly stork-like birds were devouring the hoppers and only deigned to move when the car was upon them: hundreds of them were strung out across the fields. At a stream, we stopped to let wash Mil off and eat a bit more.

At Katwe, a tiny salt lake was separated from Lake Edward only by the road. Elephant tracks led to the lake over flat sandy-spongy soil. An antelope ran off as we stop to pee. As the road climbed higher, we could see several imposing crater cones now to our west: we had driven a U shaped route around the south end of the Ruwenzori mountain range. A rickety bus is the only other traffic. Mil tried to drive barefooted but the pedals hurt his feet so I continued to drive on toward Fort Portal. The road suddenly got really lousy and I could barely focus I was so exhausted. I had been driving most of the time since we left Beni at eleven and it was nearly seven: less than two hundred miles in eight hours! I simply couldn't go on. So Mil dug out his shoes and drove to the town while I slept.

It was dark and we had trouble finding the hotel: outside the few major cities, most towns only had one hotel. The manager apologized that they were renovating the rooms and had no running water. No matter, we piled into the bathtub and poured the warm water over ourselves. Ah, we felt ever so much better that even the mediocre dinner tasted fine. So tired, we immediately went to bed.

In the morning we spoke to two fellows who had been hunting crocodiles in the Semiliki Valley. Now they were taking the skins to Nairobi, but offered us one they said had skin too bumpy to use. We asked their advice on whether to drive directly to Kampala or try to see Murchinson Falls. "Don't bother," they said: you'd have no hope of getting a boat and the scenery was dull. "Nonsense," insisted the colonel who was a railroad administrator, "Murchinson Falls is well worth seeing and parties who have booked the boats often have room for two more. Helps pay the costs!"

The crocodile hunters were right about the dull scenery and the lack of boats. As we drove to Butiaba, the port on Lake Albert, a town of maybe 5 houses and 150 native huts, the forest cover became less lush; the trees grew half dead over low grasses. Rather weird. Then small escarpment led down to Lake Albert: flat and calm and uninteresting. Termite ant hills, usually red from the clay soil, became brown.

The Commodore appeared at the office with bad news: one boat was being overhauled, the other booked for a departmental trip. He doubted they would have any space, but we could ask at the Masindi Hotel where tours spent the night. The hotel was very reasonable hotel: 37/s for room with dinner and breakfast. The hot bath with running water felt so wonderful I began singing arias. But our foray into the bar seeking a place on the boat was totally useless. The man with the moustache seemed in charge: no, the boat was full and it was an official party. Then, after some winks and nods, he announced pompously that we could come for 125/s each. Outrageous: that was the cost of renting the entire boat.

The Assistant District Commissioner, annoyed at the avarice, said that perhaps we could use the provincial boat if we could find other passengers. So I made the rounds of other guests. A Belgian couple had reservations in two days. They had driven to Juba from his border station, planned to circle through Kampala to the Congo. They ran their car radio for entertainment, sitting outside their bedroom on the verandah.

When I approached Keith, a road surveyor who was born in South Africa, he thought the boat trip was not worth the effort. Indeed, he would like to blast the rocks at the falls and divert the water over a precipice so it would be more spectacular. "You can hardly see it now." He'd been overland to the falls from both sides. Hearing we were from America, he then blasted *Life* and *Time* for their horrible reporting that condemned the system of apartheid. Keith supported separating the races and felt that the British efforts to provide medical care and education only made the natives unruly. Of course he also supported the Belgian approach in the Congo because they were tougher on the natives than the Brits in Uganda. "That's what we should do, that is the solution," he exploded into his beer. How he wished that the British government would just leave the country, "though they'll never do it, being British!" he signed.

An former Indian Army Major, now working in Uganda fisheries, hissed through his teeth as he argued that the Belgian "solution" could work in Uganda if it were settled locally, not by sentimentalists in London. "Must keep the natives in line. I'll slap a boy if he's cheeky. If I have to pay a fine for doing it, I'll pay a fine." He also had America on the mind: "Supporting Neguib in the name of democracy is not sensible," he complained, referring to the recent revolt against King Farouk in Egypt.. "If we go from here, the Americans must come in to fill the vacuum. What America doesn't realize is that Britain must keep her empire. Without it, she is sunk. And not even America could take over all the burden of our colonies."

We ate dinner with a chap who'd driven a truck out from London two years ago and stayed here since. Clearly we were not the only road trip enthusiasts, but most were tourists, not reporters. Listening to the many dissenting voices in the bar, I realized that in Uganda we had been meeting with administrators and with Africans committed to eventual independence. These whites were not settlers, but they resented any change to their privileges. All were determined that I should appreciate the errors the Brits were committing. None was interested in seeing the Falls.

Next morning the ADC joined us for breakfast. He'd already been to his office and learned that the provincial boat wasn't available anyhow: the fisheries headquarters in had booked it indefinitely because their own boat had hit a hippo. "Someone told us the African Queen was still in Butiaba, " I ventured, thinking of the terrific movie starring Humphrey Bogart and Kathryn Hepburn, and envisioning a feature story aboard it. "Well," mussed the ADC. " it is really not sea-worthy, but I'll phone and ask if you can go on it." He tried, but the line to Butiaba was down.

The ADC was swell, he apologized for not being able to help. If his wife weren't in Jinja having a baby and he weren't living in a hotel, why they would've worked out something for our "mutual edification." As we drove toward Kampala, I thought how lonely the ADC must be without his wife and surrounded by all these whites who hated the official policies!

Halfway to Kampala, the rain came down in sheets, the road was a river. The rainy season had arrived early for the lake region, according to the table in the Road Book which showed annual rainfall in different parts of East Africa. Early! Rains weren't due in the Tana River region for another month, but what if those were early too? If we didn't get across the sands to Somaliland before they came, we had been warned we might not make it.

My gloom continued in Kampala where we booked into the more expensive hotel which had a guarded parking area. The car badly needed a general check-up, but it was Sunday. Most Indian businesses are open, but not those run by Europeans. The Economic Service Station was open from 8:00 am to 12:30 pm, then 2:00 to 4:00 pm. So Monday we left the car for the day, complaining particularly about the steering pulling to the left. But when we picked it up at four to use for the evening, Nick told us the springs were half gone, with the coils resembling bed springs, and one of the leaves was bent backwards! Another day to wait.

I had phoned V.M. Clerk, MBE, owner of Narendas Rajaram & Co Ltd. which exports long staple cotton to India and England, to request an interview. It was Sunday so I did not push to see him that afternoon because Mil wanted to go swimming and I was under the weather.

When I met Mr. Clerk the next morning, a Hindu despite his name, I interviewed him poorly, especially after he told me about the African dance he arranged at his factory on the evening before. His guests, whom we could have joined, were the ubiquitous John Gunther collecting more information for his *Inside Africa* book. Another well-known writer, Santha Rama Rau, was also in Kampala at the time and would have been at the dance. I had met Santha in India when she was talking about her book, *Home to India*, at the Gymkhana Club. Her book was published just after she graduated from Wellesley in 1945, at 22! Since then she had written travel articles for the *New Yorker* and *Harpers*, just as I hoped to do. I admired her but was also envious of her accomplishments.

Missing the dance added to my gloom, but worse was my inability to write up my impressions of the Congo and sort out the contradictory colonial policies of Belgian and Britain. I couldn't think. I felt a failure. Driving through Africa, writing travel stories with a political slant, was supposed to be my chance to prove myself. Yet I lost my clippings, my manuscript, even my New York agent's address. I chastised myself for being lazy, for spending much of Sunday reading a trashy novel. We missed Murchinson Falls, lost things, missed dances, and now – I couldn't write. I hated myself. Irrationally, I also hated Santha Rama Rau. Because she is here, because she had published, though perhaps not analyzing issues as deeply as I could do. If I would only start to write. That caused this inability to write? Was I scared. of being wrong, of being rejected? How silly. Why couldn't I work? Why?

Determined to do something, I walked to a typical Indian shop and interviewed the owner, Shankar Das. He specialized in selling records and records native music for His Majesty's Voice in London. "Natives like to buy these records," he said, "but also jazz. English buy both classical and jazz recordings while Indians only buy their own songs." In addition, natives buy clothes, sheets, bikes, and gramophones from him.

The humidity and heat were pressing, so I broke custom and asked him for a drink, feeling both very embarrassed and very professional. Most friendly, he waved me to a seat, and tea. He had moved to Kampala from Mombasa where he was a nominated member of the municipal council. Seeking a seat here would be a waste, he says. "One must please those who are in power. We Indians know who will eventually take over the country but now it is difficult to act at all. Everyone is suspicious of others."

Shankar Das felt that Kampala was more tolerant than Nairobi or Mombasa. He didn't think the British would let settlers run things "because it is all that is left for them to boss," he smiled. "Also it is better for both the Africans and Indians to have the British stay for some time. I am an East African, and I hope to make my future here."

Next morning we checked out of the hotel, packed up, and took the car to the garage once again. Hoping to leave as soon as possible, we hung around their office while Nick gave us a new set of springs, replaced the coils, and tried to fix the steering again. Nick thought we should change the shock absorbers from the Armstrong ones that came with the car to the stronger Girling ones. But both of us were tired of delays and thought that perhaps we could ask the Girling agents in Nairobi to supply them cheaply in return for an affidavit. So we left Kampala midday.

It poured. The road beyond Jinja seemed worse than before. Mil swore that we were hitting bottom at each corrugation, of which there were 1000 per inch, it seemed. Now he became gloomy and foreboding. "It's too bad we have a left hand drive, less resale value in Kenya," he muttered.

"Who's thinking of selling it" I flash. "We'll go if we have to tie it together." "Poor husband," I thought. "He looks so unhappy driving. I feel horrid too, when the can shakes and bumps over the ruts. His hair is long and curly, he looks so tired."

We decide to stop for the night at the Busia Border Inn so we could tackle the escarpment in daylight. The morning was clear as we set out for the long drive to Nairobi: afternoon rains did not extend beyond the lake region this time of year. As before, the roads were lined with smiling natives going to or from the market. And once again, the mood of the land changed as we drove into the Rift Valley: the few Africans who were walking ignored us. We munched cheese and fruit as we drove, and did not stop anywhere for photos or a drink.

By the time we neared Nairobi, it was after dark. The moon, though only in its early quarter, shown clear light on the road, and on the police checkpoints. The police were tired, and perfunctory, hardly looking into the car once a white face peered into their flashlight beam. We knew our way to the Queen's Hotel, and turned in without a second thought about the becalmed capital.

We made final preparations for the drive to Moghadishu. Mil took the car in for more checking while I counted food and supplies. Tension in the city was more apparent. The atrocities committed by the Mau Mau during the

Lari massacre had divided the Kikuyu. The sympathy that Kenyatta had garnered with his calls for nationalism was tainted by that barbarism though his role, since he was in prison, was unclear. The Indian lawyers insisted to us that those taking part in the killings were rogue criminals. The white settlers clamored even more for white self-rule.

A reporter's role is to observe, to try to understand, and to record. I could do no more. The city was depressing. No more talk of selling the car from Mil. It was time to leave.

We packed up the car, vowing for an early departure. Which we didn't do. Farewells and good wishes, were offered by our fellow hotel guests as we finally drove off toward Thika and, we hoped, London.

# Part II

---

## Crossing the Horn of Africa

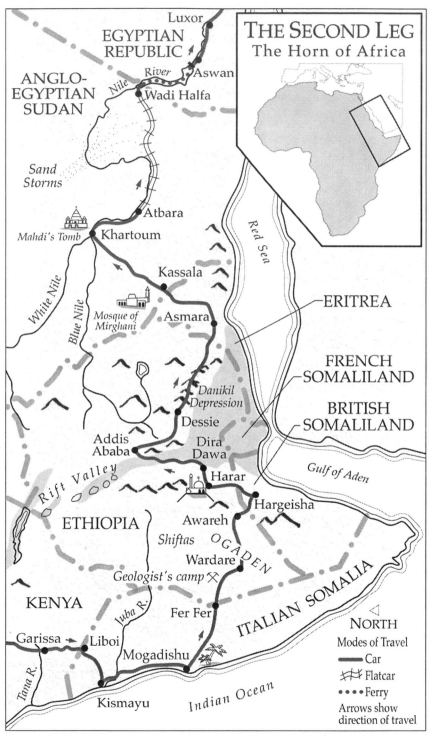

Map Second Leg

CHAPTER 18

# To London by going east

W E LEFT NAIROBI IN A CLEAR MORNING – I'D LIKE TO SAY
early, but Mil and I aren't good at early starts. There
was so much to pack and stow into our little car – on the
roof, in the trunk, in the back seat, under the front seats.
At Thika we stopped for gas, and food. This town – a main
street of six or eight stores, and the *boma* or government compound – is on the edge of the Highlands, on the edge of
civilization. From there to the Indian Ocean is bush – wild,
dangerous, primeval bush with only a gravel road to prove to
animal and native that the white man has arrived.

Thika is famous for its pineapples, and its trout fishing
when there is no Emergency on. With Mau Mau terrorist
gangs roaming the hills no fool would go into the jungle alone.
No one would dream of spending the night in the bush!

We certainly had no intention of doing so.

I stowed the pineapple and we pushed on. It was 226 miles, the map said, from Nairobi to Garissa, the next town, but it was also 5000 feet down. That meant lots of curves and turns on an unpaved road. Still we were sure we could get to Garissa by the evening. We had to. You don't camp out in Mau Mau land, and you don't sleep out in the elephant bush. An elephant can squash a little English car in no time. But you don't drive at night through the bush, either, the insurance man warned us. Animals will charge your lights. Of course your insurance covers damages...

Mil had bought a paper in Thika, and after we'd eaten some sandwiches I began to read it to him as he drove. "Mau Mau gang believed heading for Thika", the banner headlines warned. "Gang last reported circling east of Thika along the ridges of the Highlands." Mil stopped the car, and read through the article, frowning. "Shall we go back to Thika?" he queried. "There's a hotel there."

We sat overlooking the pineapple plantations and debated what to do, each of us giving the pros and cons, not really trying to convince the other. By then we'd realized we wouldn't get to Garissa til midnight, if we were lucky and no elephant challenged our way. Worse, the map showed Garissa on the far side of the Tana River...and you had to cross the river by "ferry," one of those rafts with African crews pull you by cable, I assumed. So even if we got that far we'd have to wait for dawn, and a crew, to cross into Garissa.

Yet if we went back to Thika we'd arrive at dusk, hardly the best time to meet up with the hunted Mau Mau if they were around the town. And the little hotel was probably full. Mostly, though, we hated the idea of turning back, once we started. Even for a day.

But really, it was the Rains that decided our course.

Beyond Garissa the trail to Somaliland is a bog half the year. A hint of moisture and your car is glued into sticky mud. Already the monsoon clouds hung low on the horizon. A day might make all the difference. We had to beat the Rains. We would drive on, we finally decided, beyond all the villages, then camp before we reached the elephant lowlands, off the road where no one could see us.

We drove on past the last of the sisal plantations; where that hardy hemp-producing cactus won't grow the soil must be poor, indeed! When the tin mailboxes petered out we knew we'd left the European area behind. The plateau of Kenya's White Highlands began to crumble toward the arid bush leaving phallic symbols here and there, testimony to the primordial land we were entering. The road twisted down, losing altitude steadily. The map showed crossroads, impressively titled **Mile 81**. A feeble path wandered in. A few natives, the women strung with beadwork. In Nairobi I'd bought some beadwork sewn on leather to circle the arm, like these women wore. It had been made, the clerk said, by the Wakamba tribe. As I waved through the open window they caught sight of the red and white design, and giggled. I could imagine them gossiping later:

"And that white woman, in the little green car with the stuff high on the roof, she is one of us; she wore our beads."

Then, for miles, nothing.

Literally. There was not even a way to get off the road, no possible place to camp. Finally, a few trees. I guess we should have known that where there is a drop of water, there too, would be natives. But we didn't think. It was getting dark and we had to arrange the car so we could sleep inside. We found a hard patch of gravel leading up and away from the road, hidden from the road by a pinnacle of granite. The night deepened quickly as we removed the front seats and balanced them on the roof.

With the primus stove going full blast, you don't hear much. I was stirring up a hash from a tin can, and Mil was arranging the car for sleeping. I thought I heard him call, and turned directly into a nodding African.

"Jambo, rafiki" I squeaked, swallowing my tonsils – and hoping he was a rafiki, a friend.

"Jambo, memsahib" he returned, smiling widely.

Our retreat had been discovered! But the man seemed friendly enough. Mil produced a cigarette, but the noise of the primus prohibited any conversation. As quickly as he had come he melted back into the shadows...only to appear for coffee, accompanied by the elders of the village near which we must have stopped.

The car bed was surprisingly comfortable and I fell asleep quickly, despite the coffee. Suddenly, I awoke in a sweat, my senses triggered like the shutter of a camera. In an instant I could see all, hear all, fear all. For in the distance, unmistakably, drums!

The air in the car was suffocating; the windows were rolled down only a crack... too small for a hand to get through, with or without a panga. I'd been dreaming about pangas, and the dread Mau Mau that wield those deadly knives. Instinctively I glanced up toward the window, and caught my breath...for something fluttered. I blinked my myopic eyes and stared. Only the mosquito netting, caught in the door to hang over the opening. After all, there were tse-tse flies in this part of Kenya. And Mau Mau too.

Drums! Sounding heavy across the bush.

My nerves were so taut I thought I'd explode. With effort I reached across under the sheet and touched my husband.

My clammy hand woke him, and I felt him stiffen too, as he heard the sound.

"You hear it too?" I whispered.

Mil was silent for a moment, listening. Then in a sleepy voice which shattered the tension, he said, "It's probably a wedding celebration. Go to sleep. We've got a long day's driving tomorrow." He squeezed my hand and rolled over, but I knew he was listening, too.

Still I wasn't paralyzed any more, though I wasn't exactly soothed. So I sat and reached in my shoe for my glasses; I always feel better when I can see. Not that there was much to see. A tangle of thorn bushes surrounded the car except where the rutted path ran back to a gravel road, the main "highway" from Nairobi to Garissa. And back to the village. Were the friendly Wakamba the ones now beating on the tom-toms? Or was it the Mau Mau gang? I must have sat, wondering, for hours. The drums got louder as the moon rose. It felt like a spot light; our car was the stage. A wind came up, rustling the bushes, making them move and dance to the noise. My mind manufactured nightmares and played them out before my horrified eyes.

"Mil, we've got to move", I hissed, feverishly tearing my clothes off the steering wheel and shoving my key into the ignition.

Mil sat up, abruptly, banging his head on the roof.

"Can't reach the pedals to drive", he observed much too sensibly. "Can't see, either."

Now that I could see past the steering wheel I remembered the car seats were piled on the hood of the car.

"At least we could roll back on the road, if anybody comes," I said, defending myself, but feeling rather silly. The wind had cooled the car; Mil's kiss calmed me. And we slept.

THE DAWN CAME UP quietly, grinning wryly at my fright. I felt initiated, and happily alive. Before I could finish dressing, in fact before I could even find my shoes so utterly did I tangle everything in the night, there was our African neighbor. He was also grinning, but happily, pleasantly. I felt small and foolish for my fears, and greeted him delightedly.

"Me Catholic teacher," he explained, indicating a battered sign down the road away. In the daylight we could see how poorly we were hidden, for the gravel road curved around below us. Our kerosene lamp must have been visible to everyone walking along the road. No wonder the teacher had found us. I walked to the sign and read "Catholic Primary School."

"School, where?" I asked.

"Me." He replied emphatically.

"You, boys, sit and read where?" I asked again, dramatizing like charades.

The teacher nodded, and beckoned me across the road and up a small path. Behind the thorn thicket was a trim round hut with a layered conical roof; beyond in the bush I could see the tops of other huts. His house, not his school, I thought, wishing I had more talent at acting. But then, perhaps his school met here, in the shade of the thorn trees.

On the packed earth before the hut a little boy was squatting, staring at me from round black eyes. A young girl, the teacher's daughter I assumed, looked up only briefly and with a shy smile went on with her work. She had half a large dried gourd in each hand. A gunny sack of grain sat by her feet. She would scoop some into one calabash, toss it into the other, blowing gently so that the husks floated away. She had her working clothes on; a faded print calico tied about her waist, a man's tee shirt, a bandana on her hair.

An older woman, who guarded the colorful striped reed

basket which held the sifted grain, wore even less. A faded loin cloth, a few beads and a bracelet. Her punched ears held no ornament. Unlike the peasants of India who wear their jewelry constantly as a walking bank account, these women seemed to have only colorful inexpensive ornaments which they put on for market or festivals.

When I returned after breakfast to say good bye, several neighbors of the school teacher were gossiping with the women; they were resplendent in striped sarongs and had beads in their ears. I couldn't resist pulling out my camera. They were happy to pose for me – a mere woman; but their men folk ran down the path thinking, perhaps, I was the evil eye. We women laughed at the men's timidity, and exchanged some feminine shrugs. They giggled some more over the sweets I offered them, hard candies, wrapped in cellophane. The eager youngster had grabbed a sweet and stuffed it, paper and all, into his mouth. I demonstrated how to take off the paper and suck the candy, though I didn't really want to eat it after the lush breakfast we'd had of grapefruit juice, scrambled eggs, toast, and instant coffee.

Chattering happily and sucking the candy loudly, the women walked off down the road. We waved as we drove past them a few minutes later, bouncing along on the corrugated road. One brave girl rode with us for a mile or two until we came to a large clump of trees. A dilapidated old bus sat on the grassy shoulder as if it had stopped there once, and just couldn't go on. Milling around it or sitting under the trees was a score of Africans. Our passenger gave a whoop, and in moments we were surrounded by the happy crowd who fingered the car inside and out, found the candies and devoured them. With pantomime we learned that there was indeed one-boy-and-one-girl coming-together, a wedding, and that the drums had been part of the celebration.

The sun was bright in the sky and, as we talked with the Africans, the heat also began to rise. Even under my wide straw hat I could feel the sun burn. The photographs we took of the group are so black and so white that people are mounds in a glistening sea. Much less chipper, we drove on.

We kept the windows wide open despite the red dust that drifted into the car in clouds. Mil's white tennis cap, which he kept on in the car to cut the glare, tanned brown, then red, matching the color of my arm which I mistakenly stuck out the window. I tried to write in my notebook, but the grogginess of the day and the bumpiness of the road made this impossible. Then I drove awhile, slower and slower as the holes in the road got bigger and bigger. We must have been down to fifteen miles an hour when, with a flapping and a hissing, a huge ostrich lumbered onto the road. For a moment he gawked straight at us, then whirled and took off down the road. It was such a funny sight, this big footed bird running down the road, his baby sized wings beating up and down. We clocked him up to thirty-five miles an hour before he angled off the road and into the bush.

Feeling much better, we stopped for a refresher. First, Mil untied a jerry can on the roof and, while I held the funnel, poured gasoline into the car. Then it was our turn. Into the rest of the grapefruit juice I dumped glucose until the liquid became crystalline, like molten sugar drops. Too sweet, and unpleasantly hot, this beverage was lightning energy. The challenge ahead of us beckoned invitingly. So what if most people said we couldn't get through, just the two of us in our little car? Where were our servants, where our guards, they all asked. Or where was our jeep with four-wheeled drive? Or where was our rifle and revolver to use against wild animals, or wild tribes? We were headed across the desolate Somali desert, aiming for the remote mountain kingdom of the Ethiopia. We were determined to drive into Addis Ababa and to have enough car left to carry us back down from the mountains to the deserts of the Sudan. From there we would follow a more usual route, tracing the Nile to its delta before crossing the width of the continent along the Mediterranean coast.

That was our plan.

I was daydreaming, automatically dodging the worst bumps, but not really driving. There were no cars to miss, nothing to look at beyond the monotonous bush. All the bush animals and birds were taking a siesta, and I also was, half way.

A rude tug on the steering,....thud! A flat, already! The steaming sun bored down as we got out to change the tire. The spare was on the bottom of the boot. On top of it sat a tin trunk full of canned food, tins of crackers, the medical kit, toilet paper, Kleenex. Odd shaped cans were tucked in every crevice, under the struts, around the spokes. The tools, the cooking utensils and the primus all had their place. And all had to come out onto the road.

It was a monstrous pile by the time we got down to the tire. The tin truck was so heavy we had to empty half of it before we could lift it onto the open dropped door of the boot and pry out the tire. The sun beat down mercilessly, turning every can into a hot potato. Even to touch the blown tire Mil had to put on gloves. I stood over him trying to give him some shade, fanning and dripping and feeling miserable. Then all the cans and tolls had to be fitted back into the boot. It seemed to take hours. Curious giraffe watched us.

We washed off with water from the canvas bags that hung on the side of the car. The water was lusciously cool, probably a mere 70 degrees! Yet neither this nor the glucose-

These Reticulated Giraffe
are indigenous to the
Kenya/Somali bush

grapefruit revived us. We were limp, exhausted, discouraged. If a tire could do THIS....

Driving along again, bumping, creaks and groans coming from the poorly packed boot, clump-clump coming from the top-heavy roof rack, the miles seemed endless. The heat waves produced mirages: puddles on the track, oceans of the bush. The car movement was not unlike a boat. I sat, mesmerized, outside myself. What were we doing here? What crazy notion impelled us, Mil and me to drive through Africa?

I floated along, dulled by the heat. The bush became the Indian Ocean. Once more I was on board the boat, full of enthusiasm, not knowing the dangers, the fear, the heat. Could that have been less than three months ago?

"Look! The river!" Mil shouted, startling me out of the heat-induced stupor. "We must be near Garissa."

Groggily I looked out over the sandy plain with its spiky thorn trees. The only new thing I noticed were the piles of discarded tin cans, sardine-size all the way to kerosene tins, leftovers from some wartime army encampment left rusting and useless. Then ahead I saw a wall of green, a thick tangled jungle, abruptly rising to over fifty feet, in stark contrast to the low, dusty wasteland. The shade of the forest was almost gloomy after the glaring midday sun, but beyond we could see a shallow muddy stream, the miraculous source of all this lushness, the Tana River. We searched the banks for a sign of the ferry, and found none. Instead, the road turned downstream slightly where, to our amazement, a Bailey bridge appeared, undoubtedly put up by the troops during the war.

How could it be that in ten years no one had bothered to tell the Automobile Association office in Nairobi that there was a bridge across the Tana? But what did it matter? This bit of information about the non-existent ferry was the last information of any sort we had about the roads beyond Garissa until we got to Egypt. At that thought, the audacity of our venture struck me full force, as if, up until then, I had not really believed it was going to happen. The challenge of the trip, the exhilaration, the fearful anticipation, all welled up in me at once, as though I were caught on the top of a giant roller coaster, suspended for a moment before the plunge began.

I looked over at Mil, the stiffness of his deep sunburn giving him a stern expression of concentration as he drove. In a flash of understanding, I realized that the trip meant something different to Mil than to me. To him it was a challenge of the car, a sort of super steeplechase, and because he was not a trained mechanic, though he knew a great deal about the inside of a car, he was forever worrying over Bublee. To me the trip was a challenge to become a crack reporter, an exercise in international understanding, a curiosity's urging to see things for myself, and a rude bit of pride which wanted always to say "I told you so" to all those skeptics who kept saying, "You can't, you're a woman."

So here we were, at the edge of the adventure. Garissa itself looked very much like the edge of civilization. The road forked beyond the bridge and we followed a wide beaten earth road down the main street. A collection of adobe houses, perhaps twenty of them, was strung along one side with two larger whitewashed adobe buildings facing them. Before one, the only general store on the road, grew a carefully tended flowering bush. The other building was made colorful by decorations painted on the walls: a green leafy branch, a red and blue copy of the British flag, even a blue and yellow airplane. Above the designs was printed "Special Hotel" and "IbrahimYusuf." As we drove slowly by, Ibrahim Yusuf himself came out proudly, thinking that perhaps he had customers for the night. We merely asked him where the office of the District Commissioner was, and, crestfallen, he pointed over toward the river.

The DC had already gone home to lunch, a messenger told us, but that his house was just there. With an expansive gesture he included all four of the two story adobe houses clustering at the edge of the green jungle near the river. On top of each house was a cage built of wire screening. We were later told that the heavy growth by the river cuts down any little breeze there is, so that the only tolerable place for the Englishmen to sleep was on the roof.

Our plan, not really thought out, was to get the DC to stamp our passports, find someone to repair the tire, and then push on, driving all night. We were only the second day out of Nairobi, and already we were a day behind plan. Being in a rush, we were not disposed to wait an hour or so until the DC returned to his office. Rather we drove over to the nearest house and asked for him. The servant showed me right into the house where the family was eating: Mr. Browning, his wife, three children and a governess. Hastily apologizing for intruding, I said we'd come back after we had eaten, and started retreating, although slowly, for I dreaded going back into the heat from the cool interior.

"But where will you eat?" asked Mrs. Browning, sensibly. I said we had tins for food. "But where?" she repeated. "It must be hot in your car. Why don't you bring your things in here and eat?" She turned to the tall Somali servant, "Ahmed, bring beer."

I didn't protest. I just went out for Mil and the food. A wash and a beer, and we both felt alert once more. Both Brownings came and talked to us as we finished off crackers and cheese. I tried to offer them our Thika pineapple but they wouldn't take it; indeed Mrs. Browning gave us six oranges as we left on our way back to the office with the DC. "Of course we can speed you through," said Mr. Browning. "I'll put my driver to work on your tire right now. But I really suggest you wait and go off in the early morning. If it doesn't rain, you won't have trouble getting through unless you miss the track. And if it rains, well, you'll be stuck for several days and nights. Might as well get rest while you can. No, I wouldn't suggest your going out so late in the afternoon. You'd only have to camp in the bush. We can't offer you anything much better; the new guest house is only half finished. Our English governess is using the old one. But at least it has walls which will protect you from the tigers."

I gave a double-take to Mil over that, and started to explain that we slept in the car, not outside. But I was interrupted by a red-haired man who strode into the office, his sports shirt and checked cap a distinct contrast to the neat white shirt and trousers of the DC.

"Don't let him ruffle you," he grinned at us, "I'm the Game Warden and I ought to know. I always sleep out. Tigers don't bother you unless you have something they want, like water. The DC sent me a note to come meet you. He said you are going to Somaliland, and in that little thing outside. My, my. Have you lots of provisions? During the war the convoys used to get stuck for months – well, for weeks anyhow. Course they tried to run them all through the rain. I was out away this morning, and ran into some puddles. Nothing stops my Power Wagon though. Last week I got into a bog, but the front of this Wagon has a winch so we drove some stakes and attached the pulley, and the Wagon pulled itself out as nice as you can believe."

He said all of this with a serious expression on his freckled face. Then his whole face relaxed. "By the way," he added, "when you get to Kismayu, give my regards to Reverend Cheese." I burst out laughing, despite his dire words. "We've already met the Reverend Cheese, in Lamu," I told him, "but we will get to Kismayu all right."

Poised as we were for the venture, there was no thought of giving up. Like a beginner at skiing who, in a reckless moment, goes up to the ski lift, and would rather break a leg than ignominiously ride down the chair-lift again – we were committed. The tension of the night before had only heightened my perception, made each success a victory and each difficulty a defeat. At that moment I was on the crest of enthusiasm, bubbly and very young.

My mood was catching, and Game Warden Cooper suggested we go hunt crocodiles since of course we weren't leaving til morning. It seemed exactly like the sort of crazy thing we ought to do. So off we went in his pet Power Wagon, following the river northeast, Cooper explaining over the roar of the engine, "This is all part of my job. Those crocs are vermin, useless. We're trying to exterminate them. They are always eating the natives or their cattle."

At a particular dense section of jungle, Cooper stopped the car and led us on foot single file through the quiet greenness, two armed guards bringing up the rear. The still air hung with the smell of elephants. In the merest of whispers

Cooper indicated that here the elephants sharpen their tusks and there they roll in mud before they come to drink. Of course, the elephants only come early on the morning and again at dusk; in between, their bathing spot is a favorite sunning place for the crocodiles.

Despite his assurances, I kept seeing elephants in every shadow, but flashing yellow birds and fleet waterbuck were all there really was. Finally we came to the river. On the opposite shore were two long reptiles, languorously sunbathing. We circled back into the musty jungle to come out again directly opposite them, but somehow they heard our movement and had disappeared into the muddy water. Upstream a herd of cattle was being watered – no crocodile there. Disappointed, we made our way back through the jungle, tramping to the chorus of laughing baboons.

Cooper kept going through the town, crossed the river and went downstream this time. It was nearly dusk now, and the chances of shooting any crocodiles were small. Still, we were his guests and he wanted to amuse us. Off hand, he explained that there weren't too many crocs left near the town, since he had been hunting them for almost a year. Those yet alive were extremely wary of humans. Almost to illustrate his point he indicated a group of crocodiles far ahead on the opposite shore, three or four green brown adults and one light tan baby. One guard was walking ahead of us, and in that instant the crocodiles heard his step. Flop, and all of the reptiles had slid effortlessly into the muddy water, hardly making a ripple.

We walked on along the shore, but there were no more crocodiles to be seen. Back in the shadows of the jungle we noticed a village whose huts were crude and round in contrast to the square adobe huts of the Garissa Somalis. "Riverine tribes," explained Cooper, "of uncertain origin.

Probably started from leftover slaves. In any case they have been enslaved by the Somalis of Garissa. They are pagans, not Muslims like the Somalis, and are forced to do all the hard or dirty work."

While he was talking to us we saw the young tan crocodile slither back onto the opposite bank. Cooper gave us a warning glance, and then circled back, noiselessly. Suddenly a shot rang out, 300 feet across the river, but Cooper got the reptile where he had aimed with telescopic sight, in the mouth. Instantly one of the guards waded across the river to retrieve the body, apparently without a thought to all the full-sized crocodiles that must be lurking in the mud. The other guard went back to the village to get a pagan "slave" to skin the body. Cooper poked at the reptile with his boot. "His belly is nice and smooth, make a pretty pair of shoes. No time to cure it, but I'll have the boys salt it for you and send it round later tonight." I smiled at the thought of another crocodile skin to add to those two useless dried ones we still carried; but this one has stayed soft and pliable. It is still around the house somewhere; perhaps I should get some shoes made of it.

Only one brick room of the guest house was completed. As yet there was no bath, no toilet. The bungalow and a nearby swimming pool were being constructed by the prisoners. Forced help is always slow. It was nearly dark, so we took soap over to the pool and scooped up water to shower ourselves and our underwear. It wasn't the cleanest bath. Inside the room was one camp cot. We had just decided that I would sleep in the car when Cooper appeared with another cot, two mattresses, and two camp chairs – all his regular equipment. "When we go on safari, we do it in comfort," he teased. "Only novices like you rough it. Have a washstand too, and a canvas tub, if you want to borrow them."

At that point Mil offered him one of our mugs he had just filled with Scotch. He sipped. "Well, at least you are civilized enough to have whiskey. Here's to your trip. You know, this is how I stay young. Used to be in a Gurkha regiment until the war. They thought I should retire. Instead I came out here with the Locust Control. You know, that United Nations group which is trying to control locusts and map their migrations. Had to do a lot of running around with that group. That's why I like this job better, I can write my own ticket as far as my safaris go. Wouldn't think I was forty-five, would you?" He looked pleased at my protests. "Now don't you frighten my giraffe, will you? If they get scared their throat muscles won't work and they die of starvation." He continued in this vein, giving us footnotes on animal lore that sounded like Ripley's "Believe It or Not." So fascinating were his tales that we were nearly late for dinner with the Brownings.

It was a very pleasant evening, quite unlike our dinners with the other DC in Meru. Warily, I avoided politics, and we talked mainly about problems of administration of the district with the DC, of the household with his wife. Mrs. Browning recounted the problem with their piano. "It lasted well enough up near Thika where we were stationed before. But in the damp heat of Garissa has stretched the wires out of tune, and now even the boards were warping. My husband refuses to allow the children to practice on it while he was home, but I think that the sound of the children's scales was always pretty bad, even when the piano had been in tune," she laughed. We retired early, they to their screened cage on the roof and we to the brick room, leaving behind the pineapple this time. The weird noises in the bush, shuffling and padding, did not keep us awake long. At the first light we were up, and discovered tiger tracks chasing waterbuck not 100 feet from where we had slept.

Faced suddenly with the plunge into the wilderness, we hesitated, almost unconsciously. Mil checked and rechecked the car, found a leak in the spare oil tin which means searching for a new one, changed the oil. I repacked the whole back seat and got out food tins for three or four days. We drove as far as the Browning's to fill up the water bags, then on to the main street to top up the petrol tank from an oil drum in front of an adobe store. Mr. Yusuf was standing near his hotel. A photograph seemed called for – which took more time. Our early morning start was no longer so early. When we could think of no other reasons for the tantalizing stalling, we got in and wished ourselves mutual good luck, and drove off.

CHAPTER 19

# Kismayu carousel

THE ROAD WAS TOLERABLY SMOOTH; THE PUFFY CLOUDS AHEAD looked white and harmless. The excitement retreated before monotony and we settled into the usual pattern of hourly shifts in driving. Mil had the first stint, and for a time the road was smooth enough for me to scribble in my diary. We came to an unmarked fork and turned to the left. Perhaps a mile beyond, we came to a sign painted on old kerosene tin: Go Right. There were no tire marks beyond nor was there space to turn around, for the sand was loose and treacherous off the packed track, so Mil carefully backed up to the fork and we went right.

This little incident destroyed some of our nonchalance. Suppose we did take the wrong way? As we came to a stretch of hard baked earth the proper direction became harder and

Entering Italian Somaliland at Liboi

harder to know, for there was no track at all. Only openings in the bushes suggested the usual route. It was with relief that we got back to a rougher section where the mud had caught the impression of tires in the depression where water must have stood whenever there were rains. Sometimes we could maneuver around the ruts, but mostly we had to pick our way through them, riding the ridges.

In the sparse bush, buck and rabbits ran for cover from our sound, birds perched in the naked thorns like blossoms, and once we saw two small camels lope away. Then the bush thickened, and the road became more rutted. The map shows this area as swamp. Dik dik scampered away at our approach while under the larger acacia flocks of francolin clustered, their blue feathers a brilliant contrast to the dreary brown-green of the bush. Tall inquisitive giraffes, solemnly munching mimosa leaves, peered down at us. Their skin was covered with a golden brown scale pattern etched on ivory, a rare coloring found only in this remote corner of the globe.

Beyond the swamp the road improved again. We began to wonder about all the warnings. Clearly the difficulties came from the rain, not the road – the danger is in getting stuck. So far the day was dry and sunny. Still we did not dare to stop for lunch but ate cheese and crackers as we drove. Across the flat we made good time; already we were at the border, called Liboi on the map. This place consisted of one oil drum painted with two words, "Liboi" and "water", and a bent yellow iron post looking more like a parking-meter than a border stake. In a whimsical mood I posed by the border sign in my jeans and loafers, a sort of twentieth century adventurer.

As we drove on into Somalia the vegetation became slightly thicker, much of it a prickly bush which seemed to have no greenery. In one rutted stretch parts of trucks and various old tin cans indicated a spot of enforced encampment during a rain. Accidentally, we hit the bottom of one rut, and it splashed. We stared around. The road surface itself was dry, but the burned grass earth had sprouted a green fuzz, like the hair on a boy's face just before he starts shaving. Walking along the road we saw two tall naked Somalis, balancing bundles on their heads. As we approached one man reached for his bundle and in moments he was wearing a sarong to cover himself. As I looked back I could see him carefully folding it again.

The ground cover was becoming obviously greener, confirming rain within the last few days. The road had already dried on top, but water was visible in the pools and ruts. At one very large puddle we had to slow down and honk: finally I had to get out and throw a clot of mud at them before several horrid looking warthogs would take themselves out of their mud bath. During this by-play, three men appeared from the bush, all modestly draped in muslin, each carrying a stake in one hand and crude leather sandals in the other. The nattiest of the three, whose toga-draped cloth was almost white, wore a French beret over close cropped hair; the other two had fuzzy hairdos that looked like poorly given permanents. They stared curiously at me while I did the same to them; out came a smile when I pointed my camera, an indulgent smile as though I were the childish primitive and they the age-old wise men. But there was also an avaricious gleam in the expression of the man with the beret, and I was glad we could get in the car and leave.

Off to the side, deep in the bush, a lengthy caravan of nomads was moving into the fresh grasslands which would appear with the rains. Just so the rains don't come today, I thought for the hundredth time. So far so good. Already the border station for Somalia was just ahead. Beside the police lines, a row of adobe huts gathered behind a low barbed-wire fence, there were a few beehive-like nomadic tents pitched by the road. On either end of the striped road barrier were small adobe offices.

To save time I took the passports into one while Mil checked in with customs. I entered an almost bare little room, and in the gloom nearly ran into the Somali official who had risen to great me. "Good night," he nodded, in pleasant disregard of the sun, "prego sit." "Good night," I echoed, and sat. In moments he had leafed through the passports, studied them, and stamped them. "Kismayu?" he asked. "To Kismayu, and Mogadishu, and to Addis Ababa," I replied. But the other towns meant nothing – Kismayu seemed the limits of his world. Without another word he picked up the passports and went out with them. Mystified, I watched as he walked over to where Mil was talking with the customs man and gave him the passports. Of course, I reminded myself, this is a Muslim country and women mean nothing at all.

Feeling snubbed, I went back to the car and poured myself a drink from the thermos, wrote down the mileage, swept out the cracker crumbs from the front seat. Still the three men were talking and gesturing under the acacia. When my impatience got the better of judgment, I joined the men. The carnet details for the car had been entered in a log which showed that only three vehicles had crossed the border that year! But the customs man said we had to pay one shilling in fee. Mil was suspicious because the man asked for a shilling; we had been told that the currency in Somalia was a surcharged lira. But the customs man had pulled a shilling from his pocket and kept insisting that everybody used that kind of money.

Perhaps, we thought, this border post still used shillings because it was closer to Garissa than Kismayu. But even if his demand were legitimate, what could we do? As budgeter, I had carefully allotted our shillings so that none would be left-over once we departed from East Africa. In fact I had been congratulating myself that we had a mere four cents left. The only tack I could think of was to impress upon him our diplomatic status and to declare that we never had to pay fees. But before I could interrupt the argument the man had switched his request to cigarettes; a pack of Mil's cigarettes more than pacified him.

Just as we were walking back to the car it began to rain. Somehow the white clouds had turned gray when we weren't looking. We rushed for the car and hardly got the windows rolled up before the downpour began. For a moment we sat staring at each other, unbelieving. Then without a word Mil started the car and we inched forward. Luckily Mil hadn't pulled off the road, so he had only to hold on a straight course across the suddenly treacherous surface. The road was of the same cotton soil in which we got stuck in the Congo, but here it was less packed, so the first drops of rain turned it into a slick soupy bog. For a time we were able to continue

251

steadily, driving in third, because the tires still bit into dry soil beneath; but soon we began to skid and slither. As abruptly as it had begun, the rain stopped, the clouds were puffy once more, and the hot sun beat down on the wet road.

Just as I was about to say something about good luck, we hit an even wetter patch, careened wildly, and skidded sideways in the track. Mil got out to push as I gunned the motor; there was a sudden lifting and before I could turn the wheel, we ended up in a sort of ditch off the road.

A caravan of nomads trudged up the road, camel bells clanging, men and their beasts loping through the gooey mud. Behind them came a herd of cattle, skinny looking animals with long horns. We waited, fascinated, until the procession passed. All this movement had trampled the road and once we got the car righted, with both of us pushing, Mil steering through the window, we drove along more easily for a time. When we got beyond the hoof marks the skidding began once more; the whole progress, like a crab, seemed more sideways than forward. We struck a bump and the car, out of control, plunged off the road again. The mud held tighter this time, to our shoes as well as to the tires, and we moved with effort, as though shackled. We tried digging the mud away, but when this didn't help, I started gathering dead branches from the bushes while Mil hauled out the wire cleats. We forced both branches and cleats under the tires, trying to give them purchase. Half an hour of this and we resembled elephants that have just rolled in the mud; but at least Bublee was free.

By now the road had dried a little and we skidded only occasionally as we pushed on. The road itself alternated between an ordinary farm track and sections which looked almost built-up and rolled. The rolled part had taken on a glassy finish from the rain which was much harder to navigate than the more uneven surface. We came to a smooth part again, and inevitably got stuck. It was dusk when we finally got the car free the third time. The air felt heavy with rain; we could see this in-and-out routine going on all night. It seemed more sensible to get off the main track and camp for the night. Naively we thought the nomads, too, stopped for the night and as long as we were somewhat distant from the road, we wouldn't be bothered by stray prowlers. We drove slowly, surveying the bush which was much thicker now than it had been earlier in the day. Finally Mil spied a suitable camping site well back from the road, and scouted out a way to drive in. Just off the rolled surface was a slight depression which looked harmless enough. But as I turned the car off the road toward the camping spot, the front wheels sank to the hubcaps in the boggy ditch. We were thoroughly caught.

"Can't budge her now," said Mil disconsolately. "Guess we'll just have to camp here. Tomorrow the mud may dry out a little. Let's just hope it doesn't rain in the night." He had hardly mentioned the word when a few raindrops spattered down. But as the light went out of the sky a bitter wind came up and blew the rain clouds on. Stars came out directly above, but the sky was rimmed with clouds which hid the moon. I lit the lantern while Mil tried to start the primus but the wind kept blowing it out. Only after he rearranged the trunks in the boot so that the primus could sit in the shelter of the car did he succeed in lighting it. The roar of the flame rivaled the noise of the wind. I could hear nothing else as I went about heating soup, frying sausages and potatoes and onions. It was too muddy to sit outside the car, so Mil sat half out the front seat and I stood hovering about the primus.

I had just put the instant coffee in the mugs and was straightening up to reach for the hot water when I felt I was being watched. Staring at me was a tall ragged Somali.

At my glance he faded back into the shadows. Perhaps he was frightened as I, impulsively, reached forward and let out the pressure on the primus which hissed and was silent. Sounding above the gusting of the wind were more camel bells. Squinting into the bush I could see moving shapes humping past off the road among the thorns. Mil had come up behind me; in the flash of his torch I could make out the procession of heavily laden camels, each one led by skinny children, piled with blankets, or tent skins and supports, or shrouded women.

They passed on into the shadows, and once more only the wind whistled. We rolled up the windows and sat cozily in the car, sipping the hot coffee. Is this what we came to Africa for, I wondered, to be stuck in the mud in the middle of nowhere? Couldn't we have taken the easier route by taking a boat down the Nile Valley, I asked myself. And miss Ethiopia? myself retorted. Will we get to Ethiopia? came the taunt. "Bunji," I asked aloud, "how stuck are we?" "Stuck," he replied shortly, and pulled me close to him. It did not seem at all odd to forget our plight in several long kisses.

We were roused by the distant jangling of bells, a thinner sound than the hollow clank of camel bells. "Must be the cattle belonging to that caravan that passed," Mil guessed. "That means men. If they find us here helpless, the temptation may be too much for some of them. As long as we're stuck, we're real sitting pigeons. We'd better try to get out of this ditch before any of them have time to think about bothering us."

Quickly we packed up the boot again, wrapping the dirty dishes in old rags, and started collecting branches where the headlights illuminated the bush. Then we tried the rock-and-push technique, but the ditch was too deep, and the rear tires were not holding. Every time we rolled back a little deeper. Exhausted, we stopped to rest and Mil switched off the headlights. We both sat smoking cigarettes, wondering just what would happen when the herders appeared. "There will certainly be more than two of them," I whispered, as if silence made us somehow safer. "Still, they will think we are well armed," Mil whispered back. Tense with anticipation, I murmured, "There's always the advantage of a white face, authority and all." Then I wondered whether this was an advantage. They'd think we're rich, and worth robbing. So we sat, waiting, staring into the blackness. Strangely, the bells did not seem to come closer, though their clanging, wafting on the breeze, was irregular, almost haunting. Suddenly I realized what had happened. The Somalis were detouring around us, driving the herd through the bush. "Mil," I said, my cracked voice exploding in the silence, "they're going away. They must be afraid of us!" Momentarily saved, Mil switched on the lights and went back at his digging.

If the words broke the inactivity of our fright, they also re-impressed me with the seriousness of our situation. If the nomads were on their way all night, we just couldn't sit here and wait for a brave one or a desperate one to come along and attack us. We must get help. They won't be afraid of a woman, I thought, and forgetting that I had my jeans on, I walked into the glare of the headlights, candy in one hand, cigarettes in the other. I was sure that somewhere in the bush the Somalis were watching.

Almost immediately an old man limped forward, supporting himself on a stick. Behind him rose a babble of voices, protesting. As if in slow motion the old man took a cigarette, tasted it, then pushed it beneath his toga-draped cloth. Having secured his prize, he stared in turn at me, the car, and Mil, then raised his chin toward the shadows and stepped back across the ditch. A signal, of course – I held my breath. Did it mean he had found us friendly, or merely harmless and thus easy game? I managed the widest smile I had, and leaned far across the ditch to give the old man a candy. Immediately there were other hands reaching out for the sweets and cigarettes, though none of them dared to cross the ditch into the bright glare of the lights. When I had nothing left I began to gesture to them to help push, trying Swahili and Italian and English, all mixed up and very half-made-up. The men looked baffled, and began to fade back into the night. Urgently I begged them, visions of their sneaking back in the night, piercing the tires, and then waiting for us to come out to death or capture, kept flashing through my overworked imagination. Back in Garissa I had joked about what a good story it would make, being captured by Somalis. Now that jest haunted me.

"Get in the car," Mil called, "let's show them what we mean."

"Push, push!" I screamed at the men as I started the engine. "Push, unh! Push, unh! Mil repeated, imitating native style. None of the Somalis moved. "Roll, gun, roll, gun," I said over and over to myself, trying to keep my imagination in check. Suddenly, almost as one, the whole crowd of young Somalis surged forward, rolled and pushed, once, twice, and three times, we were out. They had practically lifted the car up and out of the ditch and placed it on the road straight and ready to go. Jabbering and laughing, their voices in the night brought back my fear. I gunned the motor, and yelled at Mil to get in, fast. Hands came through the window, and I reached for more candy. Their words were becoming a chant: shil-ling, shil-ling, shil-ling. Mil jumped in, shovel in one hand, lantern in the other. Hands followed him too, and he pulled his cigarettes from his shirt pocket, threw the whole pack at the forest of arms as I let out the clutch. We lurched forward, the engine coughed, but held. The lights entranced a few stray cattle still on the road, but I managed to swerve past them without skidding. Beyond, the road was clear. Our only enemy now was the mud.

For miles we ran in low gear over sluggish ground. Even though the wind had dried the surface somewhat, it was tricky driving. Soon both I and the car were overheated. A smell like burning rubber permeated the car. Finally, where the ground seemed firmer, we stopped to look. Mil checked under the hood while I broke out a new tin of grapefruit juice and souped it up with glucose. Mil came back to drink his share, puzzled. Everything was in perfect order. Just then we heard a loud plop from the back of the car. It was a large blob of mud which had fallen from the rear bumper. Mil squatted down to flash the light under the car and found the whole bottom encased in mud. Under the fenders the mud pressed so hard upon the tires that the friction had caused the smell. Mil jacked up the car, and the two of us pried at the mud with shovel, jack handle, and tire iron. After an hour's work the pile of goo beneath each wheel looked more like elephant droppings than anything else I could think of. "Looks like Bublee had an enema," I laughed.

The strangeness of the predicament and the humor of the results revived the spirit of challenge. We were no longer afraid, only tired and determined. Mil took over the driving. With her burden gone, Bublee ran easily over the smooth sandy road. It was after midnight. Though I tried to sleep, I only dozed off fitfully. Unexpectedly we came to a fork in the road, where there was none on our map. Mil got out with a flashlight to search for some sort of sign, but there was none. Some camel drivers, asleep under a tree, awoke enough to gesture toward Kismayu to the right. The left road looked like a better way; we hesitated, and finally went the way they pointed. Almost immediately the road deteriorated to something resembling a stream bed. The overhanging thorns pricked at the tarpaulin. It was already my turn to drive again, and groggily I took the wheel. The track seemed to go on forever. There was no sign of nearing the town. I drove carelessly, bounding from rock to rock, dodging tree trunks, skidding in sandy patches. By now I was convinced that this could not be the proper route. Surely no truck could get through the tangle.

Still there seemed no point in going back to try the other road. We were in a triangle of land bounded on the east by the ocean and on the west by the Juba River. We'd have to reach one, the ocean or the river, sooner or later. It looked like later. My hour of driving was up and Mil bestirred himself. I sat half asleep, watching the track. Suddenly Mil stopped. At last a sign post. He got out to examine the weather beaten board, but all the writing had long since disappeared. The road became increasingly sandy, but just as the going was getting difficult, we reached a section which was cobbled with rocks and concrete blocks. A black mound loomed ahead. It looked like a sand dune, I thought, shaking my head to see whether I was awake or asleep. Through my blinking eyes I caught the flash of light and the movement of my head made it dance around, like a carousel. I shut my eyes, then opened to stare again. But there were no lights, only another dune ahead. Was it a mirage? Could I be that tired? Impatiently I waited while we crossed the sand and mounted the next dune. There indeed was the carousel again, arrested in movement this time, as deliciously gay as any ordinary carousel ever appeared to a country child. Mil stopped the car in amazement, we looked at the scene, then at each other, and began to laugh, perhaps a bit hysterically. The town, strung out along the edge of the shore was ablaze with electric lights, at three o'clock in the morning! But what made the vision seem round was a cruise ship of some sort, all its lights glowing, sparkling in the water as it rocked in the waves. A fairy tale ending to an incredible day.

CHAPTER 20

# Pink sands, pink grapefruit

*A*N EARLY MORNING FLY, BUZZING AROUND MY SLEEPING BAG, woke me after what seemed like only minutes of sleep. I lay still, trying to remember where we were. The soft lullaby of the waves urged me back to sleep, but the sun was already hot and soon the sleeping bag would be intolerable. I opened my eyes and squinted across the water. The ship was still there, looking less romantic in the daylight. I felt in my shoe for my glasses and looked around. We were not as far out of town as we had thought, for just over the dunes was a pile of fishers' shanties. As I watched, a tall thin Somali, dressed only in a breech cloth, tracked over the sand to spread his fishing net to dry. He was trailed by four or five children in various stages of nakedness. When they saw us, a loud chatter began, which rose to an even higher pitch as Mil wriggled out of his sleeping bag and walked across the sand to the car. Here was indeed a contrast they could not understand: white people who own cars sleeping on the beach.

It was after three in the morning when we had finally reached Kismayu. Despite the bright electricity the town had been completely quiet. One large house had a guard at the gate: the house of the *Residente.* The *hoteli* sign pointed down along the beach but after driving back and forth along the seafront, we gave up trying to find it. Instead we drove beyond the electric lights and bedded down on the sand for what was left of the night.

More children poured across the sands until both Mil and I were surrounded. From a distance they bombarded me with questions; one of the more daring ones rushed up to touch the sleeping bag. I was too preoccupied with my own problem to be more then vaguely annoyed. The night before, after we parked, Mil and I had rushed into the surf, pulling at the thick cotton soil which caked our arms and legs. Not thinking of the morning, I had slipped off my wet, dirty clothes and had put on my tough, but somewhat transparent, nylon pajamas. Now with this youthful audience, just how was I to get to the car?

Mil had unlocked the car and was already examining Bublee to see how she had stood that nightmare ride. Squirming in my mummy sleeping bag, I managed to grab Mil's larger bag and unzip it. Then with what dignity I could muster, I draped it over me toga-like, slipped out of my own bag, and walked to the car. There I sat, feeling utterly foolish to be so wrapped in a hot blanket in a day already warm. Thus I remained until we rode out of town far enough for privacy. Then recklessly we washed in our remaining water and put on clean clothes. Even thus we were hardly dressed to pay a call on the local governor; yet that was what we had to do.

Not that we had planned this. I was in no interviewing mood. Mogadishu and paved roads were still a full day's drive away and rain could still impound us for weeks anywhere along the way. Despite the advice of Reverend Cheese to spend time in Kismayu, we were determined to push on immediately. The trouble was we had no gas, and no money. At first we looked for a tavern or store where we might cash a traveler's check and get some food. We had no more luck with this quest than we had with trying to find a hotel the night before. Every time we went around the town we ended at the only recognizable landmark, the *Residente*'s house. Out near the docks I tried my Spanish-Italian on some rummy looking sailors; but they shrugged apathetically and muttered

Italian cupola on Kismayu beach frames the cruise ship

"banco, banco." When we did find a bank, a sign said it wouldn't be open til ten; it was still only seven o'clock!

The next time round the *Residente*'s house I decided we should go in and ask for help. Perhaps he could get the bank manager to give us money right away. It was already so hot that my shirt clung to my legs and my blouse was no longer fresh. Uncertainly, I approached the low bungalow and announced *"Residente"* to the servant who appeared. He vanished and in a few moments the *Residente*'s wife appeared, a short crumpled housecoat drawn over pajamas. Her bored eyes brightened at the sight of a European but immediately dimmed to polite interest when I began my halting request. She waved her hand in one of those expressively hopeless gestures which at the same time welcomed me into the cool dark interior of the house. A houseboy fetched Mil and we all sat in heavy chairs under the one fan in the house trying to keep awake on repeated cups of strong bitter Italian coffee. Mil gave up first and relaxed into a light sleep. Signora and I exhausted my Italian and her English and then carried on a desultory conversation through her houseboy.

When Signora finally gave up trying to make conversation, I talked a while to the houseboy. He had worked for the British colonel when they had occupied Somalia and had, briefly, followed the British colonel to Mombasa. But Somalia was his home, he grinned when I asked him why he had come back, "and soon," he added softly, "this land will belong to us again."

Of course, I thought sleepily, it's already promised to you by the United Nations. Vaguely I wondered why I hadn't seen signs of the trusteeship and promised myself to ask about it in Mogadishu – if we ever got there. In the heat, and exhaustion, getting to Mogadishu seemed about as possible as getting to the end of a rainbow.

At length, a rotund man in white shorts and shirt ambled in and bowed in a lazy military manner. His heels would have clicked had he been wearing shoes instead of sandals, I thought, as I heard his fleshy knees smack. With an envious glance at my sleeping husband he departed toward the other side of the house, questioning the houseboy who tagged along behind him.

Uncertain what else to do and afraid of falling asleep, I asked about washing up and was taken through a shady courtyard into a sparsely furnished room. Beyond this unused guest room was a complete bathroom. An extra bathroom, electricity! For the moment, Italian colonization impressed me. This Italian couple seemed more lonely, more "native", than those English in Garissa with their out-of-tune piano. But the amenities here! I thought, turning on the water, and nearly scalding my hand.

Signora had hardly poured out fresh coffee and served us with delicious pink grapefruit when Signor returned, full of apologies. He had not been eating breakfast, as I supposed, but had been out talking to the bank manager. Indeed we could cash traveler's checks, any kind of checks. But this bank was a small branch bank, and it would have to await clearance from the bank in Mogadishu. That should not take too long, not more than four days.

"Four days! And rain in the air." I sighed, wondering how I could have been so stupid as to spend all our East African shillings in East Africa. I think the *Residente* found our impecuniousness rather strange too.

Then Mil leaned forward earnestly and began in his best diplomatic manner. "But see this card," he urged, holding out the engraved calling cards which said impressively: Millidge Penderell Walker, III, Vice-Consul of the United States, New Delhi. The Signor visibly brightened. "Won't this allow the bank manager to cash a check immediately?"

"A diplomat, why that is different!" exclaimed the *Residente*. With new purpose and more charm he once more went out to talk to the manager.

"Marvelous, Mil , I hope it works. Imagine being stuck here

for the next four months if it should rain!" We toasted each other with coffee, and ate sweet crackers the wife offered us.

The *Residente* looked pleased, if warm, when he rushed back. We were not prepared for his words. "No, the bank cannot cash your check without word from Mogadishu." He spoke the name of the town with a reverence bordering an incantation.

It is a magical town, I thought, it doesn't really exist for us because we shall never get there. I think I would have cried except that I was so emotionally battered from the strain of the last few days. I wasn't listening to the *Residente* as he chattered on looking very pleased with himself, not until Mil said "What?" rather sharply.

"It is all right," repeated the *Residente* in careful Italian. "I give you money! You give back in Mogadishu. Here," he said peeling off hundred shilling notes from the roll which he pulled from his pocket. We were embarrassed, astounded. But in the end there was nothing else we could do but accept his offer, though we only let him give us two notes instead of the five he wanted us to take. Then he wrote down the name of a friend of his in the secretariat in Mogadishu and simply told us to give him the money! With that we departed, full of coffee and directions, and amazement at the trust of this man. It was even stranger when we walked into the secretariat some days later and gave two hundred shillings to his friend. He accepted the money and our story as casually as if the notes had been worthless paper instead of $14. each. "The value of a white face," I mused to Mil. "Imagine what a scoundrel couldn't do!"

THE FERRY ACROSS THE Juba River outside Kismayu typifies, in retrospect, the contrast between Somalia and Kenya. The Juba is the only year-round river in Somalia and is wider and

Cable ferry across the Juba River

swifter than the muddy Tana. The cable ferry was sturdy and permanent looking, the African crew neatly clothed. But though they smiled wanly at the Memsahib and her camera they did not sing or joke. Perhaps it is merely the difference between the tribes, but I got the feeling that the distance between white and African was wider here, more so just because of the amenities, the better cable ferries. For these things were built exclusively for the Italian colonists – the message of the United Nations had not yet spread. Most Somalis did not understand that the cable and the running water and the toilets would soon belong to them. I found myself wondering exactly what they would do with them, when they got them.

Or with the luscious pink grapefruit. The Somalis did not seem to eat them though I have never tasted grapefruit with such delicate flavor. We bought a dozen right by the ferry from a man carrying baskets of them to be sold in Kismayu. It was not only the heat that made the fruit delicious, for we gorged on them when, the following day, we finally reached Mogadishu.

You should be able to drive in dry weather from Kismayu to Mogadishu in a day; the distance is only about 325 miles, and a road at least exists. By now our start was distressingly late, though our mood was gay. Confident that we would reach Mogadishu that day, I insisted on stopping frequently to take photos. We even thought it was funny when we missed the track and drove down an irrigation ditch for miles. So did the small urchin we picked up in the fields to guide us back to the road. His delight in riding in the car far overcame his pungent odor; and when we dropped him by the oasis where we picked up the road again, he seemed to have grown inches, so suddenly straight was he standing.

The map read Marguerita. But the town was Somali, with square huts, each with its walled-off court. At the edge of the huts was an imposing well. Mounds of camels were clustered about it, and at the strange sound of a motor-car they rose, as dust before a gale, looking more like shifting sands than any real sandstorm we saw. Their owners were sophisticated compared to our nomads of the previous night. Lying relaxed in the shade of acacias or curled behind the stone wall surrounding the well, they hardly acknowledged our existence. A few men were drawing water from the well and pouring it into the camels' water troughs. They looked up at us with a pitying incredulity, as though wondering why anyone would be so foolish as to prefer a car to a camel. Indeed the car was very unsuited to the environment. All the jogging had loosened many things causing new rattles and coughs. And when, in the increasing gloom of a late afternoon storm, we switched on wipers and lights, they did not work; something had happened to the generator.

All afternoon we watched the rain clouds gather. But the road continually improved. At first it was narrow track varying in quality and color from sickly white, glaring sand, to rich red treacherous clay. Then we worried about rain. But gradually the road widened, became graveled, if pot-holed, and even the curves were banked. We stopped worrying and began to admire the scenery. We were near the ocean again, but the sand dunes towered over the car cutting off the view of the ocean. The dunes themselves were unbelievable; rolling as waves, peaked as stiff whipped cream, and tinted pale peach, or delicate pink, or ivory. Herds of camels frothed across the horizon; goats nibbled the prickly grass which tufted the base of the dunes. These were special desert goats, I noticed, with their water bags hanging awkwardly beneath their tails. The children-shepherds climbed the spiky acacias or feathery pepper trees to wave us along. It was entirely enchanting.

Then the storm broke, and without lights or wipers, we were forced to stop. The rain quickly passed, leaving a slick but passable road. We drove while there was any light in the sky. As the dark closed in we turned off the road to wait til morning.

So near and yet so far! Only sixty miles from a soft bed and clean sheets. Perhaps nearer. Over the dunes from the road, along the coast, the map showed several towns. Back near the pink dunes we had noticed a turn-off for Brava, Somaliland's sea resort and the main town between Kismayu and Mogadishu. We were somewhere in the delta of the Webi Shebelli, if the mouth of a river that never reaches the sea can be called a delta. Before the war the Italians built irrigation networks along its banks until the point where the residue water bogs into the salty marshes just short of the Juba River. At one time the river must have emptied into the ocean but now the dunes have blocked its course and turned the backlands along the river's new course into the best farming land in the country. Thus we supposed there must be farmhouses nearby. Twice we heard four-wheel drive jeeps churning along the road.

The wind was high, but Mil managed to light the primus in the lee of the open boot. Hot soup helped our tempers, but not too much. There is something about continual strain that upsets normal reactions. Usually we were keyed up to excitement, could ignore both major and minor difficulties. But every so often, as though a balloon had burst, our ability to cope gave out; everything became too much. This was one of those nights. The expectation of reaching Mogadishu, after all the problems, had keyed us higher than usual. The disappointment left us lower than ever. We could hardly speak civilly to each other, inevitably taking out our frustrations with words. We couldn't even convert the seats into beds for that meant putting the seat frames outside and it was too wet for that. So we curled up in the seats and growled.

With morning, stoicism returned. Stopping only for grapefruit juice spiked with glucose, we headed for Mogadishu. Here and there were fields which looked as though they once might have been irrigated. Closer to the city we did see irrigated farms, but there was still no sign of people. The desolation continued until we came to a tarmac road only about fifteen miles outside of Mogadishu. Already the road was crowded with camels and donkeys ambling slowly under their loads of clay pots and wood and hay and empty kerosene tins. Happy again, we joined the procession over the dunes and, at last, into Mogadishu.

CHAPTER 21

# *Somalia in Transition*

From the dunes, the view of Mogadishu was a picture from Arabian Nights. The impression of dazzling whiteness took shape in the houses and shops, irregular, two-story buildings jammed into the least possible area. Against the sparkling white, the pink sand looked almost red. An azure sea picked up the color from the blue minaret and glorified it. The sky, only shades lighter than the sea, was a smooth velvet backdrop for puffy little clouds. Really, had we arrived on our private flying carpet it would have been more appropriate.

Bublee almost pranced down the dunes and through the broad paved main street to the seaside promenade. Here green was added to the color scheme – a wide park rimmed the stone walk around a memorial arch. Down the narrow alleys of the old Arab section we could see date trees breaking

the expanses of white walls.
Here and there were rocket
shaped towers of the smaller
mosques. These older Somali
mosques were built without
minarets, unlike the tall
and graceful Arabic-looking
azure spire we had seen from
the dunes.

Down the alleys, too,
were street lights and telephone wires. Somehow this
did not seem as surprising as
the very precise policeman
directing traffic from his
round concrete safety island
at the town's main cross-

A traditional Somali mosque
gleams against the blue
of the ocean and sky

roads. His khaki shorts and shirt were made more conspic-
uous by the addition of loose white sleeves and white gloves.
The police pin on his black beret glinted in the sun. The
general effect was not unlike the black and white striped
wooden umbrella under which he stood, for his long black
legs were as straight as poles while his arms, outstretched,
were striped: white sleeve, black arm, white glove.

With one long white finger he directed us, unasked,
toward the hotel. This street, which also led to the market,
was thronged with women. City women swished by in long
crinolines, their heads and shoulder, but not their faces,
draped in white or black shawl-veils. Their sandals clicked as
they walked. The barefoot desert women, balancing mats or
baskets on their heads, moved without noise. But their gaudy
sarongs of orange and black, pink and purple, drew attention
nonetheless. For modesty, all but the poorest of these desert

Women in downtown Mogadishu
display distinct dress styles,
but all cover their heads

women wore an old sarong from the waist down. On top of this they draped another over one shoulder and twice around. Even the most raggedy women had amber beads around their necks and some sort of cloth for a head shawl.

By contrast, I was almost undressed, in a skirt and short sleeved blouse, both distinctly dirty. But as I went up to the desk of the Croce del Sud, I couldn't have cared less. On the contrary, I strode in like a conquering hero, jubilant. We had gotten to Mogadishu – surely the worst was over.

For once I didn't even ask the price of the rooms, but just said we should like a double room for a week. A week! The word itself was relaxing. A whole week in one place, in a civilization of pink grapefruit and Italian wine and vinegar artichokes and coffee-bars which serve cappuccino in break-fast-sized cups. A week of pink sandy beaches where we could lie and let the tensions seep out. Worry over pangas and rain and wild Somalis and cotton soil had built up fan-tastic pressure, much more than we realized until they grad-ually subsided. After Mogadishu, though we went through some fairly bad moments, we were never quite as wound up again. Perhaps this very nonchalance was what got us through. But in Mogadishu, we were so certain the worst was already behind us that we were able to relax and enjoy a very merry week. As new-comers in a lonely foreign colony, we were feted as royalty.

By foreign colony I mean non-residents, most of whom

were employed by the United Nations. In 1950 the name of Italian Somaliland was changed to Somalia and the colony became a Trusteeship under the United Nations Charter. The administration of the country was to continue temporarily under Italy until 1960 when the country was to be fully independent. To supervise this gradual handing-over of power, an international advisory council with its permanent secretariat was set up in Mogadishu. For this reason many more foreigners from more countries than you might expect to find in this remote corner of Africa clustered in the city.

Many Italians were still living in the country, both in the administration and in private business or farming. Whether or not they should be called "foreign" I don't know. It was Mussolini's idea that the Italian colonies in Africa should become an outlet for Italy's excess population. Thus most colonists were sent to Africa with all costs paid by their government. In Somaliland they were given irrigated land along the rivers and told to establish a home. World War II stopped all migration. Those men who were not drafted into the Italian army for their invasion of British Somaliland and northern Kenya in 1940 were interned by the occupying British forces the following year. After the war, many colonists never returned. Those that did often came back only to sell their lands and depart once more. Naturally the administrators would all leave once the Trusteeship was terminated. When we were in Mogadishu there were still five thousand Italians in the whole country, but the number was quickly decreasing.

The Arabs actually formed a larger group of some 23,000 persons settled entirely in the towns. Yet certainly they were permanent residents, for their ancestors came over from the Arabian desert only a few centuries after the Somalis themselves migrated to the area. Sometime earlier, the Bantus, who are believed to have been in original possession of the

Horn of Africa when it was perhaps a more hospitable region, had wisely departed south. Indeed, so torrid is the whole Horn that I could not understand why Italy or anyone else had ever wanted it for a colony. I said as much, one afternoon on the beach, to our host, a knowledgeable member of the UN staff.

"Look at the map," he said, rolling over and drawing Africa in the pink wet sand where he had been sitting. "When the Italians finally got themselves established as a nation, most of Africa was already a colony of somebody. Because every other European nation had colonies, Italy wanted some too. When they tried, and failed, to take Ethiopia in 1896, they really lost face. You can get the Italian administrators here pretty mad by reminding them that Italy is the only country in modern times which was defeated by an African army. Naturally, after that, the Italians felt they had to get Ethiopia as a colony. They held on to the coastal ports in Eritrea from which they had launched their expeditions. Then they rushed over here and pressured the local Sultans into giving them more rights. That way, Menelik, the old Emperor of Ethiopia, was cut off from the sea and also from the modernizing effects that any wide contact with the West might have brought. So when Italy finally decided to take over Ethiopia in 1936, they just walked in." He turned back to his sand map. "Then all this corner of Africa, all but these little bits of British and French Somaliland, became the Italian Empire of East Africa."

"I used to collect stamps," I said somewhat irrelevantly. "They always said 'Abyssinia' on them."

"The Italians always called it that, so now the Emperor prefers the more ancient name of Ethiopia."

"If the Italians really only wanted Somaliland as a foothold for the conquest of Ethiopia," I asked, "why on earth did they agree to come back here now? It must cost them a lot of money, and they haven't a chance of re-conquering Ethiopia."

"They didn't have much choice," he answered. "No other country wanted this thankless task. And I suppose their government thought they should help take care of the Italians who still had interests or capital here." He paused thoughtfully. "Prestige, too. The desire to finish a job, and do it better than other colonial powers. Goodness knows Somalia is a challenge. Such a poor country, one foot in feudal times, the other in today. The Italians have quite a job trying to make the country ready for independence. I am afraid that with our commission watching over their shoulder, they are being pushed to go too fast."

"Really?" I remarked a bit sarcastically. "To us Somalia looks like another colony. Does the Trusteeship really mean anything?"

Our friend frowned at my purposely provocative question. "Come, there is still time for a dip before it gets too dark. Look how far out your husband is swimming!" And we raced for the water, he added: "Drop by the office tomorrow and you can see us trustees at work."

WE HAD A PREVIEW of how the trustees work when we attended a cocktail party later that evening. I am not one to disparage cocktail parties. Far from it, I enjoy both the drink and the people; and I know from experience that the odd bits of information dropped at such affairs will often be more revealing than hours of cautious official replies to carefully-phrased questions.

The party was in a staff member's house, one of those two-story vaguely modern whitewashed blocks-of-a house that you can see in Rome or Los Angeles or New Delhi

– comfortable enough, but completely without character. The Italian contingent had taken over the balcony; the UN staffers milled about somewhat closer to the drinks. None of the three members of the Advisory Council had as yet shown up, though all were reputedly in Mogadishu.

"No doubt there has been another fight about the motor-cars," laughed our English host.

"Mais oui," giggled a French secretary. "How silly, two autos, three advisors." She added in a darker mood, "Of course, there are not often <u>three</u> advisors. <u>They</u> don't have to stay here all the time, not like we do."

"Come now," chided the host. "Your tour is almost finished. And there are worse places to be stationed." In the same patient, almost patronizing tone – a result, perhaps, of his job – he turned to me. "You know that the Advisory Council for this Trusteeship consists of representatives from Egypt, Colombia, and the Philippines. These men are politicians; with eyes on their future in their own country. Being sent here is rather like exile. What is even worse, they don't agree, indeed no one agrees, about what the Advisory Council is supposed to do. If one member tries to do something, suggest some scheme, another is bound to disagree, and not only for reasons connected with the colony. No wonder they get frustrated and ask for leave, or recall. Last year we had eight different advisors; and, at that, delegates from all three countries were here together only a third of the time. Honestly, though, I prefer it that way. Since politically the Advisors can't really make a stand on anything, it is better from the staff's point of view that they don't interfere at all."

Just then the host's wife joined us. "You had better go to the door, Jonathan. The Philippine representative has just arrived, in the big car."

"Moments later the Colombian delegate arrived in the

small car, and the French girl, still giggling, remarked, "I guess the Egyptian will not appear tonight. He does not at all speak to the others, and he will be furious about the auto. I do not understand why there cannot be three autos, even little ones. So many memos, always about who gets the car big tonight. Why do they want to drive? There is no place to go. Nothing to do either, but drink." At that she headed for the table again, to get a refill.

"The Egyptian couldn't care less about cars," put in a tall red-haired American woman. "He is here to work. Egypt wants Somalia to join the Arab bloc as soon as the Italians leave. So their delegate has to travel all over the country preaching Muslim solidarity and reminding the Somalis that back before the "hated" colonists came, all this area was united under Islamic rulers supported by the Ottoman empire."

"My dear Dorothy," teased her Lebanese husband, Gono Deeb, "you quote their line so well I almost think you believe it!" He continued to us, "But it is so. Every time I go out on a field trip I find that an Egyptian has been there before. Not always the delegate. Already over fifty Egyptians have come here as school teachers. If they find a promising youth, they ship him off for free schooling in Cairo. Probably as many as four hundred have gone by now. When you consider that almost no Somalis have any education at all, you can see what this will mean in five years. The Italians are now educating some of the brighter clerks to become administrators and have sent two hundred of the best to Italy for university work. You can see the lines of controversy already forming between the two groups, with the tribal leaders hating anyone with education because they themselves are illiterate and fear anyone who can read. We're trying to push education now, and so we've suggested that Somali become the language instruction. To do this we had to invent an alphabet because til now, Somali has been only a spoken language. But these old boys oppose the use of Somali and insist that Arabic continue to be used. They give religion as their excuse, because the Koran is written in Arabic. They say if people could read Somali only, it might weaken Islam here! You can bet the main reason is the old chiefs don't want a lot of educated youth who might become rivals for tribal authority." Gono Deeb paused a moment to munch a cheese straw. "Fascinating country," he said. "Mil, you're a political scientist, what do you think will happen after 1960?"

"Most people seem to think that Egypt will just take over," said Mil.

"I wouldn't be too sure of that," replied the Lebanese. "The Somalis want to unite the so-called Five Somalis: Italian, British, and French Somaliland plus the Somali areas of Kenya and Ethiopia. This is more important to them than any idea of united Islam. They are Muslims, of course, rather fanatic ones, but a Muslim from Cairo might find some of their customs here very different from those prescribed in the Koran. I think the Egyptian, because he tries to tell the Somalis how to pray and govern, will only get into more trouble. He was stoned by some tribals not too long age." The Lebanese was only too correct. A few months later the Egyptian delegate was found stabbed to death in an alley.

WE MET GONO DEEB again when we visited the UN offices the next day. His knowledge about the country was phenomenal. As a Muslim, speaking Arabic and with a dark olive skin, he was far more acceptable to the Somalis than a European would have been. He seemed to have an impartiality toward the problems of the country and thus would be a good man to explain to us just what the UN was doing in Somalia. At our query, Deeb went over to a map of the country which hung on his wall. "These red lines show all the trips our staff has taken, collecting complaints as well as information, observing the administration at work. I was up here last month," he said, pointing to an area on the Ethiopian border where the Juba entered Somalia, "observing municipal elections. There are a few settlements of Somalis along the two rivers. Organizing this election wasn't easy; but holding elections for the legislative council will be a real corker. The administration will do the actual work, of course, but we must make suggestions, see that the voting is orderly and secret. Here in town we act as a sort of clearing house for petitions on subjects which range from an objection to the way an Italian doctor examined an infant to complaints of wholesale arrests and detentions without trial. The little problems we try to settle here, but those with political overtones usually end up being sent to New York. I suppose all this is useful. But actually I think the mere fact that we are here is more important than anything we can do. We are a sort of world conscience."

Deeb went back to his desk and picked up a pile of reports. "Here is a sort of by-product. No matter what else happens, at least we collected a lot of statistics and surveys concerning the country and the people. I like this sort of work best. It's intriguing going out into the bush. I even took my wife once," he added, shaking his head, "Never again."

"But why?" I asked, a bit indignant at the apparent slight on my sex. After all, his wife seemed a very capable sort of person.

"Let's walk over to the house for coffee and you can ask her yourself," he replied, obviously amused at my quick defense.

We left the cool shelter of the squat adobe buildings that housed the secretariat and crossed a parched lawn under the withering glare of the midday sun. Sheltering under feathery pepper trees was a small frame house, not at all appropriate for the climate: it seemed to enclose rather than exclude the heat. Only the constant ocean breeze – the house was practically on the beach – made it habitable. While our husbands talked about routes and cars, Dorothy speculated about the house.

"Probably one of the temporary wartime buildings that were never torn down. I think this was probably an officers' mess because of the way the bedrooms are arranged, each with an outside door. And of course it is hotter than the adobe houses. Still it is no worse than New York in the summer; and there is much more room for the children to play here than in that city. It was ideal til this year, but we've run into the schooling problem. Up til now I've taught the boys myself from a correspondence course. But the oldest is nearly ten, and so next month I am taking him to Beirut to put him into an international school there. It probably would be better to leave the other one there too, they are such companions. But I'd have absolutely nothing to do then."

Can't you go along with your husband on his tours, and maybe write articles about it? No one in the States knows a thing about Somalia, even where it is." Dorothy started to answer, but I rushed on. "Or couldn't you teach women here in town? Surely there must be many things to do."

"I've already tried giving homemaking lessons. A few Italian women came. Seems that all the town women are in strict purdah. I haven't even met an aristocratic woman the whole four years we've been here. Then I tried going along with Deeb once." She laughed. "Didn't he tell you about it?"

When I shook my head, she continued, "The trip was exciting, going back into tribal areas. Because we traveled by jeep, of course I wore shorts and a shirt. The trouble happened one afternoon, just as we were leaving to go back to a government rest house nearer the river, I had had a scarf around my head, but it was slipping, so I untied it and my red hair tumbled out. It was apparent that up to that time the chief had thought I was a man, for he came over to me and touched my hair. A Muslim that had been to Mecca may henna his beard, so red hair had special significance to the chief. He asked Deeb whether it was dyed, and he said no. Then he turned back to me and put both hands on my breasts just to make sure I was really female. I blushed frantically, but I didn't want to insult the chief so I just stood there. He walked around me, feeling me, just as though I were a horse for sale. And that is exactly what he thought I was. He offered Deeb a whole herd of camels for me!"

"That is quite a compliment," Deeb said, for he and Mil had been listening too. Most wives are worth only four or five camels. So naturally the chief couldn't believe that I would refuse. Since then I've been a little afraid he might try to kidnap Dorothy, so I won't let her go outside the city. She's the only woman with red hair in the whole of Somalia."

EVEN IN A SKIRT, no tribal chiefs offered to buy me the next day when I met a whole roomful of them. Perhaps they were too startled at the politeness shown me, and thought I was an important person. The meeting took place in the office of the representative of the Sinclair oil company. Probably no other person in Mogadishu could assemble these proud chiefs. But the company was searching for oil in the desert lands controlled by the chiefs. Even the most isolated chief knew that from the poorest soil can come black water, enough to make him and his whole country rich.

"It is really pathetic," Tom had said earlier, over a cup of Nescafe which he had brewed himself in the apartment kitchen of the newly completed office and bachelor quarters. "The land is so poor. Every year they are five or six million dollars in the hole. Right now Italy antes up most

of it. Where it will come from after 1960 no one knows...
unless from oil. And so far it doesn't look too good. We've
already sunk quite a few test wells, with no luck at all. To top
it off, we've run head on into tribal rivalry with our labor
problems. The first time we set up to drill we had to hire
local boys to help, to drive cars or grease motors. Nothing
complicated. But a machine is no camel. Takes some time to
teach these fellows anything cause they've never even seen
an engine before. They learn fast, though, and so we asked
the better drivers and repairmen to come along when we had
to move to another location. Moving all that gear is no easy
matter, and we were furious when they refused. Only one
budding mechanic came with us, and then ran away within
a week. We thought they were plain lazy, or wanted to blow
their money on camels and go back to their tribe. This happened several times with our crews getting madder all the
time. Then we drilled near the first site and all our boys from
that first well, including the mechanic, came back clamoring
for jobs. It finally came out that they loved the work but
didn't dare come with us into an area controlled by a clan or
tribe from the rival tribal federation or group. They might
have been beaten, robbed, maybe even killed. The mechanic
said he didn't worry about himself, but the men from the
other tribes threatened to put sand in our gas and break the
drills if he kept working in their territory."

"Is there anything you can do about it?" asked Mil.

"We tried to get the chiefs together to talk about it, but
none of them would go into the other man's territory. Finally
we invited them all, the tribal heads and the big boys, who
are chiefs of the federation, to come here in an hour. Stick
around and watch, if you want."

Tom led me into a wall-to wall-carpeted room. "Have
to impress our visitors," he grinned. He went back into his

apartment and returned in a moment wearing a tie and coat. Two or three at a time, the chiefs drifted silently into the room and sat down on the carpet around the edge of the room. If they were a bit startled to see a woman there they carefully did not show it. But I did see an eye or two staring when Tom handed me a cigarette, lit it for me, offered me the only chair in the room, and then stood while I sat.

Soon, the room was packed with white-robed chiefs. Hangers-on blocked both doorways. These men looked younger, wore sarongs with ordinary shirts over them; one or two had on shorts. Tom nodded at them and said that some were young men who wanted work with the company and were trying to pressure the chiefs into reaching some sort of agreement.

At last the interpreter felt it was time to begin. For ten or fifteen minutes Tom poured forth extravagant words of praise for the country, the chiefs, the tribes. No matter how flowery Tom's phrases, the interpreter seemed to go on better, embellishing the words with gestures. The crowd had shut out the cooling breeze and the room became stifling. Tom's cord suit was rumpled with sweat, the heat made the scene undulate, and I thought that the dark faces, swathed carelessly in white turbans, looked like corks on a frothy sea. Tom's words came as through a sea shell over the murmur of comments. "You want riches," he told them, "like Saudi Arabia. So you must help us find the oil. You have said men from one water-hole cannot work at another water-hole. We must take men with us who know how to watch over the machines. You did not learn to care for a camel in a day. It takes time. So we have decided, to keep peace among you, we will hire half our men from each tribal group, some from every tribe in whose territory we will work. You honored chiefs must see that the men work and do not waste money and time in fighting."

As the interpreter ran on, Tom leaned over. "Don't know if this scheme will works or not; but we must try it. Just maybe, the rivalry will make them all work better. If they could, it would be a real help to the country. You can't really call it a country now; just a bunch of sheikdoms." Almost as an afterthought he added: "It would help, too, if we found oil."

The murmurs stopped when the interpreter finally came to the proposal, took imaginary handful of men from the two tribal groups and pushed them together graphically. I noticed for the first time that there seemed to be an invisible line drawn down the center of the room. The two sides glanced at each other. But there was no other indication of deep rivalry. They would accept it for now, and see. Then with the impressive dignity, and some relief, they rose; the tide went out.

Tom went back to his kitchen and in moments returned with two tall gin and tonics. We stood on the balcony watching the gathering glide into the streets. "And silently steal away," I quoted. "Don't they frighten you sometimes, Tom? They seem so, well, untamed. What would they look like in business suits? Do clothes make an outlaw?" Looking down into the deserted, sun-baked street, sipping my drink in the cool of the shadows, I felt very foreign and sad; once more Africa had eluded me.


THAT EVENING THE FEELING of distance was intensified. We had supper with a very young French couple. When we entered their room-and-a-half apartment we left Africa. Surely this was Montmartre, if not the Left Bank. The wife was an artist, and her vivid primitives, in all stages of completion were piled against the walls. Primitives, European style. Not one had an African theme. Her husband, Claude, was a translator for the United Nations staff, a job which was for him a drudge, but one that gave him time and money to pursue his avocation:

poetry. They were happy to be in Mogadishu because it meant a job that supported them, a maid to watch the baby, and time to paint and write til their pent-up emotions were eased. Perhaps then they might want to go back to Europe, for recharging as it were. Now they were sufficient unto themselves. Somalia had no reality for them – they could have been anywhere in the world. For an evening, we were glad to escape with them into French philosophical speculation aided by tasty French food and excellent wine.

More direct in their mode of escape were the young men involved in the oil search. In Mogadishu after a month in the bush, these boys indulged in spirited drinking parties that were part of the hotel noise. There wasn't much else for them to do. All day they sat in the hotel café progressing from espresso to bitter Italian aperitif to beer to whiskey. On the whole they were a lighthearted group, making fun of the harsh life in the bush. Perhaps their week in town was harder for them to take; from their point of view there was absolutely nothing to do.

"Swim?" said Phil, "why should I swim? I can stand under the shower and get the same effect. Did you ever feel such sticky water?"

"I'll bet it'd poison you if you drank it," said Bob.

"Nonsense," rejoined Jim, "the stuff is good for you. They say that before the war the Italians in Brava used to carbonate the local well water and sell it for mineral water."

"It couldn't taste as salty as this," insisted Phil. "The water in the Ogaden is better than this. Sometimes I think they don't get it from the wells at all, but just out of the ocean. So why swim? You can drink all the sea you want right here."

THE AMERICAN BOYS SAT at their table all day; every afternoon a table on the other side was occupied by Somali youth.

Generally, they ignored each other. But one young engineer with a wider curiosity than the rest had struck up an acquaintance with them. One afternoon he stood us all to an aperitif. Usually, the Somalis said, they drank one bottle of soda between them. They liked to sit in the café, because it represented to them their share in status. Before the war they claimed that they had had to get off the street if an Italian walked by. They would never have dared to dream of sitting down at a table with Europeans. All of them knew a little English as a result of the British occupation. During that occupation they had joined the Somali Youth League, now the most powerful political organization in the country. Even though they were among the leaders of the League they were not entirely certain about their own future. It was not only their small amount of education that set them off from the bulk of Somalia's population, but also the reason they were educated. They were all waifs, whether by reason of illegitimate birth or an intertribal or interracial marriage. Brought up outside the tribal structure, they were sent to missionary orphanages where they often became converted Christians. Now they were set on attaining respectability by returning to Islam and marrying into a tribe.

These young Somali leaders talked til dusk about their political plans and how they were going to unite the Somali people. "Our flag," said their leader, a tall thin youth who still used his Christian name of Joseph, "has five stars for the five Somalilands. We will have no trouble uniting with British and French Somaliland, and Kenya. After all, they are colonies and so will soon be free. But Ethiopia, that will be trouble. You Christians, you are too tender to Ethiopia, but she is not tender to us. Already she comes across our borders to arrest our people. The Emperor wants Somalia back as a part of his country like it was under the Italians."

This statement startled me a little. I had grown up thinking of Ethiopia as a heroic country defending itself against a dictatorial Italy. Trying to think of Ethiopia as a possible aggressor required some reshuffling of my mental reference system. I thought of that little ditty: "Little fleas have lesser fleas upon their backs to bite'em; and lesser fleas have lesser fleas, and so on *ad infinitem.*"

ONE MORNING I WENT, in my official capacity as correspondent, to visit the biggest flea – or what had once been the biggest. The Italian government offices were in a group of pretentious classical buildings. Inside was a jumble of offices, all dark and piled with papers. Behind one such pile I found a kindly old administrator whose job it was to tell the world, or such of the world as found itself in Mogadishu, what the Italians were doing with their ex-colony. He recited a list of figures which did indeed show progress in the improvement of the position of Somali; but they even more clearly showed how little the Italians had tried to do for the native population before the war.

"Look at the school program," he said, with a British accent he had picked up in a prisoner-of-war camp. "Before the war most children didn't go to school at all. There were only about forty primary schools in the whole country. Now we have over three hundred primary schools, some middle schools, and even an academy for training civil servants. Maybe three hundred schools doesn't seem like enough for a population of 1,250,000. But remember that four-fifths of the Somalis are nomadic. We even have plans for traveling schools, ones that will migrate with the tribe. We also are digging wells in the back country, so perhaps a few more tribes will settle down and cultivate the land. Right now only ten percent of the area is under crops. About half the land supports pasture; but the other forty percent is and most of it always will be, pure waste land."

"Wasteland," he emphasized. "I used to think Italy was poor, before I came here. You know, Italy is spending about fifty million American dollars on this country right now. That is a large amount of money, for Italy."

"Wasteland," he repeated again. "You will see much of it when you drive to Ethiopia. But the road is good to the border, so you won't feel the waste. When you walk over it, or ride a camel over it, the wasteland gets into your thinking. I've seen so much of it." He added rather ominously, "I hope you will not be forced to know the wasteland too well."

As I left, he said, "There is a guest house at the border. I'll arrange for you to stay there. Just report to the *Residente* whenever you arrive and he will put you up." We shook hands. "And remember, Italy is a poor country compared to yours. We had to think of our own people too. When America almost stopped immigration, we had to find some other place for our people to go. Here we only settled on unused land, no worse than your forefathers did in America." I had a sudden image of Indians sending petitions to the King of England or to the Pope.

"Now," he concluded, with the slightest trace of bitter-ness, "you make us age the country, like wine, give them the best things of life, like wine. But," he made a hopeless little gesture with his shoulder "the Somalis do not like wine. You look at the people up country and decide for yourself what will happen in 1960."

CHAPTER 22

# *Wastelands in contention*

THE WEEK WAS UP. THE CAR HAD BEEN REPAIRED, A NEW GEN-
erator installed, the tank and all jerry cans filled with
gas. We spent half the afternoon seeking kerosene for the
primus and finally found some in the back of a very dark
general store. I was not the only female hunting cooking oil.
As several young Somali girls stepped back into the blinding
light of the afternoon carrying pots or tins of kerosene, they
posed unwittingly for photos – some of the best I shot.

One final time we drank cappuccino in breakfast-sized
cups, even though it was tea time and not morning. The cafe
did not open til a respectably late hour of nine and we were
due for an early start. Mogadishu was no longer a haven – it
had become only a stop on the road. When we had finally
reached the city it had seemed that nothing ahead could be
as difficult. Now we were not so sure.

Tom came by the hotel for a farewell drink and tried to persuade us to stay on a few more days in Mogadishu. "After all," he kidded, "there's nothing in the desert that won't be the same next year: same sand, same thorns, same camels."

"Same problems," rejoined Mil, "might as well get on with them."

As he realized that we were intent on leaving the next day, Tom let his usual beaming face sag into sadness. "I'd planned a special beach party for you tomorrow night," he complained, "it's too late to move it up to tonight. I never thought you'd really go so soon." For awhile we all sat silently. I could tell Mil was looking at the sunset, wondering what sort of day would be coming up. Suddenly Tom brightened. "I know, at least we can go out to Afgoi and celebrate. You kids go get dressed. I'll be back in half an hour." And he rushed off happily.

"Why, he's going to miss us," I told Mil as we changed. "He's been so gay and generous. I hope at least we've amused him. He must have a lonely life."

"But honey," replied Mil with his amazing clairvoyance, "a man like Tom is lonely wherever he lives. Distractions are just harder for him to find here. In a way it probably makes life for him more challenging, maybe even more rewarding."

Tom was as proud of his restaurant in Afgoi as if he had built it himself. It was charming: a green-blackness of trees surrounded the garden where we sat watching a spirited game of bocce ball. In the background you could just hear the soft gush of the waters of the Webi Shebelli. Afgoi itself was the center of the Italian plantation area some fifteen miles west of Mogadishu. The restaurant, unlike the capital city, had retained a purely Italian atmosphere. The food was authentic and delicious, the crowd gay and full of song. All that is the best from Italy was evident that night. Yet still it was colonial. The Somali waiters stood around the edges of the room grinning at the lack of dignity shown by their onetime masters. Indeed, in their flowing gowns they looked more sure of themselves than the guests. We speculated about 1960, wishing for a crystal ball, for Somalia and for our trip. If we had known the troubles that faced us within the next few weeks, perhaps we would simply have put Bublee and ourselves on a boat for Europe. Not knowing the future has value along the lines of "fools rush in."

As it was, we drove out of Mogadishu next day while the morning was still fresh. In moments the tarmac road took us up and over the sand dunes that guard the city, and dropped us into to the interminable desert. Bublee ran well with the new generator; as a precaution, though, we drove for hours at a time with the lights on to avoid any chance of overcharging.

Whenever the road neared the almost dry riverbed, the trees would thicken and under them a mosque or a hut or a police station would hide from the sun. Otherwise we were alone with the thorn bushes, buzzing quickly along on a smooth, well surfaced road which paradoxically improved as the landscape grew wilder. It was the best road we had driven on in Africa. It, like Somaliland itself, was part of Mussolini's dream. He planned this road as the major communication link between Mogadishu and Harar in Ethiopia. From Harar a road would lead to Addis Ababa and then back to the sea through Asmara in Eritrea. That was to have been our route, too, for the army maps we got in Nairobi showed a solid red line all the way. But in Mogadishu we had been warned that this beautiful road existed only on paper; the section across the Ogaden to Harar had never been completed. The foundations had been extended a few miles beyond the border to Ferfer; then the desert took over. The oil men advised us to take a round-about route via British Somaliland; that way, they assured us, there is at least a camel track to follow. All their warnings seemed unnecessary that first day. As the old Italian had said, the desert looks almost romantic from a well-paved road; we were to feel the desert soon enough.

Passing another vehicle became an occasion. A few Italian semi-trailers lumbered by us toward the capital. The driver counted on almost no traffic, I suppose, for with five or six passengers crowded into the high front cab, the driver did not have much room for maneuvering. We saw no other sedans at all, but several Land Rovers were parked near the cotton gin at Villaggio Duca delgi Abruzzi – a rather long name for what would hardly be a crossroads in the United States. The cotton gin was cooperatively owned by the local Italian farmers. We had heard in Mogadishu that there were plans to let Somali farmers join too, if they wished.

The sun was merciless, reflected off the barren desert. The elevation was slowly increasing. The pull and the heat eventually made the engine water, and even the battery water, boil. We tried running with the hood slightly open, but this didn't help much. Near Bulo Burti we found a half-built stone church which gave some shade, and stopped there to let the engine cool, and incidentally to eat some lunch. Mil kept the engine running, for just letting it sit in the penetrating heat would not have cooled it very quickly. A Fiat jeep churned by, screeched to a stop further on, and backed up to us. A trim, if heavy, Italian leaned out and introduced himself as the Provincial Commissioner. Then he turned to his driver and told him to help Mil fix the car for he had seen Mil leaning over the engine and thought we were in trouble. When he realized the car had over-heated and there was nothing we could do but wait, he produced a bottle of red wine to help the time speed past. In turn we offered him a drink of our warm grapefruit juice which he wisely declined.

Leaving us to finish the beverages, he chugged off, promising to warn the *Residente* in Belet Uen of our coming.

I'd finished writing in my diary and was trying to balance accounts of the last week while Mil was checking the tires and letting air out of them. "Golly," I called to Mil, "do you know Bublee cost more than both of us put together! $21 for gas, and $16 for repair. The hotel was only twenty shillings a night for the room – $20 for the week! With all that entertaining, we spent only $10 for food and $5 for all those aperitifs! Another five dollars for washing and three dollars miscellaneous. That's it."

"Don't forget that silly orange prayer hat you bought," Mil teased. "What did you put that under? Entertainment? And those sandals you have on, didn't you just buy them?"

"Oh, they don't come under any daily expenses. I have a special category for personal things. They were only 30 shillings together; that's only a bit over four dollars." I did some more figuring. "Even including the shoes and hat, that's $84 for a week in town and two days on the way, so we're well within the ten dollar a day budget. So there, I'm glad I bought them".

We sipped the wine slowly, and by the time the bottle was finished the car was cool enough to go on. I promptly fell asleep, and was awakened only when I felt Mil slow down to stop. "Look, there's the Commissioner again," he laughed. And there he was, sitting calmly under an acacia tree drinking another bottle of wine while his driver sweated out changing a flat. We offered condolences, returned the empty wine bottle with thanks, and asked him to have an aperitif with us later in Belet Uen. It all seemed so civilized.

It was already dusk, and we began to think we had passed the turn off the town since the road went straight on up to the border. Suddenly, as we rounded a curve, we could see a few electric lights twinkling in a gray depression to the left. No longer startled by lights in the midst of nothingness we simply drove toward the largest cluster and found them ringing a small outdoor cafe. Not surprisingly, there sat the *Residente*, having his aperitif. He waved for us to join him after first dispatching a servant to open the guest house for us. We sat on rudely fashioned chairs under the bare lights which were only slightly softened by the Mimosa branches waving slightly in the evening breeze. Beneath the unsteady tables the sand and dust had matted to a soft carpet. It was pleasant, but still frontier. The light seemed to intensify the gloom beyond; like an actor on the stage. This is perhaps how the Italians wanted to live here in Somalia, I thought, oblivious of the people and life outside the circle of light.

The guest house was pure luxury with running (unsticky) water, shower, and a flush toilet, a convenience we were not to enjoy again until Addis Ababa. There was a pantry alcove next to the bathroom, replete with a kerosene refrigerator; ice for drinks, no doubt. Our kerosene was too valuable to expend on so much comfort, though, so I put the grapefruit in a bowl of cold water instead. The furniture in all the rooms – living, dining, two terraces, and bedroom – were brightly new; the inner spring mattresses looked so inviting that I wondered if we could stay awake long enough to eat. The *Residente* had even sent over sheets for us to use. I couldn't help comparing this guest house with the unfinished brick one in Garissa where we had slept on the floor. We showered, filled the water bags, and decided to eat.

The bungalow had a cook hut out back meant for a servant; it seemed a bother and undignified to use it. I had just set out the primus on the terrace wall when the Provincial Commissioner arrived and insisted we eat dinner with him at the cafe. Full of energy, in contrast to our thoroughly exhausted demeanor, the Commissioner arranged for our passports to be stamped during the night so that we could leave early in the morning. On second thought, he also gave us a letter for the border police, to speed our way through customs. And although we didn't ask, he ordered a soldier to go with Mil in the morning to buy petrol from the government supplies. Over dinner we talked about his experiences in the old Somaliland and his brushes with tribal warfare. It all seemed as distant as if we were discussing a movie. Yet next morning, after a hurried cup of coffee, we ourselves drove onto this movie set ... where there was no kind director to call "time", and no doubles to take over when the action became dangerous.

THE SOMALI BORDER GUARDS at Ferfer were smartly turned out in khaki shorts, shirts, and caps, standing at attention with their rifles by their sides. Despite our letter from the Commissioner, it was over an hour before we could continue. The actual formalities didn't take long. I helped a Somali clerk fill in the carnet while Mil took the passports into another office. This man was an Italian, and apparently lonely, for he kept Mil talking for half and hour. I amused myself by walking through the border camp, a collection of square mud-and-wattle huts occasionally shored up with a sheet of corrugated iron, the whole surrounded by a stockade: posts interwoven with grass. Beyond the stockade were the skin-covered rounded huts of the nomads. The women were frankly curious about me, touched my skirt, and compared the color of their sand-bleached feet with my naturally white ones. In turn I admired their amber necklaces worn even by baby girls and took a picture of one slender woman whose stringy hair bunched about her face. They made me understand that only unmarried women wore long hair; the mark

Nomadic huts, woven mats covering a collapsible
lattice framework, are easily moved

of a matron was short hair or a shaved head bound under a
scarf. For once my haircut was in style.

We held our breath as we drove past the raised barrier
and crossed into Ethiopia, for we were expecting the worst
from the Ethiopian customs officials. We had no "move-
ment pass" which the Ethiopian Airways chap we met in Nairobi had suggested we should get; we had no special automobile permit which the Automobile Association had told us was required. We had only our carnet and an expired visa on our passports. The original visa was good for four months; we had been unable to extend it because,

Somali nomads wander the
Ogaden ignoring artificial borders

contrary to our expectations, there was no Ethiopian representative in Kenya. How we were to explain this, and in what language, I didn't know. We'd debated changing the date ourselves, but most of the visa was in the Amharic language and we had no idea whether the date might appear in a different scrip.

Counting on female charm, I presented the passports myself, entering a small office, so dark that the dark face of the official was almost invisible. But not his welcoming smile. "Donastily," I murmured, having just learned the word for "hello" from the Somali women. The man barely glanced at the passports, returned them, and gestured to a further hut across the road. "Preliminary check, I'll bet," I told Mil as he drove the car over to the hut and parked under a tree.

A plump genial man came out of the hut and up to the car. I tried my "donastily" on him, and he replied in English, which he said he had learned from a Swedish missionary in Dira Dawa. He stamped the carnet, warned us about the road, and we were through. We got back in the car not really believing the good luck.. Then as we were backing into the road a soldier ran up and held his arm. "Oh, oh, here it comes," I moaned. Not understanding the soldier's gestures, Mil went back after the customs man. The soldier was a bit wild looking, his khaki uniform was rumpled, and he swung his rifle about frightening abandon. Twice he tried to get into the back seat, and I wondered whether we were to be plundered or accused of smuggling. It was neither, according to the custom's official. Each vehicle which passed through was assigned a soldier as guard. Mil looked at the soldier and had the same reaction to him that I had. So we politely declined the offer saying that we had no space for him. This was not entirely true, as we could easily have rearranged the back seat to make space for me. In fact, we felt we'd be safer without this unkempt soldier who had seemed extremely surly when he was told we had refused his services.

Suddenly it occurred to Mil to ask the customs man which side of the road to drive on... still the left. Armed with this superfluous information – we didn't meet another vehicle for days – we drove off.

Just beyond the huts I noticed a milestone with a face, – Mussolini's perhaps – on it above the words: imperial strada. I wanted to take a picture, but Mil didn't think we should stop within sight of the custom post since we had repeatedly been warned that picture-taking was against the law in Ethiopia. Hardly had we passed the milestone than the imperial road petered out into a gravel track, and we cut our speed accordingly. The only remnants of Mussolini's dream were a few plank bridges which crossed deep-out stream beds. From the violence of the gashes, it would seem that the rain, which averages a mere three or four inches a year, must come all in one cloudburst. Despite the bridges, we noticed tire tracks running around them, crossing the stream beds at distant points, then joining up with the track again. Did this

Mil checks a plank bridge over
a wadi in the Ogaden

mean the bridges wouldn't hold traffic? Mil tested each one carefully: two we went over, another we went around. There were other gullies with no bridges and each crossing had to be surveyed for rocks too big, or ruts too deep, for our light car. Several times in the depression we scraped front and rear bumpers, and were glad Bublee's overhang was as short as it was. Still, somewhere in the Ogaden is a guard from the rear bumper. We only noticed it was missing when we stopped to fill the tank from a jerry tin. I was very glad Mil had been driving!

The road wound around flat-topped limestone hills which were covered with a low thorny scrub. Not surprisingly, the area was deserted with not even birds to vary the monotonous scenery. There was still enough gravel on the track to make reasonable time except where sand had drifted or water carried off the smaller surface and left exposed the rocky base. The desolation made us look forward even more to a stop at the geologist tent. Tom had told us that the oil company was surveying in the Ogaden and they had set up camp near a dot on the map called Lamma Bar. We had expected to reach there in mid-morning. When we finally spotted the camp midway up a hill next to a half-build Italian stone chapel it was well after noon. Three tents were pitched in the lee of the tent. Beyond them was a Higgins trailer, an army "six by six", a "Power Wagon", and a small tank. At the sound of an engine, the camp swarmed with Ethiopians in various stages of undress, obviously still groggy from napping. Most retreated in surprise before the sight of a female, but a mechanic, who had been fiddling with one wagon when we drove up, informed us in slangy English that the geologist, Metaysic, was out and that he usually did not come back until sunset.

Assuming that we planned to wait, the head servant,

Abda, motioned us into the trailer where he had already set out two glasses of cold, but horrid tasting, water. We sat on two folding chairs squashed in between the bunk beds and the removable table. The canvas flaps were down to keep out the sun, and somehow it seemed a bit less hot inside than in the unstructured glare. Abda brought some apple juice, also cold and much better tasting. As we ate our own crackers and sardines, we leafed through the *Saturday Evening Posts* and *New Yorkers* scattered on top of and under the bunks. First Mil, then I, moved onto the bunks. Clinging to this haven as shipwrecked sailors to a raft, we began to invent reasons for staying.

"We really ought to talk to this Metaysic about the condition of the road," suggested Mil.

"He should know which route is possible," I said, in capacity of navigator. "This map gives two first class roads on it, and we know neither exists. Maybe he can draw a route for us."

"Besides," added Mil, "Bublee is so hot; she will go better at night."

"Well," I hesitated, remembering the nomads we had met on our way to Kismayu, "we could leave very early in the morning. But it does delay us a day, if it should rain."

"This fellow Metaysic is probably lonely and would like to see us." Mil returned sleepily, "Let's toss a coin."

"Never mind," I managed to say before we both fell asleep.

ABOUT FOUR, ABDA CAME in with more juice, turned the radio on for us, and at my request, gave me a guided tour of the establishment. In one tent were four Ethiopian soldiers, sent along with the expedition to guard them against *shiftas*. Right then I decided we would spend the night safe in camp. Abda shared the largest tent with the cook, two mechanics, and two drivers. The third tent was badly torn, and was only used for storing supplies. The cook had rigged a tarp from the back of the chapel to serve as his kitchen. The baby-sized frig, like the lights and radio, ran off a portable gasoline generator. All water, cooking and washing, came out of the five hundred gallon mobile tank which was filled whenever anyone went to report or collect supplies at the drilling camp in Galladi, west of Wardere. It seemed like a long way to go for water, and indeed they sometimes went into Ferfer instead. But mail and magazines were flown into Galladi; besides Metaysic, or his Ethiopian assistant who shared the trailer, were apparently always glad for an excuse to see their friends.

At that point, the boys would have been glad to see Metaysic. He hadn't come in yet, and it was late. The setting sun took all the harshness out of the bleak landscape, picking up a pink tint in the sandstone out-cropping. The sight was blotted out when Abda turned on a string of yellow lights hung from end to end of the camp. We opened some tins and – ah luxury – had the cook stir up the soup and heat the lima beans. While we ate Abda told us why everyone was so worried. Three weeks before Metaysic got lost and wasn't found for twenty-four hours. By that time a driver had dashed over to Galladi and returned with all the Somalis at that camp. They'd even hired another twenty Somalis at the local well and were planning a complete sweep of the area. An airplane had been radioed for and hospitals alerted in Belet Uen, Mogadishu, and Dira Dawa. When Metaysic drove in the next day, all alone – he had not been "found" by anyone – he insisted he had never been lost at all, had merely been too busy surveying to return to camp the night before. Later that evening Metaysic told us his own version of the story, concluding that had he known about the search he would most certainly have hidden a day or two to make it all worth while.

Remembering all the fuss the time before, the two drivers, a mechanic, and the four soldiers piled themselves and their woolen overcoats into a truck and went out into the blackness to search for Metaysic. Perhaps ten minutes later another set of lights appeared over a hill and made directly for the camp.

Metaysic climbed out of the cab of another Power Wagon and greeted us as though our presence in camp were a most usual occurrence. He was a short, wiry man, with long sun-bleached hair standing almost straight up in a tangle. His litheness made him seem younger than his 32 years; in sloppy khaki shirt and pants, high boots, he looked perfect for the part. On the other hand Desta, his assistant, looked reasonably trim, though he tended to imitate his boss in every other way.

Abda lost no time in producing a Scotch and water which Metaysic drank chugalug. "Cuts the taste of the water," he laughed, relaxing into a chair outside the trailer. "Those silly yellow lights," he said, "make me feel like a side show attraction. The experts say yellow lights aren't supposed to draw bugs like white ones do. Guess nobody educated the bugs here in the Ogaden, huh, Desta?"

Food appeared, as nondescript as ours had been. As they ate, Metaysic gave a running commentary on our trip. It was very unsettling.

"Road is easy to Scillave. Can't miss the turn, there's a well that's always crowded with Somalis and their camels. Don't go straight, though it looks better. Road just stops after a bit. Turn right and go until Wardere. If you can. That part's really rough. Uphill for seven miles, nothing but sand. We go though in these here Power Wagons in four wheel drive and our fingers crossed. Three jeeps turned over there and once a car was stuck for three days. Pretty much every man for himself out here. Better not try that stretch at night. If you get stuck going up, maybe you should turn around and come back. Dangerous to stop. *Shiftas*, you know. Haven't heard of any trouble in this month, but there's always a first time. That's why we have those four soldiers...aren't they back yet? Used to be six. Wasn't a Somali around when we set up camp in January. Now they steal our triangulation flags if we leave them unattended. If they see you stuck, anyone is likely to turn *shifta*. Got a gun? They all carry guns, but it's a part of their dress. Lot of them don't work, were left over after the war. I suppose some do work, and that the ex-soldiers know how to aim, though I've never seen one shoot anything at all." He gulped the rest of his coffee. "Don't let me change your plans."

CHAPTER 23

# Crossing the Ogaden: shiftas and sand

THE ALARM WENT OFF AT 3.30 AM; DESPITE THE CONSTANT drumming of Metaysic's words in my head, I must have slept. The cots and mattresses we had been loaned were much more comfortable then our car bed; but with only one blanket I had shivered when the wind blew gusts in my face, and sneezed from the dust. We washed ourselves awake, drank coffee from the thermos, and were out of camp before dawn even stained the sky. Then, as the light began, the thorn bushes looked abloom. Birds, gaudy ones in purples, maroons, and yellows that seemed to have taken their combinations from Easter eggs, others in faded colors with beaks larger than their heads, perched on the angular branches or skitted across the road in front of the car.

We approached the last bridge. Metaysic had said was

passable, but Mil still checked it before motioning me to drive across. The bridge held all right, even though the boards were rotting, but the front tire picked up a six inch cleat. After all the talk of *shiftas,* it didn't seem wise to chance the desert with no spare. Mil changed the tire and we headed desolately back to the geologist's camp. They were just getting up. The mechanics took the tire and worked on patching the eight holes in the tube while we sat down to breakfast. It was a very hot eight o'clock when we finally pulled out of the camp, with many thanks given and good lucks received.

Back through bleakness, the birds had fled. The only thing which flapped was my old straw hat which I'd tied on my head with a scarf in hopes it might somehow keep me cooler. We left the car's hood hooked half open, hoping the wind would help cool the engine, but soon we were all boiling.

As Metaysic said, you couldn't miss Scillave. Long before we got there, the sand ahead had seemed to undulate, as a mirage. This turned out to be backs of hundreds of camels milling about around the large stone wells, one on either side of the road. The road crossed a slight depression which must become a stream bed one or two days a year. The course of the river was marked by much larger, fuller acacias, and in the shade of these trees lay camels, and sheep, and even a few scraggly cows. Perhaps these cows belonged to the inhabitants of the six grass huts which lined the road just before the Y. We turned right, away from the graveled road and onto what looked like a stretch of lovely back sand.

"Mil, this can't be right," I said, uncertainly. Mil stopped the car to check the map while I walked across the road to a group of Somalis to ask them if this was the way to Wardere. The Somalis took one look, and ran, from me, or my hat I wondered. We backed onto the gravel road and went up it a few miles, but there was no turn-off. So once again we started across the sand.

It is like sailing, driving across the sand, heeling first on one side, then the other, riding the ridges as waves, allowing for the push of the sand as we slither around corners. We tried to avoid running along the troughs because the high-piled sand scraped the bottom of the car; rocks or chunks of wood hidden by the drifting sand could easily knock a hole in the sump or bang up the exhaust. For a time the sensation is almost pleasant, and I pooh-pooh Metaysic's warnings as meant for greenhorns. I relaxed enough to notice that the vegetation was changing from low scrub thorn to less frequent but larger acacia trees. Every so often a bush had been broken over and its top branches burned as though a hasty meal had been prepared right there. Occasionally the whole tree had burned, setting fire to the area around until sooner or later the fire would reach a wide stretch of sand and burn itself out.

Imperceptibly, the road began to climb, and the sand got sandier. I said so to Mil, and he said it wasn't possible, and we were still arguing about this when we ran into a particularly big drift. We had to go out into the heat to fasten cleats on to the rear tires and lay down wire mesh sand tracks. Then PUSH – or rather a series of rocking pulses such as we'd learned that time we got stuck near Malindi. Suddenly, Bublee and I were up and away leaving Mil behind, trudging up the incline and dragging the wire mesh. Stuck again, repeat process. This time I drove for almost a mile, daring only to stop at fairly level spot. Then for some time, a reprieve. Next time we were stuck I did the walking. Again, but now we were really stuck. We tried the mesh, we tried jacking the car and collecting sticks to push under the tires,

As the elevation increased slightly, Bublee became stuck in the sand

still the car wouldn't move. Next we tried excavating the sand from under the chassis; still stuck.

Deflate the tires. Rock and accelerate, rock and accelerate, til Mil was absolutely exhausted. There was no question of turning back; if the car went any direction it could only go forward. Mil staggered to a near-by acacia and sat beneath its half-shade. I rushed to mix glucose with juice, orange this time.

"The powder dissolves more easily when the juice is hot," I observed to Mil, "at least that is an advantage." Mil growled back. Suddenly I felt terribly guilty: I am the committed feminist, the great believer in equality, shares on everything, one hour driving each. But even though Mil was still weak from his jaundice, in all this heat he has been doing most of the work: digging while I collected branches, walking while I drove. Abashed, I went back to the car and pushed

An exhausted Mil found a little
shade under an acacia tree

sticks under the front wheels, fixed the rest of the juice and gave it to Mil. I decided gaiety was the only thing, and Mil did look like an illustration from the Rubaiyat of Omar Khayyam: a glass of juice and thou beneath a tree... As I took his picture I noticed a large black bird sitting on a nearby stump. An even larger, nastier bird circled above, a vulture!

"Good God," Mil muttered, "the vultures are in a hurry." With a sudden spurt of energy he was back at the car, letting out still more air from the tires. Bublee struggled and spurted as Mil rocked and I gunned the engine. Unexpectedly she suddenly lifts, almost air borne, and I was off, tearing almost literally from low to third, to second, to first, to second...., to third. Slaoosh, and I skidded to a stop. I could hardly see Mil, and waded back along the track to help him carry the mesh and the jack and the shovel.

"Couldn't you run around and jump in when she starts to move?" I asked, after Mil has refused to let me do the pushing. We rocked and gunned again, and this time I knew the feeling of the lift and screamed to Mil to come. He only pushed harder, and Bublee spurted ahead. I honk and he ran along the side, still pushing. "Get in," I screamed, and somehow he does, and we're off. For mile it is skid and go, grinding from gear to gear, I have never felt so a part of a car, or imagined that a car was human. Bublee chuffs and gurgles, responding to the sand and not to the accelerator which I have to floor most of the time... except that there was no time as we struggled up the hill.

Time only began when we topped the crest and bumped along a rocky track. Somehow knowing the climb was over, Bublee choked on a vapor lock. We stopped under the first tree to let her rest, chasing away a flock of untended goats from their shade. Mil pushed some crackers and cheese at me: he'd already eaten his while I drove.

"You must be tired," sympathized Mil, "you realize it was four and a half hours ago that we left Scillave? You've driven for almost all of it, except when we were stuck. Better let me spell you." And in a moment, continued. "Good thing those were only vultures and not *shiftas*." He leaned over and kissed my sweaty cheek.

A camel caravan was plodding up the road behind us; it seemed best to continue. Over the next rise we caught a glimpse of palm trees, a white minaret poking its finger up behind them. Permanent square grass huts, round skin huts of the nomads, rose out of the sand. Quickly the scene was populated with camels, goats, and people. Wardere!

To the left of the road was a barbed-wire enclosure housing government offices. There was even a sentry at the guard box which, strangely to me, faced town. Wouldn't attacks come from the desert? We drove into the yard to ask for directions and road conditions. A pleasant official pointed out the road to Awareh and assured us that is was much better than the one we had just come over. We prayed so. Almost as an afterthought he asked to see our passports, leafed casually through them, seemed to wave us on as he retired to the cool of his hut-office. As we were backing out, several men rushed out of another hut and ran towards us, arms waving.

More soldiers for guards, we thought, and resolutely continuing backing. Just as we started forward one man reached the window and yelled at us something that sounded like "customs". I looked at Mil and he looked at me; our reaction was the same. We drove on, pretending not to understand, waving a gay goodbye to the six or so men still standing in the sun. Both of us remembered the stories we had heard about self-appointed customs officers who demand contributions from every vehicle that passed the town, for in the desert each settlement is law unto itself. Only much later did we learn that it was all quite legitimate: though Wardare is several hundred miles from the border, as the last town in Ethiopia proper it actually is the customs point. We should have stopped.

The road was better, a level sand track bordered by bush. Vegetation seemed a bit more abundant, some of it must have been the famed aromatic frankincense and myrrh. The thorny acacia was still everywhere, but fuller mimosa also abounded. In the shade of these leafier trees we would often see clusters of brilliant blue francoline, or flocks of long-necked brown fowl busily gossiping. Jackals and rabbits scampered across the road. Gazelles leaped and bounded: delicate long ones, shorter grayer ones, and a sort of greenish Dik Dik. Bright blue bustards and less flashy brown and white birds circled lazily. But again, though the road was crisscrossed with hoof marks, not a person or herd was to be seen.

Bublee was making boiling noises, and a rattle under the car grew perceptibly worse. We hardly heard the convoy until it stopped there before us: two Thorneycrafts, a Power Wagon, and an old British army truck, all bearing the symbol of the "Locusts". The English leader of the Locust Control expedition jumped down and greeted us as though we were long time friends. We stood in the shade smoking, while all the cargo riders jumped off the trucks and practically disappeared into the bush.

"They do that. The bush seems so sparse, yet they can just melt into it," observed the Englishman, with affection in his voice. "Yet I haven't seen a *shifta* all day. Too dry. Should have rained, but hasn't, guess the Somalis are all busy searching for water. Still, the acting DC in Awareh made me take this guard along." He indicated a nattily dressed Somali Scout, whose turtle-necked blue sweater over khaki shorts and khaki turban with blue badge was quite a contrast to the Ethiopian soldiers we'd seen in the last few days who seemed to sleep in their uniforms. "Where's you guard?" he asked, as we pulled off the track to let the convoy pass, "Aren't you worried about the *shiftas*?"

Lightheartedly, we dismissed the question as we waved good-bye for we were confident the worst was behind us. The sand was less and less red, and the road took on a more solid base. Still there was a sandy overlay, and you had to watch the track every minute to avoid the sudden rock outcroppings. Crossing dry stream beds, the way would often split into five or six separate sets of tracks wandering far apart across the sand. We were constantly worried that one set might be a side road which would get us thoroughly lost. There was no way to tell one road from another. Sometimes, too, there were deep depressions where rain obviously collects; there the track became sun-baked ridges, miserable to drive across. Sometimes these ruts were partly filled with branches, which helped us see, if not miss them. As the sun set, the slanting rays exaggerated every bump and we barely crawled along. The night had closed in before we reached a cluster of huts, dimly lit with oil lamps. Mil got out and checked with the guards; they were Somali Scouts. This settlement was Dik: we were entering the Reserve Area, technically Ethiopian land at that time, but administered by the British. Somehow, we felt safer as we pushed on toward Awareh, 47 miles away.

At night, the road was deceptive. The rocky parts were often so smooth we thought the road had been paved. Then the track would divide itself in a run across a sandy stretch, and seem to be a six-lane highway. We saw headlights: a broken-down truck being escorted back to Dik by a jeep-load of Scouts. They waved cheerfully at us we passed. Again we felt reassured.

We were both so tired that we switched off driving every half hour or so. To stay alert we started a game of "My grandmother went to London and with her she took..." only changing the name of the town to Hargeisha. I can still remember almost half the alphabet, it's as indelibly etched on my mind as the trip itself: grapefruit, francoline, elephants, dik dik, chewing gum, (that's not fair for "c" said Mil, but it stayed), bambuti, aphrodisiacs. This diversion lightened our spirits though we were both very tense.

Headlights again? No, a Somali lion, lacking the majesty of a maned king of the forest, was mesmerized by our headlights. We turned them off a second, and he was gone. Further on, a barricade of bush blocked the road, and fear came back with a rush. So many people had warned us that the *shiftas'* favorite trick was to block a road, attack you when you stopped to move the bush. Without a second thought I careened off the road into the blackness in the right, bouncing and barging away full tilt and didn't let the accelerator up for at least five miles.

Anything to occupy out thoughts. Mil taught me a complicated version of "Twenty Questions", and we played it without thinking, all the gaiety gone. Lights in the distance, a whole cluster. No electric ones, these, but the blue-white glare of the pressure kerosene lamp. The Somalis in a coffee hut pointed yonder to a tent when we asked for the DC. It was after nine.

Our headlights swept a dark brown tent, and a stocky man came out. "Why, hello," he said, "were you looking for me? I'm the DC here. Vaughn-Davis is the name. Come in and meet my wife. We're just having some sherry."

The front section of the tent was made more comfortable by rugs over the tarp on the ground. Easy canvas chairs and small non-mobile tables were the only furniture. But various cases and trunks were stacked to make a bookcase. A flap concealed the camp cots. In its own compartment behind was a tin bathtub and a commode. A second tent beyond housed the kitchen. Even in my tiredness, the romance of a tent appealed to me; it seemed so much more appropriate to the environment than we did with our automobile.

My hands were so shaky from tenseness and tiredness that I couldn't hold the sherry glass without spilling; impolitely I gulped the glassful. Mrs. Vaughn-Davis signaled the bearer to fill it again. This time I managed to be more polite as the warmth of the company and the drink relaxed me.

"You do look exhausted," Mrs. Vaughn-Davis sympathized. "Have you just come from Hargeisha today?"

"No," I replied, "that's where we're going. We came over from Lamma Bar today, where the Sinclair geologist's camp is." I started to tell her about our false start and the flat tire, but her husband broke in.

"Where is your guard? Did you drop him in the market?"

"We didn't have one," answered Mil. "An Ethiopian soldier offered to come, but we said we didn't have any room. Actually, he looked so untrustworthy we thought it would be safer without him."

The DC stared at us, incredulously. "That was foolish. I know those soldiers look like rogues, but so far there has been no trouble with them." He shook his head, still amazed. "You were lucky to get here, you know," he breathed softly, "that's a dangerous route. Didn't you know that the old DC, a brigadier-general he was, too, got himself shot dead a few months back. Of course it was a fluke; he was riding in a jeep. But the *shiftas* have been mighty bold since then. Speared a Locust chap, but he's recovered. Worse, last week they dared to attack a truck-load of Somali Scouts just outside Dik. Had themselves a tidy little battle. We've had double patrols out since then, but of course that's only a gesture. Did you see any signs of *shiftas*?"

"We aren't sure," Mil said, "but about thirty miles back it looked like as though someone had laid an ambush across the road. We didn't stop to investigate."

The DC was nodding his head. "That's near where the fight was the other day. God, you were lucky."

I must have paled at his words. I don't think I had really been frightened til then. Mrs. Vaughn-Davis looked at me, suggested tactfully to her husband, "They'd probably like a wash. Couldn't they use the DC's house for the night? I'm sure they could do with a good rest."

"Of course," agreed the DC. "The house has been vacant since the DC's wife moved out. You see I'm just acting DC til his replacement comes. I was just assigned here a month before the old boy died, and I'm really only Assistant DC. Come, I'll take you over. The place is a mess, but there are beds with rubber-foam mattresses."

"You must come back for dinner," said his wife, and I gratefully accepted, offering her the cans we already had taken out for our meal. The dinner was much better than could have come from cans, and we ate hungrily after our twenty-hour day. The DC kept looking at me, and then at his wife, and murmuring how lucky we were to have gotten through. Apparently, even without red hair I would have been worth one or two hundred camels. He was inclined to agree with the Locust official that the dryness of the season was in our favor. "The Somalis love their battles," he said in the tone of an exasperated father, "but they love their camels even more. Now they have to search for water; but after the rains start, they will take blood for any slight, imagined or real. Supposing a fellow is hurt falling off a truck he has no business riding on. He will blame the driver and go collect his family to fight the driver and his family, and fight to kill!"

"Incredible," said Mil, feeling very happy we heard all these tales after, not before, we crossed the Ogaden.

"We've tried to stop these feuds by hitting the Somalis where it hurts. We fine the whole tribe, five or six shillings a male for a serious clash, and then hold the necessary number of camels until the fine is paid. This keeps the tribe busy for a few months, earning their camels back by working on the road, building walls, and so on. But as soon as their camels are back, they are at it again."

The night wind was chilly, and he got up to close the front flap before continuing. "The Sinclair boys have had quite a time with the tribes, too. The Somalis fight vehicles as though they were alive, throwing boulders at the windscreen, breaking spears against doors. Once a truck was put out of commission when someone built a bush fire under the differential. Luckily the fire was caught before the whole truck burned. You said you met an oil man down in Mogadishu, Tom something-or-other. Did he tell you why he is confined to the city? He's really an expert on drilling, but he got caught in the middle of a feud, and had to shoot his own way out. In doing so he killed a Somali. Too dangerous for him to come up-country again. The whole tribe is out for his blood." He gave a half smile. "At least it's an interesting place!"

WE WERE TOO EXHAUSTED to have nightmares. In fact we felt exhilarated at having finished what we felt surely must have been the Trip's Worst Day. Next morning we as eager as ever. After we had breakfast with the Vaughn-Davis', Mil went off with the ADC to find out more about administering desert tribes. The problems were particularly difficult in the Reserve Area. When the Horn of Africa was divided up among Britain, Italy, and Ethiopia, the interior boundaries were never fully recognized. It was a border incident near Wardere that had given Italy an excuse to invade Ethiopia back in 1936. Somalia and Ethiopia were still quarreling over the line. When the division was made, no one knew or cared much about the barren plateau where the Somalis grazed their herds.

Over forty percent of the tribes from British Somaliland graze their livestock in the Ogaden. Since the British first went into Somaliland in 1884-86 to protect the tribes in exchange for trading concessions, the British claimed the right to protect the tribes irregardless of where they moved. The Ethiopians, whose penal code is considerably harsher than that of the British, also claimed the right to administer law to the tribes whenever they strayed into Ethiopian territory. The distinction between Ethiopian and British Somalis is most confusing. During World War II, the British military administration partitioned the Horn by tribal migration routes rather than by neat lines on a map. Thus the 25,000 square mile Reserve Area was attached to British Somaliland because the nomadic inhabitants go back and forth. Two years after we drove through, the area was officially ceded back to Ethiopia, over protests of the Somalis themselves who tried to appeal to the UN by asking a very fundamental question: how could Britain give away something it never owned? The basic problems remain: a clash of authority between the Ethiopians and the British who still have rights to maintain liaison officers and police within the Ogaden to protect the migrant tribes.

"A logical turn-about of our rights here in the Reserve Area," the DC had said, "would be for Ethiopia to demand policing rights within our borders. So far they haven't tried that though they did try to get Italian Somaliland after the war. Instead they are now trying to persuade the Somalis to join Ethiopia when we eventually pull out. Not a chance of that, though. No love is lost between the Copts and the Muslims, even in their own country. The Ethiopians are very much afraid of this United Somaliland idea and accuse us of continuing to foster it. We started the idea during the war when we tried to unite Italian Somaliland with the British Somaliland and the Ogaden, but the Ethiopians wouldn't buy that. I think they would like to take over all of Somaliland themselves, especially French Somaliland, so they'd have the railroad. No matter what happens internationally, here on the border trouble will increase when we leave. The Somalis won't recognize the Ethiopian border and will certainly fight, even over this place."

His arm indicated the barren desert and a flagpole surrounded on three sides by wattle huts. The flag was a local, unofficial one, bearing the English name for Ogaden: Haud. A marketplace faced the open end of the U. Mrs. Vaughn-Davis and I, followed at a discreet distance by five Somali police, wandered through the area while the men talked. The police kept off the herds of curious children by their official stares. But they wouldn't help me persuade the women – there were few men in the market – to let me take their pictures. I tried some dodges, for which the Rollie is useful, of looking one way and pointing the camera another. Mrs. Vaughn-Davis said there was some belief that if you die you won't go to heaven if there is a likeness of you, such as your photo or painting, still on earth. That and shyness, she thought, made the women hide from the camera.

Beehive huts of the nomads were grouped very near the bazaar and we walked over to them. My companion called these huts *agal*. The covering of these mobile homes was not skin, as I had always imagined, but grass or bark fiber mats. I caught sight of a few desert women, lean and tall, dressed in plain bleached cloth tied over the shoulder. Their scarves, usually in faded reds, added the only color to the drab surroundings. The settlement women, who lived in the wattle-and-daub huts called *arish*, wore bright sarongs with equally bright loose-fitting shirts on top. As if that were brightness enough, most of them had large black or white head-coverings. But I did see one woman with a European-type dress over a sarong, both in bright and clashing colors; her scarf, too, was colored. Some women were cooking on charcoal braziers, others chased chickens, one was milking a cow; most simply stared as we passed. Suddenly we came on a very differently dressed woman. She wore a full length, full-sleeved dress in a odd diamond and flower pattern over which she wore a white knit jerkin. Her shoes were laced, and rather new. But it was her face that really startled me: she wore sunglasses, and her hair was caught in a bulbous scarf. Later I would have known she was an Amhara, the aristocratic group that rules Ethiopia. She had no shyness at all, and quite ignored me while I took her picture.

As we neared the government compound, we were back in man's territory. Unlike the women, the men posed for pictures. A regal old man, all in white, with a white-tipped beard, must have been a chief. His two equally tall companions wore red-checked sarongs – like something on a beer-hall table – and yellowing shirts; both had headscarves and turbans to guard against the sun.

We found Mil and the DC talking to another Locust Control chap who was complaining about the lack of cooperation he was getting from the tribes. Somehow the Somalis had decided the gammexane powder, which the Control people put out to kill the locusts, also killed the goats. He wanted the DC to help. A felt-hatted Ethiopian waited to talk to he DC; he wanted help on a matter of taxes. One Somali tribe, which grazed the whole year in the Ogaden and thus technically were not of concern to the British, had consistently refused to pay Ethiopian taxes because they claimed the area was British. The Ethiopian tax collector wore a dark suit coat over thin shorts. His dark glasses and unshaven face somehow combined to make him both haughty and distant; the Somalis, equally proud, carefully ignored him.

CHAPTER 24

# British Somaliland sets
# a different pattern

*L*ATE IN THE MORNING WE DROVE ON TO HARGEISHA, CAPITAL OF British Somaliland, taking with us various letters from Vaughn-Davis including a highly classified official report. Security was good between the two towns and the ADC was not concerned about his unofficial couriers, but we were about to leave so his dispatch would arrive more quickly. The drive, though no super-highway, presented no difficulty. Most of the way the scenery was extremely barren, becoming a real sandy desert for about ten miles. We looked at the sand drifts on either side of the gravel road and felt very lucky not to be out there pushing. Dust clouds on the horizon were raised by herds of migrating camels. Then, far down below in the greenery along the river bank, we saw the modest little capital. Until the war, Berbera had been the cool-season capital of British Somaliland while Upper Sheikh was the hot weather capital. Apparently the constant moving bothered no one; nomadic habits are natural to the area. But the war-time military administration moved the capital to Hargeisha because of its better communications. The returning civilian administration had just followed suit.

There are three macadamed streets in Hargeisha, and we went up and down each one several times trying to deliver the classified report. At one end of the streets the Somali huts clustered; closer in were the adobe homes of the Indian traders and the two-storey stone shops of the Arabs. At the other end of town was a small cantonment area lacking the permanence and assurance that cantonments in India exhibit. Government offices and the British Club were between the business and European residential areas. The whole town was cut by the dry river bed that we had crossed on the Irish bridge several times before we even realized it was a "bridge."

With the help of a police *askari* we finally traced Mr. Appleton to his office. He immediately asked us to lunch with him the next day, Sunday. "We're worried about the rain," I explained, "so we think we had better push on. But thank you anyhow."

"Look out the window," he instructed. "Those clouds are raining along the border. Better wait a day for the roads to dry. Besides, the Ethiopian customs are closed on Sundays. You're staying at the Club, aren't you? I'll pick you up about eleven then. Thank you for the report." As we were leaving he added, "Oh, and by-the-by, I wouldn't cross the river after six tonight. Flash floods from the rain, you know; can't drive across the bridge. But we've just finished a foot suspension bridge; before that if the river was running, there was no way to cross it. I live on the other side of the river, and before that bridge was built I spent many a night here in the office.

Don't play with those floods; the water often comes like a tidal wave and people are always getting drowned."

Actually Mr. Appleton was an hour off. I watched the river bed carefully from our plain little room in the Club which, without running water and with little furniture, resembled a room in a pleasant summer cabin. At seven there were only a few puddles from a local shower in the river bed. A roar and a swish, and the water was over six feet deep. As I watched, I shuddered with premonition.

Fortunately, the Italian Club was on our side of the river. We ate there with Attila Morassi, a small sincere Ethiopian citizen of Austrian and French ancestry whose wife was a stunning petite Italian. He acted as a sort of local representative of the Sinclair oil company whose truck convoys, running between Dira Dawa and Galladi, used Morassi's garage and repair shop and guest house. We had looked him up to check on road conditions and his news was not encouraging. The last convoy to come over from Ethiopia had been held up four days by rain. Still, he cheered us, the rain on the border that day didn't look too heavy. He himself was driving a Power Wagon to Dira Dawa on Monday and would be glad to have us accompany him. That way he could pull us out of ditches if we got stuck. He warned us about the customs men at the border town of Jigjiga. When we mentioned our expired visa, Morassi looked at the passports, and checked the Amharic writing. Then he strongly advised us to extend the time limit on it ourselves just to avoid any chance of trouble. With only slight guiltiness, we did just that.

The dinner was cut short by my first really bad attack of diarrhea. I crawled unhappily into bed, and stayed there until Mr. Appleton collected us the next morning. Meanwhile, Mil had taken the car to Morassi's garage for a check over. Amazingly there was nothing basically wrong. The battery water was low from all the boiling, but no one in Hargeisha had distilled water. Morassi suggested we catch rain water next time we hit a shower. "It will give you something to do while you're stuck," he teased.

At the Appleton home, a Pimms spruced me up and the odd bits of Mrs. Appleton's domestic gossip put us all in a gay mood. The month before, their old *ayah* had gotten sick and had gone home to her tribe: seemed her city boy-friend got annoyed when she threw him out so he had her cursed. Then the Appletons had made a mistake when they hired a new *ayah* who was a member of a tribe different from the rest of the servants, and was caught one day angrily chasing the bearer with a panga. They were lucky they still had their bearer. So many of the best servants had been recruited to work for a new oil refinery in Aden; 150 boys went, and considering that there are only 150 Europeans in Hargeisha, nearly every family contributed – rather like sending sons to battle, commented Mr. Appleton, wryly.

"Is Egyptian influence as strong here as in Somalia?" Mil wanted to know.

"We don't allow Egyptian teachers in the Protectorate, but I imagine that there are as many of our Somalis studying in England or in other Commonwealth countries. So far only four or five are officer material. Trouble is the their lack of previous education. We've only just opened the first secondary school in the Protectorate. Until recently, the Somalis refused to attend secular schools. The Egyptians have an advantage in being Muslims, yet I think the Somalis are more suspicious of them than of us. Strange as it may seem, the Somalis like us. Some of them have begged us to promise to stay ten or twenty years. It won't be that long, though I imagine some British administrators will have to help out here for many years to come. You know that many people at home in England would like us to hand the desert back to the Somalis right away. After all, this country costs the British taxpayer about a million pounds a year. But we must stay long enough to set up the country so that the fellows here have a fighting chance of maintaining some sort of government; can't have anarchy like there was when the Mad Mullah roamed, when was it, dear?"

"1900 to 1920," his wife replied promptly.

"That time," Appleton continued, "we 'retired' to the coastal towns and left 'our' tribes with arms to use against the Mullah. After perhaps a third of the Somali males had gotten themselves killed off, we finally sent the army in to take back control of the desert. No, we can't let that happen again."

"Is that why the country's so, well, untouched?" I asked. "The Italians may not have done much for the Somalis, but they did something about roads and irrigation and electricity. Generally, I'm partial to British colonialism. But here, it seems as though no one was even trying."

Mr. Appleton sipped his Pimms thoughtfully before answering. "Where do you start, after an attack like that?" he laughed ruefully. "Let me say in our own defense that we've never wanted this particular bit of desert, and though it is a challenge, it's also both a big expense and a big headache. The money we've put in here has mainly been for administration, something Ethiopians have never done for "their" Somalis. The Italians, in fact, rounded them up as forced labor to build all those things you listed. You know, sometimes it **is** a great temptation when you see all those Somali men doing practically nothing. But that's not the way we work, we try to teach or persuade, not force. We've had about two decades between the Mad Mullah and the war, and another decade since to civilize the country. Thirty years isn't a long time, especially when you're working with a group of people who still live essentially as they did in Biblical times." He added, following that tangent, "You know, that the frankincense and myrrh probably came from here; the Somalis grow it down nearer the coast."

We sat down to a meal of Indian curry which, contrary to all health rules, suited my stomach very well. Indian spices were easy to buy in Hargeisha because of the large number of Indian merchants even though few were permanent settlers, unlike the Indians in East Africa. Yet because the Protectorate had started out under Aden, which itself had been administered for many years as part of India, the Indian colonial influence was great. In fact the rupee had been the official currency until 1950 when East African currency was adopted.

Over an incongruous dessert of English trifle I asked the Appletons how they liked living in Somalia, especially since there was no job security.

"Well," grinned Mr. Appleton, "I'm not worried about the future. Someone will always need a good administrator. For now, I'm happy. I like the Somalis, the work is challenging; also we get yearly home leave with free transportation out and back and we pay no income tax." "And," chimed in his wife, "there's lots of sun for the kiddies, and servants to help me. With the home leave, we really don't feel too cut off from home. Next year we'll leave our son in school in England. Still we will see him every summer." Mr. Appleton added thoughtfully, "I've been here ten years now and, you know, this is home. Things have changed so fast at home it might be harder to adjust in England than it is here in Somaliland. It's good to feel wanted, and useful."

By morning the river had stopped running, indeed it looked so dry that it was hard to imagine the torrent of the night before. We were up early, gulped a self-prepared breakfast, and packed the car, all before seven. Mil went off to check with Morassi while I waited til the manager came in to settle the bill. I had already checked the rates in the visitors book and knew the price for the room only was twenty-five shillings a night, not cheap considering the plainness of the room, but still we were glad to have had one. I also knew that we had exactly 58 shillings left. With a tax of some sort our bill should have been 53 shillings and I planned to give the rest as tip. This simple little transaction turned into a huge quarrel. Monday was the manager's day off and Mrs. Cox, a battleaxe sort of woman who was the assistant, decided that we should pay for room and meals because, she said, it was not written down that we booked for room only. She kept insisting that it didn't matter that we did not eat a thing here, we must still pay for 72 shillings. When I demurred she got quite nasty and said that she had been there when we came in and that we had asked for room and meals. Apparently she had heard us ask if we could get extra meals in the Club, thinking that a hot breakfast might be wise. The manager, to whom we had been talking had said no, so we booked for room only.

By this time Mil had come back and said we were to go in half an hour. I told him the problem. We could try to cash a traveler's check, though if we had to wait til the banks opened, Morassi would have left and we would have to face the rain alone. In any case, we were not anxious to have leftover East African shillings since it is my experience that you usually must exchange left-over currency at a loss and I knew shillings would not be useful in Ethiopia. Thus cashing traveler's check practically meant throwing money away, and we couldn't really afford that. Besides, I was furious at Mrs. Cox's attitude, and determined to check the price listing before we tried to change money. Mr. Appleton, whom we consulted, said Mrs. Cox had a reputation of "clawing the wall", but begged off trying to reason with her by saying that Hargeisha is a small community and he had to live there. Morassi offered to help, either with talk or the loan of some shillings and Mil was all for accepting a loan. But by then my pride was involved so I phoned the Club secretary, and he readily settled for 53 shillings. I had made Mil go back to pay the woman, knowing I'd blow up if I saw her. Although she accepted the money from Mil, she insisted the difference would remain a "bad debt."

With that unpleasant memory and worried anticipation, we left Hargeisha. It was already 9.30; dark clouds were gathering ahead, and it was obviously raining in the northwest. After we climbed out of the river valley, we headed directly toward the clouds. We held our breath. The engine started missing – from dirty petrol or too much sand, who knew? The low battery water had somehow affected the cut off so we ran most of the time with lights. The road itself had a gravel topping and we made good time, passing rich carpets of green grass with sheep and goats and even a few cattle nibbling hungrily, passing barren stretches where the rain had not yet fallen.

When we turned off the Borama road toward the border, we were going southwest. Rain clouds threatened to the right and left, but ahead it seemed clear. We were feeling relieved when suddenly the road became a mass of deep mud ruts. We followed Morassi's every move: off to the shoulder, way round to a by-pass and across half dry mud, back to the main track and down the middle ruts. If we should get stuck we felt it would have been better to follow his lead. Mil was driving; I became the weather-watcher. The lightest shower would have turned the by-passes into lakes, the ruts into rivers. A drop of rain splashed off the windshield, teasing us. Ahead on the flat plain a single adobe building stood out marking off the road. A truck was parked by the building and Morassi stopped to check on the road. We also got out to fill up the gas tank while we had the chance.

"We must quickly go," said Morassi, "that truck has engine trouble, nothing more. Perhaps they are fixing it. So far you are lucky, already look at that rain, and worse is the road ahead. Hurry we must."

We looked; just behind us the sky was black and streaked with rain. We hurriedly continued. The scrub turned into steppe as the altitude increased; not a tree in sight, but there was green fuzz everywhere, and in some places knee-high yellow grass. Livestock increased and for the first time we saw horses grazing. The rain that grew the grass also gummed the road. Puddles had collected on the road and several times when I was driving I splashed the distributor enough to stall the car. As the road got ruttier, we couldn't always follow the Power Wagon tracks; it could clear rocks which would have made a sieve out of Bublee's undersides. The slipping and sliding, and watching the rain clouds gain on us, held our attention. We hardly noticed the town in the valley below until, suddenly, we were back on a surfaced road, back after a lapse of centuries, into civilization.

THE CUSTOMS POST AT Jigjiga is closed from 12.30 to 3. When we arrived at the barrier at the entrance of the town, it was 1.30 Had we been alone we might well have sat there, fuming, for an hour and a half since the guards looked with distrust on our visa since part of it was in English. Morassi quickly explained that Mil was a diplomat on his way from a post in India, and surely there must be some communication from the American Embassy explaining our coming. To our amazement the guards in charge checked a list from Addis Ababa and then explained sadly that our name wasn't there, but since Morassi knew us, we could go into town as far as the customs shed. For safety's sake he sent three soldiers along as guards. We left one guard, our car, and our passports at the customs shed; the rest of us piled into Morassi's truck and went into town to eat.

Red-checked cloths, bottles of every sort of aperitif made the cafe seem European. We thought it premature to celebrate, but Morassi bought anise for all of us, including the guards. Pleased, one guard went back to encourage the customs and to take the passports on to immigration while we ate. The plump Ethiopian owner of the restaurant bustled out herself to serve us, joking gaily with Morassi as she plunked down a plate of nondescript meat, another of eggs, another of cooked greens. Two men entered the cafe and Morassi waved them to join us for coffee. Neither spoke English so we worked over a few polite phrases in Italian and French before they rather abruptly left. Morassi explained that the one was a police spy; the other was assistant governor in Wardere. They'd just come in to look us over.

Guilty I asked, "Do you think they know already that we didn't stop for customs in Wardere?"

Morassi laughed and said that even if the incident had been reported the office in Jigjiga wouldn't hear about it until next year. He then explained that top-ranking officers such as assistant governor were political appointments from high ranking local families; this young man visited his station as little as possible but lived in Jigjiga instead. Since we had come through his area, he wanted to meet us. The policeman was a spy for the government in Addis. "You see, the Emperor, he cannot altogether control all the Rases or dukes. Everyone plots against everyone else. Not now do they plot to fight and murder like before. But for money and rank and for who will be the next Emperor; these things go on, like opera comique." He looked sideways at the remaining guard, but the guard was playing with his empty aperitif glass and dreaming. "Harar province is more under the Emperor than the others, because Haile Selassi and his father before him were dukes here. The Emperor is modern, compared to the other dukes, and the people like him. But tribe is more important than country and of course the Emperor is not a Harari. His family is Amhara, the top dogs."

Morassi's slang, which he used generously, often confused me. I choked on the coffee, trying not to laugh. He grinned back, and tried again. "You saw the assistant governor. You saw he was taller than me. But that cop, not. And see the fuzzy hair on this here guard. On top are Amhara like the governor, tall, skin almost as light as mine, a Copt. The cop is not a Copt, ha, ha, but a Muslim, from Harar. Probably got some Galla blood in him so he's a bit darker. This guard calls himself a Galla; but see his nose and fuzzy hair; probably has slave blood in him."

Although Morassi's division of the peoples of Ethiopia was too facile, we later found that there were indeed three main groupings of Ethiopians classed by religion and ethnic origin. The rulers, those who speak Amharic, have Semitic ancestry, though by now well mixed, and are Coptic Christians. The majority of the population is mixed Semitic-Hamitic and is Muslim. Around the southern borders live Bantus, generally animists. Due to widespread slavery which still continues in remote areas, this Negroid strain has been well mixed with the others. The Harar Muslims fit somewhere in between the top and second group, and form the aristocracy of the Ethiopian Muslims. Over and over we heard the echoes of Morassi's words: "You'll almost never find a Galla who's an official. They do the work while the top dogs pansy around."

Back at the customs' shed, everyone was confused. The diplomatic passports and visas issued in India meant we were very important, or that we were spies. A group of spectators and underlings quickly gathered and soon Morassi was talking more with them than the uniformed officials. A uniformed man sauntered up and asked to see the passports. I couldn't tell what he was, but he was not a customs official. He looked, after Morassi's lecture, to be from a low social level and I whispered to Mil, "Surely that man isn't anybody. Why doesn't Morassi look for his top dog?" Morassi turned on me, sternly. "Let it be. This is Ethiopia. What the top boss says doesn't always go."

This seemingly aimless talking went on. Impatient, I wandered into a back office and began what turned out to be loquacious and useless negotiations with a large fat man who towered over a desk stacked with yellowing piles of papers and files. A guard had followed me into the office, and when the older man decided my Italian was indecipherable, he sent the guard for an interpreter. Having heard my problem the big man waved me back outside, and indicated a distant office; I had to see the immigration official first.

By now Morassi was concluding his harangue with the multitude, and with amused cries of cheering, we were, very abruptly, off into the ancient kingdom of Ethiopia. Morassi explained later that intrigue is so rife, group decisions were often easiest to get. That way, no one was responsible. If we had gone from one office to another, we might have spent a couple of says there. Clearly I had been too impatient!

# Part III

Old civilizations confront the new century

# CHAPTER 25

# Harar: island in the desert

HE ROAD PAVEMENT STOPPED AT THE EDGE OF TOWN, BUT THE gravel was well enough surfaced to stand all but worst ravages of rain. It wound gradually up, past little groups of round huts hiding beneath a few wind-battered trees. Crockery pots, upside down at the peak of the roof, served as chimneys. In the long light of late afternoon these pots almost looked like spires, gave a civilized appearance to the otherwise wild-looking outposts.

As we climbed, the wilderness softened, the fields seemed lush, and the red berries on the coffee bushes caught the afternoon sun. Morassi stopped at a roadside stand to buy some melons. Everyone knew Morassi; they all swarmed down to his truck: the old Italian woman, her pretty dark daughter, and several Ethiopian girls. Dusk was in its last

Round huts use crockery pots as
chimneys; note the threatening sky

light as we topped a rise to see the fabled walled town of
Harar on the summit of the next hill. The flat-topped houses
were jammed next to each other, irregularly, like children's
blocks fitted carelessly into an oval basket. Two long-fingered
minarets varied the silhouette, made a town out of a beehive.

Looking at an ordinary map of Africa you cannot appreciate the tremendous influence of terrain. Even a physical
map, showing clearly a few points of very high ground,
cannot really convey the island character of the Harar plateau. On all sides stretches fine beach sand, or pebbly sand,
or rocky sand, pinned to its place by tufts of wiry bush. It
is the starkness of this sand-sea and the suddenness of the
height that is so impressive, truly a magical island created for
gods alone, and populated with a million fairy-tales. Thanks
to Morassi, our entrance to this magic town was as smooth
as a landing of a flying carpet.

Not til the next day were we able to visit the town; it was
too late to see anything. Just beyond Harar is Lake Aramaya;
we stayed at a small Greek inn on its shores. The old Greek
widower also knew Morassi, and soon a spaghetti dinner
with passable wine was on the table. In the lamplight, the

one common room looked overstuffed with heavy furniture, overhung with rugs and draperies. We could hear the lapping of the waves as the wind began to rise. Morassi told us that the desert tribes to the south often come all the way here to bathe, using as soap a special yellow fruit they collect. But when we left, early, it was too cold for bathing; all we saw were hundreds of oxen drinking the cold water.

After the Greek went to bed, Morassi told us about how much he disliked his first name "Attila" and how he met his attractive young wife. "I used to live in Addis, and one day when I was driving my truck down a narrow lane I nearly ran over a girl on a bike. I only dated the girl once or twice before her old-fashioned Sardinian mother began to ask when were we to marry. It was all or nothing. She's ten years younger than me, and old-fashioned like her ma. But maybe she can grow up. She is mighty pretty." He sighed. "But, oh the home influence. Sometimes I envy drivers. One of them has bought twenty-five virgins. Not on what we pay. But like most of the other drivers, he hauls water for his tribe in my trucks. Most of the men like to buy camels, to save money. But not this boy. Trouble with virgins, once they aren't virgins, they lose their value. You know, virgins are even more valuable here in Ethiopia because you can have only one wife at a time if you're Christian. So when a girl goes to her husband the first time, the mother of the boy goes along to see that the girl is really a virgin. Virgin price is so high, only old men have the money. But there's lots of divorce. The younger men get the hand-me-downs."

His folk-knowledge of the Galla was astounding. He told us that every married woman is supposed to get a plot of land from her husband where she can raise *khat*, a sort of intoxicating tobacco which everybody loves to chew. The raising and selling of *khat* is a female monopoly, and from the money the women receive they buy themselves hair ornaments and other little luxuries. They also pay for their hair treatment. After washing, their hair is oiled with butter, which of course soon turns rancid, then parted in narrow rows with each row tight-braided close to the scalp. Morassi insisted that most women have this done only once a month, and just leave it that way, smells and all, until the next time.

As the wind increased, it beat the trees and waves into sighing, Morassi asked if we believed in spirits. All the Ethiopians believe in *zaar* or spirits, he said. The Christians say that God was displeased with Eve for having too many children. Whenever God visited Eve, she hid half her children because she feared God's wrath. During one visit God asked her where all her children were. She replied that all her children were right there with them. So God said any other children Eve had would become *zaar*. There are good *zaar* and bad ones. The Ethiopian women have all night *zaar* gatherings at which they chew *khat* and dance. In the moan of the wing, I could almost hear Eve's children calling!

Abruptly he changed the mood. "This business of driving to Addis. I've done it myself, once in a Volkswagen smaller than your Austin. But the road, she was better then. No one drives now except them Fiat trenta-quartos – you know, them thirteen ton trailer trucks. Everyone'll tell you to go by train. But if you are still going to do it, let me warn you. Always follow the lorry trucks. Those boys, they are smart fellows. They know what they do. Even you think they are crazy, you follow their ruts. Most of them bridges are out. In the driest season, mostly the river beds are dry. In the wet time, you cannot go through. Now, the rain is just beginning. Maybe you get through. But you know the sound if a flood comes? Like thunder, but it just goes on and on. If you hear, and are in a river bed, do not stop for anything, just run, run, if you want to live."

"Where is the map," he asked, "See, here we are. All along here is mountain. Here is desert. The road, she follows the edge of the desert. So every river drops off these mountains and goes banging across the road. Like putting the road along the bottom of a waterfall. Silly place for a road – but it follows the French railroad. Old Emperor made the French put it down there even though all them bridges made costs fantastic, upkeep fantastic. We truck everything we can. Old Emperor didn't care about costs. He was afraid the French, 'fraid if they put their railroad to Harar they'd just grab the city. Nothing to grab down below. At least, if you get stuck, you can try to flag a train. Probably won't stop. Everybody's scared silly of them savages, the Danakils. They don't want women. They collect male parts for necklaces, they do. But you won't see any. They keep to the real desert. The road is in the scrub. Suppose you can always walk the tracks back to a town. Once you get past Awash the road is OK. There is a railroad bridge on the Awash. That river has cut itself a whopping big canyon. Could never get across without a bridge. From Dira Dawa, Awash isn't so awfully far, hundred-fifty miles maybe. You can do it, maybe, but be careful."

He looked at our apprehensive faces. "I know. I will find all out for you tomorrow. You look at Harar, and I will meet you in Dira Dawa hotel for lunch. I will tell you what will happen."

Harar was like a movie set, a medieval town put down in the middle of green pastures which were criss-crossed with highways. And indeed it is a town out of its century. Primarily a trading center for coffee today, it once was on the main slave route from the Negro interior of Africa to the insatiable slave markets in Arabia. When the great Emperor Menelik II decided to prohibit the French from building their railway in the highlands, much of Harar's trade shifted to Dira Dawa on the foothills below, where the railroad runs. All this has happened within the last century. Egypt briefly controlled this plateau and the near-by coastal areas from 1875 til 1885, a fact of history that may well encourage present-day Egyptians to dream of recapturing their "lost" empire. Since 1887, Harar has been a Muslim city within a Christian Ethiopia, jealousy preserving its distinctiveness as well as its religion. No wonder the whole town spreads a sleepy, almost deadly, aura, as if the whole population, by chewing enough *khat*, had forgotten its ignominious present and was dreaming of the glory of old.

The width of the streets in the beehive town is measured to allow for loaded mules. Cars park outside the walls, under wide-spreading mimosas. This too added to the unreality. I half expected the guard who stood near the footpath entrance to ask me for my admission ticket. I was also afraid he might see two cameras which I had hidden under my light cardigan. Morassi had said that there is a law against taking pictures anywhere in Ethiopia. Like most laws in this strange country, sometimes it is ignored, and sometimes dreadfully enforced. "Better you not take chances," he said. So we decided I alone should take pictures on the old theory that women aren't worth bothering with anyhow.

The variety of costumes was tantalizing. Dodging around narrow corners, tripping over shallow steps in the path, I would pursue a woman in gaudy red or vivid orange. Just as I would find a fairly empty stretch and dare to take a picture, she had vanished. Merchants spread their goods along the narrow passages, making them even narrower. Some school children spied me photographing a withered old tailor pumping a foot-level sewing machine. For a dreadful minute I thought they were going to run at me. Instead they ran screaming into a school yard, and moments later a dour looking woman came out to see what the commotion was about. She was wearing the distinctive Harari embroidered dress which some people say is a local variant of the sixteenth century Portuguese costume. I couldn't resist the chance, so I wheeled and took her picture. As she realized what I had done she grinned widely, and strutted off!

At the far end of the town was an open market place. Most of the sellers were country women with dark skins and roughly braided hair. Although there was no real gate in this part of the wall, the wall itself was low enough to climb over. Beyond the wall the hill fell away steeply, but the women, carefully holding their large painted leather bags of *khat*, climbed up and down as easily as if the hill were level. In the distance, purple hills rimmed the horizon. The town was indeed magical and made me feel quite pleased as though I had made a personal discovery.

Then we hurried back to the parking lot, for the clouds were gathering. Near the entrance, where autos were not supposed to be, an ordinary American car, looking giant-like in the narrow alley, was honking its way towards us. Squeezed into a doorway with several annoyed Hararis, we could just make out an elderly American couple in the back seat, a TCA sticker gleaming on the windscreen: technical cooperation administration, American aid. I was glad that our car was British, masking our nationality.

We were easily in Dira Dawa for lunch. Indeed we had checked into a columned hotel with its spaciously formal gardens and bathed before it was time to meet Morassi. Yet the luxury of a clean bedroom and hot running water could not cure my black mood. The drive down from Harar was breathtaking. Though the road to the escarpment was still under repair – by American engineers on a World Bank project – the escalator down the precipitous side was newly asphalted. It was still clear enough to see, as from an airplane, beyond the foothills into the desert sea beyond. Perhaps the very tameness of the trip took away something from the excitement. But I was still feeling piqued over Harar, like a child taking an Aprils Fool's chocolate to find a cream center laced with pepper. Here was to be my romantic city, my excursion into the last century. And then, in an instant, the twentieth century came crowding back, with all the problems involved in the do-goodness, and the insensitivity, of American aid programs.

Morassi's news didn't leave me with much time to sulk. Reports were not good. There had been a lot of rain in the hills west of Harar. Most of the rivers were flowing, and several of the giant Fiat trailer-trucks were days overdue. We were all a bit upset at this, and at Morassi's suggestion we hurried to the railroad office to check costs and possibilities of shipping the car as far as Awash. The cost was unnerving, over a hundred dollars, but the real stopper was the Frenchman's estimate that we would be lucky to obtain a flatcar within ten or fourteen days. A few days might have been livable in Dira Dawa. It is a wide-stretched colonial-looking town. The hotel was especially nice: when the railroad was first built the 440 mile trip from Djibouti to Addis Ababa took three days because the French only dared to run the railroad during the day. Passengers spent one night spent in Dira Dawa and another in Awash. Today the trip takes 36 hours non-stop.

But two weeks was too much time to waste. The drive seemed safe enough, if we were careful. The challenge was one of stamina, and skill with the car. Stoically, I agreed we must try to press on. Mil, on the other hand, confided, "I'm rather looking forward to tomorrow. It will show just what we and the car can stand." And it did.

CHAPTER 26

# *Flash floods along a ruined Italian road*

W E LEFT DIRA DAWA AT FIVE PAST FIVE IN THE MORNING IN A depressing drizzle and in a dither. It had rained more heavily out of town, and some heavy lorries had rutted the road quite recently. This, at least, was reassuring: someone was still using the road. Although we had to drive carefully, and slowly, we reached mile 39 in fairly good time. This was to be expected. It seems that the old Italian road had been hastily repaired thus far about six months before by the American engineers working on the Harar-Dira Dawa highway. The Emperor was paying a state visit to the Harar project and then, rather suddenly, decided he wished to visit the famous hot springs at mile 39 on the Dira Dawa-Addis Ababa road. This being Ethiopia, of course the road was checked, holes filled in, ditches and streams bridged, and one or two Bailey-bridges flung across the larger rivers.

"I'm awfully glad the Emperor wanted to take that hot bath" I laughed to Mil, "though it must have been an expensive one." Then, as anything resembling a road halted abruptly at a large muddy field and one whitewashed building, I moaned, "but what a pity that the hot springs weren't further along."

The contrast was truly amazing, although the road that far had been a poor track by any standards. But, as we soon realized, the biggest difference was the existence of bridges. Now there simply were none. Hardly had we passed one ditch than another was there, around the bend. We had expected this, though perhaps not as frequently, and followed Morassi's advice to "follow the diversions." At the first diversion we promptly turned off the main track and as promptly got stuck in mud. With a few rocks under the wheels we were easily out, but curious, I went back to the main road to check. A huge hole gaped in the track. "I guess the truck drivers do know what they're doing," I reported to Mil.

After that, whenever we saw truck ruts leaving the main track, we stopped. Mil would reconnoiter the diversion while I spied out the main track. The diversion would by-pass the bridge approaches, meander through bush and miniature rapids down to the riverbed – wet or dry as it might be – then climb up the other side. The main road would usually lead over a built-up approach to the edge of the ravine where the concrete piers of the bridges still stood, but that was all. Always we left the car clear of the river, surveyed the track, moved rocks here, and filled sand there. After all, a track passable for a Fiat giant was not always ready for a Bublee Austin; the clearance on those trucks was almost as high as Bublee herself! Having built our own way across, we would then have a go, one person driving and the other directing...

and listening, over the roar of the motor, for a warning murmur that presaged the dreaded flash flood.

So it went, over and over: big flat dry river beds, tiny steep wet gullies, muddy slippery stream beds. Any illusion of speed soon left us; we could have walked faster. But for a time, at least, it was exciting in its challenge. The sky ahead had cleared. I told Mil, as I stood ankle deep in mud heaving at a rock with the shovel, that I was bucking for my Girl Scout's badge in the Road Building. We kept it gay for hours. Mostly Mil drove and I sat in the front seat clutching the dripping shovel, ready, like a minute man, to pop out, and start digging. Our speed was so slow that flies swarmed in and out, settling on my sweaty arms. Usually squeamish about squashing insects, I began to swat them with my hands. Somehow this made me feel battle-hardened, ready for anything.

The emergency brake wouldn't hold on the steep climbs out of the river and onto relatively flat land. It was a case of run and gun: if you made it, you made it; if not, you had to back into the riverbed and try again, if you could. It was devilish to get going again once you are stalled in the mud. All the while you know while you're down there in the gulch that you may not have that second chance, not if a flash flood comes.

This may seem remote and foolish, this talk of flash floods, if you've never seen one. We knew better. In the little hospital in Dira Dawa were two Catholic priests who only the week before had started the trip in their four-wheel drive jeep station wagon from Awash to Dira Dawa. Long familiar with the track, they were careless about checking each streambed and got stuck in a few inches of water in one of the larger rivers. At least they knew what the roar meant, and wet cassocks clinging, they ran for the bank. They didn't quite make it before the tidal wave swept down upon them, but they were close enough to the shore to grab some bush and save themselves while the jeep disappeared into the flood, carried like a twig. The story was going round that the next day the jeep (1) was found fifteen miles downstream in perfect condition, (2) was never found, (3) its pieces were found strewn all over the desert. No one seemed to know what really happened to the jeep, but the priests were in good condition, considering. Every single person we met in Dira Dawa told us this story. No wonder we were careful.

In the distance a rock-strewn hill materialized into a stone-hut village as we crawled nearer. It looked very close, nestled on the next ridge, but between us and the village was the biggest river yet. The high bluff of the first road crumbled into the water; nothing was left of the original bridge across the narrows of the gorge. Lower downstream we found the remains of a second bridge. Up river perhaps only a quarter of a mile the railroad trestle arched the gorge gracefully, securely. The river was running so swiftly that there was no sign of a truck crossing; the sand was also unrutted, showing that no truck had gone by since the last flood, whenever that was.

This time our surveying took a long time. Mil found a steep straight crossing that had a rock base; up and down stream was only mud. But the water was up to Mil's knees. There was no help for it. We bundled up Bublee for her swim: stuffed rags around the distributor and spark plugs, and took off the fan belt, Bublee waddled through like a duck, then clumsy from her dip she skidded on the bank and slipped back into the water. We piled more rocks over the mud, but every time the tires spun the rocks free and the car slipped on the goo. With the water so deep, Mil didn't dare back into the center of the stream, so we tried inching up the bank. Mil would race the car and then pitch forward an inch or so til the slipping began; I would rush to jam rocks behind the wheels, dump more stones in the muddy place, then get set to push for the next inch or two. In our feverish activity, we hardly heard the roar. It sounded like a train. It was a train, glory be. Almost hypnotized we watched the little toy engine crossing the willowy span. As it toot-tooted disdainfully, we both broke out in too tense a laugh. Like a prisoner reprieved from execution, we set to work with a will.

At last we struggled up over the crest practically at the foot of the village of Gota. This dot on the map was a water halt for the railroad. We helped ourselves to the fresh spring water as an Italian couple peered suspiciously at us from behind a reed fence surrounding a pukka house. Beyond Gota, the way seemed more desolate. The last pre-rain ruts disappeared and we were on our own to figure out diversions. Incredibly, since the hot springs four hours before, we had gone only **six** miles.

For two miles we drove steadily, without a stop. Then we came another wide river with running, but more shallow, water. Automatically we tumbled out to survey. This time the banks were steep but the sand approaches were wide and hard packed. After building up the track with stones, Bublee crossed easily: we decided we had graduated.

The map showed that we were driving across the watershed between two river systems, both of which empty their rushing, foaming water into the salty desert marshes. For another ten miles we had a respite; we practically ignored the dry shallow gullies which crossed the road; even those with three or four inches of water posed no challenge, only effort. As we neared Afdem, a stop on the railroad, we passed an Imperial Highways truck that was loading furniture from the railroad to take to a mission in the hills. A Locust Control jeep passed us, heading up river into the bush. We were hungry and, as passenger, I made some cheese sandwiches for us to eat.

Near the railroad stop at Afdem as we were bumping across a level pasture, we saw a most unlikely sight: a Chevrolet pick-up. We passengers greeted each other in amazement, glad to find other fools. The Italian and the Ethiopian both spoke at once while a third man, his skin and features almost a cross between the other two, hung back at first. They were all bubbly in ebullient French. We did manage to decipher that they had come only from Miesso, the next major railroad stop. The road was very bad, and a river some twelve kilometers on was running high. In turn we conveyed our meager information; what else could we say but that the road was lousy, awful, but not so impossible that we had not been able to get this far. If we can, you can, especially over our nice new bridges. As we talked, the clouds over were darkening. With a wave, we all scooted for our cars and rushed off, at five miles an hour.

In our hurry, we become a bit careless at the next river. Instead of checking every hole and puddle, we splashed through, the theory being that a little water was better than a lot of mud. But when we tried this idea to cross what appeared to be a broad shallow puddle, we sank down and down, as into quick sand. Clouds over the hills, the possibility of floods in the rivers, and there we were, supposedly serious adults, playing mud pies in the middle of Africa. I dug a canal with my hands and the water rushed through. Mil constructed dams to keep my canal from draining the whole lake instead of concentrating on our pond. More canals, more lakes. The mud dried quickly, but not fast enough. We dumped roots and stones into the puddles and built a rock road in front of the tires. Out came the sand-tracks, and lo, out came Bublee. We were stuck for over an hour!

We drove on, chastised, looking like natives of the country covered as we are from head to bare toe in clinging brown mud. Again we checked every crossing, every puddle. If this slowed us, it seemed worth it. A couple of rivers surprised us by having concrete Irish bridges still intact. Then we came to a real dilly, the one the Chevrolet people warned us about. Even the truck diversion was impossible. The incline to the river was in our favor, being much steeper down on this side than up on the other. But the drop was a sharp fifty feet on either side. Clearly a flood of only four or five feet would fill the entire ravine with water. Our crossing would have to be fast; we would be in danger every moment we were in the defile. We desperately wished the car were lighter, that we had shipped off our heaviest trunks by railroad. We had considered this, in Dira Dawa. But the thievery is rife along the railroad and our chances of losing whatever we sent were quite high. The alternative, to ship by air freight, was sky high. Morassi assured us it wasn't necessary. Now too late, we were sorry.

Mil at last found a crossing some hundred yards downstream but he wasn't sure whether he could maneuver the U-turn necessary to head the car across the flowing river at its shallowest. But he would try. First we waded to clear the path of the biggest rocks: the water at least cleaned my muddy loafers. Then we packed the approaches with great care. We were ready. We paused to look and listen apprehensively, but all was quiet, if overcast. Mil drove carefully down the slip, along the sand, across a rivulet bordered with mud: a precise bit of backing and turning to position Bublee for a run across the river and up the bank. Mil stopped the engine so we could loosen the fan belt, making me jump with fear. Even my own breath sounded like the roar of a flood to my staining ears. We worked the fan belt loose and I stood

behind the car, ready to push. Back in the drivers' seat, Mil
gunned the engine, then settled into a strong second gear
for the crossing, declutched to low for the ascent. I hang
onto the gas tank lid and on the fender, half pushing, half
steadying myself. I almost fell as Bublee spurts ahead. We
were on top.

"That is enough for me," I moaned, sinking onto a rock,
dead tired, still scared. Mil came back to fetch me, exultant.
It was a skillful exhibition of driving, but I am exhausted.
His kisses helped, but I was still numb as we pushed on. The
clouds in the hills were obviously raining. I wished we'd come
last month or last week or that we had started yesterday,
anything to be beyond the rivers then. I was tired of wading
through little lakes, of feeling where I can't see for holes or
rocks, of slopping back to the car in squishy loafers. The
shoes were ruined, but I wouldn't dare walk into a puddle
barefoot and hit rocks: rather the shoes than my feet. I was
tired of making "V" stream beds into "U"s, of jumping out to
survey, of listening for rumbles. I was tired. I was exhausted.

But we had to go on. Surely we were near Miesso, but
the railroad was on the wrong side of the road according to
the map. We passed a small town with a water tank reading
Mullu, then came to a bridge that was whole! Miles yet to
go and already it was getting dark. Into gullies, into gulches,
into ravines, into puddles, into mud, into rivers, wearier, and
wearier. Each time we are about to enter a riverbed my ears
grew large, surely rabbit-like like Harvey's. But I couldn't
joke, for fear was growing with the repetition and if I spoke
surely my fright would show, and once let out, it would no
longer be controllable. As usual, fear is worse than the event.

The river was medium-sized. With the flashlight I picked
out three concrete pillars where the bridge used to be; close
downstream a short span of trestle marked the railroad.

The diversion was clear even though there were no ruts, for the bank was heavily overgrown with thorns. The descent was not too abrupt; the river bank across the stream was only some sixty feet away. It looked like an easy crossing. I scrambled down the bank, glad that for once I was wearing my jeans and had rolled them down: the thorns can scratch badly. I waded and stumbled into a series of deep ruts at the edge of the water. My pant legs got wet, but by that time such minor discomforts meant nothing. I felt up-stream with my feet and decided the bottom there was solid enough, so I waved Mil on. Drive to the left, I indicated with my flash as he came through. But he plowed straight on, and began to skid as the rear wheels slid into the ruts. The car settled back, the rear wheels half in the water, the whole car angling up at nearly forty-five degrees. Rocking the car only makes the rear wheels slide further downstream til the right wheel was wedged against a large rock at the top of small rapids. Discouraged, Mil found the wire mesh tracks and we pushed and shoved trying to straighten the car again. A light rain began to fall, slicking the thin layer of mud over the rocks on the ascent until we could hardly walk without slipping.

I heard a sound like a distant thunder, but it kept rolling. "Must be a train," I said to Mil. He straightened, searching for lights on the track. The roar became louder. I got a bit panicky. "Push," I screamed to Mil; jumping in to steer. I gunned and he pushed, but we only skid back. "Rocks and bush for the front tires," yelled Mil back to me, his voice cracking with a tear in it, a cry. "Lord," I murmured, dead sober, and sprang out to comply. My hands were sore and one finger bleeding, but I no longer felt the tear and pulled rocks out of the track with a newly-found strength. But before I could get back into the car to try again the roar was upon us.

I flashed the torch at the stream and watched with

351

terrified eyes. In seconds Mil was beside me at the front of the car, holding my hand, striving to keep the fear from this glance. With the roar comes foaming brown water – like the head on root beer. Pushing the foam was a two foot wave of water that covered the rear wheels to the hub. "Let's do something," came a voice above the roar, eerie and wailing. I recognized it as my own, and the spell of terror broke. Without thinking – as if I alone could hold the car against the force of the water. – I rushed into the water behind the car just as another wave of water washed past raising the water level another foot and a half. "Rocks," I hissed, more to myself than to Mil, as we both try building a barricade. This too seemed futile. The water was still rising, steadily now, as if someone has just unplugged an enormous bathtub. I stood staring at Mil, the rain gently caressing my cheek, or was that a tear? "Let's, let's..." I began, wanting badly to think of something, and it came, "let's take everything off the car. Yes, let's lighten it, and then, if the water comes higher, at least we'll save our own stuff." Almost gaily Mil answers, "Yes let's."

We were geniuses at unpacking. As Mil pulled things from the roof I kicked off my soggy shoes for better toe holds and ported the stuff up the hill. All the carefully stowed boxes and cameras and notebooks and bags came out of the back seat and were added to the pile. All this in moments, truly record-breaking. It was steadying to be doing something, anything, not just staring. The water licked higher and higher, but slower and slower. Mil jammed more rocks under the wheels fearing the new buoyancy of the car may make it more, not less, vulnerable. But the river seemed at its peak, perhaps eight feet above its mark five minutes before; the panic and fear subsided. We stood weakly by our trunks watching the brown foam bubble down the stream. After interminable minutes the river ebbed ever so little, then more and more. The back end of the car was above the water and I opened the boot. "Cheers, it is dry inside," I muttered, searching for a tin of fruit juice and the glucose. The crystalline mix never revived us so wonderfully! Mil had eaten nothing all day, and I'd hardly nibbled at the cheese. We sat on the rocks, close together. The misty rain cleared and a half moon shone through. At such times, how close we were. Perhaps it was a strange time to exchange vows, but under such terrible pressure one's need for the other, one's weakness, become so apparent.

After a cigarette or so we off-loaded the rest of the roof, rearranged the rocks behind the wheels and, with one or two jerky tries, slid the car out of the ruts and up to safety. It was nine; in sixteen hours we crossed a hundred streams and driven a hundred miles. Too tired to go further, we camped in the middle of the road, within sight of the railroad bridge. The valuables we dumped back in the car; the rest of the load Mil covered with the tarp and left it where we had piled it. We hadn't planned to camp and had no wash water, little drinking water. The muddy stream only took the top layer off our crusted bodies. Still grimy and sticky, we gulped down the left-over sandwiches, finished the spiked juice, and slept.

NOT A SOUND DISTURBED us, and we awoke only as light unveiled our privacy. Although the day before we had seen buck and jackals and wild pigs, no animal had poked at our provisions. Two tall tribesmen stalked by on long thin legs; but they carried only spears and looked more alarmed at seeing us than vice versa. Perhaps they were Galla not like the ferocious native we'd seen the day before, swinging his shotgun as though he knew how to handle it, who was probably a Danakil. If he were, he was the only one we ever saw. For breakfast I made coffee with the last of our drinking water, opened a tin of grapefruit sections I'd been saving, and spread some deviled meat on crackers. We had almost finished repacking the car when a railroad crew chuffed by on a little flat car to inspect the bridges after the flood. They slowed for the bridge near us, and called over to see if we were all right. I felt friendly toward all Frenchmen and all railroads right then.

An hour, three and a half miles, and four stream-crossings later we came to another flooded river. Bits of foam clung on bushes already several feet clear of the water. Beyond the river we could see a water tower that we knew must be in Miesso. The flood here must have been over ten feet. On the other hand, the bottom of the truck crossing was solid with concrete, for immediately below the crossing a small waterfall began. If we had gotten this far before the flood, we wouldn't have been stuck in this river, with its smooth Irish bridge. If only we hadn't have been stuck in the silly mud-puddle. But it didn't matter, we were still in one piece, with the worst behind us.

Mil waded across the river; though the bottom was fine, the water was still running nearly three feet high. We'd have to wait for the water to ebb. So I sat in the car, catching up on my diary, while Mil hiked into Miesso to check on the road ahead. Our map showed only two rivers in the forty mile stretch between Miesso and the bridge at Awash. Two rivers, then the way was clear to Addis. We were very pleased with ourselves and with Bublee.

The car was a grandstand seat, for the river had formed rapids above the road. I could hear the falls below. So all the tribesmen had to use the crossing just before me. The cattle they drove were sure-footed, but many of the goats lost their footing and were carried over the waterfall, below which, somewhat bruised, they managed to swim and struggle ashore. An old man led a young girl to the stream and looked at it uncertainly, then tried the crossing while she stood very close to the car since we'd parked under the only shade nearby. She shyly looked away when I said hello, but she didn't move when I snapped her picture in color to show all the red and white bead necklaces circling her throat and falling down upon her bare breasts.

Galla beauty adorned with bracelets and necklaces, shaded by a basket on her head

The river had gone down nearly another foot before Mil came back. I was fidgety and wanted to hurry on to Awash, for already clouds are gathering in the hills. My left foot had begun to ache from a scraping I'd given it somewhere the horrible day before, so I pulled out the first-aid kit, for something to do, and gave myself an impressive white bandage. By then Mil had arrived on a jeep with three Ethiopians, all in shorts and shirts. They backed up to the river and wound out a rope for pulling. One waded over with Mil and on seeing the loose fan-belt decided we had engine trouble. He started to take the carburetor apart before Mil succeeded in conveying, in sign language with a grunt or two in French, that our only problem was the river water. The rope would not reach across the river so Mil tried to cross unaided. He actually managed to get through the deepest part of the stream and half the way up the other side before the water penetrated to the distributor and stalled the engine. A heave from the men, and we were out again.

Shortly, when the engine was dry, we followed the jeep for three and a half miles into Miesso. The driver led us past the railroad station to the French station master's house where we parked near the small warehouse. Back a little distance from the railroad line was a long low structure proudly calling itself the "Greek Hotel". A squat mosque with a lighthouse for a minaret crowded close to the railroad track; on a hill beyond was a small round Coptic church with a thatched roof; between these two houses of religion, mud huts of the natives were scattered along the road.

We planned to push on to Addis and were filling our water bags when the Ethiopian second-in-command of the station hurried out to meet us. It was he who had sent the jeep to help us, and was now asking us to join him for coffee at the hotel. He spoke a little English and seemed anxious to practice it. It seemed impolite not to accept even though we were anxious to leave. So we went into a small dark room, perhaps twelve by fifteen, that served as office, lounge and dining-room for the "Hotel". The Ethiopian kept asking Mil why we didn't wait a few days for the water to go down. He kept repeating that the Arba River was the worst river crossing; it was there that the priests had lost their jeep the week before. Despite his warnings we were still determined to try; we kept reasoning that we could always come back to Miesso.

In the middle of this exchange, a Land Rover and a Chevrolet pick-up roared out of the west and headed for the station master's house. We rushed over to find out where they came from and caught up with a group of Ethiopians as they had entered the house. A light, almost Arabic looking man, was already greeting the French station master. He turned to us as we approached and introduced himself, in French, as the regional commissioner. He explained that he had charge of the six districts in the area and was on a two-day inspection tour from Arba to Afdem. So he had not yet been over the road we planned to use. But he suggested that the station master phone ahead to Arba, the next stop on the rail line, and find out how that river was. The contact was efficiently established; "ne passez pas," came the reply. A Fiat truck-trailer was stuck in the river and the floods of the previous night had turned the giant truck so that now it was heading upstream, broadside to the crossing. It would be impossible to get it out until the water went down, it might take days, or weeks, for who knows when it will rain. "Til then, nothing can cross, not unless you can get that little car of yours under the truck," the Frenchman joked.

I must have looked as dejected as I felt. A week, two weeks, in the metropolis of Miesso. The regional commissioner was talking, almost dictating, something to the Frenchman. He turned back to me and said kindly, "You shall take the train to Awash. The first flatcar that comes is your, monsieur will see to it." This small matter finished, he turned without waiting for my thanks and strode into the house to attend to more important matters.

So began two days of waiting. The Greek showed us a row of box-like rooms, each crammed with two small beds and one night-table; we picked the first one preferring the greasy cooking smells to the stink from the bombsite toilet at the end of the hall that might have flushed once upon a time. I watched the villagers cook their food over charcoal braziers made of empty kerosene tines, and watched them eat the porridge with their hands. I took pictures of men trampling straw in a mud pit to repair the walls of their huts and of the boys playing among the stone ruins of several never-completed Italian buildings near the railroad tracks. They were a motley bunch, their ragged clothing testifying to their poverty. Many of them had running sores on their legs and almost all of them seemed to have an eye disease, probably trachoma. Yet they were gay, even silly, when they had time off from their shepherding to play. Several times I followed them and their herds back down to the river which rose and fell and rose and fell.

Mil haunted the train yard noted every flatcar being pulled to or from Awash. But always the Frenchman said it was promised to someone more important than the regional commissioner. I, too, began to watch the trains come and go. It was easy to tell when a train was due, for the yard beneath the water tank filled with women. Every train stopped for water, and the pipe that ran from tank to tank leaked. The whole town filled its bucket and tins with the railroad's well water.

One train stopped to discharge a passenger as well. A burly young American, a Protestant missionary, was on his way back to his mission station at Ghelemso. That night we all had dinner at the Greek's, and we were immediately sorry. Up til then we'd been eating from our supply of tins, except for coffee. The greasy food was not eatable, nor did our insides like it. Youngheart, the missionary, said he could eat anything, and did. He had been working in the mountains for four years, and often had to go down to Djibouti to bring back books or trunks of clothes or food for his new baby. Otherwise he and his family lived as the Ethiopians lived. There were no roads to Ghelemso so of course they had no car. In the dry season you could sometimes get a truck into the town, but usually, from Asebe to Ghelemso, they had to ride on mules. The mission had neither truck nor mules, but it wasn't too hard to hire either one.

He talked til late at night about the problems a Christian

missionary in a nominally Christian country trying to convert anyone to Christianity. "Of course we are here to convert Muslims not Christians," he explained. "Before the war not many missionaries were in the country when the Italians threw everyone out but Italian Roman Catholics. We're back now, but carefully regulated: a special area for each mission, and no conversions in the Amharic areas. Trouble is, the students who come to our schools, and then to our services, are mostly Copts, not Muslims. We can't let them join our church even if they want to. If they joined and the government heard about it, out we'd go. Emperor's worried about weakening the Christian solidarity against the Muslims – they're almost fifty per cent by population. But the whole religious problem has become political so we convert almost no Muslims, aren't allowed to convert Christians."

"If they are already Christians, why should you want to convert them," I asked.

"But don't you see," he cried, "these Copts aren't really Christians. They've got all sorts of pagan ceremonies mixed up with the Bible. Their worship is all show; they don't feel it with their hearts. And, oh, the sins they commit and call it marriage. Defames the holy sacrament. Yet we can't help these poor sinful creatures." We asked him to explain. "You see, marriage within the Coptic Church is so strict and the punishments for inconstancy so severe, that most church members have only a common law marriage, which is as easily dissolved as entered into. Technically the Coptic Church does not recognize these marriages, but the church does nothing about it, except symbolically. In their church buildings there is an inner sanctuary for the priests; circling this core of the church is a wide aisle where those church members with legal marriages may stand and receive communion. But all those members with common law marriages may stay in the outer circle, or if there is none, they must remain outside the church. Otherwise the priests do nothing to change this sinful practice. Surely," he exploded, "that is not Christianity."

"Isn't it better for their church to tolerate local customs than to alienate the people by being too harsh?" Mil asked, describing to him something of the inverted Christianity of the Mau Mau. "And certainly," I insisted, "there are enough European folk-ways like Christmas trees or Easter Eggs all mixed up with our sort of Christianity to make one pause before complaining about other people doing the same thing."

From there we were into theology and social ethics. Mr. Youngheart talked so persuasively that I began to think he was trying to convert us! Although we parted still defending our own views, the arguments helped the evening pass quickly. He left early next morning in a truck he had hired from some Greek contractors to take him to Asebe.

These Greeks, relatives of the hotel owner, had a lumbering concession about ten miles further up the road to Addis, though not as far as the Arba River. One afternoon Mil accompanied them to their concession in a jeep. Almost the whole way they ground along in four-wheel drive. The land was higher and flatter than before, making the eroded channels of the streams even more precipitous when those we had crossed. Even so, I think we would have tried it – after all Addis was only fifty miles and two rivers away – except for the trailer-truck nicely blocking the Arba. Sitting in Miesso was discouraging. We had quickly exhausted our conversation with anyone who remotely knew English or could vaguely understand our French or Italian. Several times over, the Ethiopian assistant station master described his lonely life without his family who were staying in Addis until he received a better assignment. The problem, which he would enlarge upon the as the _tej_ – a local cross between mead and beer – warmed his indignation, was that he and his family were Amhara; it wouldn't do to bring his wife to live among the savage Galla.

The only other English-speaking Ethiopian in Miesso, a lad named Mikeal, had a very different outlook. Although he too was a Copt, his mother had been a Galla and he said he felt more like a Galla than an Amhara. Indeed he told us cynically that he remained a Christian only to keep his job. "See if you find a Muslim Galla in any decent position," he had said bitterly. "Those Amhara treat us like slaves. I am lucky. The Locust Control people wanted a look-out to live among the Galla. I will be treated like an Amhara as long as I stay a Christian. Also I could go to high school and learn English, because I am like an Amhara. The Amhara say that to them religion is more important than tribe. They mean you can be converted to both, but you must be both a Copt and an Amhara. Amhara, I hate them. Copts, I hate them. I am a Galla. Our time will come."

Every mealtime, the whole Greek family gathered in the main room of the hotel. Perhaps it was wrong to call them Greeks, for their immediate ancestors had lived in Egypt. Years ago an uncle had moved to Harar when the Egyptians held that town. When Menelik recaptured Harar, this relative had found his Christianity an advantage. Gradually many of the extended family had moved south from Cairo, settling in Harar and later along the railroad until there were cousins in almost every village between Djibouti and Addis. The Greeks in Miesso still considered themselves Greeks even though none of them had been outside Ethiopia.

Besides this family of Greeks, the only other European living in the village was the French station master. Most of the time while we were glumly stuck in Miesso, he was in Awash and points between checking on the repairs and exploring the situation of the Fiat in the Arba river. He was afraid that the truck might tear loose in a big flood and crash into the railroad trestle below. As a result, even the railroad crews were trying to clear the road even though the railroad and the trucks are competitors. However slow and risky the trucks are, they have the great advantage of being able to go more places, as long as what is left of the roads hold up.

Late one evening the Frenchman came back to Miesso complaining, "Ah, it is no use. The truck she is caught like the mud is cement. Even another flood, she will not budge. No danger for the trestle, I don't think. We'll wait another couple of days and try again. Rains, ha, they are not was bad as locusts. They swarm on the tracks and are like grease if we run over them – so we slide all the way back to Djibouti. Ha, ha." But we didn't laugh. We were thinking of three more days in Miesso. Seeing our discouraged faces he winked at me and said, "Ha, ha, smile! You must not wait. I have a surprise. Maybe tomorrow comes a flatcar for you."

Although the through Djibouti-Addis train ran more or less on time, there seemed to be no real schedule for the freight trains. We watched all the movement on the trails throughout the next day, and finally, at dusk, we gave up. While I was heating soup on the primus in our bedroom and opening a can of some tuna, the Locust boy, Mikael rushed in with the good news. "She is here, she is here, your little flatcar. You must hurry, she wants to return." And hurry we did. The train from Awash dropped the flatcar and chuffed off toward Dira Dawa. In the dim light of the torches, Mil drove up two planks and onto the flatcar which had been shunted onto the siding. Mikael secured the car with tremendous hawsers, and then we waited. There was no sign of activity and the Frenchman was no where to be found. Finally I persuaded

Mil to come back and finish eating while Mikael watched the car. Nervously, Mil bolted his food and went out again while I packed up our things. Several hours went by. The flatcar was still standing alone on the sidetrack. Not knowing what else to do, we loaded the car and climbed aboard.

A jolting and shaking awoke me at two to find our flatcar was being attached to a freight train. Almost immediately the train started crawling away from Miesso. The car began to sway, like a hammock. Worried, Mil checked the ropes, but it was the train, not the auto itself, that was swaying. Relaxing to the movement, we dozed until, with a clatter, the train lurched to a stop. Through the gloom we could see a water-tank: we were already in Arba station and beyond it the Fiat truck in the middle of the river! A short passenger train clacked by, and then once more the train started up. As streaks of gray appeared in the sky ahead, I pondered the problem, and finally, pretending the flatcar was a dhow, relieved myself, precariously, over the edge. Then, in the privacy of the desert dawn, I managed to have a fairly complete sponge bath before changing to clean clothes.

Even from the security of the railroad trestle, the next river crossing looked difficult. How luxurious to be high above the gully enjoying our breakfast – of tomato juice, Nescafe from the thermos, and graham crackers – instead of surveying the track and constructing a bridge. Almost immediately the train slowed, and wound carefully over the deep canyon of the Awash. Much lower in the canyon we could see a battered but still usable vehicular bridge. Confined in its narrow crevice, the river ran foaming and plunging over boulders and tree trunks. In seconds the river itself was out of sight, and the canyon closed up till, looking back, it no longer existed.

While we waited for the shunting engine to untangle us, a

trainman brought us a letter from the Frenchman in Miesso. "Cheers and bon voyage," he wrote, "but remember, I don't know a thing about your flatcar." We blessed him.

CHAPTER 27

# Addis Ababa: capital
# of feudal Ethiopia

THE RAILWAY HOTEL IN AWASH HAD A VINE-SHADED TERRACE
and clean toilets. Otherwise Awash was hardly more of
a place than Miesso. Just beyond town we found the tent of
Mikael's Locust chief O'Leary, and stopped briefly to deliver
some letters. O'Leary was still drinking coffee, sitting in the
shade of his tent flap, when we drove up to his barbed wire
enclosure. "Have to keep the goats out of my things," he
explained as let us in. Turning he yelled out "co-<u>fee</u>" to no one
in particular, and motioned us to sit. He wore British tropical
shorts and long stockings, and spoke with a soft Cambridge
accent, despite his name. We had hardly sat down when a
young Ethiopian girl came in bringing two mugs of coffee.
She unobtrusively withdrew, not back to the open kitchen,

365

but into the tent, and came out some moments later in a clean dress and sat on a stool just a little behind O'Leary.

Her presence seemed to relax him, and he began to talk about his life, partly explaining, and partly justifying himself. "It all started out in rebellion, you know, the father wants his son to go up to Cambridge even though the son doesn't want to do; the father expects his son to take over his business, and the son objects. Well, I went up to Cambridge, and had a wonderful time until they kicked me out. Never cracked a book. But I rowed a crew for the College. Had a friend, brilliant. We always argued; it was a game to disagree. He wanted me to study, take this course. Rebellion again. When I flunked out, we had a real bust up. I drifted around London, refusing to go back to Liverpool and my father's business. Next thing I know, I'm off to fight in Spain. Anything to get away from my father. I didn't know the first thing about politics, still don't. Later my mother wrote me that my friend also went off to fight in Spain, and had been killed. The awful thing was, we were on opposite sides. He was an idealist, and fought Franco. I had just joined up with the first man who asked me. I kept thinking, maybe I killed him. Herded sheep in South Africa til the war; shipped all over the Middle East in the army. Then this. Never stay long in a spot, don't like ties, nothing stronger than this," his arm included both girl and tent. "Guess it's not much of a life," he apologized to himself, "but, well, it suits me."

FROM AWASH TO ADDIS is all up. Between Dira Dawa and the Arba River the road had wandered over a plateau about four thousand feet high; then it had dropped over a thousand feet into the depression of the Rift Valley through which the Awash River roars. Our speedometer clocked 141 miles from Awash to Addis; the map showed that we climbed from three to ten thousand feet, then descended two thousand feet into the high meadows where Addis stands. Outside Awash volcanic ash stretched for dreary miles. But the ash was useful in road repairing and for the first time since Nairobi we saw maintenance crews at work on the roadway. The plateau around Adama resembled the steppe near Harar, but the road kept going up, over a mountain rim, to Moggio. I assumed that at one time this road had been finished, but neglect and use – first by military vehicles and then by those giant Fiats, had worn off any gravel topping leaving bare the uneven base. Once more we drove slowly, often stopping to moving a rock or the fill a hole. Back in a wide valley beyond Moggio the road had been resurfaced with ash or gravel. The scenery, too, had changed. The lower plateau had been treeless and windswept; the mountains were thickly covered with untended forest. Now we had dropped into fertile savanna, liberally sprinkled with trees, especially a silver-green eucalyptus. Sheltering under the trees were rectangular stone huts with corrugated tin roofs as well as the traditional thatched-roof round huts. Even the huts varied from those we'd seen, for these had horizontal reed decoration below the thatch roof. We still saw no other horseless carriages, but in the villages were two-wheeled gharries pulled by a horse or donkey.

At a tiny crossroad we almost collided with a country gentleman astride a handsome horse who had stopped in the middle of the road. Over his head the gentleman held a large black umbrella to shield his face and turbaned head from the hot sun. Yet over his light weight white cotton toga he had thrown a heavy black wool cape. His jodhpurs were nearly concealed under the folds of the toga but his highly polished boots glistened in the sun. His companion, walking, was barefoot, his toga less generous, and his head bare. His frizzy gray hair framed a face whose dark brown color was no darker than his master's, but a broad nose and fuller lips indicated his ancestry probably included a slave. He had a lesser servant helping him, a dark-skinned youth wearing shorts under his skimpy shoulder cloth. In utter contrast to this feudal panorama was the tall light complected Ethiopian to whom the gentleman was talking. As a sign of respect the younger man had removed his felt hat, but otherwise he showed no traditional deference. Rather he stood straight in his pin-stripe business suit, joking with the rider while I scrambled out to photograph the scene.

Suddenly, at Bishoftv, not twenty miles from Addis, the

Crossing centuries:
feudal privilege confronts
modern practice

narrow gravel track gave way to ambitious four-lane asphalt. In a burst of enthusiasm Mil pushed down the accelerator, then regretfully slowed; beautiful though the road looked, it was full of potholes. A plane roared overhead, and for one awful minute I wondered whether perhaps we had driven onto a landing strip by mistake – there were of course no other cars. No, the plane landed at the army airfield just beyond the town. At last we began to pass cars and trucks going both directions. The edges of the road filled with strollers: men in jodhpurs and tunics, in shorts, in slacks – all wound at top with the toga-like shawl; Amhara women in ankle-length dresses of white or natural cloth, white bandanas covering their balloon like hairdos; young Galla maids in brighter cloths, the tight braids showing their scalp beneath.

The eucalyptus trees cast dark shadows increased by the

smoke of many cooking fires. We hardly realized we were in the city until the road abruptly left the eucalyptus shelter and climbed a steep hill. Imposing stones of the never completed Italian opera house loomed on the left, a row of shops and two-storey buildings lined the right side of the road. At the crossroads stood a policeman. We were at last in Addis.

Bublee struggled up the hill and spattered to a stop on level ground. So interested had it been I been in the people, so intent had Mil been with the road, that we hadn't noticed that the fuel gauge was down. It didn't show empty, but it never did; we should have known that quarter-full was a warning. An ignominious entrance to Addis, stalling right in the center of the capital, but at that point we didn't much care, so glad we were to arrive.

While Mil untied a jerry can I went over to the policeman to ask directions to the Pension Goddar which Morassi had recommended as cheap and clean. But the Ethiopian could not imagine that people in cars wanted to go anywhere but the Ras Hotel which we had passed coming up the hill. At length I gave up and tried a beauty salon with a French name. The proprietor gave clear enough directions, but cited as landmarks buildings which of course I didn't know. Vaguely annoyed with arriving so late in Addis that finding anything in the smoky dusk was difficult, I started back to the car. But there was a store called New Delhi; surely an Indian must own it and he would know English. But the owner was out, the clerks had never heard of the pension even though it could not have been more than three or four blocks away, for the built up center of town was no larger than that. Knowing no more than before, I went back toward the car.

To my horror I saw that Mil was gone but the car doors were unlocked. In seconds I thought of all the dreadful things which could have happened to him – my imagination was not tired. Then I saw him some distance up the street, half hidden by a heavy truck with USIS written on it, talking to a blond man. Cynically I thought that no American in the foreign service would know where the cheap pension was, but anyhow I walked over to join Mil, eyeing our own car carefully, suddenly aware of how dirty and messy all three of us looked. Apparently the young man, Dick Post, did know where the pension was; he was sketching a map for Mil when his wife Ann came out of a shop and stared at me.

"Lordy, aren't you Tink?" she gasped, using my college nickname. It took me a moment to place her, because she had been two years behind me at Radcliffe, and her name had been Hawkes then. "Come have a drink and a hot bath," she suggested, "you can find the pension later." It didn't take much persuasion before we were following the truck to their house. After a delectable bath it seemed too late to look for a place to eat so we supplemented their prepared dinner with some sardines for hors d'oeuvres. By then it seemed silly not to spend the night on their convertible sofa. We never did find the pension, though we were in Addis nearly a week.

The Post's house was a one-bedroom bungalow in what I assume might be described as a middle-class suburb of the capital. In actual fact it was the only cement house in the neighborhood, the others being large rectangular *tukals*: a reed wall foundation covered with mud and straw under a corrugated tin roof. Every yard was filled with the ever-present eucalyptus, a gray-silver-green variety that at this altitude grew into a large bush or a small tree, but not into the pillar-like trees which abound in California. Otherwise there was little other ground cover to help disguise the transitory nature and the shantiness of the capital. The royal family and the titled elite live their exclusive lives behind the walls of their fiefdoms, often in modern splendor. Embassies house most of their staff within their own compounds. Except for the downtown square that we saw when we first arrived, much of the rest of the town looks as it must have the day after the inhabitants traded their round tents for huts when Menelik II set up the capital in 1894. Only then, of course, the eucalyptus forest was newly planted and so the ugliness of the shanties lay exposed. Now, looking at Addis from the hills beyond, the capital appears to be a sea of silver waves with the main square a brown stone island in the center.

In this eucalyptus sea stood the Posts' house in which they had been living for about six months; before then they had stayed at the Ras Hotel. The house still had that just-moved-into look, as if the second delivery of furniture had not yet come. Actually, Ann had explained, they were lucky to have what they did. Like mostly newly married, fresh from college, neither of them had any savings. Dick had just began working for the State Department when they had received their assignment to Addis where he was to be "loaned" to the Information Service. They read in the post report that everything they might need for the two years ought to be brought in. Almost no imported goods were available in the capital and what little there was cost three or four times its worth because of the expensive transportation. So they were forced to buy basic furniture and a limited amount of canned good in the States and have it shipped in by the government. This had meant taking a loan through a special fund for government employees. "So, you see," Ann laughed, "we're practically mortgaged to the State Department."

To economize, the Posts ran a simple house with Ann doing all her on cooking over an impossible little kerosene stove which she supplemented with a charcoal brazier when needed. One boy acted as house-cleaner and washer. We gave him our dirtiest laundry and I coped with the rest in the bathtub at odd moments during our stay. One evening when the Posts had to attend a cocktail party, I stood in as cook. Suddenly I felt very domestic, more than I ever had in New Delhi where we had lived in a "pavilion" or sitting room/ bedroom/bath area of an Indian home. We had converted a servant's room behind the house into a kitchen which was always hot and so I had simply avoided it entirely. In Addis, perhaps for the first time in my marriage, I felt the urge to settle down; a weak little urge, but there. Despite the stove, the dinner was good, especially the crab cocktail and the muffins; there was no resemblance to our slapped-together road meals.

We talked late, telling the Posts of our adventures; they had their own to relate. Two weeks before, over a long weekend, they had driven south to visit a well-reputed Swedish missionary hospital built just on the edge of the escarpment. The trip had taken much planning. First they had to obtain a permit to travel from the Ministry of Interior. Next the Ethiopian Foreign Office had wanted to know why the Posts were going out of the capital and had sent an official over to talk with them and with the people who were to accompany them: another American from USIS, an Englishman from his Embassy, an Italian mechanic-driver, and an Ethiopian interpreter. Finally everyone was notified of clearance and a truck was fully stocked for emergencies. They left the capital before sunrise and, after a very hard day's driving, got to the hospital that evening where they spent two interesting days with the missionaries. On their way back they were stopped by the police in the only town they had passed through. The travelers showed their travel permit and their passports, but the police were adamant: they insisted that the Posts had no travel permission which they recognized: they would have to speak to the local chief of police and the security officer.

Since it was Sunday, the group would simply have to wait til the next day. The next day the police chief said that he had to talk to his superior who would not be in town until Tuesday.

"I could see this going on for weeks," said Dick. "No one there would honor the travel permit: indeed their attitude toward the center was rather cavalier. They kept saying that strangers were simply not allowed to travel in their region without permission of their bosses. Since the police were under the Ministry of the Interior, and since the travel permit came from the same Ministry, we didn't know what to do; we were completely stymied."

At last Dick persuaded them to let the interpreter go, for he was not a foreigner. The interpreter swiftly returned to Addis and informed the Embassy who informed the Ministry of the Interior who informed the local police chief. But nothing happened. The Ministry simply was not recognized by the local men in power. Another day went by, then two. The group sat in the back of the truck and played cards. At first their guards wouldn't let them leave the vehicle, but eventually they were allowed to set up an emergency camp in the shady courtyard of the police barracks. Ann and Dick slept in the truck, the others in a tent which they had brought along for emergencies. Very early the fourth morning of their captivity, when their food had almost run out, their interpreter returned with a squad of soldiers from Addis who, with a show of force, recaptured the Posts and their truck, and escorted the group back to the capital.

"We were grateful," Dick concluded, "that this was postwar and local chiefs were forbidden to maintain their private armies. Then, I supposed, we'd have been held until ransomed, for surely the Emperor wouldn't have started a civil war over us!"

"It was so strange, that happening along a main road," Ann put in. "When we were really helpless, the time we took mules into the interior to visit the wonderful cave-churches at Lalibala, that the time the local governor couldn't have been more helpful."

Their talk only emphasized the prevailing disunity in the country. Mil and I wondered what would have happened if we had been waylaid, who would have come to our aid. Dick suggested that we get a travel permit for the rest of our journey in Ethiopia, and that he would get us a small American flag to fly as we drove. "If you look official, perhaps you won't be bothered. Most of the bandits or shiftas would rather not be involved with government, it is getting stronger all the time. Of course this wouldn't help in a situation like ours when the local authorities just wouldn't accept federal authority. But the road to Asmara is fairly frequently traveled, much more than the part you came over. There should be no trouble."

"It is a funny country," mused Ann. "Take this book, for instance, it's called *Government of Ethiopia* and it's by an Oxford don, Margery Perham. She has written a lot on Africa, and done so very fairly. Just because she is fair, and not hopelessly pro-Ethiopian the way Sylvia Pankhurst is, the government won't let her come to visit the country. Yet everyone reads her book, there is nothing else as good in any language. She has a translation of the myth about the queen of Sheba and how, through trickery, Solomon fathered her son, the first Emperor Menelik. That's a story out their own holy book, so they can't mind that. But what Miss Perham says about lack of control annoyed the Emperor, I guess. The country just can't stand criticism, even if it is honest. That is why you're not supposed to take picture; they might show that the condition of the people isn't as modern and up-to-date as the government propaganda says."

"Maybe they are reacting from Evelyn Waugh's *Black Mischief*." I laughed at the remembrance of the satire. "It was a bit cruel."

"Maybe," Ann said, "but whatever the reason, the people here are still afraid to meet foreigners. It's taken me nearly a year to know a few Ethiopian women well enough to be invited to their homes; I doubt they will ever dare to come to mine."

"The government is so scared of foreigners that they hire advisors from different countries, and play them off against each other," explained Dick. "British, American, Swedish, and French governments are limited in the type of assistance they can offer, and told where the projects will be. Only recently the Russian opened a large new hospital here in town." I nodded. We had already seen the Russian's modern three-story building with bright beach umbrellas and painted metal chairs set out on the second floor terrace. Since the Russians have no diplomats in the colonies of Africa they are making a bit of a show in Addis. As for their espionage, of which we heard so much in Kenya, it seemed very limited if not non-existent.

"But all the foreigners, *ferengi* they call us, no matter what nationality, are taboo," continued Dick. "The government sees intrigue in every shadow, in every harmless talk you might have an Ethiopian. As a result, the Ethiopians avoid us like a plague.. Only the most secure Ethiopians, those on the top, would dare to be seen with a foreigner outside official functions or in the offices." He sighed. "Makes our work very difficult. I only hope it will change. Of course, they have every right to be suspicious. Look at their history, the way Britain and French and Italy kept dividing the country into spheres of influence. It's like giving away a dying man's clothes while he watches."

"Do you suppose," I asked Mil, "that was why that young fellow in the bank this morning looked so scared when we asked to see him? He's the younger brother of an Ethiopian in their Embassy in New Delhi," I explained to the Posts. "His brother was so grateful for our friendship in India, it was almost pitiful. He and his wife and their two kids were as good looking as they come, but very dark by Amharic or Indian standards. They had a hard time keeping servants, for the color prejudice is still strong among the low classes there. Sometimes they were even snubbed at diplomatic receptions. Anyhow, he promised us his brother in Addis would show us how an Ethiopian lived, and what he ate. But today when we met him at his office the brother practically shrank at the thought, even after he had read his brother's letter introducing us. I'm sure he will never contact us, though of course he promised."

The only Ethiopian I really talked to the whole time we were in Addis was the private secretary to the Emperor. I had gone to visit the Indian Ambassador to gather some material on Indians in Ethiopia for an article. Sardar Singh was a magnificent specimen of a royal elderly Sikh. His uncut beard had turned snowy white; indeed he looked like Santa Claus with a turban. Ultra-nationalist from his early association with the anti-British freedom movement in India, he commented vociferously on the role of the colonial powers which more or less invented the three Somalilands in order to play their old "divide-and-rule" game. There wasn't much else for him to talk about. Indians in Ethiopia were so few that they played no role at all in the culture or power struggle. In the cities were Gujerati traders, both Hindu and Muslim; a few South Indian Christians taught in mission schools. The total number was less than 1300. Unable to produce enough facts for a story on Indians in the country, Sardar Singh suggested I try to see the Emperor and said he would make an appointment with the Emperor's private secretary, Ato Tafari Work.

I didn't think there was much chance of meeting the Emperor, though of course I should have liked to. From all sides I'd heard of his formality; mere protocol practically obviated a meeting arranged only a week ahead. Nor had I, in the female's eternal cry "a thing to wear" because one must dress formally for meeting His Imperial Highness. Still, I decided that meeting the secretary might prove interesting.

Ato Tafari Work's office was in an old Italian villa in a large and comfortable room that might have been a library. As if to emphasize the formality, he wore a cut-away coat – though without tails, striped pants, and white shirt with a formal silver and black striped tie. He was a small compact man, with bright piercing eyes. It was not I who did the interviewing, but he. After quizzing me about the troubles in Kenya he went on to ask details about our drive across the Ogaden. Every time I asked him about Ethiopia he suddenly got rather deaf. He also promised to call, and I also knew that he wouldn't.

One afternoon, however, I did have a pleasant encounter with an Ethiopian, the neighbor of the Posts. Unfortunately it couldn't be called a conversation, his English was hardly more fluent than my Amharic. I had been scrubbing away on my washing when I became aware of an incessant pounding from the yard next door. Peering through the reed stake fence which separated the two houses I could see a barefoot Amhara woman preparing beer by pounding *gesho* leaves in a wooden barrel with a heavy wooden post. Remembering the admonition so often repeated that taking photographs was NOT allowed in Ethiopia, I carefully did not ask permission but quickly took the shot. But one of the many children playing in the yard and in all stages of dress and undress spotted me and began to yell. With a startled look in my direction, the woman fled into the house while I tried to placate the child with some sweets.

At that moment the father of the brood came out and with a courtly air invited me to come through the break in the fence. He was a tall man with black wavy hair, good-looking by any standards, with features, if they had not been very dark brown, could have been Italian or Spanish. His combination of clothes was amazing, yet he wore them with such assurance that he looked perfectly proper, without even that hint of embarrassment I feel when someone surprises me at home while I'm wearing shorts. Over an undershirt he wore a wool vest; the suit coat thrown over his shoulders was old and battered, and from a different suit than the vest. Beneath these he had on what I assumed was the bottom half of an old tunic; under a tunic he should of course be wearing jodhpurs, but he wasn't. Alone of the family he wore shoes, old army boots half tied, with no socks. Later, when he decided that the whole family should have their picture taken, new sandals were found for the youngest girl.

The father was fascinated by the Rolliecord camera, so I showed him how to focus and he soon had his own children and some strays posing for him. The children, wearing odd bits of fourth or fifth hand clothing, seemed unconscious of their rags; all of them had that sort of certainty of position that allows a proper Bostonian to drive an old car while all the nouveau riche use Cadillacs. The oldest daughter, per-haps twelve years old, wore her hair puffing up a high snood; the middle daughters were apparently growing their hair since they covered their heads with kerchiefs; the youngest girl wore only a few curls in front to relieve the severity of a shaved head. The little boys also had tufts of hair left from shaving, but elongated, like a cockscomb. Several of the children were several shades darker; their noses flatter. I never dared ask whether they all the same mother. Nor did the woman come out of the house again while I was there though I could hear the children talking to her. The baby cried while sister held up his face for a photograph; they both were sitting on the door sill, the only flooring, inside or out, that wasn't just straw scattered earth. Then the mother flew at the sister like an incensed hen, and in a flurry of white, the baby disappeared. For all this apparent poverty, the man was a moderately well-placed civil servant; when he went off to the office his jodhpurs and tunic were the Addis version of what a white collar worker wears.

Down the street where the gravel gave way to mud, the *tukals* had thatched roofs with pottery chimney pots. But to prove its claim to the modern age, one *tukal* had strung bare light bulbs on top of its three chimney pots. Where the smoke went, I don't know. This *tukal* was, presumably, still middle-class. Beyond the main bazaar were rows of stone hovels, reminiscent of Italian slums, paint peeling off the walls. Here the little girls, fetching water in old tin cans, wore the Galla beads around their necks; the women had tight-braided hair and carried round clay water ves-

Ethiopian neighbors reveal the poverty of the middle class

Raised wooden stall in the Addis Ababa
market; customers in typical local dress

sels tied on their backs. Evidently the racial line is also
economic.

The market was a glorious place, perhaps because it was
so unlike the close-packed alleys of Indian bazaars. Rather
it was an open area, cluttered with temporary looking structures of wood, always with the tin roof. Around the edges
were stone and concrete-block stalls. The merchandise itself
held no glamour: under most of the tin roofs were yard goods
with a few ready-made nondescript items of clothing hanging
from the roof supports. Along the stone verandahs sat rows
of tailors, each behind his own machine, ready to make up
your cloth while you watched, if necessary.

Near the tailors, using the verandah as their shop, sat
sellers of silver, both men and women. Plain wedding rings
and crosses to be worn as amulets were arranged on the stone
floor; a few bracelets and silver beads were also for sale. All
the jewelry was extremely crude in execution, yet its very
crudeness gave it charm and I haggled awhile for a Greek cross
hung on beaded string. The trader wore a Muslim skullcap
though I noticed a topee behind him on a ledge should he
need to look Christian for customers or police. His coffee-
skin covered features there were Semitic in the extreme. He

certainly had all the bargaining acumen normally attributed to his race, whether Muslim or Hebrew in religion. I nearly bought a silver incense urn which I certainly didn't want; when I refused the urn he passed forward various other silver objects from or for churches: chalices, ornate keys, and large crosses for bearing atop poles. But I nearly bought a black and white rug made from the skin of the Gezira monkey.

Further along the row an Amhara woman was selling horns and swords and silver tipped canes, all necessary accouterment for the well-dressed man. The open area of the market was almost carpeted with straw mats for sale; scattered on top of the mats were straw baskets, and the little straw umbrellas which were commonly used for the sun than the rain. However, no self-respecting gentleman used straw umbrellas in the capital anymore; de rigueur were the black cloth ones. Hemp and leather were also piled here and there.

But it was not the goods, but the people, that fascinated me. Every ethnic mixture was there: Semitic, Hamitic, Negroid, all jumbled in countless variations. It was easier to type the shoppers by their clothes than their features. The Amhara men wore jodhpurs, mostly without shoes, and all of them had a long cloth for the toga shawl. Under the toga some wore a white tunic, others an old suit coat; some had on both. Others wore ordinary shirts; a few had on bush jackets. Occasionally a man would be wearing the cape of the countryside, but many more kept warm with a sleeveless sweater. The Amhara women, too, brightened their invariably white long-skirted, long-sleeved dresses with knitted woolen jerkins. The dress of the Galla women was more ragged, less than white, some looking like flour sacks rudely stitched together. One young girl, her hair braids running round her head, carried her baby papoose style in a leather sling decorated with sea shells. The head peeping from the sack was incongruously covered with a red-check gingham bonnet. Most Galla women pulled their shawls over their braided hair while the Amhara women wore white head-pieces. One woman wore nothing on her frizzy hair which crowned her head as a cap of mushroom. The men, on the other hand, wore all manner of head-covering: caps, tropical topees, turbans, felt hats, prayer hats, berets. The children sported odd bits of hand-me-downs, so that one would have only pants, another only a shirt; but almost everyone wore a small cross on a string around their necks.

I wore my cross to dinner that evening, but not before, on Ann's insistence, I had thoroughly boiled it. Skin diseases, she had explained, are easily contagious. Mil teased me about my sudden religion, but I assured him that the cross was so primitively done that no one would know it was a cross when I wore it, and I was right too. He seemed relieved that I hadn't bought more things, and even more relieved that I had come home, self and camera intact. For although I knew there was law about not taking pictures, I also knew that there were many strange laws in the country which most people ignored. So I chose to ignore the regulation and take photographs, such quick ones though that many were spoiled. Only one man, a bookseller in a tidy little reed hut, waved at me to stop and shouted threateningly. Most of the other men gave me a sly grin or a haughty sneer, while the women, proud of their beauty, generally struck a pose, like women anywhere will do.

One day we bumped around Addis on the roughest city roads we'd ever encountered looking at the Coptic churches. The traditional churches were hexagonal, following the pattern of the earlier round huts. The ambulatories that divided the congregation were clearly demarcated though. Because there were no services taking place we were able to walk the middle aisles of these churches as well as the outer ones, and look more closely at the art work on the walls. I was somewhat more intimidated about taking pictures of such landmarks. Instead we bought some parchment paintings of saints copied from monasteries. A fascinating contrast between Eastern European art and African primitives, these paintings continue to symbolize for us the contrasts that are Ethiopia.

The major monument in town, the statue of Menelik II astride in jumping horse, graced the small park just above the built-up business district I thought it seemed like a harmless enough picture. But Dick warned me that a tourist had his camera confiscated for taking just that picture only a few weeks before. Challenged as I often am by the senselessly forbidden, I took a shot from the moving car on the theory that perhaps movement would give reality to the horse. In fact, the picture simply looks fuzzy.

While I was busy washing clothes or photographing the market, Mil had seen to the car. Bublee had withstood the pounding amazingly well, but it took the mechanics a lot of time to clean and tighten the car. As a gesture to our adventuresome-ness, the manager of the garage, an engaging Austrian, put Bublee back into shape with all the labor free; we paid only for the parts. So friendly was he that he asked us to dinner, and promised us the use of his trading company's guest house in Dessie, the main town on the road to Asmara. In the garage Mil also discovered the true ending to the story of the priests and the flash floods; he saw what was left of the jeep: a fantastically tortured mess of metal. The mechanic swore he could make it run again; if he did, he must be part magician.

Our car ready, the clothes washed, a check cashed, and we were ready to leave. There was no point in waiting around trying to meet Ethiopians. We treated the Posts to a farewell dinner in the wooden-beamed dining hall of the Ras Hotel, the only decent restaurant in town. The chatter of foreign languages once again emphasized the isolation of the *ferengi* in this isolated capital. No wonder the favorite sport in the capital was big game hunting, anything to get away.

Yet the barriers of distrust were breaking. An American professor from Oklahoma Agriculture & Mine College, who was teaching at the new agriculture school in Jimma, had dropped in for lunch that day. He regaled us with a description of the reactions of the first batch of students to arrive at the school. Naturally the boys chosen to attend any school were picked by their fathers' position and not by any aptitude for or interest in agriculture. The upper class Amhara whom they represented looked down upon working with the hands as a job only fit for slaves. "This is nonsense for anyone studying agriculture," exploded the professor. So the Americans had set out to change this attitude. They set up dormitories where all students were required to make their own bunks and straighten their own clothes. All personal slaves or servants of the boys were sent home. Apparently a few of the boys left on the heels of their servants, but most stuck it out and were already adapting to this very strange American idea of doing work yourself. The Oklahoman thought that if the students learned not a thing more, just the fact they had worked in the dorms or in the field was practically enough to reorient their whole thinking. "That's what those people need," he almost growled, "a good shaking up. If the Amhara don't learn, and they probably won't, then there's going to be a revolution."

This talk seemed so strange coming from a dedicated scientist who at home would probably not have known his own Congressman's name. But his practical nature had been affronted by the intrigue of the country. He was still furious over a commission he had sat on which had been formed to pick a site for another agricultural college. After much travel, deliberation, and expense the committee had chosen an area with ideal soil, not far from the capital. Then, blandly ignoring the committee which he himself had set up, Haile Selassi announced that his own personally controlled province of Harar would receive the school even though it already had several other colleges. The professor perfectly understood the political reason for the choice of Harar; what he couldn't understand was why the Emperor had ever set up a commission and wasted all that effort and money.

Dick suggested that this action was typical of the Emperor, for the man was caught between his history as the absolute ruler and his own belief in constitutional monarchy. Sometimes he was one, sometimes he was the other. The important and amazing thing was that Haile Selassi had become as progressive as he had. In particular, the Emperor was pushing education, for during the Italian campaign nearly all of the few hundred Ethiopians with even passable education had been slaughtered. To modernize the country you need educated men to serve the state. There was such a long way to go. The Year Book on Education listed only 600 elementary schools and four secondary schools in the whole country with its seven million people! Yet so ambitious was the Emperor that a university had been started with seventy-two students, including one girl. To hurry the process along, the Emperor often paid for schools and foreign staff out of his own purse since government revenues were low even though an income tax had been reluctantly put into effect in 1944. Besides education, the Emperor had just established a sort of indirectly-elected advisory council as a step toward representative government.

Still, I was inclined to agree with the Oklahoman. The dominant memory I have of Ethiopia is its feudalism. Surely this is an anachronism in the twentieth century, I thought. Sooner or later, the country is bound to change. Remembering Mikael's words from Miesso, I would bet on sooner.

# CHAPTER 28

# A beautiful rollercoaster drive from Addis to Asmara

T HE MORNING MIST HUNG HEAVILY OVER ADDIS ABABA AS WE drove out of the capital; thus hidden and beautified, the city for the first time resembled its name: new flower. We had already wound high up a mountainside before the first sunrays penetrated the valley, glinting across the eucalyptus like reflecting so many silver coins. For a moment even the treeless steppe was softened as the oblique rays that made each drop of dew into a tiny light-bulb. The road climbed steadily between rocky hills, each crowned with its own collection of round stone *tukuls*. Not a tiny level space was left uncultivated so that the sheep had to scratch their food from the almost perpendicular rock. Then the valley widened and as we reached the crest the land beyond gave the fleeting illusion being an unbroken plateau, gently ridged. As we stared the sun licked away the mist and the plateau seemed to develop cracks and gashes and chasms for which the ridges were mere camouflage. It was almost as if geological history were repeating itself, creating this amazing panorama before our unbelieving eyes. Incredibly, this was mountain scenery turned upside down, with the jaggedness and steepness at the bottom of the canyons, the soft rolling plains at the top. The map labeled this area the Shoa massif.

Gentle streams sometimes used the road as a riverbed; the whole world was new-green and damp. We drove through Alpine pastures, stretched almost level and laid as a carpet on the top of world. Tiny pastel flowers, blue, purple, and white, poked their heads just above the grass cover and nodded violently in the wind. Their size and colors contrasted sharply with the big gaudy tropical blooms you might expect to find at this latitude. The round grass fences protecting huts from roving sheep etched a design on the grass carpet. We stopped to photograph this pastoral scene and for the first time the altitude, which must have been nearly thirteen thousand feet, impressed itself on me. The sun on the car kept us warm even with the windows open. Outside, the wind snapped at my skirt and cracked it like a sail; I pulled on a sweater but still I was chilly. Walking perhaps ten feet into the field for the picture, I had to push my way back against the wind; by the time I reached the car I was exhausted and panting.

The road itself was of crushed gravel, with many excellent stretches that were tantalizing without being satisfying, for just as we had dared to increase our speed above thirty miles an hour there would be a gaping hole and we'd have to brake. The reason for the ruts was soon apparent. While outside of a few towns we saw no other cars on the open road the whole day, many trucks of all sizes, but mostly the thirteen-ton giants, crawled up and down the hills going in both directions moving slowly, at a man's pace. Their drivers were usually Italians or Greeks or Armenian though there were a few Ethiopians too. All were friendly and would wave as we passed, when we were able to pass. The road itself was barely more than one way and the trucks drove down the middle. Coming up behind them with all their grinding and moaning, our horn was useless; it was often ten or fifteen minutes before the driver would realize we were there. Sheepishly, as if he suddenly realized we might have been there for hours, he'd pull his giant rig off the road and almost salute as we whizzed by – at twenty-five miles an hour! There was less wait behind the smaller trucks, for they usually had riders clinging precariously on top of their load of produce and who would wriggle forward to knock on the cab for us. Often the cabs were also filled with people, but not to overflowing as they had been in Somaliland, for with all the curves and climbs, the driver had to have enough room to maneuver. Whenever we had stopped for eating or filling the gas tank or taking a picture, all the trucks behind us would pass and their drivers would lean out, asking if we needed assistance. Somehow we felt very protected, as if all the trucks formed our personal bodyguard.

Skimming along the top of the world we could see for miles on either side. To the left, layer upon layer of huge gashes slashed the plateau until, in the distance, the far side of a deep canyon rose abruptly, indicating the valley of the Blue Nile. Ahead and to the right the ridges piled up behind each other til they touched the sky. Spying the American flag fluttering from our baggage rack, two peasants bowed low in obeisance to an unknown authority. They stood as statues, beneath their tiny straw sunbrellas, clad in flowing robes of yellowing cotton, their heads bound in a tight turbans which looked more like bandages than hat. The long white

Ethiopian peasants, in accordance with feudal tradition, bow in obeisance

shawls that wrapped their shoulders covered them so well that I couldn't tell whether they were male or female. Their costume, too, was unique; we saw no more like that again. As we passed them I had the oddest feeling that they had, like the sleeping beauty, just awakened from a distant time when you humbled yourself before any powerful or unknown thing. I wondered whether they stood there all day, bowing to the huge trucks as well.

For some time we followed a ridge, rather more rugged and barren than usual; then, unexpectedly, the road turned directly toward it. Only when we were nearly on top of it did we see the tunnel which must have been a feat to construct in the crumbly shale. We blinked the lights, honked, and then plunged through.

On the arch above the tunnel we could still make out the word "Mussolini." Blocking the view as we first came out of the tunnel stood a large defaced monument; the only writing visible on it was the year of construction, 1932. Sitting around the base of the monument, as if they were in the corner park and not perched high on a mountain crest miles from any apparent settlement, half a dozen ragged boys huddled in stripped blankets and one man in jodhpurs and tunic. What they were doing there we had no idea; they didn't ask for a ride, didn't even hold out their hands for

Monument to Mussolini at the tunnel entrance

food or money. They simply gazed at us while we gazed at them, posed eagerly for a picture, then went back to their chilly sunbathing.

Beyond the monument, the plateau fell away into a steep escarpment dropping over five thousand feet in a breath-taking plunge. So abrupt was the drop we could see only parts of the road as it ribboned back and forth to the floor of the plain where the tin roofs of the houses of Debra Sina glistened in the sun miles below. In the valley, the road turned and snaked its way northward following the escarpment. Beyond the town in the east we could see far over the barren plain as it sank into the Danakil Depression, miles below sea level. The only features enlivening the dull backdrop were the mirror-like lakes in which the plain, like a dish tipped slightly toward the Red Sea, had caught the raging waters of the mountain streams and dammed them into salty marshes and ponds.

Down we dropped, through all the seasons from early spring to mid-summer, through the latitudes from the Swiss Alps to the African desert. Our ears hummed and caught, as in a swift elevator. The sensation, like the scenery, was

exact position. Of course it didn't matter, with only one road, you couldn't get lost.

Only when we came to Combolcia did I find us on the map. A large monument to *Il Duce* marked the only road junction between Addis and Asmara. Here was the turn-off for most of the huge Fiat trailers and the lumbering oil tankers. Instead of climbing the tortuous hills back up to the Shoa Massif, they veered east across the across the desert to the Red Sea port of Assab. Our road turned west and began a long but not particularly steep climb up the escarpment. Back we went from August to June to early April; on again went the sweaters. Both the road and the scenery improved with the height. Greenness returned, and dampness. Waving trees replaced the stiff naked thorn branches; there were sheep as well as goats pinned to impossibly steep slopes.

Up and over the top, the road turned north into a valley. Sheltering from the wind in a slight indentation in the plateau, was Dessie. It was a large town, its many European style buildings giving it an Italian rather than an Ethiopian look. In the business area we saw mostly Italians tending shops... or were they Greeks or Armenians? They all spoke Italian and had dark complexions. We asked one shopkeeper where the A. Besse compound was and he courteously jumped in his car to lead us there. The letter from Addis made a great impression on the Greek accountant who received us. Immediately he sent for the Indian manager who rushed over from his house on the other side of the compound to show us a luxurious guest house with living, dining, bed, and bath rooms plus a small kitchen. A Galla maid cooked dinner from our tins while we indulged in a lengthy hot bath. The maid had her hair braided into the tight strip braids of the traditional Galla style. From a distance I had never noticed that women wore a thin front braid that followed the hair line and buffered the front to back braids. Nor had I realized how taut the skin was between the braids. It must hurt, that hairdo.

The next day's drive was through the heart of Ethiopia's ancient kingdom of Aksum; most of the people we saw could have belonged to almost any century between then and now. Even the tents of the Imperial Highway Authority looked authentically ancient though their mission was modern. Outside Dessie the grass carpet spread over terrain that looked like an ideal golf course; surely if the British had colonized the country, tees and greens would have quickly been added to the rolling hills. The level area did not last long. Almost immediately the road began to lower gradually into a wide river valley that opened back onto the Danakil desert. A prison, a cluster of houses, several half ruined stone buildings which might have been a factory, and a small *ristorante* clung to the last bit of level ground before the road shot abruptly back up the towering escarpment beyond. This *ristorante* was the first of the many small truckers' restaurants which lined the road to Asmara and, as always, several large trucks were pulled to cool off while their drivers enjoyed a coffee or a beer. Although it was lunch time we pushed on, anxious to get out of the heat. Bublee went slower and slower as Mil was forced to shift from high to third to second. The grinding of diesels echoed against the hills miles before the trucks came into view. Even at our slow speed we passed them, a hare to their tortoise. Further on, as we rounded a curve from which the road could be seen serpentining behind, we stopped for lunch while the trucks, like the tortoise, inched past us and won the crest.

Then began a giant roller-coaster: up and over rocky ridges fit only for grazing, down into narrow valleys, often marshy, filled with people working in their fields. The valleys were rimmed with eucalyptus woods and round reed huts. In one valley, perched on a small dry island in the marsh, stood a ruined Italian church in a sort of watered-down Gothic style. Up we shot again, and down, over and over, each ridge between five hundred and a thousand feet high. One valley would be wide and short, the next long and narrow; this one had a tiny jewel of a lake, the next a marshy swamp. At one larger settlement there was a sawmill though all the valleys we saw were practically treeless except for the soft, immature eucalyptus. At the outskirts of a large settlement was a sign-post announcing the town as Mai Cheu Ham, even though, on the map, this place was at least ten miles inland from the road. First there was a *tukal* colony which served as police barracks. Next came a tin roofed whitewashed building bearing the legend: Sudan Interior Mission. We had been told to stop at the Mission, which was said to be located in a place called Enda Mohoni, if we needed any help, but since it was Sunday and all was going well we preferred not to bother the missionaries. We decided the name, rather then the road, had moved.

Looking at the apparently smooth walls of the valley it was impossible to predict where the road would go next. As we began to climb, it seemed the road perversely picked the tallest mountain to scale. The ascent was the steepest climb of the day, twisting and doubling back, looping above itself. Near the brow of the mountain we stopped along an empty stretch to refill the gas tank. Looking to the east, the desert lay inert and lifeless, miles below. A cattle path wound up to the road from a small village in the crevice beneath us. As I watched, a black cloaked figure danced up the path, showing the purple and scarlet lining of his cloak as he jumped and pranced. Was he in a trance dance, or simply crazy? Leaping past me, he jigged over to the car where already three of four herders were shoving and pushing to look through all the windows. A tall Amhara with a generous turban of almost Indian proportions stood aloof from the group for a moment; then he too pushed forward and began to shout about "shillings." I couldn't imagine where any of them had come from, but they began to make noisy remarks to each other and

Ethiopian herders peer into our car

at Mil when the demand for shillings was not met. Suddenly their tone turned from a supplicating to a threatening one. I hopped in the car, shoved some candy out of the window, and we summarily drove off.

At the top of the crest, perhaps a mile beyond, was a collection of tin-roofed *tukals*. Sitting on the roof of a lower shed were three children with dome-like hats, black and white striped. I decided to try taking their picture. They watched idly until I was within two feet of them: then they began a slow retreat to the end of the roof and down across the meadow. I held out candy, the same cellophane wrapped suckers I'd been using right along, and the boys looked at it longingly. Still they continued to back up, motioning for me to put candy on the ground and leave it there. Three adult men walked up so briskly that I could not but be impressed at their speed in the rarified atmosphere. One man, seeing the boys cowering behind the shed, strode over to me and shook my hand, accepted some candy and promptly ate it, paper and all. All the while he kept up a running monologue directed toward the boys, chiding them for their fear.

At last the tallest boy came shyly forward, bowing and extending his hands cupped to receive the sweets. Having survived the ordeal, he swaggered back to his friends and grandly gave them each a piece. I ate one also, by way of demonstration, and the boys began peeling off the cellophane. All the while the man's piercing voice ran on; I began to understand that he was posing them for me. Smiling my thanks I took a close up of the boys; not one moved as I went near them, though the looks they gave me were a mixture of fear and curiosity. At close range I could see that the hats were made of coarse natural wool woven somehow to produce the striped design, then gathered into an impertinent spire and topped with four or five tassels. For warmth, the boys draped animal skins over theirs shoulders but their knees and feet were bare. When I had finished, all three men gravely shook my hand and escorted me back to the car where they graciously accepted the cigarettes Mil offered them.

As we continued Mil confessed that he had been somewhat worried when he saw the three men approach, particularly after that noisy reception we had had earlier. He grinned at me in his crooked crinkly smile. "I even had the wrench out ready to use. Guess I'm silly, huh?" But I didn't think so; I kissed him as he drove.

This time, as we wound down the mountain, a longer, wider, valley opened up below, running north. As the twilight etched the outline of the ridges behind us, it seemed as if we had finally come off Mount Olympus into the highlands around it. The land was drier, and rockier, the *tukals* of stones with thatched roofs. Checking the map I decided we should be in Quita before it got dark. Yet soon it was pitch black and not a light showed on the plain. The road surface improved and we drove faster, wondering where we were. Suddenly ahead were red tail lights of a truck lumbering ahead of us.

Quickly we overtook it, not bothering to honk, for here the road is two car widths wide. Then for another hour, only darkness. I was beginning to feel annoyed at the map and at my navigation. We couldn't be lost, we were somewhere between Dessie and Asmara. But where was Quita?

We weren't prepared for such a small place. Quita consisted of one small *ristorante*, a petrol pump, several *tukals*, and many parked trucks. When we asked for a room we were given a tiny square box even smaller than the bedroom in Miesso. I took full advantage of my uniqueness as perhaps the only woman who had stopped at the place in ten years. The servant brought a washbasin into the room, and also a small commode. Mil had gone off to find the inevitably smelly toilet, had used the great outdoors instead, and was a bit jealous of my little luxury. The restaurant had three family-sized tables covered with soiled gingham. For dinner we ate a thick soup, with a can of our own Vienna sausages added to it. After one swallow of their sickly sweet coffee we settled for hot water into which we stirred our own powdered coffee. It was sleep more than food that we wanted: we'd been driving steadily for fifteen hours. Back in our little box, we covered the beds with a layer of DDT powder, lay down on top in our own sheet sleeping bags, and immediately slept.

By the first rays of the sun the *ristorante* looked more rundown than I'd thought. I woke with the certainty that bedbugs were gnawing at my legs; imagination again. We had planned to buy gas here, but the pump wouldn't open til eight o'clock. The thought of spending three more hours in the cubicle, or in the greasy restaurant, was not encouraging. We gulped our instant coffee, and speedily departed.

The road was a ramp between a complex of sheer-cut canyons, earth brown at first, then lighting vividly as though on fire into brilliant reds. Gradually the red softened into

Coptic priest with
parishioners before their
cave church near Agula

dazzling pink between layers of steel gray, or blue or green. While the color lasted, the scene was almost too beautiful; we kept stopping just to gaze, or to take pictures. At length, like cotton too long in the sun, the colors began to fade; the panorama was over.

Near Agula we stopped to see a Coptic church cut into the rock wall. As we waded across a stream and scrambled up a steep hill, children from the fields beyond caroled our arrival to the priest. He stood tall and regal, turbaned and shrouded in white, his haughty features completely Semitic. Behind him was a wooden door leading into the church. It appeared that an older, cave-like entrance had been filled in with rocks and plaster except for a door and a small window cut in above it which was covered with chicken wire to keep out the bats. This main door was set into a section of the cliff which protruded from the rest to form the top of a cross. On either arm of the cross was a door, each cut directly into the rock; the cliff area around the door had been whitewashed to give the impression that all three doors were made the same way. On the north side the hill fell back and almost the entire length of the church was visible, but both to the east and south the church melded into the cliffs. A few crosses whitewashed on the walls were the only attempt at decoration.

As we examined the walls we were joined by a gentleman of the village, his hair and goatee as white as his toga and jodhpurs. He led us back to the main door and motioned for us to remove our shoes. We entered the gloom, padding across straw laid on the mud-packed floor. With all three doors open we could see the priest standing by a large stone cross set into the center of the space which seemed to form a Greek cross. Actually the rear of the church was rectangular, but a small curtained area in each corner made the open space symmetrical. With a taper to light the way, the priest led us to one curtain on which were pinned two pictures, one a serene Mary, the other a fierce demon. Reverently the priest drew the curtain and beyond there appeared only a pile of ashes until he thrust his taper into the enclosure to show a relic box, undoubtedly the pride of the church. In the other corner, partially hidden behind curtains, was a crudely carved confession box.

Four pillars surrounded the center stone cross and probably served to divide the sacred heart of the church from the ordinary members during a service. Apparently this division did not apply outside of services, for the priest encouraged us to examine the columns for their crude carved crosses. There were so many questions I should like to have asked, but neither the priest nor the gentleman seemed to know any European language. Murmuring our few words of Amharic, we bowed our thanks, and moved from the darkness of the Middle Ages back into the sun glaring upon our twentieth century vehicle.

For awhile longer the highway traversed the ridge; then the ridge itself began to break up as we reached the edge of the plateau. Just outside Adigrat the road ducked into a narrow valley which gradually widened into a new step of the plateau. Rows of young eucalyptus lined the newly asphalted road. The climate at this lower level is much more amenable to European settlement; the town was thoroughly Italian. We saw more of this town than we wished to because we kept circling its center, hoping to find a petrol pump. Between

Addis and the border of Eritrea we were warned that gas was only sold in Dessie and Quita, but we had thought, not realizing the precipitous nature of the route, that we could do the entire six hundred miles on a full tank and two full jerry cans. Still, we had expected to fill up in Dessie or Quita, but the pumps were open very short hours, and we were in a hurry. By the time we got to Adigrat we knew we could not dare to leave the town without more gas. The moment we drove around the town's main square we were besieged with little ragged boys shouting "benzene". The price they quoted was so high we knew immediately it must a black-market, so we drove off, searching the town for a regular pump. Eventually we were forced back to the square where we bargained down the price of a jerry can of twenty liters to thirteen Ethiopian dollars – versus the regulated price of about eight and a half – or something over a dollar a gallon.

The border between Ethiopia and Eritrea was unmarked: the good road and the border of eucalyptus were the same on both sides. Encouraged by the less rigorous climate, and despite the poorer soil, more Italians had settled in this area. They left behind many towns, all Italian in style, with plastered houses and window-glass. Any one of them seemed more of a city than the Addis, even the ghost town of Decamere with its boarded-up houses and vacant staring shopping area. Bordering the road between the columns of trees were more and more road signs, strange relics of the pre-war era when the Italians drove on the right; the British and now the Eritreans prefer to keep to the left. High on a hill, as a sentinel to the city, was a deserted hotel, reminder of the power that had been defeated. Then Asmara at last, badly in need of a coat of paint, but a proud colonial town. It was more European in flavor than any African town we had yet seen, and consequently the least interesting. In fact, Asmara was a let down after three days driving on the top of the world along what was to us the most spectacular, most unpredictable, most beautiful drive in the world.

# CHAPTER 29

# Asmara: what future?

ALBERGO ITALIA WAS A SMALL FAMILY HOTEL SUCH AS YOU might find anywhere in southern Italy. The owners were grey-haired Italians who had put all their life and savings into the enterprise, but unlike many of their compatriots in Asmara, they had no intention of selling out just because of unsettled political conditions in Eritrea. "I am telling you instability is good for hotel business," the old man insisted, his eyes twinkling mischievously. "Only when all was stable, my hotel, she had not an easy time. That was forty years ago when I first came. We had not money, but the other Italians also had not. They could not afford my hotel; almost I could not afford it too. But ah, after the invasion of Abyssinia, of Ethiopia I mean, all changed. Much money everywhere, and many Italians soldiers to stay in my hotel. Then came the

British troops and I must to know English. After the war also were coming many big men of the United Nations, to Eritrea and to my hotel. Now is many European people coming, as they say foreign experts, and many newspapermen. Next year who knows, but must be some who move around and stay at my hotel."

Contentedly, he settled still deeper into his chair. I could almost see his mind totaling receipts of these yet-to-come visitors. Then abruptly he sat up and popped his eyes. "You people are too thin, you do not like my lasagna and spaghetti? All Italians in Asmara come to eat my food, but you Americans, you do not come. Hundreds there are, your soldiers, but at that place Radio Marina. None they come here. Americans like not spaghetti?"

WE ASSURED THE OLD proprietor of our fondness for good, authentic Italian cuisine and later devoured every fattening strand of a luscious many-coursed dinner. I couldn't understand why the Americans at the radio base never came to Asmara for a sample of the hotel's delightful cooking, not until we had visited the base. With a friend from the American Consulate in Asmara we went out to the Commissary at the base to replenish our supplies of canned food and buy more tampax. Refuting the old man's claim that Americans did not like spaghetti, several rows pallid canned spaghetti lined the Commissary shelves.

"Why, Mil, would anyone eat this canned paste when they can drive into Asmara for that lovely food we had last night?" I demanded. "Do you suppose they're afraid to eat in a local hotel?" I wondered, remembering the fear of eating in Indian restaurants so many Americans felt in New Delhi.

"Maybe they just prefer to ignore the whole fact of their existence in Eritrea so that they can make believe they are in some base in the Mid-West," he suggested. Certainly the whole base was the army's version of suburbia. There were recent American movies and American products filled the shelves of the Commissary. American beer and liquor were served at the club, and at the soda fountain you could order American ice cream or an exact facsimile. The wooden duplexes provided for families were unimaginative, but we were told that each one had a refrigerator. All those things which seemed distinctively American were available yet it wasn't America; rather it seemed sterile and dull. Later I said as much to the vice-consul while we consumed hamburgers and milkshakes at the soda fountain. "Just think what all these people are missing, staying cooped up at the base. I'm sure if I had to live here I'd escape every moment I could, wouldn't you?"

"Well, yes, probably," the vice-consul replied, "but you must remember that most of these GIs are draftees; neither they nor their families had the least desire to leave the States and most of them cannot wait to get back. Meanwhile, the more like their hometown this base is, the happier they are. Not all of them of course," he added. "The regular army men, most of them, are more adventurous. They will go any- where for a girl. There really isn't much else in Asmara that they don't have here. It is probably better that most of the men here don't like the town. This way we avoid incidents. And I think, too, isolated the way it is, the townspeople treat the base like a ship...a place that lays in stores, lets the men go into town on a weekend, but otherwise is not part of their life. This way anti-American groups cannot accuse us of meddling in politics. Such an accusation would be the fastest way of losing this very valuable base. You know, as a relay center, this station is absolutely vital." He glanced around the booths. "I think it is better this way. The soldiers can go into town, or anywhere in the country, if they want to. But we do everything to discourage them."

"What an unreal existence," I insisted. "It's nice to have a milkshake, and I am a pig eating a sundae on top of all of that. But I'd go crazy living here. Given the choice between here and Asmara, I'd pick Asmara."

"But Asmara is unreal, too," he countered. "It's an Italian town set down on this last bit of plateau before the desert. It has no more to do with the country than the base does, perhaps less. Keeping up the town costs Eritrea money; while the base contributes heavily to the local income with rent and with wages. Look carefully," he admonished, "Asmara is a dying city."

"ERITREA IS A DYING country," echoed a young Muslim politician to whom we had repeated this opinion the next afternoon in a tiny apartment in Asmara. "Whatever identity we had we lost when the United Nations federated Eritrea to Ethiopia in 1952. But it doesn't matter. Eritrea never had a real existence or reason beyond serving as a base for Italian expansion. What little development the Italians did do here was entirely for themselves: roads, houses, clean markets. They didn't care one finger what happened to us. Why, we received more education in the few years the British were here than in all fifty years under the Italians." He glanced around the room. "That's why all of us politicians are so young. We got some education. Our fathers do not know what is going on."

"At least they know that we have just become a colony of Ethiopia," jeered a thin faced, long-haired youth.

"Nonsense," retorted the other. "It is Ethiopia that will be our colony. We have the education. And now that Eritrea and Ethiopia are federated, there are as many Muslims as

St. Mary's Orthodox Church with its twin
towers and imposing entrance gate
dominates Asmara's central plaza

Christians in the country. If we can convert the pagans, we
can dominate the entire land."

"If ," exploded the youth, "and when?" he challenged.
They were ignoring us in their own controversy, yet I felt
that this argument had taken place over and over until each
had said his part by rote. Campaign speeches, I thought,
left over from the recent elections to Eritrea's Assembly and
Parliament. The youth was warming to his own defense.
"Partition would have been better for the Muslims. Let the
highlands with their Christians go to Ethiopia; Massawa has
always been a Muslim port. It was Turkish, and then Egyptian, before the Italians came. It should have gone to Sudan.
That's what we wanted," he declared with a flourish. Then
he lowered his tone to a conversation level. "But nobody
else did. Sudan was afraid of the idea of partition; someone
might suggest the whole pagan and Christian southern part
of Sudan be split off from the Muslim north. Ethiopia was
also afraid of the idea of partition because of all her Muslims. What a mess the imperialists made with their arbitrary
boundaries," he sighed, "but I suppose it would be even more
of a mess trying to redraw them. No one ever wants to lose

something they already have. You ask Yassein about it," he directed, as we rose to go.

MOHAMMED YASSEIN WAS THE representative of Sudan in Asmara, and the first Sudanese to hold that position. It seemed an impossible coincidence, but Yassein and I had been in the same seminar on local government back in London. I remember a dreary spring day in London, one of those days that starts with a promise of sun and ends in a full drizzle, when the seminar was ending. The quiet Sudanese talked of going home to the sun, back to his job in the civil service; and in a burst of friendship that parting often brings, we exchanged addresses. When Mil and I first planned the trip to Africa I had written Yassein at his address in Khartoum, asking him about visas. He had replied promptly and cordially from Asmara saying that he would arrange the matter for us when we arrived in the town.

When we met again in Asmara I was surprised at the superficiality of our former acquaintance. I had not realized that he was one of the top Sudanese administrators in the Sudan, nor that he was so old, for I had quite wrongly thought of him as a contemporary. In London we had never discussed politics; I must confess that at that time I was not entirely sure where in Africa the Sudan was located and I certainly did not know that the name Anglo-Egyptian Sudan referred to the fact that Sudan was a Condominium under the joint rule of Britain and Egypt. Thus I had not realized that although his English was impeccably British, Yassein himself was somewhat anti-British, as all good Sudanese nationalists were in those days.

But as a correct civil servant, Yassein refused to discuss politics with Mil and me beyond an intense statement that Sudan must quickly get its independence. Rather, he devoted himself to showing us Asmara, and extending to us the most gracious hospitality. At first we took his kindness to be an exclusively personal matter, but as we met more Sudanese we found that this warmness and pleasantness was practically a national characteristic, one that impressed us all the more when contrasted with the haughty secrecy of the Ethiopians. This apposition of temperaments was vividly illustrated at the border between the two countries.

The drive from Asmara to the border at Tessenei was uneventful. Once we were outside the town, the country and the people were drab and impoverished. The plateau, which was four thousand feet high at Asmara, began to fragment and the land grew poorer as the road descended until even grazing it would be difficult. Already we were in Muslim territory, a land of desert and oases. Near Keren and again near Agordat the vividness of the greenery only emphasized the bleakness of the rapidly disappearing brown hills. Domed straw huts of the natives and empty concrete square bungalows of the ex-colonizers were grouped around the water supply. The oasis women wore colorful gowns of reds and oranges instead of the dirty white dresses of the Copt women. Already the weather was torrid, and we stopped for a beer, one beer between the two of us since we had only sixty Ethiopian cents left. The beer was fifty cents but when Mil left the waitress the last cents as a tip, she ran out to us at the car to return it!

THE CHECKPOINT OF TESSENEI was tucked into a green niche in the valley of the River Gash. As we crossed the trickle in the deep riverbed we could see a flood control dam which, we had been told, was used to irrigate a small cotton scheme. It had been started by the British army in imitation of the larger and very successful Gezira scheme in Sudan. The town itself was primarily a government outpost and consisted of several out-of-place two-story frame houses and a cluster of the more suitable adobe homes. We stopped briefly to meet the district officer, a friend of Yassein's, Saleh Haneit. It was wonderfully cool under his trees. The orange squash had ice in it from a small factory in the town. Indeed, this small community on the edge of the desert had both running water and electric lights. As one of the two Eritreans trained by the British to take over high administrative posts, Saleh should have had a much more important assignment than this border district. As a Muslim, however, he was out of favor with the Ethiopian rulers. When we left to go on to the customs, Saleh suggested we come back for tea, intimating that we would be with the customs for a long time.

We understood why Saleh had not offered to come with us to customs when we met the officials there. All of them were Copts, and the presence of a Muslim, even though he was the district officer, would not have helped us a bit. These officials, probably annoyed at being exiled to this Muslim outpost, were tiresome and suspicious. One by one they opened our bags, spilling the contents, examining under-wear, demanding that I take a tampax apart to prove I wasn't smuggling something, though what there is in Ethiopia that anyone would want to smuggle out I couldn't imagine. Even when I protested that we had diplomatic passports one man kept digging around in my suitcase, not with a smile, but a sneer. I had been full of ideas for Ethiopian tourism to exploit that spectacular drive we had just experienced. "They'll have to change their attitude toward tourists ," I grumbled to Mil. "You know they don't want tourists, or any foreigners, to come bothering them," Mil laughed. "You'd better wait before you try opening a tourist agency."

At last the customs men had finished, and after a hurried

tea with Saleh, we drove past the checkpoint and encountered a sign reading "road unfit for driving." It was as if the Ethiopians, secure in their superiority, wished to tell us that Sudan was a barbaric land. The sign intimidated us at first, yet the road was neither better nor worse beyond Tessenei than it had been before. I was already back to normal driving speed when we came to a bridge with a gap in the middle of it. It was obvious we couldn't stop in time, so I merely accelerated and Bublee flew across. I'll admit I was frightened momentarily, but more, annoyed. Why couldn't they mark the one bridge and not the whole road?

HERE IN THE EMPTINESS between the two countries, all that was left of the Ethiopian plateau were weird outcroppings, like huge ant hills or backs of prehistoric dinosaurs, protruding from the pebbly waste. In other places enormous granite boulders were piled as if in play. I wondered whether Hanuman and his monkey soldiers had flown about Africa as well as India, dropping some of their rocks as they went. As the desert widened, the road ceased to be a road. A series of whitewashed rocks simply led us across the desert. Mil took out our newly acquired compass to check direction just in case. The customs had taken so long that already it was dusk, and sometimes we could not see from one rock marker to the next. At last a light appeared: the Sudanese checkpoint. The officials were full of smiles as though they were immensely pleased with themselves and their work. The actual formalities were quick and efficient; but we struck one snag. No guns were allowed to be brought into the country without a permit. Since we did not have such a permit, we should have to check the revolver with the border guards or leave a deposit of money. We protested at first, not realizing that officials are to be trusted in the Sudan; but eventually we left the gun behind and continued into Kassala.

For a second I thought we were back in India. The Dak bungalow could have been lifted out of any Indian town; even the name was borrowed for originally Dak (post) bungalows were at post stages, conveniently one day's horseback riding apart. A long sheltered front verandah overlooked a well-kept garden. In the ceiling of each bedroom a four-bladed fan droned continuously. Behind the bedroom was a dressing room and a bathroom which was nothing more than a square room with a drain set into one side. Water was brought in buckets for a dousing type bath or for dumping into a large tin tub. The only difference with usual Indian Dak bungalows was that the commodes were not placed in the bathroom, but in a section of the bungalow far to the rear; apparently this arrangement was preferable due to the intense desert heat.

While we were waiting for dinner, we had long cool drinks in the garden, talking with the Sudanese District Commissioner, Mirghani El Amin, and an English judge who had been in the Indian Civil Service before the war and, like so many of his fellow civil servants, had transferred his service to Africa. Both men warned us not to try the desert drive to Khartoum alone. Only the week before a Sudanese lawyer who had made the drive many many times had lost his way and driven in circles until his car ran out of gas. Then foolishly he had left his car to walk back to the main track. He had been found unconscious; perhaps he would live. The rules of the drive seemed to be: never go alone, check in and out of every police station, never leave your car if anything happens but just wait for rescue. Also, since it was so hot in April, it was better to drive at night. The DC said there was an official from the Khartoum police in Kassala who would be going back shortly so the DC would ask him if we could go along with him.

I KEPT THINKING OF Kenya, trying to imagine and English judge and a Kenya District Commissioner having dinner together, but could not. Granted that only recently had any Sudanese held the post of District Commissioner but they had been assistants for many years. Few enough Europeans in Kenya would sit down with an African, and when they did there was an undercurrent of effort. Here in Sudan the occurrence was obviously usual. I wondered how long it would be before Kenya had its own African District Commissioners? Or be about ready, as the Sudanese were then, to receive their independence. No wonder the Sudanese seemed happy.

We had hoped to spend several days in this desert town, but early the next morning, the DC sent word that the police officer was leaving that same evening. We had to go with him or risk waiting a week or so for the next convoy. With the message, the DC also sent his assistant, Umar, to help us see as much of the town as we could in one day. The town itself was small, and amazingly clean. Even the market retained none of those stifling smells which some tourists find romantic but to me are merely repulsive. The stalls were straightly rowed and neatly kept, most of them selling cloth or foodstuffs. We poked our heads in several of them, and because of our escort, were immediately invited to enter and sit, a courtesy we could hardly ignore. Inevitably a warmish, sweet, sticky squash appeared which we had been instructed was necessary to consume. We met a Greek grocer, an Indian cloth merchant, and an Arab grain seller before walking across the street in the blazing sun and immediately going into the Modern Café for more liquid to revive us from that exertion.

In the filtered light of the cafeteria, I surveyed the other

customers, for in the glaring light of the street the Sudanese had appeared all white cloth and black face. Now, for
the first time, I noticed the various tribal scars etched into
their ebony faces. As you might expect in a café calling itself
modern, many of the Sudanese were in western dress; but
many more were enfolded in the loose white traditional
gown, their heads encased in yards of casually wound cloth.
Also, of course, this being a fairly strict Muslim country,
there were no women to be seen.

SOON WE COULD DRINK no more of the warm orange squash, so
Umar took us to the town hall to talk with various officials
and hear details about the municipal elections which had
been introduced into the Sudan during the Second World
War. Here, happily, we were served with hot tea, gently fla-
vored with mint, but still much too sweet. Two officials, their
white clothes making their dark faces appear even blacker,
took turns explaining statistics and graphs with such bubbling enthusiasm that occasionally I found their rounded
soft-spoken English impossible to understand. Even the
more sophisticated DC, to whom we talked later, could not
contain his excitement and fascination with the problems
of administering his area as independence approached. We
were thoroughly captivated, we were rooting for the team.
In one day I became more emotionally attached to Sudan,
more personally involved somehow in the outcome of their
venture into self-government, than I had become after two
years in India.

Umar was indefatigable. He reported to the DC that we
had seen the town, all but the mosque of Mirghani. If the
DC gave his permission to borrow the jeep, he would take us
there right then. Thus it was that in the hottest part of the

day we found ourselves, to our surprise, careening across the scorching desert with a jeepful of Sudanese.

"Umar," I shouted, "why are we going out of Kassala?" Above the roar of the engine, Umar shouted back, "We go to see the small village where Sayed Ali Mirghani was born. He is the leader of the religious Muslim group we call Khatmia. That is why he is known as 'Sayed.' But did you know that the British made him a knight? The British also made a knight of Sayed Abdel Rahman el Mahdi. Ha, ha. They are both knights, and now they fight a political duel. Ha, ha, ha." His laughter was echoed by his friends, with much comment in Arabic.

"But before you said that Mirghani was a religious leader," I protested. "Why is he in a political duel?" My question caused the laughter to start again. Nor did Umar try to reply, for the roar of the engine as the jeep churned along in four wheel drive was just too loud.

Ten or fifteen minutes later, we approached what looked like a series of low mud walls. As we drew closer we could just make out the slightly higher adobe roofs rising above the walls. Not another person was so foolish as to be out in the midday sun. Beyond the village, set at the base of a massive granite outcropping, was a half-completed mosque, modest, almost severe, in its lines, and completely dwarfed by the natural spectacle towering behind it. Whatever ornamentation there might have been was flattened in the glare. With hardly more than a cursory look at the mosque we all made for the shade of the tower. The relief was immediate, and as we sprawled on the sand Umar turned to me and said in a soft rolling voice, "You must remember, in the Sudan we fight only for religion, or water."

Looking beyond Umar across the desert, past the entirely treeless village, I watched the sun rays as they glimmered

The unfinished Mirghani Mosque near Kassala, Sudan

and shone across the sand, creating a mirage of ponds and water. With only a little imagination, I envisioned hoards of white shrouded black warriors swarming at each other, the sun glinting on their swords. The image persisted as Umar continued: "You know we have elections this year, the first parliamentary elections for Sudan. The DC told you this morning that after the elections Sudan will have self-government. Then within three years all the British civil servants will leave and we can determine our own future: whether to have a federation with Egypt or to stay completely independent.

That is what the officials must say; that is what most foreigners think the election is about. We intellectuals know better. As I said, the most important thing in this country is religion. You think the peasants in this village know the difference between Egypt and Britain? You think the nomads in the western desert have ever heard of federation? Of course

417

not. In this election, every man will vote as his religious leader tells him."

Umar had started pacing up and down, and the effort of walking and talking had covered his face with perspiration. In the shade this merely made his black face darker, but once as he turned in his pacing his face caught the sun, and a thousand sparkles glistened, their rays jumping off his face; it was a momentary vision of a halo. Suddenly all religions, all miracles, seemed not only believable but natural; I wondered if the deserts were necessary for real piety. Umar sank to the ground and began wiping his face with a huge white handkerchief. Then he tied it round his head as a sort of makeshift turban. This alteration of his western dress somehow made him look more real, or was it more heroic, a rebellion of mind against the global standardization of dress as a feared standardization of souls?

WE DRANK DEEPLY OF cool water from a thermos. Savoring his drink, Umar grinned as a new thought struck him. "Water is the most precious thing in a desert. Those who live in oases must often move to seek more or better water; they become more daring people, maybe more superstitious. Those who live along the rivers never wish to move, never wish to change. This village is not a real village, but a sacred place; Mirghani's family comes from a river village; his followers are river men; his religion is conservative; and politically he wishes continue some sort of close ties with Egypt. The great rival of Mirghani is el Madhi whose father swept in off the endless desert with his whirling dervishes. Now his followers, whom we call the Ansars, revere the old Madhi as a sort of saint. So the religion of these desert men is unorthodox, and also their politics. Some say el Madhi wants to become a king; others say he is pro-British. But politics doesn't really matter to the followers. If they vote, they will vote for el Madhi or for Mirghani. Tomorrow they could switch their political positions and still their followers would support them. We intellectuals know this. The foreigners, even the Egyptians, do not know this. Egypt spends much money sending us teachers. The teachers try to tell the people how to vote. Ha, ha, ha. As if that made any difference!" He rose up to his full six feet, a study in black and white, and in stark contrasts. With an unmistakably British accent, and a definite mime, he said: "Religion's the thing."

Back at the Dak bungalow, we had hardly finished bathing and eating when Ahmed Awad, the police officer, appeared, eager to start off across the desert for Khartoum. By the time we had the bags packed, the gear stowed and the water bags filled, it was tea time. The hot liquid revived us momentarily, and without a second thought we were off across the fabled trackless waste. Yet at first it was hardly trackless. A single railroad track ran like a surveyors guide line southwest. A telegraph line strung on metal poles marched along side. Car tracks ran up and down along both sides of the railroad, but there was no level crossing. Finally Ahmed's driver decided to cross the rails, and without checking the way at all, he bounced the car up and over the built up rail bed. The car hung briefly at the top as though stuck, then scraped down the even steeper decline. Without pausing to see whether we could cross, the police car blazed off in a cloud of dust. We maneuvered the rails at a smoother point, then followed the dust cloud at a great distance.

The last sign of hills faded away; the horizon was perfectly flat, its monotony broken only by the hump of the rails and the masts of telephone poles. The ground, which had been pebbly near Kassala, became heavy earth. We passed a beehive of a railroad village: round huts with conical white roofs to reflect the heat, their black little peaks, like pinheads, held the image to the sand, for everything shimmers in the desert and seems to float away. There was one solitary tree before the beehives; I saw my first Sudanese woman there, watching her child play in the shade. A convoy of four battered trucks stormed past heading for Kassala and enclosing us in their black cloud. Just as we came out into clear air, the night came down without warning. Now we had to trail Ahmed's car more closely, within sight of his tail light. But the dust cloud was smaller since we were both going slower. Still we tended to follow him off to the left to miss the dust cloud; the road was as wide as the desert.

WE TURNED WEST, AWAY from the guiding railroad, then south again following a newly dug ditch, which I could only imagine was some sort of irrigation canal. I was driving now, while Mil dozed, and I noticed that old car tracks seemed to cross the ditch. The police car kept on, but slower and slower. I wanted to stop and tell him I thought we were off the road, but it seemed presumptuous, and I wasn't at all sure. For perhaps fifteen minutes we followed the ditch, veering all the while both south and east when we should have been going west. Finally Ahmed stopped and with a long grave face admitted that he was lost. Very tentatively I suggested the earlier crossing, for after all it was Ahmed's role to lead. With no difficulty we found the crossing of the ditch which Ahmed said was a new road that would connect Kassala to the cotton bowl along the Blue Nile at Gezira.

Soon even the yellow grass had disappeared and except for a few wispy thorn weeds, the sand and rocks were bare. In places the sand was soft enough to hold car tracks. In other places the solid ground showed no sign of previous travelers; we could have been the first. Striped oil drums, heavy with rocks, assured us periodically that we were still on the way toward Khartoum.

Mil and I switched off regularly every hour, the dreary flatness of the way made it hard to fight off sleep even when driving. We sipped at coffee each stop, and smoked incessantly. The night air was cooler than the piercing heat of the day, but it was still hot. Time went on in a drowse. It hardly seemed midnight when Ahmed stopped his car and announced it was time to eat. We had prepared nothing beyond asking for bread and fruit from the Dak bungalow. I pulled these out, and rummaged about for a jar of cheese; I did not feel like eating much. Just then Ahmed called to us to come. On the far side of his car he had set up three camp stools and a small table which now held a bottle of whiskey and three glasses. "My driver doesn't drink," Ahmed laughed, as though excusing a backward child, "so he has gone off to eat by himself. Cheers!" The whiskey wakened both senses and hunger, and in no time we had polished off the entire fried chicken Ahmed had provided, munched some unleavened bread, eaten our bread and cheese as a savory, finished off with fruit, coffee, and small sticky Sudanese sweets.

On we drove, under a clear starry sky. We seemed to be on a pebbly table land now and in between the oil drums we could only hope the direction was correct. Then unexpectedly we saw firelight ahead and soon came to a cluster of three adobe huts. A truck was pulled up before one hut which had coffee and tea for sale. Four or five men were standing about and Ahmed's driver checked directions. Apparently this was some sort of crossroads, though not a road or a car track was discernable. On we went again, once more alone in the world. As light was streaking the sky we came to another such cluster of huts, and this time we stopped long enough for a glass of mint tea.

A policeman, on camelback, loped up to the cars and saluted Ahmed even though he was not in uniform. Ahmed explained that he had informed the police of his trip and the date of return, and that this man had come out along the road just to check to see if he had safely returned. This was standard procedure, Ahmed insisted; but of course the police were especially careful since he himself was police chief of the area. I wanted to ask him more about his work, but we were all too groggy for any sort of conversation. Instead, we hurried on to Khartoum, racing the heat of the new day.

IN A FEW MILES we came to a police checkpoint and soon the landscape began to put green back into its brown color scheme. We crossed irrigation ditches and wider canals, all filled with a thick gooey liquid: a little water and much sand. Paralleling railroad tracks, the road turned south across the now sluggish, chocolate-colored Blue Nile and into the tree-lined streets of Khartoum. People were dodging mud puddles in the street, queuing for the trolleys. Mud puddles, so close to the desert! There was no drainage system so the infrequent rain just collected on the road until it evaporated. I noticed it was after seven when Ahmed's car turned up a side street and stopped in front of Khartoum's other hotel; the hotel, the Queen's, being too expensive for our budget. Thanking him profusely, and extracting a promise to meet us later in the week, we said goodbye to Ahmed, went up to our room and slept.

CHAPTER 30

# Khartoum on the verge
# of independence

*M*AY IS SUPPOSED TO BE THE HOTTEST MONTH IN THE SUDAN, and it was hot! The day after we arrived the Muslim month of fasting, Ramadan, began. The combination of heat and fasting was enough to bring daytime life in Khartoum to a standstill while nightlife bloomed. Fasting, according to Islam, means not eating or drinking a single thing from sunrise to sunset; but as soon as the cannon at the mosque goes off each evening, the eating begins. It goes on, fitfully, until the cannon goes off again to mark the rising of the sun. Not surprisingly, we found that most of the Sudanese Muslims who kept the fast slept through much of the day, for going without water in that heat was sheer torture.

The offices begin work at eight; by ten, during that month, they would nearly be deserted. We were told that, formerly, the British administrators always used to take their vacations during Ramadan since no work was accomplished anyhow. Certainly the two-story, columned government office building which faces a large, park-like square was more like a tomb than the heart of a growing nation. We had gone there searching for Osman Abdullah, a senior civil servant and a friend of Mohammed Yassein's. Though his entire staff had gone home, Osman was still at his desk. He rose to greet us cordially, smiling from his entire countenance. He was a small man, as Sudanese go, but still four or five inches taller than I. His build was slight and he was wearing the usual white shirt and trousers. Yet there was something commanding about his appearance, the sort of thing you normally meet only among royalty. Later I found out that Osman's father had been one of the first highly trained Sudanese civil servants, so that in terms of power, Osman did indeed come from royalty.

But the most impressive feature about Osman was his tribal scars. Impolitely, I kept glancing at them, revolted just slightly at first, and then completely intrigued. The hollow of each ebony cheek had three sideways V's cut into it, each a glossy charcoal brown because, once cut, tribal scars are treated with medicine to prevent smooth healing. This causes each mark to swell with scar tissue which is several shades lighter than the skin. My first reaction was to feel sorrow that such a handsome face had been so mutilated; but as we saw Osman again and again I began to accept, even to appreciate, the beauty the scars were supposed to add to his face.

Osman was the first civil servant we had met who had the scars since they are considered old-fashioned by most educated Sudanese. The next evening we met him for drinks on the breezy lawn of the Queen's Hotel. I was teasing him about drinking whiskey during Ramadan. He rubbed his hand lightly over his cheek before replying. "Social pressure is a strange thing. My wife makes me fast during Ramadan; she says it is for my soul, but what she really fears is what her family would think if I were so godless as to break the fast." He stopped a moment, controlling his anger. "You saw the office yesterday, no one was working. Public opinion thinks it is better if we fast than if we work. How can we build up our country if for a month every year no one works? I try to work, but it is hard. When I can no longer stand it, sometimes I sip water. My wife would scream if she knew. I think my job is more important than superstition. But there is no point in making her unhappy. She will never know whether this is lemonade or whiskey that I am drinking." He lifted his glass and finished the highball. Unconsciously, I watched his cheeks as he swallowed; the dim light from the scattered lamps picked up the scars but left his face shadows.

"These scars are all the result of social pressure," he commented after a moment. "My father had scars of course, but he wanted his sons to be modern. My mother must want what my father wants. So when the age came for the ceremony, I was the only little boy of the village that was not cut. My grandparents were outraged, but could do nothing. Then one day, two or three years later, my mother and my father both had to go away. While they were gone my grandparents took me to be cut. My father was so furious that he wouldn't speak to his parents until they promised never to interfere again with his children. But for me, I kept the scars. The wounds would never have healed entirely, for the cuts were deep and the medicine they put in had already started to work. So my father decided it was better to have full, correct scars than half-hearted ones." Osman smiled a little self-consciously as he said: "I'm told as scars go, these are well done."

In the pause, the buzz of insects around the lights rivaled the hum of conversation from the crowded lawn. Osman fingered his cheeks lightly. "I used to be ashamed of the scars. But, you know, they can be useful. When I was the District Commissioner in the South, most of the people in my district were pagans who are still very suspicious of us northerners because it was always northern Arabs who were slave traders. Arabs don't use scarring. Because I have scars like the pagans do themselves, I think the people trusted me more than they do other northerners. You know the British kept the South a closed area. Not only Arabs and Egyptians, but even other Sudanese were prohibited. Muslim teachers were kept out but Christian missionaries were allowed. It may have been reasonable in 1900, to stop the slave trade; but it was not fair to keep us out for so long, or to fill the southerners with fear of us. Our South will be our biggest internal problem, as your South is to you. Even now there are demands for a separate state within the Sudan. How could they govern themselves? Most of the people there are very primitive and completely uneducated. Yet even there the Egyptians are trying to win votes. Did you see the picture in the newspaper of the "dancing Major"? That was Major Salah Salam, an Egyptian army officer and member of the Egyptian cabinet. A big man to risk his dignity in a tribal dance!"

"But why do the Egyptians care so much about this election, Osman?" I asked.

"Water," Osman said simply. He filled his empty highball glass from the water pitcher, and held it up, symbolically. Turning the glass in the light he asked, softly, with an edge to his voice: "Did you know, even though our family lives along the Nile, that we cannot draw even one glass from the river without permission of Egypt? A farmer's crops may be withering, but if he uses Nile waters to save them, he can be put in prison! Years ago the British in Egypt made an agreement with the British in Sudan to give some 97% of the Nile waters to Egypt. As long as the British were here, Egypt was sure to get her water. Naturally Egypt is afraid that an independent Sudan might feel the percentage was perhaps unfair." Osman drank his water slowly. "Egypt does not care about us, only about the water. If we develop our own country, we must use more water. We are trying to find more water ourselves, by draining the swamps in the south. But Egypt wants that water too."

"Then you will vote for the UMMA party of el Mahdi," I said brightly.

"Oh no," replied Osman sharply. "My family is from the river valley, I will support Mirghani. But make no mistake, Mirghani is no child. We are not going to walk out of British control right into union with Egypt. There is much sympathy today with Egypt. No one liked King Farouk. Naguib, you know, is half Sudanese. But Egypt has its own problems. We would be foolish to put our country under theirs. Then we would never develop."

ONE OF THE REASONS for looking up Osman had been to check about conditions of the road between Khartoum and the Egyptian border, and to find out what sort of permission we would need. Osman had phoned several offices early in the morning when people were still working, and they all had promised to meet us at the Queen's. Azis Osman of the newly formed tourist agency, was the first to arrive. We soon realized that Aziz's enthusiasm far out-ran his experience, but he had looked up various regulations for us. "You absolutely cannot drive alone across the desert from Wadi Halfa to Aswan. Always there must be two or more vehicles, unless you are guided by plane like that Austin man Alan Hess was when he went through last month. You could hire a taxi to accompany you, but that would be very expensive, two or three hundred American dollars. It is better you take the boat; it goes once a week and is not very expensive and you can put your car on a barge."

"Couldn't we get special permission to drive, Osman Abdullah?" I begged. "We want to drive the whole way."

Osman smiled kindly. "Especially for you, I would never ask that. I would not want you to die in our Sudanese desert. It really is dangerous, you know. The Nile there cuts through the most treacherous part of the sandy desert so the trail must make a wide arch to the east to avoid the worst of the shifting sands. Even so, the oil drums that mark the way are often covered with dunes. It is too easy to get lost. With two cars, at least you can plot your direction." Osman paused a moment and looked earnestly at me, as though reading my thoughts. "Of course you could go without permission. Most of the desert is in Egypt so once you are past our last check point in Wadi Halfa, no person will stop you. But the sand might. I would ask you not to try anything so foolhardy, Irene."

I smiled guiltily, while Aziz continued: "I also learned that last month a carload of Britishers became lost between Atbara and Aba Hamed. Four of them were dead before their car was found, but a fifth passenger was still alive. They hadn't even tried to drink the radiator water. What amateurs! The track in that part of the desert never goes very far away from the railroad or the river. I do not understand how they could become lost so close to help."

Aziz was still speculating on this accident when Mohammed Effendi arrived. Mohammed was from the State Railroad. Osman had told him over the phone that we wanted to drive as far as possible, and then to take the cheapest possible transport to the Egyptian border. Hardly saying hello,

Mohammed declared, "I have bad news for you Walkers. This is the driest part of the year, and when the Nile goes down too far we cannot ship automobiles on to our barges. Maybe with this next boat it is still possible, but after that, no. You must catch that boat or wait about three months. Today is Monday. You must put your car on the freight train which leaves Wednesday. Saturday you take the passenger train to Wadi Halfa. The train arrives in Wadi Halfa next Monday morning only a few hours before the boat leaves."

"But we don't want to take the train," I protested. "Surely we can at least drive to Wadi Halfa. You said the track follows the railroad, didn't you, Aziz?"

"You are allowed to drive that far without an escort," Aziz began, but Osman put in: "You may drive to Wadi Halfa, but it takes as much as six days. To catch that last boat you would have to leave tomorrow morning."

I wailed softly, but Mil more constructively asked, "How far north is there a fairly good road? You see, Mohammed Effendi, partly we want to drive whenever possible, it's sort of a dare, but partly we are getting rather short of money."

"Well," said Mohammed thoughtfully, "I don't know much about the road, but there is a freight yard in Atbara. I think we could arrange for your automobile to be shipped from there. But you see, the freight train and the passenger train go several days apart. You would have to stay for three days in Atbara, and there is no hotel there. Besides, you have to hire a guard for your car while it is on the flatcar; the railroad cannot be responsible for it. I can help you here, but you may have difficulty finding a good man in Atbara. Surely it is better for you to wait in Khartoum and send your car ahead."

"Mohammed Effendi," Mil pursued thoughtfully, "isn't the passenger fare rather expensive? Then on top of that we must hire a guard. Wouldn't it be cheaper and easier if we just drove as far as Atbara, then put ourselves on a flatcar along with our auto?"

"If we take the flatcar," I injected, but everyone ignored me.

And so it was decided, despite many objections from Mohammed who obviously did not approve of a woman on a flatcar. Mil's plan cut our stay in Khartoum very short, but here was no help for it. The pressure of time and money pushed us forward faster than we liked. Always there was something we did not see, or someone we had not met, some sleep we had not caught up on. But then, isn't there always?

We always got up early in Khartoum, earlier than we liked. Our box-of-a-room was airless at night so we slept out on a tiny balcony which was cool enough until the first rays of the morning sun began to play on the whitewashed wall. The showers in the hotel were inconveniently across the upstairs lobby; only at such an early hour were the chairs and sofas still empty of the various members of the Greek owner's large family whose frankly curious stares annoyed me. With this up early routine plus staying up late, we were able to crowd an incredible amount of experiences into our five days in Khartoum.

Our daytime visits were dogged by the sun; I began to dodge its glare with an intensity I had never felt before. Each office was a haven from the shimmering light. Wet and thirsty, Mil and I would drop into the chairs closest to the fan. Our smiling Sudanese host, whether at the administration or at the garage, would produce ice cold lemonade for us, and chat pleasantly while we gulped the forbidden liquid. Not even stoicism was evident in their attitudes. As the day wore on and I wilted further and further, my admiration grew of what I nonetheless considered foolish fasting. Yet bound up with this rational reaction was that questioning, could I do it if I wanted to? Was this whole fasting month more a proof of one's self-discipline or physical prowess than of one's religious fervor?

We rushed from office to office, trying to finish business while the clerks were still working. Usually the top men kept working until one or two, but after noon it was hard to get into the buildings: even the guards had locked up and gone home. We had to arrange for the flatcar with Mohammed Effendi, have the car checked and the oil changed, cash our rapidly diminishing travelers' check at Aziz's Travel Bureau.

Also I had a professional call to make. The Sudanese elections, in order to ensure a minimum of political influence from the British administrators or the Egyptian teachers, were being conducted by an international committee consisting of an American, an Englishman, an Egyptian, three Sudanese, and an Indian as chairman. Naturally India dispatched her able Election Commissioner, Sukumar Sen, whom I knew well from my research in India. I was anxious for his comments on the comparative problems of elections in the Sudan and in India. As I talked with him it became quite clear that working in a foreign country without your own staff presented a multitude of problems quite apart from election machinery. Sen was, for example, often forced to write his own letters while in India he had his own efficient staff. His wife was finding the heat of Khartoum unbearable even though New Delhi is no cool mountain resort. Yet for all the annoyances, Sukmar Sen was rapidly working through the problems of holding the elections in a country with a literacy rate of about 2%, a figure which makes India's 10% rate seem high.

One statistic that particularly fascinated my feminist side was the fact that there were twelve women on the voters list.

In the regular elections only men had the vote, but to give a little extra weight to the educated voters, all graduates of high school were given an additional vote in a special Graduates' constituency. Only twelve women in the entire country of eight million people had such an education!

Sen's offices, like all the other governmental buildings, were in Khartoum. Indeed the entire area of Khartoum is rather like a cantonment area for the older, original, Sudanese city of Omdurman which is situated on the other – west – side of the Nile. Osman took us around Omdurman late one afternoon. Through deserted streets we circled, looking at a new school and the old market; everything seemed sterile in the blinding light. The heat seemed to sink through hair into the brain and fog it. I appreciated why almost everyone in Omdurman wore a turban or a topee. When we got out of the car I crammed my floppy straw hat on, regardless of my appearance.

Osman thought we should see the bullet-like tomb of the old Mahdi and sent us to look around the museum while he waited in the car. Afterwards he posed for me in front of the tomb when I insisted that a picture without figures was barren. "But promise me you won't show it to any Sudanese," he bargained. "You know I'm anti-Mahdi." We walked deeper into the old lanes of the market area as the shops began to open, half-heartedly. Occasionally men on donkeys would clatter past, but there were few shoppers about. Osman led us to a boarded-up corner shop owned by a rich friend of his. The old merchant and his four sons crowded eagerly around us as we sat on the grass mats within the shop. With his sons translating, the old man told us of his two trips to England, of the cold and of the glory of London. Tea was brought, but only Mil and I sipped ours. A cannon boomed. Without an interruption in the old man's tales, more tea was poured, and everyone drank. When we went out once more into the streets they were as lively and crowded as they had been empty and uninviting. I poked into various shops, looking for a memento of Sudan, and finally found a small wooden camel. Only with the greatest firmness were we able to persuade Osman that I wished to buy it myself, for with that depth of Sudanese hospitality, Osman wished to give us everything in the shop.

This wonderful hospitality of the Sudanese was almost overwhelming. Our evenings were filled with two or three engagements, and still we had to turn some down. One evening Mil and I had made separate commitments and had to apologize to our hosts for the mix-up. Ahmed, the police officer, showed us the garden at the confluence of the two Niles, the elephant's trunk from which Khartoum gets its name. Under colored lights strung through the trees we sat on wire chairs and drank lemonade in the garden, then had dinner on top of a nearby restaurant. Perhaps because of his cautious policeman's mind, Ahmed did not dare to drink whiskey in public. Unlike Osman, who observed Ramadan more for his wife rather than because of social pressure, Ahmed outwardly conformed to the strictures of his religion.

All evening parties were on lawns, for the heat of the sun more quickly leaves the gardens, but lingers in the walls and houses. An Egyptian colonel, deputy commander of the Egyptian troops in the Sudan, mixed his guest list with English and pro-British Sudanese to balance his own pro-Egyptian friends. During the first part of the evening politics were avoided, but in the after-dinner relaxation, the groups separated themselves on the lawn and you could hear two versions of the same story by simply moving chairs.

At another international party I was most impressed to meet the two Americans who were representing the United

States at our Liaison Office...not an Embassy because Sudan was not yet independent. Both men spoke fluent Arabic and had an easy informality with the Sudanese which may have been helped by the informal nature of a Liaison Office. More important were the capabilities of these two men who, oddly enough, were both of Irish descent and Catholics: Sweeney and Murphy.

Briefly, one evening, we went with Osman to a cultural evening at what before the war had been the second-echelon British Club, but had been unable to maintain a color bar against the multinational British army during the war nor afford to hold it after the war. Although, as the country prepared for independence, Osman could have joined the fanciest club, he explained "I have no desire to rot in the first layer club, and this one is better for sports."

At all these places the guests of all colors mixed and always there were European women present. At no public place, whether market or hotel or club or party, did we see a single Sudanese woman. I asked Osman and Aziz and Ahmed to let me meet their wives. They were full of excuses: extra cooking during Ramadan, knowing no English, not feeling well; Aziz had the best excuse: he was not married because he wanted to a girl he could talk to. "Why are our woman not educated?" he lamented. The responses from around the table suggested that women are happier that way. I held my comments; how could I know what their women thought? But no one offered to help me meet a Sudanese woman. I was amazed at their reluctance, for even in much more orthodox Afghanistan I had been able to meet Afghan women in the shelter of their own homes. Eventually I realized that this reticence probably had more to do with their pride than their religion. We met and knew these men in a western modern frame; their homes were traditional joint households, crowded, under the sway of the old grandmother, with no place to entertain foreigners. Perhaps, too, there was the lurking worry over their wives' reactions after meeting a liberated female; might they get ideas?

But finally, on our last evening in Khartoum, we were invited to the home of a Sudanese. We had been out visiting the university in the morning, and talked to the very able principal, Ibrahim Ahmed Ibrahim. He had shed some light on this puzzling question of the position of women in the Sudan when talking about the education of his only daughter. Most Sudanese girls never go to school at all, but in the capital there were grammar schools for girls. After that his daughter had attended an all-girls Greek high school and had passed with high marks, Ibrahim Ahmed himself expected her to go on to Gordon College, the liberal arts section of the university. She would not be the first. Already there were eleven co-eds in a student body of 550. The girls flitted between classes modestly veiled in a toup, a lacy version of a shroud; but in classes they sat unveiled. Apparently this freedom had frightened his own wife, and she had forbidden his daughter to go to college. Ibrahim was disappointed, and hoped that next year his wife might change her mind. But the affairs of the girls are left to the women, and no man other than her husband can interfere. Since most women start having children as soon as they are married, this conservatism is bolstered generation after generation.

Ibrahim Ahmed showed us over the campus. The new student dormitories were light and airy, their in-turned architecture blocking out the glare of the sun and their simple arches owing more to Arabic history than to their British colonial rulers. These buildings were somehow illustrative of the major differences from Makerere College in Kampala. Both colleges grant London University standard degrees;

but while Makerere seemed to be attempting to foster a "modern," rootless culture, Gordan College was striving to recover and re-emphasize its own distinct blend of African influences and Islam.

Ibrahim Ahmed emphasized that the school of medicine decided against the granting of London degrees because the curriculum would have had to be changed and less emphasis given to tropical diseases. For the arts course, London had agreed to accept credits in Arabic literature and in Islamic law. Most of the courses were taught in English, but that was primarily because 70% of the teachers were Europeans, another 20% Egyptians, and only a few Sudanese. He was particularly proud of a brilliant young economics teacher, Saladin Fawzie, who had just returned to the Sudan after receiving a Ph.D. at Edinburgh. We found Fawzie in a small room littered with graphs and statistics from a survey of town housing which he was doing for a resettlement scheme. We talked a long time and then he invited us to his home for cocktails later that same day. At last, I thought, I shall meet a Sudanese woman!

Fawzie met us at our hotel, and took us to several curio shops before we went to his home. His completely British manners and mannerisms belied his skin coloring, and I forgot to remember his origins when I exclaimed over an intricate silver filigree ring with a hidden compartment for poison. I reminded myself that I had a wooden camel and that our budget had been stretched by the expense of the hotel and the railroad; and with the greatest reluctance, so I put the ring back and we left the store. As we drove out beyond the fashionable section of town toward the new complex of small university houses, Fawzie handed me a small package. His western informality withdrawn, he said with flowery formality that this was a gift from the Sudanese

436

in tribute to our interest in the country and as a reminder in times to come. It was the poison ring; and I felt terribly embarrassed, but or course I had to accept it.

We were met at the door by Fawzie's wife, a very blonde Dutch girl whom he had met at a conference while studying in Edinburgh. They and their daughter had just arrived in Sudan. Fawzie had had offers of jobs both in England and the United States, but his sense of nationalism had urged him home to be in the Sudan "during its momentous years." Since he had never been to the South, he was planning to go during the next college vacation; he hadn't yet told this to his wife. She had enough problems coping with the ostracism from wives of the foreign faculty. Another Dutch wife was friendly, but the English wives were not. I watched Fawzie closely as he talked, following his enthusiasm, as he switched from personal problems to economic development and back again. He deplored the social difficulties he and his wife were having, but said they had weighed these factors before they had returned to the Sudan. While he was talking he smiled at his wife and her tiny worry-lines turned into accents of a smile; it was clear how in love the two were.

Touching the poison ring I had on my finger, I realized in amazement that for the first time in my life I could understand emotionally as well as rationally a love that challenged society. Mil and I had often talked of racial prejudice and its ingredients. Having grown up in China, Mil was happily free of the problem. His parents' friends were of all nationalities and races, so he had no situation to react to, as I had. It was as if up to that time I had been confronting prejudice with defiant actions and by doing so unwittingly encouraging its persistence. I reflected on our weeks in Kenya and was aware of how aggressive my anti-prejudice feelings had been there. It was different here in the Sudan. Fawzie and Osman were my friends, not my Sudanese friends, or my colored friends, but simply my friends. In my admiration of them and my attraction to them I had felt no need of any anti-prejudice. Suddenly I felt released from this burden of collective guilt, free at last to see beyond the skin to the heart and mind of a person. Watching Fawzie's serious face, remembering Osman's engaging, scar-accented smile, I felt as if I had somehow achieved my own independence of spirit.

CHAPTER 31

# To Aswan by train and boat

I NCREDIBLE AS IT MAY SEEM, IT WAS ONE HUNDRED MILES NORTH of Khartoum on our drive to Atbara that we found the first tree large enough to cast any shade. Majestically the tree rose on the barren desert, visible long before the row of low adobe buildings just behind it. As we pulled to a stop in the precious shade, we could see that the building which the tree sheltered was the district government office of Shendi. Clustered around under the tree were a few sleeping goats and cattle; the inhabitants of the village seemed to prefer the more constant shade of their homes. A few men, guards perhaps, lay drowsily on string cots in front of the office. They stirred slightly when we stopped and listlessly got to their feet when Mil went over to the office. Osman had phoned the DC from Khartoum telling him that we were coming through. We had hoped for a cool rest, perhaps even a glimpse of a traditional tribal home. Apparently Ramadan was too much for the man; no one was in the office. But then it was already after eleven.

For five hours we had been driving through a furnace, one that got hotter as the sun grew more intense. The car absorbed, and now radiated, the heat. Sitting in it was just bearable when there was wind from the movement of the car; it was sheer torture to stay in it when we stopped. Standing in the breathless shade of the tree I looked around for a well where I might wash, for my face felt caked from sand and dried sweat. But nothing was visible of Shendi except low mud walls; if there were wells, they were within those secret confines. All our water bags were filled, but with prescience of desert folk, I was hoarding our own supplies. Wiping off with cologne helped a little; I decided that a small drink of water was in order. There was still the clink of ice in the thermos as I poured out pure water; the thought of any crystalline glucosed grapefruit juice was merely sickening in all that heat. But as I started to moisten my parched lips with the cup I noticed that the men on the cots were glaring at me, hate and envy vivid on their faces. "Ramadan," I exclaimed out loud, "Oh damn," and hastily poured the cool water back into the thermos.

Mil was checking the tires, letting out more air as the heat had increased the pressure. When he finished the sweat had made rivers in the mud on his face. I used cologne on his face too, explaining the lack of drinking water. He started to protest that we weren't observing Ramadan, but a glance at the staring men confirmed my reactions. Instead, we fed water to the Bublee which had been boiling for some time despite the extra fan blade which Mil had had put on in Khartoum. Mil had left the motor running and by then the thumping of the boiling water had stopped. Cautiously Mil unscrewed the cap and slowly we filled the radiator. We drove out of sight of the men, gulped our ration of water, and once more continued under the merciless sun.

Whatever I had expected, when driving along the Nile, it was not this pebbly trail across nothing. Surely we should have a glimpse of the mighty river, seen a palm tree or two along its course. Instead, all morning we had crossed an unrelieved desert. Only the map told us that not far away the Nile moved sluggishly toward Egypt. Somewhere, too, over to the west, the river suddenly changed its character and bounded down the Fifth Cataract. Yet all we could see was more sand, more slightly mounding pebble hills. The road was where you made it, anywhere across the flat desert as long as the oil drums of markers were still in sight. We passed a few trucks, as often on the left as on right. Who should care about traffic rules when there was only the sun to enforce them?

The long morning had seemed endless; now this state of self torture seemed normal existence. The heat reached an apex of penetration beyond acceptability yet it had to be endured. Slipping into a state of semi-trance, I kidded with Mil that the next stage was nirvana. My joke made no impression on him; his own lethargy was too consuming. Fighting off ennui, I tried to write, but the bumpiness of the track made hen scratches of my efforts. There was nothing in the unvarying scenery to interest a second glance; reaches of pebbled earth, tiny islands of yellowed grass with clumps of hay sitting on top of the sand carpets like a paper-weight against the wind. Occasionally a small thorn bush, black against so much yellow-brown, rose bravely to a height of two or three feet. Once, in the distance, we saw odd shaped mounds of adobe construction; if they were houses, they were completely unlike the low, flat dwellings we had seen in the towns and villages. It was nearly time for a driving switch, so I roused myself enough to take a picture of this novelty.

After that we met no cars, saw no people, no camels, no goats, no trees. The track markers were at greater and greater intervals. Our torpidity was so intense we could hardly talk; yet this alone kept whoever was driving from a stupor which might make the other lose control of the car. We exhausted the subject of the trip and somehow got onto a recital of our ancestors past, present, and future. Our assumed interest in this subject grew as the noise of the boiling radiator increased from a distant pounding of waves to an insistent thumping of an urgent caller. What could we do? There had been no shade since Shendi; stopping in the sun helped not at all, for the slight breeze of movement compensated for the pull of the engine. We could not wait for evening, the track was indistinct enough to be easily missed in the dark. Besides, we had no idea of the exact time the train would leave from Atbara. Freight trains apparently had none of the precision which is traditionally associated with the once-a-week passenger train.

We didn't feel like eating. Once when we changed drivers we took another sip of water. The bumping in the radiator boomed across the stillness; it seemed less terrifying when we were moving. The road was poor; but as we were veterans by now this hardly warranted a second thought. Nor did we feel any danger, for the track crossed and recrossed the empty railroad line. The boiling engine bothered us, but only a little; in our lethargic mood we were even beyond worry. It was merely a case of endurance, of pushing on until we got to Atbara, or until we couldn't go any longer.

On the speedometer, mileage increased, though to us one mile or ten were the same. I welcomed the mileage markers as proof that we were not simply going in circles.

The brilliant ball of the sun seemed always directly overhead and so was useless for direction. Twice we saw somnolent villages, or perhaps deserted: there was no sign of life. Then the track rose along craggy hills. Briefly and suddenly there was a glimpse of the Nile, a chocolate snake winding its way through brown banks. No green thing relieved the picture. At the same time I was aware of a strange silence. I looked quizzically at Mil but he was staring ahead. There was the bridge across the Atbara River. In the gully beneath the river puddled and trickled. Ahead we could see the criss-cross pattern of the railroad yard.

Now Mil too noticed the lack of noise, "It's gone dry," he let out, rather like a sigh. He let his foot off the accelerator for a moment, and let in the clutch. There was still a slight gulping as though the engine were gasping its last. Mil instantly made up his mind. "There must be a little water left. We can make it." And coasting much of the way in, we did. Circling the railroad shed for the shady side Mil left me with the steaming car and went off to find someone in the deserted yard. Groggily I checked the speedometer: hardly more than two hundred miles in nine hours driving. I sloshed off my face, but still my mind was miles distant from my body. I watched myself drink, hold water for Mil to rinse, offer him water; but my body did all this from habit. At that moment I could have believed in any number of the mystical religions that preach multiple existences or pre-knowledge. I saw the Greek yard foreman come up to us and refuse to put the auto onto a flatcar, and Mil argue back just as if I were seeing a re-run of an old movie. I heard myself ask for a Mr. Black and knew the man would reply that Mr. Black had already left for his vacation in England. But I was not worried, for I knew, after much cajoling and threatening and pleading that the man would give up and let us drive the sweltering Bublee onto the single vacant flatcar. By then the sun was setting and the man probably wanted to go home for his dinner, or a drink.

The idea of a drink was like a beacon. Mil told a Sudanese urchin to keep an eye out on the car, and we accepted a lift to the Rest House with another Greek. We walked into an empty building, for the Muezzin had called to break the fast, and all the staff were out on the back lawn guzzling food and water. There was nothing to do but wait impatiently until their hunger was satisfied; then at last we were served. Only after several sour lemonades and a thorough soaking dipper bath did I come out of my fog. Even the same wrinkled clothes felt cleaner. Meanwhile Mil had been trying to find someone who knew what time the train would leave that night. Another guest in the Rest House phoned a friend who referred us to a Mr. Garfield. Over the phone Mr. Garfield said that the train was not due to leave before midnight, so why not join him at the Club after dinner. Somewhat pacified, Mil also poured water over himself; then we tried eating the fare at the Rest House, which seemed reasonably good, but beyond liquids I could not touch a thing.

At the Club I was grateful for the dim lighting, for the feeling of grubbiness returned. I wondered about the advisability of putting a gin and tonic on top of my empty stomach, but Mr. Garfield was so hospitable, and so reassuring about our getting on the train "if he personally had to go down to the yards and order it" that both Mil and I began to relax. Sensitive to our exhaustion, Garfield soon bore us off to his house to rest. He checked with the station and learned that the expected departure would be about three in the morning. Leaving word that we were to be called an hour before the train was to depart, he fed us omelets and put us to bed.

I awoke with a start. The quiet darkness and the clean

sheets confused me a moment. Sensing it was late I reached for the clock on the bed table: four o'clock! I was up and dressed in seconds, swearing mentally at whoever had forgotten to phone us. Then I realized that Mr. Garfield was on the phone; it must have been his talking that woke me. I sat down on the porch and waited for him to finish. No, the train hadn't gone yet; it was expected to be rather late and the man would phone us in plenty of time. The house-boy had appeared with morning tea. There seemed little point in going back to sleep for only a few minutes, so Mr. Garfield and I sat talking while Mil still slept. He seemed glad of female company; his wife had gone back to England a month before to spend the Easter holidays with their son. In a few weeks his annual leave was due and he would join her in Bournemouth. But even a few weeks as a bachelor had made him lonely. Still, he found his work rewarding, both emotionally and financially; he had like the Sudanese when he had been in the Sudan during the war and had been eager to return. The short term of his contract did not bother him, rather he was most optimistic about the ease of transfer to the Sudanese of the railroad and the government too, as long as the Egyptians did not take over. Indeed, he was much more upset about rumors of anti-British rioting in Egypt right then and urged me to think carefully about shipping the car to Cairo, not trying to drive.

Mil got up when breakfast was ready, about five; we had just finished when the phone call finally came through. Mr. Garfield drove us to the flatcar, ordered several workers to fill up our water bags and the radiator while he sent back to his house for drinking water. Still with no signs of departure, we urged Mr. Garfield to go home for a bit more rest while we clambered up onto the flatcar. Mil stood around watching, but I promptly went to sleep again in the front seat. Only

Bublee riding backwards on the train
from Atbara to Wadi Halfa

after the muezzin called did the train pull out; dimly I realized that the crew all wanted to drink until the last possible moment since they were planning to fast throughout the torrid day!

And how torrid that day could be we soon began to find out. The auto had been placed backwards on the flatcar so that there was less breeze than we had when driving. Almost as soon as we were under way, the sun rose as well and we could feel the temperature rise minute by hot minute. To shut out the glare, we ranged the raffia seat mats over the windshield, hung scarves on the windows. Eventually I put on my floppy straw hat on the theory that more layers between me and the sun, the better. I would have loved, at that moment, to put the car into purdah; even my usual undeviating allegiance to feminine rights would have rejoiced to procure a veil of any sort. I dozed a few times, but was soon too uncomfortable to sit still. Already the air outside the car was as hot as that inside; the gusts of wind that blew into our car were laden with sand. We tried closing the windows and opening the doors a crack. Still the sand drifted in: a veritable dust storm.

We passed some sort of maintenance station. No glittering beehive houses here; only two or three huts clustered by a clump of palm trees. Nearby, most unexpectedly, was a small factory processing some sort of desert chemical. After that, the scenery had only a negative quality. For a time we could see car tracks pacing the railroad; then they disappeared behind a rim of hills. Here was the dangerous part of the journey for autos. I felt a slight prick of remorse at our not accepting the challenge; but the heat precluded real regret. In fact, as far as self-immolation is concerned, I began to feel we had chosen the worst way. It was hardly noon; there were six more hours of torture. Nothing seemed really to help. I was waiting for the torpor of the day before to take over so that I could forget the place and the heat until it was all over. But something more pressing protruded upon my consciousness. Despite the heat and my perspiration, I had to go to the john. Soon the need became a critical problem. Many of the box cars were going empty to Wadi Halfa to haul back goods brought from Egypt by the boats. I had noticed many riders in these cars. This potential audience hardly encouraged any dhow-type maneuver such as I had employed before. As necessity was forcing a decision the train jerked to a stop at a motley collection of huts and one larger adobe structure which proclaimed the stop to be Abu Hamed.

The station house was jammed with reclining bodies, for the station provided a bit of that rare entity in the desert: shade. I had wandered over to look for a WC; but I was too embarrassed to ask any direction for there was not a woman in the crowd. However the station consisted only of two rooms; wherever the WC was, it was not there. So I walked forward along the train, hoping to find an empty box car or a sheltered space between some cars. There were some houses in the distance, but I had no idea how long the train would stop and it didn't seem wise to go very far away. Suddenly I noticed a car which looked like a Pullman. Vaguely I supposed it was being hauled to Wadi Halfa, and assumed it would be empty. Still, I thought, there must be a porter or a guard on board. Surely he would let me use the john. Quickly I climbed the steep steps and knocked, deciding that embarrassment in front of one was better than near-shame I had felt in the presence of the masculine throng at the station. Urgently I banged louder.

At length a white gowned porter answered, but despite my earnest pleas and gestures he gave me to understand that his boss was in the car, sleeping, and would have to be asked. Confused at this turn of events, I could only cling to the side supports of the steps and wait. Although it could not have been long, I was almost completely wilted before another Sudanese appeared, this one in his bathrobe. "Please," I said too loudly, "may I use your WC?" Not a flicker of amusement crossed his face, bless him. With practiced savior faire he gestured a slight bow, and led me through a dim corridor past a shaded sitting area. Motioning me forward, he shut a door behind me. As my eyes grew accustomed to the gloom I realized I was in a bedroom. Under other circumstances this might have been amusing or compromising, but neither thought entered my head. I looked for, and found, what I had been looking for, then washed in the tepid tap water. In the corner of the bathroom was a shower which at that moment seemed the greatest of luxuries. I just stood and stared, visions of relief dancing more insistently than sugarplums the night before Christmas.

Reluctantly I withdrew and returned to the now pleasantly dim sitting area where my Sudanese host was lounging. Feeling some sort of explanation was due, and undoubtedly looking for excuses to stay in the comparative coolness of the salon, I explained that my husband and I were riding in our auto on the flatcar. The Sudanese was aghast. "How impossible," he cried, stirring to his feet, "you must not ride out in the sun. You will become ill. No, you must ride with me. There is much room here." I will confess I did not protest. Quite eagerly I went back after Mil with news of this incredible luck.

Mil also had a surprise for me. He was talking in the shade of a shed with a South African girl. She and her English husband were driving from London to Cape Town in a vintage Bentley. All the tires on their car had given out in Yugoslavia and for weeks they had waited for the odd size tires to be ordered and to arrive. This delay had drained their pockets. With a bravado that probably masked shame, she boasted that since then they had traveled by borrowing money here and there along the way and which they would eventually try to pay back. It had taken them three days to drive just to Abu Hamed from Wadi Halfa. The road had always been in sight of the railroad so it was only tough going. "But from here to Atbara," the girl said grimly, "frankly, we're worried. But we ran into a Greek contractor here in Abu Hamed who had a pick-up truck. He says he will help us along to Atbara if we want to wait for him to finish his business. We've been here in Abu Hamed now for two days. Richard is always working on the motorcar, but I have nothing to do, no one to talk to. Perhaps tomorrow night we shall leave. If we are lucky we will be in Atbara before the sun gets too hot the next day. Wish us luck!" she pleaded.

Back in the salon, books and diary in tow, our host introduced himself as Mohammed Abdul Gallender, a railroad engineer on his way from Khartoum to Wadi Halfa on a routine inspection trip. He had changed from his pajamas and bathrobe to white shirt and trousers, but he still looked sleepy and I apologized again for waking him. Brushing aside my hesitations he insisted he was delighted at the company on what otherwise is always a dull trip. Immediately he had the porter serve us iced lemon squash, but did not join us as he was observing Ramadan. He told us he was half Turkish, that he had studied in Cairo and London. "I was in London once during Ramadan," he smiled. "For three days I tried to keep the fast. But it was so hard to find a place to eat about four in the morning. What was worse, it was June, and the days were eighteen hours long! No, I could not keep the fast there; I nearly became ill trying."

The afternoon passed drowsily. None of us was up to long conversations with the heat and the lack of food. It did not seem proper to eat in front of Mr. Gallender; but we did drink more water. We took turns napping in the bunks. I was reading a rather dull novel and decided to try balancing the budget instead. Bublee's train ride of $47.50 really hurt financially; the boat ride would cost another $22.50. Our flatcar trip cost us a mere pound each; Mr. Gallender's was hospitality beyond price. The boat ride for us was going to cost $21.00. As never before on the trip the pressure of finances loomed depressingly large. Especially after that encounter with the borrowing travelers, I determined we would have to cut expenses in every way to avoid such a necessity on our part.

Precisely at sunset the train stopped in the middle of no place: everyone wished to eat. Mil and I went back to the car to forage for tins and for clean clothes. Sticking his hands into the boot, Mil came out with them covered in a reddish goo: the shoe polish had melted and run all over everything! The porter added our supplies to his own and shortly produced a welcome meal. The evening was not cool, but the contrast with the penetrating heat of the day it was invigorating and we walked about on the still desert for nearly an hour. Back on the train, Mil and I showered and went to bed in Mr. Gallender's bunks while he, gallant gentleman that he was, slept on the floor of the salon. I felt distinctly guilty, but courtesy implied that the female should have a bed; certainly he could not have used the other bunk.

Sometime during the night the train moved off again, and by morning we were in Wadi Halfa. Here at least was the bright greenness of palms and large leafed acacias, the dull greenness of parched grass. Under the trees, paralleling the river, the one and two story houses and shops gave off a look of belonging and of permanence that we had not seen since Omdurman. Even the railroad station, secure under its protecting trees, looked built to stay rather than an alien form in the midst of unending desert.

We had letters of introduction to Saad El Din Abdul El Gany whom everyone called Sheikh Barbees because of his local power rather than because of heredity. We were told we couldn't miss him, and we couldn't. He was six feet of a glowing ebony Nubian swathed in snowy fill gown and loose turban. Here, surely, was the perfect Othello. A king in his own parish, he had no need for that sophistication of manner we had noticed among the Khartoum Sudanese. But his hospitality was no less sincere. Among his many activities he was caterer for the Nile boats, so immediately he swept us off the train and into the dining room of the newest river boat which was already tied up at the water's edge. After ordering a large meal for us he thoughtfully disappeared so that we could eat without his fasting perturbing our pleasure. By the time we had finished eating the Sheikh had already had our tickets checked and our car cleared. He bemoaned the fact that our last minutes arrangements had put us on the oldest steamer on the river; he would try to have us switched to the new boat if there were any cancellations. We would enjoy the trip more, he thought, in the nicer boat and both boats left at the same time.

Sheikh Barbees sent a boy with us to show us the hotel which was nearly hidden by its forest of palms up-river several hundred yards. The manager, a young man named Haylor, greeted up with something less than enthusiasm and when I asked whether if we skipped lunch that day we could have it the day we left, he curtly agreed and forthwith installed us in the cheapest room. Later he apologized, but explained he was remembering the couple in the Bentley who had not only not paid for their room, but had borrowed money from him, which he was sure he would never receive again. Indeed, we unexpectedly ran into him in Rome a month later and up to that time he had not heard a thing from them. Since he was off on the first leg of his vacation to Europe on the same boat we were, he would need all his money for traveling. Thus he had put up his guard against us lest we too beg money of him!

AT WADI HALFA WE were within the boundaries of the old Egyptian civilization. My grammar school lessons of ancient history had taken better than I knew and suddenly I was interested in the past, though perhaps not with the intensity of my fascination for the present and the immediate future. Up stream and across the river was a small ancient building, one of the oldest extant and the one furthest up the Nile. Sunday we hired a sail boat and went to look at it. By a propitious fluke of nature there are prevailing north winds so that the natives can sail up the Nile and then drift down with the current. Our boat, too, sailed up and drifted back, lazily, for there was neither much breeze nor much water current. The thrill of discovery was still on this small, half-destroyed temple; there were no noxious guides to beg money or comment with lewd references to the carved and painted relief. We explored at our leisure, then drifted back to the hotel for the rest of a relaxing day.

Mr. Garfield phoned us that evening from Atbara to make certain we were all right, and once more to urge us not to drive through a riot-prone Egypt, especially in a British car. His words were well meant. Financially we could not listen to them; but they did put us on our guard. In fact the next morning we got a preview of Egyptian anti-Westernism, for this national psychosis is motivated in all likelihood by the same basic inferiority complex that stirred in the customs official in Wadi Halfa. We had gone down to the dock early in the morning to get the formalities finished before the passenger train arrived. In minutes we had finished with the Sudanese official and had passed on to a gruff, huffing Egyptian who seemed mad at the world and intolerant of its inhabitants. There was no crush of people so he stalled over the forms. But he was actually so pitiable, this man against the universe, that my sympathy must have shown; soon he was confiding about his poor assignment and how it was so hot that he could not bring his wife to Wadi Halfa, and all the frustrations that involved. Mil finished with the passports and came over to help me, thinking I was running into trouble. Mil's presence moved the customs man, who was by then quite contrite, to great speed and efficiency. We found throughout Egypt that ostentatious dislike was usually, like this incident, only surface deep. But emotions of crowds always float on foam, frothing easily into riots. We avoided groups, but we did drive to Cairo.

The hotel was having a farewell meal for Mr. Haylor, so Sheikh Barbees took us back to the hotel where we shared a truly expansive banquet that continued long into the afternoon. No one realized until it was nearly upon us that a dreaded *haboob* was blowing. The *haboob* is the desert wind which has different names in different places. But always it is dreaded for its blasting heat. Walking into the wind was like facing molten fires. Mil rushed to the customs shed to drive Bublee on to the two-storied barge. Already large waves were lapping at the shores; the river, which had until then been like a calm mill pond, became an angry little lake. A sandstorm, fierce in its biting, descended on the town. Goodbyes were hurried as we fled from the attack. Our boat was filled and we pulled out ahead of the new boat into a heavy gale with currents more like sea than river. In moments we could no longer see the river bank, the sandstorm was so thick. Suddenly we heard a strange moaning sound from the shore, like amazed drawing in of breath. Then the sand clouds lifted a bit and the same breathless expression progressed across our boat and the barge: ah-h-h, feel that, water! Driven in front of the gale, a few drops of rain spattered down! Average rainfall for Wadi Halfa is listed as zero. No wonder everyone was astounded: it hadn't dripped a drop in seven years! Indeed those few drops, we later heard, were enough to wash out the railroad line, laid with profound belief in the zero inches of rainfall. No trains reached Wadi Halfa for nearly two weeks! Once more our luck had held; imagine being stuck on the flatcar for two weeks, or trying to drive through such raging of nature.

The amazing weather continued most of the night; the choppiness of the water lost its force on the low flat bottom of the boat, but the gusts of wind sent shudders through the superstructure. By morning the placidity of the river reasserted itself and we chugged along in this deep gash in the desert. The steepness of the valley, and its narrowness, was not something I had expected. Only rarely did the valley walls recede enough to make room for a small town. In some places the water filed the entire valley floor. Elsewhere fields clung to the rugged walls while the huts of the *fellaheen* were built up above the valley on the desert floor, exposed to all the winds and sands. Weirdly, the small fields did not stop at the edge of the water; tips of plants and large branches of trees thrust up out of the water. In stretches where the wind did not ripple the water we could see whole underwater gardens waving in the current rather than in the wind. A young Egyptian schoolteacher on board explained to us that these fields had been inundated when the Aswan dam had been raised the last time. All the *fellaheen* who owned or farmed land that would be under water had received money for the land. Most of them, unfortunately, had not really understood, had accepted the money as a bonanza and squandered it. Poor again, and landless, most of them returned to their holdings. Now they eke out crops between the floods, perhaps supplementing their income by sending a son to Cairo as a servant.

Apparently, going to Cairo as a servant is a glamorous future in this area. One of the charcoal Nubian cabin boys on the boat begged and begged us to take him to Cairo as a servant. At length we convinced him that we would not stay in Cairo but that we were willing to give him a ride to the big city. The poor man, faced with this dilemma, eager to go but not quite adventurous enough to look after himself in the metropolis, was in agony for the rest of the trip. When we were about to depart he bid us the best of salaams and returned, sadly, to the boat.

As SHEIKH BARBEES HAD warned, our boat was very old. We had a funny little room with double-decker bunks which must have been second class in the good old days. Now second class was on a small tow boat hitched to the large new boat; third class was on the barge where Bublee was traveling. Out of Wadi Halfa there had been few third class passengers; but about noon the next day we stopped at a small town in a slight bend of the river where the valley wall suddenly cut sharply around leaving an open point of land for houses. Swarms of young boys flowed onto the barge and I was suddenly fearful for the finish of the car. Indeed Bublee did acquire many scratches as memory of her Nile trip. Our Egyptian teacher friend told us these boys were going to Aswan to sit for the school leaving examination. The examination board, which conducted the exams throughout the country, was reluctant to waste several weeks so far up river so the boys went down-river instead.

The first evening on the boat, still full from Haylor's fare-well meal, we ordered only tea for supper and ate lightly of crackers and cheese. Next morning we checked food prices in the dining room and once again ate in our wee cabin. Sheikh Barbees was wealthy enough without our custom. The cabin was so small that the only place to sit was half-upright on the lower bunk, so for lunch we ate on the upper deck where I had been writing all morning. Mil then went back to his cabin perch in the upper bunk directly under a small fan. Much later, when I went down to fetch him for tea. I walked into inches of water all over the cabin floor. Hastily pulling out the suitcases and piling them on the bunks, we yelled for the cabin boy. To him this sort of flood was nearly routine. As he began to clean it up he scolded us for not calling him earlier to empty the water. Only then did we realize what had caused the flood: the cabin basin. To give the appearance of running water there was a large tank hanging rather like a medicine cabinet over the bowl. As you used the water, it ran into a similarly sized tank below. Thus when you asked to have the top tank refilled, the cabin boy would empty the lower one. We had thought the water merely drained off. Since the water from the top tank ran out the murky color of strong tea, we had asked for a jug of water instead, and had had it refilled many times. Thus the bottom tank had never been emptied and eventually overflowed. With the mess in the cabin, and with a demanding appetite after a relaxing day, we braved the prices for a proper meal in the dining room.

Time floated as easily as the boat; since everyone had said the ride took two days, we were preparing for another lovely day. I had just installed myself on the upper deck the following morning when the boat docked at a place which proved, to our surprise, to be Shellal, the last town above the Aswan dam. Because we had gone through customs at Wadi Halfa we expected simply to drive off and go on to Luxor the same day. Unfortunately the papers from the customs man were all on the large boat which was reported to be some four hours behind us. While Mil talked over the problem with an officious customs man I sat in the shade by the pier. An obstreperous hawker besieged me selling ugly dirty shell necklaces which I wouldn't have put on a cow. He began to screech at me, insulting and almost threatening. Finally, I bought one of the filthy things to be rid of him, a bit apprehensive of starting a scene which might touch off the apparent anti-European attitude of the porters and customs men. Still he shrilled at me, wealthy imperialist, paying so little for his beautiful necklaces, refusing to buy more. Just when I could take no more of it and was surveying a possible retreat, a tall policeman in khaki shorts and shirt ambled up. Peace was instantly restored. He looked at my apprehensive face and asked me why I was waiting and what was the trouble. His influence must have outweighed his rank, for he spoke only briefly to the customs official and within minutes we had the car off the barge and were free to go.

Several of the students from the boat were milling around, trying to hitch rides into Aswan. We managed to squeeze three into the back seat for the short ride and started off, expecting to drive straight on for Luxor that day. But in the few miles from Shellal toward Aswan the engine overheated and began to spurt and bubble. The weather was hot, but not that hot; nor should the extra load have made much difference on the flat gravel road. Something was wrong. So as soon as we arrived in Aswan, Mil took Bublee to a garage while I waited at the local hotel. Hardly had I sat down, book in hand, when I was besieged by a platoon of importunate guides, shrilling, shrieking, jockeying for position, caging me within a ring of heat and smells. "No, no, no guides," I insisted. "But you must have guides," they cried in return. Each had his own sales pitch which he shouted in competition with the others: "See Aswan Dam. I show best view form boat." "Take a camel across the desert to monastery. Every American want ride camel. One day go, one day come back." "I go with you to Luxor. Never find road without me. I show you the Dead City. Price cheap. How much you pay?"

I retreated before this hoard, but they followed, avarice glinting in their eyes. I found myself at the hotel desk. "Please," I begged the clerk, "make them go away." To my relief, he did, by threatening not to let them come into the lobby again. But several sly old men took up stations by the doors, like soldiers on guard, ready to pounce on the prey should it leave the lobby. I couldn't concentrate on the novel with all those eyes on me. Though taking the train from Aswan to Cairo was financially out of the question still, I resolved to be careful. For the first time since Addis I was aware of my white skin and apprehensive of its effect on the local people.

It was after one when Mil got back to the hotel. He reported that the mechanic had found a loose gasket in the carburetor and that this was probably causing the overheating. That such a simple thing could cause so much trouble and concern, and waste so much time! Already it was too late to get to Luxor before nightfall, so we checked in at the hotel. The mid-day dinner came as something of a surprise; not only was it the most lavish we had eaten since Nairobi, but it was French cuisine. Here was another reminder, along with the cloying guides and the higher hotel price, that we were back within the ordinary European tourist circuit, that a journey up the Nile had long been a fashionable winter vacation for the cream of continental society. But with the unrest in the country, tourists were few; no wonder the guides were predatory.

After dinner we went off in search of an elder brother of Sheikh Barbees who had been, until Nasser and Neguib had abolished it, a member of the Egyptian Parliament. As well known in Aswan as Barbees was known in Wadi Halfa, we had merely to mention his name and we were led to a small café. There sat Mohammed, also of extreme size but of width rather than height, talking earnestly with a friend of size almost as monumental. The two of them were squeezed into a corner behind a table filled with bottles of Coca Cola; full, empty, half-drunk, all warm and too sweet. Immediately Mohammed called for more glasses and poured us out coke, apologizing for not joining us because it was Ramadan. His friend, another politician but a Copt, continued to consume the beverage with almost sickening speed. Mohammed read the letter from Sheikh Barbees that we had brought him, commenting volubly in Arabic at nearly every sentence.

When he finished he turned to us with the exasperated expression a mother might use toward her darling child and said, "Barbees is called sheikh among his own people, but for him it is not enough. He wishes to go again to Europe, this time to see the Coronation of Queen Elizabeth. Already I have told him he must not go, but still he asks." He clucked his tongue disapprovingly. I remembered Barbees speaking of his planned trip as though it were a certainty, his handsome face screwed up in childish delight.

"Why shouldn't he go," I asked, a bit pugnaciously. Mohammed clucked again, a deep sound, followed by a snort. "Ah, he is a child of the desert. He has not lived in Cairo. He does not understand that he is nobody in London. He will tell you instead how he was honored by so many Englishmen when he went there before, how they waited on him and lived with him." Mohammed rumbled again. "They did, like leeches they lived on him, and he never understood. And it was very, very expensive. We are afraid to let him go again. He cannot afford so kingly a trip again." He let a sad smile settle over his anger, and added softly, "if he goes as an ordinary tourist, and no one honors him, it will break his heart!"

At length Mohammed stirred his great bulk and waddled as far as the door. Immediately an old black limousine rolled up and Mohammed spread himself across the front seat, next to the driver. He took us to view the "big needle," reputedly the world's largest, though unfinished, obelisk.. Then we went on to the famous, and now controversial, Aswan Dam where he sent us off in his speed boat with one of his many minions to have a closer look at the submerged Temple of Philae. Mohammed himself did not join us on the plea that he must return home to pray; I was just a happy for the boat looked too small to bear his majestic tonnage. His car was waiting for us when we returned, and a young relative took us through a colorless bazaar where the only thing I could find to buy was some cucumbers for lunch. Mohammed himself appeared at the hotel after dinner and regally occupied a small sofa as though it were a specially-measured chair. He was full of anecdotes about his early life and vignettes about the Sheikh; but though we talked well into the night, and however much I tried to draw him out, not a single comment on any Egyptian government, past or future, came from his pouting lips.

CHAPTER 32

# Egypt: Non-African Africa

THE ROAD WE TOOK TO LUXOR THE NEXT DAY BORE NO RESEM-blance to the route on our map. The old narrow way had wound through the valuable cultivatable land in the valley creating a slow and tortuous path. Sometime during the war a desert road had been built, one which climbs onto the rocky dunes which border the river gorge and goes coasting along through nothingness between hot sun and hotter sand. We worried constantly that somehow we had by mistake taken the road for the Red Sea, so desolate was the way. With the heat and the hills, Bublee again began heating up and the engine started missing. Obviously there was something more drastic wrong with it than just the loose gasket. Soon the car's compression was so low that we could hardly mount the rolling hills. In the grueling heat, with not a single tree

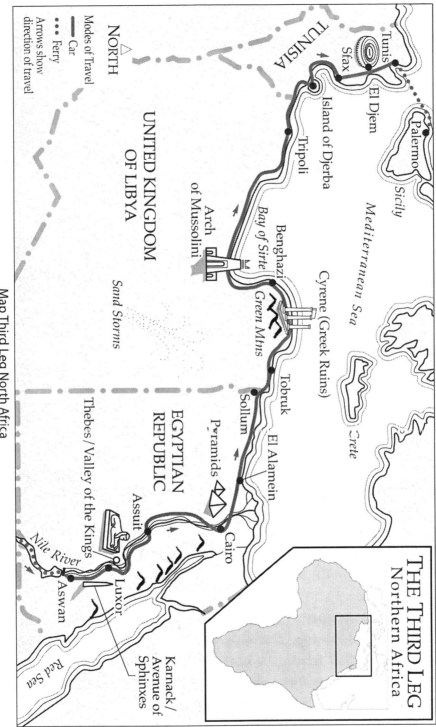

THE THIRD LEG
Northern Africa

UNITED KINGDOM
OF LIBYA

EGYPTIAN
REPUBLIC

TUNISIA

Tunis
Sfax
El Djem
Palermo
Sicily
Island of Djerba
Mediterranean Sea
Tripoli
Arch
of Mussolini
Bay of Sirte
Benghazi
Green Mtns
Cyrene (Greek Ruins)
Crete
Sand Storms
Tobruk
Sollum
El Alamein
Pyramids
Cairo
Assuit
Thebes / Valley of the Kings
Nile River
Aswan
Luxor
Red Sea
Karnack /
Avenue of
Sphinxes

NORTH

Modes of Travel
—— Car
••• Ferry
Arrows show
direction of travel

in miles, Mil changed the steaming spark plugs. This helped some and, limping slowly, we arrived in Luxor in twice the time that those hundred and fifty miles should have taken.

We checked into a sister hotel of the one we had stayed at in Aswan. It was equally a relic of the Edwardian era of British colonialism and was now steeped in an atmosphere of complacency and decadence like a ghost that doesn't yet know it is dead. After washing we went off in search of a garage where we could have the car checked again. The hotel clerk directed us to an old Coptic mechanic who ran what had once been a British-owned shop. It was too late for him to do anything that day, but he promised to work on Bublee first thing in the morning. Walking back toward the hotel we came upon, quite unexpectedly, the ruins of the Temple of Luxor. Encircled by the expanding town, the temple lay like a graveyard in an honored but forgotten spot. The long afternoon sun gave back to the immense colonnade and its guardian colossi a life that was sucked out by the glare of noonday. We wandered amidst the towering pillars and line carvings, happily unencumbered by guides or guide book, until the shadows wrapped the art in its obscurity.

In our cavernous room in the hotel, threadbare and sparsely furnished, we sipped carefully from our bottle of Scotch and discussed our plans. For several days I had been fiddling with dates, trying to see exactly how we could drive all the way to Calais in the time we still had left. From Cairo to Tripoli to Tunis to Algeria to Gibraltar through Spain to Calais the schedule was prodigious, not allowing for any mishaps and permitting us only a few days rest in the month of continuous driving. The impact of the European atmosphere which we had felt in the hotels somehow dulled the adventure; the month ahead seemed more punishment than challenge. We began to think about boats to Europe. Alexandria is a busy port, surely one could go from there to Greece or Italy. But, came the nagging question: could we afford it? Well, maybe we could ship to Lebanon and drive the short way round the Mediterranean, or talk the Egyptians into letting us drive across the Sinai peninsula to Israel and up to Beirut. From Beirut I knew the road back to Europe since I had driven that section on my way out to India. Except for one day's driving along the border road between Greece and Turkey, that route was easy enough and would only take two weeks. Still, I had been that way, and it wasn't Africa. Perhaps we should just drive west along the top of Africa til we ran out of time and money, then take a boat from the nearest port. After all, Tripoli and Tunis and Algiers all had ferry service that connected to European cities.

As I rolled those names off my tongue and traced the routes on the map, enthusiasm began to seep back. "Algiers," I said. "I've always wanted to see that town. My grandma used to recite a long sorrowful poem to me when I was four or five that went something like: 'A soldier of the Legion lay dying at Algiers; there was want of woman's nursing and a dearth of women's tears...' Or Tunis. After all, that is where Carthage was. I remember that our Latin class did a bit of a play about Dido and Aeneas: I was Dido and had to kill myself on a funeral pyre when Aeneas sailed away. Or Tripoli. Of course we must see Tripoli, not that I've been to see the Halls of Montezuma, have you?" Maybe it was the Scotch. I poured out some more in our communal glass and toasted the Marines. "From the Halls of Montezuma to the shores of Tripoli..." I sang.

The mood, unfortunately, did not last. I had begun to balance the books. We were out of traveler's checks due to the unexpected cost of the train and boat. The nearest place we could cash a personal check was the Embassy in Cairo. There was a bank in Luxor, of course, but even a cable transfer would take four to six days. We would simply have to get to Cairo on what money we had. Our first economy was to tell the hotel clerk that I did not like to eat in the morning and that one breakfast would be enough, served in the room. In fact one breakfast plus the free morning tea consisted of as much food as the two of us normally ate anyhow, but the dodge did make us feel a bit underprivileged. We would also skip the midday meal in the dining room; in any case we were not used to two large meals a day. Thank heavens, I thought, the hotel was European plan so that we could save by not eating.

Realizing how long the food would have to last, we ate heartily of the evening dinner. In the lobby, over after-dinner coffee, we met three Americans from the Embassy in Cairo. The couple was taking the night train back to Cairo but the young man, Bob Stanton, was planning to go across the Nile to see the Valley of the Kings very early the next day, and wouldn't we like to join him?

It was a fantastic morning: an excursion into antiquity, a whole course on the glories of ancient Thebes embellished with comments on art, religion, agriculture, and court intrigues. The guide was good, and Bob brought a Baedeker; from these two sources we devoured huge amounts of almost indigestible information. The day was infused with heat: with climbing over barren hills in the stark desert light and then entering tombs of remarkable coolness and placidity. Of all the long names of the kings which rolled off our tongues only that of King Tutankamen sounded a familiar cord. We spent the longest time in his tomb for it was completely intact when discovered in 1922 so that the tempura frescoes were undamaged and the furnishings for his palace in the next life were the most extensive. It was interesting to see these works of art in their original setting, but they were difficult to appreciate in the dim light and without much background information. I reflected on the inadequacies of my standard American education once again; after all, I had studied ancient history three times in high school or college, yet always Egypt had been skipped over lightly in favor of Greece and Rome.

After the tombs we examined temples, drove to view the immense Colossi of Memnon out on the flood flats by the river and wound back into the crusty hills rimming the desert to the terraced temple of Queen Hatsheput. Climbing the endless steps to the temple in the hot midday sun was physical torture; below us lay the glorious dead of Thebes, their spirits seeming to rise from the desert as the sun played tricks with the vapors. Almost four thousand years divided the kings and ourselves; life has gone on that long. It was humbling and calming thought after all the political turmoil we had been experiencing.

The present, with its immediate problems, returned with a shock when we got back to the hotel. Typically American tourist, Bob Stanton had not bothered to bargain with the guide before engaging him, had agreed to the inflated price of five pounds just for the one trip and expected us to pay two-thirds of this. We had only ten pounds left at that point. I was furious, first at myself for not having asked sooner, secondly at Bob for not bargaining, thirdly at Mil for paying what the guide asked and not trying to cut down the price. Back in our room we ate our bread and cheese in frosty silence; then I erupted. "Bob got us into this," I stormed; "now he is down in the cool dining room eating his fill. He should have paid half of that exorbitant price. You know the guides I talked to had already come down to three pounds while the hotel clerk told me that two was standard." Mil exploded right back at me saying how tired he was of living on the brink of financial disaster. "So you spend the money here," I retorted sarcastically, "and just how do we pay for the petrol to get us to Cairo? It is over four hundred miles from Luxor to Cairo; we can't make that in one day but we won't have any money for a hotel, and you don't think we should drive at night. We might not even have a car; you haven't paid for Bublee's repairs yet. You figure it out," I yelled, and with that retired to the bathroom and a cold shower.

Calmed by the shower, I was contrite but there was no one to apologize to: Mil had gone out. He was soon back, though, apologetic but pleased. He had retrieved the car for less than we had expected by doing some uncharacteristic bargaining. Then he had met a thoroughly embarrassed Stanton in the lobby. He had figured out why we did not eat the midday meal in the dining room and had diffidently offered to repay the cost of the guide. Mil of course refused, but agreed to accept a loan of ten dollars until we got to Cairo. We would still have to drive straight through to Cairo, ignoring cautionary advice; but at least neither Bublee nor we would go without sustenance.

Making the best of the long afternoon we rushed out to Karnak, taking Stanton along, and had our final glimpse of the glories of the Egyptian Middle Kingdom. We gazed at the obelisks and pylons, took pictures of the regal Avenue of the Sphinxes, and marveled at the carved relief on the elegant portal of the temple. To my untutored eye, these were the most impressive of the Thebian ruins. Wandering amidst the ruins we discovered, as countless others before us have, two such simply sedate columns set among the more typical arches that they looked jarringly modern with their straight lines fluted at the top into scrolls. Then, before we put Bob on the evening train for Cairo, we all toasted Luxor on our Scotch and some canned potato sticks.

Very early next morning, with one breakfast between us, we left the ancient serenity of Thebes for the political turmoil of Cairo. This time the drive along the Nile was as I imagined: a winding gravel road twisting between canals and tiny fields and shaded constantly by palms. We were flying our American flag prominently from the roof rack. Perhaps because of the flag, or perhaps the anti-British feeling had been exaggerated, we met with nothing more unfriendly than a stare, while smiles and waves from the children were much more common. All along the drive, too, poverty was evident. Not since India had we seen such emaciated and diseased humans as were these Egyptian *fellaheen*, their sores and swellings made all the more obvious by their dearth of ragged clothing. Here were perhaps the world's poorest people, sinking further all the time into that hopeless round of too many children for too little land. Quickly we forgot our own temporary impecunity in the face of this widespread misery.

We saw this poverty more closely during a slight misadventure. I had spent much of the morning studying our guidebook and had been beguiled by the flowery description of the temple of Cleopatra at Dendera, just across the Nile from Qena, a small town we were then approaching. It seemed to me that visiting the temple might make a pleasant diversion in our long drive to Cairo. Mil, less enthusiastic, agreed to stop. We parked under a tree near the river, by now convinced that all this talk of riots was probably referring to the volatile mobs of Cairo. Because the town had no dock, the little ferry boat anchored off-shore; the *fellaheen* with their goats and donkeys merely waded out through the churning, muddy water. I had read too many tales about bilharzia to walk happily into the river and as I hesitated the ferry man gaily scooped me up and deposited me in the boat. Then, as the passengers giggled, he did the same for Mil. The whole boatload was courteous and curious; a young girl leaned over and smoothed my hair in a delightfully winning gesture. Everyone seemed flattered at our presence, but no one had ever been to see Cleopatra's temple, nor were they at all sure where it was.

Only one path led away from the ferry across parched brown earth. We saw no canals or trees, but the land looked tilled; apparently it was one-crop-a-year flood land. We straggled up the dusty path to a bus-stop lean-to at a crossroads and joined the locals in the smelly shade. A bus arrived going the wrong way. The bus driver, a little more versed in local geography that were the *fellaheen*, told us that the temple was north right along the road and "not far." He thought we should walk since his bus would not return for an hour. So we began to walk along the dusty, vacant road under the unrelenting sun. We had brought no hats, no water, no food. The sun glared and the brown earth shimmered. At length, across a field, we saw a small, unprepossessing temple surrounded by, oh glory, some trees. Starved for shade, we cut across the stubble in the field, tripping in our eagerness, just as a bus churned by. I stared angrily at it, but it was a different bus from a different company.

The thought that we need not have walked made us all the hotter and we collapsed in the shade for a time. A nasty mongrel sniffed us and began barking wildly. His noise brought out a man from a shack behind the building who told us he was the temple guard, and that for a mere pound each we could view the fabulous art inside. At that I exploded. The fee at Karnak had been nominal; obviously this man was holding us up. Besides, the guide book said that the beauty of the temple lay in the carving around the portal and on the outside. Mil was so annoyed he just sat in the shade, but to prove my disdain to the avaricious guard I looked around the solid stone structure, took a photo of the deep-cut reliefs. In response to our indifference the guard began to reduce his price and ended by begging us to enter for a mere gratuity. His servility only made Mil more furious; I wished fervently that I had never heard of Cleopatra or her temple. To an Egyptologist, this temple may be a gem of some sort; to us, especially after the long deadening walk, it was quite ordinary. Still hot and thirsty, we made our way back to the ferry; hotter and thirstier, we rode a nearly empty ferry back across the river, eyeing hungrily a barge piled high with crates of Coca Cola. At last we were in the car, draining every container for drinking water, splashing cologne over our sticky faces.

We drove on through heavily cultivated fields. The distance line of the Nile gorge began to press closer to the river until finally the cultivation and the main road were forced to cross the river. We stayed on the east side to avoid the people and the twists and the irrigation ditches which hump the road every mile or so. In the narrow space between the gorge wall and the Nile there was nothing but the road; driving along was like following an enormous movie set since the river and the opposite bank teemed with humanity sailing, farming, fishing, bathing, eating. Then the river broadened at the large barrage and we crossed on the top of this dam into Assuit, the only major town between Luxor and Cairo. It was only about five, but we decide we had better eat something hot so that we would not have to stop later along the road.

At a corner we saw two students lounging with their bikes and asked them if they knew where there was a good restaurant. One youth, answering in French, volunteered to take us to a hotel and, giving his bike to his friend, climbed in.

The hotel was dirty and dingy so we decided to look further. Just then another student rode up on his bike and was hailed by our friend. This young man knew English and quickly suggested a restaurant near-by. He led us there on his bike and we all went in. We had soup and eggs and tea, but the boys would not touch a thing. One indeed was observing Ramadan even though he was also taking exams at the missionary school he attended. It seemed unfair to me for a Christian school to have exams in Ramadan, but perhaps they were really only quizzes. The English-speaking young man was a Copt; he kept up a stream of questions about life in America, then asked for our address. "Someday I will visit you," he announced with all the bravado of youth as we were leaving. We said we hoped he could, and with that drove off through the dusk toward Cairo.

Soon we heard the muezzin calling an end to the fast of the day and on all sides we could see banquets spread in the yards of the houses. We passed a check-point, then another, all untended while the guards ate or slept. All night the feasting seemed to continue. We drove past fully-lighted towns and lantern-lit villages; not once were we challenged or hailed. Dawn broke dramatically as we drove past the Step Pyramids at Sakkara, and soon we were washed and bedded in a tiny clean hotel in Cairo. The first thing I did when I awoke was to send a letter to Mr. Garfield, allaying his fears: the people along the Nile were as peaceful as the river itself.

CAIRO HAS ALWAYS BEEN a crossroads; we found it a jumbled and harsh combination of East and West, of Orient and Occident. The one thing the city was not was African. Rather it was modern European with its bars and cars, American with its soda fountains, Arab with its mosques and bazaars, Greek with its small businesses, plus English and French influence in government and education. But it was also Egyptian. Its sidewalk cafés were crowded with overweight men who stared at every woman who passed, undressing her with their eyes. The streets thronged with pretty dark-tanned women gaudy with their greasy purple lips, their too-short, too-tight skirts, and their sheer provocative blouses. No wonder the modest women remained partly veiled behind their flowing cloaks, their faces open but with a fluttering transparent veil that hung from a ribbon just below their eyes. I almost wished for a veil myself. Everywhere was noise: cars honking, radios blaring, obnoxious guides in their ragged gowns wheedling, waifs nagging and begging. Of refinement or manners the city had none; we could hardly leave fast enough.

Nonetheless, we spent a week in that boisterous capital, for we had projects, as always. Our very first move had to be to the Embassy to cash a check and return the ten dollars we had borrowed from Bob – only he was out of town and left us a note telling us to give it to his girlfriend Gloria. We talked to several Foreign Service officers who had, at one time or another, driven parts of the North African coast road that runs between Cairo and Tangiers. One young man, who had just driven from Tunis to Cairo, gave us his route guide issued in French by the Egyptian Automobile Association and said, a little ominously, that once was enough. Quickly he corrected himself by adding that the road was not terribly difficult, but that it was dull, not the sort of drive you would choose to make often, but worthwhile the first time. We decided to try: we had checked the cost of a boat from Alexandria to Greece and found it much too expensive. The next possible crossing to Europe was in Tunis; we had to drive at least that far.

Our Sudanese friends in Khartoum had inquired about us at the US Embassy, so we spent a delightful quiet afternoon with the Sudanese representative and told him about our trip. He mentioned that President Neguib still thought that Sudan would remain part of Egypt after independence. He also provided me with some historical materials for the article I was writing about the Sudanese elections.

WE TOOK THE CAR in for its check-up to a small Greek-run garage where we listened at length to the problems of the rotund little owner. For centuries the Greeks had lived as a community apart in Cairo, prospering mildly in their modest businesses while keeping themselves aloof from the Arabs. "White Egyptians," they were often called. Now, of course, with nationalism becoming a sort of state religion, unassimilated minorities were deemed unacceptable to the army officers in power. Either the Greeks would have to become "Egyptian-ized" or leave. The government had instituted discriminatory taxes on those businesses owned by foreign nationals to force the issue. This attempt to make Egyptians of the Greeks did not, however, extend into the realm of religion: they could remain Catholic. After all, over a million Coptic Egyptians live in the country or one Copt to twenty Muslims.

Yet we hardly recognized Cairo as a Muslim city: we completely forgot it was Ramadan. As we made our rounds of government offices seeking an exit permit we found no hint that any of the officers or clerks was observing the fast. The Ramadan stillness in Omdurman or in Shendi had underlined for us the problems of mixing Islam and democracy, of hurling Sudan's traditional society into the modern world more or less without warning. We were excited by the experiment, by the enthusiasm of the Sudanese themselves, but concerned about the impact on government of a month-long holiday. This was hardly a problem in Egypt.

In Cairo, we observed many competing traditions: Islam versus democracy, feudalism versus modernization – all with alternative interpretations and distortions – complicating the transition from monarchy to independence. The problems multiplied due to a lack of a clearly defined focal point. As a fly caught in a web, Egypt seemed confused about which strand to cut first? No wonder then, that despite its recent revolution, Egypt seemed a tired country, old under its burdens, cynical, disillusioned, lascivious, corrupt.

This was, of course, exactly what the revolution was against. The enormity of the task which the Council of Revolutionary Command had undertaken was staggering. The Free Officers Movement, headed by Gamal Nasser, had led the revolt against the king. Its members were all young officers, so to provide greater legitimacy they selected the older and well respected General Neguib as their nominal leader. The members of the Command had the reputation of being everything that Egypt was not: dedicated, honest, idealistic, optimistic. Certainly the one member of this hard-working group with whom we talked remains in sharp relief against my unsavory memories of Cairo and its citizens. Indeed, his calmness and humility made him a very different sort of politician than any we had previously met in Africa. He was not a publicity seeker fighting colonialism; he was an administrator tackling the basic problems of making the Egyptian government run.

WE HAD TRIED TO see Group Captain Zulfikar at his office but were told that he was too busy to see us. Infected by the ennui of Cairo, we did not try again, but simply left him the letter we had brought from the Egyptian Colonel whom we had met in Khartoum. Two days later, in the midst of a torrid afternoon, the Group Captain found us at our pension. Our landlady, when she burst into our room, was numbed with a mixture of fright and awe at our visitor: we were amazed ourselves. For two hours we sat and talked in the tiny entry way of the pension, its austere furnishings providing just the right backdrop for this dedicated man. Sitting rigidly erect in a straight-backed chair, the Group Captain's voice shook with emotion as he described the great things the revolution would accomplish for Egypt. "Land reform is our first priority. The wealthy landlords own some two-thirds of the land," he complained, "and they charge the *fellaheen* exorbitant rents. These pashas are so very corrupt; they are just like the king."

He talked with his hands as well as his face; his whole being gave off a sort of disciplined determination that projected enthusiasm tempered by harsh reality. With charm and modesty he admitted his own inexperience, but he was obviously learning fast and working hard. Yet with all these pressures at work, he was nonetheless observing Ramadan. When he left us it was to return to his office for several more hours of work before he could break the fast. Here was a man with a depth of personal integrity that would have made him notable in any country; in Egypt he was a shining jewel.

Trying to understand the Egyptian political scene in a hurry, we visited several newspaper offices; in India reporters were always well-informed and delighted to share their opinions. This was also true in Cairo. We found the editor of *al Akbar*, Amin Mustafa, heavy and genial, behind a huge desk in a crowded office; a full set of Harvard classics appeared untouched in a glass cabinet behind him. He insisted that the country had no real alternative to Naguib. The opposition was split. The Communists were outlawed and the Wafd Party had been banned; now some of their leaders supporting the Muslim Brotherhood "which is worse."

G. K. Reddy, whom we knew from India where he had worked for the scandalous newspaper *Blitz*, was now more respectably employed by the *Times of India*. He invited several other foreign reporters to meet us over dinner, which surprised us because his imaginary stories that he wrote in India were virulently anti-American. Of particular interest was the discussion about the growing rift between Neguib and Nasser and how Neguib was using the conservative Muslim Brotherhood to counter the radical reformist ideas of Nasser. The reporters also analyzed the growing anti-British feelings which had escalated after the 1952 riots in Cairo when the Shepheards Hotel was among the British buildings burned. Later we saw the empty lot along the Nile cornice where the Shepherds Hotel had stood. Tom Little of the Arab News Agency thought that the breech could be healed if the British would give Egypt a generous settlement as compensate for the police officers killed in the 1952 clash. Such a gesture was sure to bring forth "the latent pro-British feelings held by the Egyptians," he argued. Reddy doubted that would happen and told us that one of the French newspapers hoped that the rift between the Britain and Egypt would lead to fighting that would restore the government to a resurgent Wafd Party.

As we discussed and dissected Egypt's problems with the many people we met in Cairo, never once did we hear anyone express regret over the removal of ex-King Farouk. With varying degrees of intensity and good-will everyone was watching the Revolutionary Council. Among the foreigners we found a curious suspension of judgment as if events were simply too much to analyze. To compensate, most of them focused on their own pleasant life, swimming in the palatial pools at the Gezira Club, applauding the acts of the belly dancers, inter-dining and drinking, and so becoming perhaps even more removed from the realities of the country than is usual in foreign capitals. I confess to enjoying the pool and eating American ice cream when Gloria invited us there for lunch.

One impressive exception to this generalization was Judge J.Y. Brinton. He had devoted the greater part of his life to being a judge on the Mixed Courts but who had, since the court's abolition, been an advisor to the American Embassy. The institution of Mixed Courts was a curious carryover of the imperial era, from a time when foreigners were not subject to the laws of the country in which they were living. The Mixed Courts were composed of judges from various foreign countries governed by treaties with Egypt; the law they administered to the foreigners was the French Code. At a time when local law was often a lottery, these courts did give necessary protection, and often unnecessary advantage as well, to foreign businessmen and tourists. As nationalism grew, they became an anathema; their powers were gradually diminished until in 1949 the Egyptian Mixed Courts were finally abolished. The twenty-five years Judge Brinton spent in the service had given him a fund of knowledge about Egypt which far surpassed that of any other foreigner we met in the country. Yet even to him, events in Egypt were far from clear. Like others sympathetic to the country, he could only hope.

I had a personal project while we were in Cairo: to finish a final article on East Africa for the Calcutta *Statesman*. How many times since we left Garissa had I outlined it, started it? But the days had been too full of absorbing events and of anxiety ever to finish it. Finally, on our last day in Cairo, I sent Mil out alone to check the car, to pick up our visas, and see a movie. Even then he had to try to sleep despite the noise of my typing that went on most of the night. Still, I did finish the article and next morning took it to the post office to register it. The queue in front of the window wound snakelike half across the barn-like interior; it looked like a wait of hours. As I joined the queue, the men in line waved me away. Puzzled, I wondered whether they did not like foreigners in their post office. Yet the crowd seemed friendly enough. I decided to ask the clerk, and walked to the head of the queue. There I noticed a small sign indicating that the long queue was for men only. Next to that sign was one for a women's queue; this line had only two women before me. The clerk alternately served a man and a woman. Very quickly I had mailed the article, grateful once for the segregation of women under Islam.

We crossed the Nile River for the last time, and headed for the coast road, pausing only briefly as we touched the edge of the desert to make our last gesture to tourism: seeing the pyramids and the sphinx. In between our other errands in Cairo we had managed to see most of the other principal tourist points of interest, the mosques, the tombs, the bazaars, the fabulous National Museum. The flame trees were in bloom and the vivid red played color patterns with the lovely Blue Mosque and framed the views of the Citadel and the city's skyline. We also ate well in homes and restaurants. Mil consumed strawberries everywhere, a craving he still continues. We even took in a movie for the first time since India. Still, we were exhausted and so weary.

At every tourist site we visited, the whining of guides and entreaties of beggars marred the beauty of the scenes; more and more, sight-seeing had become an unpleasant duty. No wonder we debated whether it was worth stopping to see the pyramids close up. From the Nile bridge we could see them towering over tram lines and dwarfing the huge Coca Cola signs. Were they worth seeing closer, these trademarks of Egypt? Then suddenly the road climbed the steep limestone cliff marking off the edge of the Nile Valley from the vastness of the pebbly desert. Set in their original habitat of unending desert, the monuments took on a new grandeur; almost involuntarily we turned into the parking area. Before we had stopped the car a swarm of guides descended upon us as thick as the persistent flies which kept making footprints on my extra heavy lipstick I had applied to protect my lips from the sun.

We tried to keep a sense of humor with this insidious hoard by joking with them, but they only got nasty when we tried to refuse any guide at all. Almost sinister in their snarling, they seemed more like extras from a mob scene than like useful guides. As self protection we finally hired a small man who kept insisting that he was a guard, not a guide, but that as a special favor he would show us around. He wore a sort of military costume in place of the flowing burnoose worn almost as a uniform by most guides, and claimed to hold the record for the fastest mounting of the pyramid: eight minutes. "You have heard of me, no?" he kept insisting as we circled the towering structures. For all the by-play, the stop was worthwhile. The pyramids, colossal monuments to man's vanity, are overwhelming.

More pleasing to my romantic eye was the wily personality projected by the sphinx, especially when viewed, as it should be, from camel back. On our way back to the car the backsheesh routine began again even though with both the camel driver and the guide we had already fixed the price. Now both began that nagging singsong "thank-you-very-mush, anything you like, than queue verry mush..."

It was with the greatest relief that we sped away from Cairo and its landmarks, off across the desert on a smooth open highway. The greenness of the Nile valley and delta was soon out of sight; here nothing grew, not a blade of grass nor a scrubby bush. We turned left, into this wilderness, toward a desert hideaway belonging to Judge Brinton. For miles there was nothing to break the monotony, then ahead, jutting into the flat horizon, we saw Berg el Arab. The mud-walls surrounded yellow-brown buildings, some of stone but others of adobe, that looked hot under the glaring sun. But within the smaller wall surrounding the Judge's house, the greenness of mimosa trees and cactus cut the glare. The house, built in a mixture of Arab and modern styles, was arched off the ground so that autos could park beneath the building out of the beating sun. Sarde, the keeper's son, produced the keys from a Maxwell House coffee tin prominently displayed outside the back door as if our arrival were the most natural thing in the world. Inside the cool and silent house we felt an immense relaxing. The study was filled with books and the toilets flushed: all the comforts! The Judge had urged us to stay for as long as we wished, but reluctantly, the next morning, we pushed on.

This time we drove straight north, toward the sea. After a few more miles of empty pebbled desert the road rose over a ridge and there below, with all the beauty of priceless jewels, lay the Mediterranean, its blueness ranging from aquamarine to lapis lazuli. As if encouraged by the sight of the sea the desert itself sprouted scrubs; lean cattle, camels, and sheep munched on the harsh grass paying no more attention to the car than their ragged herders did to us.

Within sight of the sea, we turned west along the Egyptian coast that had been overrun with foreign troops during World War II: British, German, Italian, Australian. El Alamein and Marsa Matruh were names as well known during the war as were London or Cairo. Yet as we drove through these towns, they had already returned to their former inscrutable ways. The native women enveloped themselves in cloaks of checked or stripped cotton. Such vivid colors against the glittering white of the seaside towns and the pulsating blueness of the sea were a feast of brightness after weeks of seeing little but shades of brown or weathered green.

We stopped to eat lunch along the shore; a chill wind blowing off the sea made the water too cold for swimming so I waded happily while Mil studied our Sahara map with its notations about the 1942-43 desert campaign. Suddenly the sea breeze stopped; there was that expectancy of a storm. Inland we saw dust clouds swirling high into the air. The *sirocco*, the *simoon*, the *haboob*, the *ghibbi*, call it what you will, the hot desert windstorm had begun to blow. We rushed for the car and barely had the windows shut before the sand beat down in gusts, like rain. For hours the sandstorm continued as we drove along an empty coast, past mile after mile of tough scrub. Eventually the wind lifted and rain began to fall in enormous drops so that although the storm did not seem heavy the road was soon covered with puddles. "Imagine," I exclaimed to Mil, "crossing the desert and getting stuck in a mud puddle!"

Slowly the inland ridge pushed seaward until it forced the road to wind up a steep escarpment. At the beginning of the climb was once a small fishing village, the border town of Sollum. The ravages of war had left it flattened; two pukka houses had been constructed in the rubble and were surrounded by the shacks of a few returned inhabitants. On the wooden porch of the first building a large, unshaven, beery-looking man was standing, his khaki uniform so rumpled that he must have been sleeping in it.

"Oh my," I moaned to Mil. "If this is the customs man, it looks like trouble. He looks just like a pirate!" But I was wrong. As if penitent for his appearance, the man turned on his fading gallant charm as he welcomed us to the miserable outpost of Sollum. He was the police officer, and shared the small cottage and his distaste for the post with an assistant, a customs man, and a doctor. His servant produced hot tea in chipped cups which we sipped while he explained to us that the assignment to Sollum is so unpopular that all officials are changed each month. Waiting to get back to Cairo and their families, they apparently drank the month away. As senior man in the post, the policeman looked over our papers, then presented them to the customs man to sign. He apologetically explained that we must also stop at the house further up the hill for a military clearance. This was the only time throughout our stay in Egypt that the fact of Egypt's military dictatorship actually intruded into ordinary civil affairs.

The army man was much more polished looking than the policeman despite the fact that we got him out of bed. "Ramadan, you know," he smiled as an excuse. His room was almost bare, the cot, a table, and chair being the only furniture. But the walls were plastered with sexy pictures of chorus girls of all nationalities. He checked over our passports and carnet quickly, apparently looking for irregularities, while telling us about a German bicyclist who had appeared in Sollum a month before. The German claimed that he had come from Libya, but his passport had showed no stamps. Nor did he have an Egyptian visa. So the army had held him in Sollum for twenty days until Cairo decided to take over the case themselves. Concluding this tale with "but your papers are in perfect order," he bowed us out of the office and out of Egypt. Little did we realize how almost prophetic his story of unstamped Libyan passes was to be.

CHAPTER 33

# Libya: an un-united country

$f$URTHER UP THE ESCARPMENT WE HALTED AT UM SAAD ON THE Libyan frontier. The border formalities were even faster there. It was too hot and it was Ramadan and the officials really did not feel like bothering with tourists. A constable in a black fuzzy fez led us to the dazed immigration official who carefully copied our names and passport numbers, then waved us on. The customs man, a huge bulk of a figure under a white-tasseled fez, scrawled his signature on a variety of documents, including our carnet, and asked us to deliver the others at the customs point between Libya and Tunis. Feeling like official messengers of the king, we departed.

Now the road led us across the emptiness of the barren plateau. To the south of the plateau lay the Libyan Desert, that vast expanse of shifting sands that even camel caravans

484

avoid. During the desert campaign the armored units could not penetrate inland in this section of the coast. Thus the brunt of action was channeled into the narrow coastal strip. Everywhere we saw evidence of that campaign, rusted bits of metal equipment, signs saying tersely, "mined area, do not leave road," and the tragic rows of white and often nameless crosses standing starkly against the sand.

How little I know of that actual campaign, I thought; how little I know of war. How do the soldiers get buried? Surely the enemy does not bother, not in the midst of a battle. And really, I pondered, are all these nameless graves of any point? Or even the named ones? Do relatives really make the heart-wrenching pilgrimage to these desolate crosses. Surely the spirit of the dead pervades the familiar more than these deserted reaches. So I pondered as I stared, hypnotized, at the vast cemeteries, the wasted men, the dead hopes. And I remembered my own pilgrimages at thirteen, to my mother's grave, biking to a neighboring town ten miles away from my home in New Jersey. Sentimentality, I observed to Mil. Yes, he replied, but sentimentality also makes fighting the war easier: without attachment to a cause, belief that it was worth fighting and dying for, how could all these men have been persuaded into these battles? I suppose, I said, jotting these notes in my diary, that without emotions at all, people wouldn't fight, but then people wouldn't be people.

My imagination was stimulated often on these long drives when I would fall into a stupor of unrelated daydreaming, particularly when the road was too bumpy to write. Gazing at the endless desert, I thought of a plot for a beautifully tragic story. Imagine, I recounted to Mil, a young couple coming here to look for the grave of her brother, and how, one at a time, the stumble onto buried mines. Wounded, the crawl to each other and die with love on their lips.

Night fell abruptly in these eerie surroundings. With the mines and crosses heavy on our minds, we debated whether to drive all night or try to camp. Tobruk, our original goal for the day, was still hours away and it would do no good to arrive at midnight looking for food and room. Despite our trepidations at camping, it seemed foolish to exhaust ourselves the first night out on this long marathon to Tunis. At first we tried to find a likely spot near the newly-built culverts on the theory that the workmen would have detonated any mines nearby. As these culverts had replaced Irish bridges crossing the numerous wadis, the road was built up for a level crossing and there was enough of a bank to provide some shelter against the whistling wind which had begun to sweep unobstructed across the plateau. But as always, when you look for a thing, none appeared though we had seen quite a few just before dusk. It was much later than we had intended to stop before Mil saw a tiny side road; we drove off the main road and spent a cold night, huddling in our sleeping bags, tossing on the hard packed sand. All night long convoys of trucks or Land Rovers flashed past, their headlights breaking our sleep. At dawn we awoke beneath a heavy blanket of dew: not a comfortable night.

AT TOBRUK THE ROAD again went down to the sea, through a white field of crosses. We drove past blocks of adobe houses, many still unpainted, giving the town a close affinity to the desert. Beyond a minaret, a brilliant white concrete pier and water-break sliced the blue sea and protected the port. Although it was still very early most of the fishing fleet was already out for the day. We bought petrol from an Italian-looking chap and then followed the road back into the bleak brown wilderness. These long stretches of monotonous but fairly good road, excellent by the standards of the roads we had been traveling over deeper in real Africa, caused a change in our driving patterns. The asphalted road was smooth enough for me to write; Mil was even more bored when he was not driving than when he was, and driving was really not any more exhausting than just sitting in the steamy car. So Mil began to drive longer and longer periods while I caught up in my diary or balanced the accounts. I was pleased to report that our trip down the Nile had not thrown our budget too far out of line. Even including the cost of the train and boat and all the backsheesh and tips paid to the guides, we had kept our daily average to four and a half Egyptian pounds or just under thirteen dollars a day. By sleeping out all across North Africa we hoped to cut below our ten dollars a day allotment to make up the difference, and we did.

I also began to read to Mil a few notes on the route guide about the history of the area. The Ottoman Empire conquered the coast in the 16th century, but the weakness of their rule had encouraged piracy. The United States tried to stop pirates from preying on US ships by paying tribute to the *dey* or governor in Tripoli, but disputes about the amount led to a desultory war from 1801-1805. "Ah," I said, "that's where the Marines get the 'shores of Tripoli' in their anthem." I continued: the Italians invaded the north coast of Tripoli in 1912 and eventually ruled this whole area until World War II. The United Nations helped prepare the country to become an independent constitutional monarchy in 1951, uniting Cyrenaica, Tripolitania, and the inland desert province of Fezzan. "Not very long ago," I muttered.

All morning, ponderous British army trucks rumbled past us, but otherwise the desert seemed uninhabited by man or beast. Near Derna we came on a few old hill top forts; then suddenly, as if the cliff had been sliced away with a knife, a palm-festooned town appeared directly below us showing white against red soil and blue sea: color again! The road picked its tortuous way down the escarpment to this seaside oasis, smoothly, in yet another tribute to the road-building skill of the Italians who had first engineered and constructed this coastal highway. We were thirsty after the long morning, and feeling grubby as always after a camping-out. Our water supply, drinking and washing, was low and this seemed like a fine place to replenish it.

We hailed a British army Land Rover and asked generally of its riders where we might find a hotel or some place to get water. The ranking officer, a dark-haired medic with glasses, told us to follow and led us to a tree-shaded compound which was ringed with various army barracks. Popping over to our car he explained that this was the officer's mess and much preferable to the hole-in-the-adobe that called itself a hotel. He showed us where to fill the water bags and then took the thermos into the bar so that we could have ice with our water. Once there he insisted that we join him in a drink and then, with that charming English reserve, asked us if we would mind joining him for lunch which up to then we had not thought of having. Only as we sat down to eat did he introduce himself as Dan Stewart, a doctor from London, doing his national service, and craving a good conversation.

Much refreshed after this unexpected treat, we drove off toward Benghazi, following the pink coast just inland of the white dunes and always in sight of the Mediterranean with all its changeable hues. No wonder that on our map this section of the road was labeled "scenic." At length the road once more began to climb, and the colors faded into yellow; wild olive trees appeared on the dry hillside. Still the road climbed and grass appeared, soft green grass, not the cactus-like spikes of the desert. Soon the hills proclaimed their name in truth: Jebel el Akdar, or Green Mountain. Here deserted, half-ruined, square concrete houses dotted the plateau with great regularity, each bearing the legend "Ente Colonizzazione Libia." These dingy huts were all that is left of the Italian dreams of colonizing Cyrenaica. In some places the nomadic Senussi of the region were using these vestiges of colonial rule as huts for themselves or their camels, donkeys, goats, or cattle. More often a beehive shaped tent could be seen pitched near the concrete ruin which then served as barn and play pen. The fields around these huts and tents had an untended look, but wheat was growing. Once or twice we saw ungainly camels hitched to plows as a nomad tried his inexperienced hand at farming.

NEARER BARCE THE CONCRETE huts became more fancy, with peaked chimney pipes looking more than anything else, ironically, like minarets. Often these houses were lined five deep on either side of the road, each the master of a tiny plot of fertile soil. Even among the crags, wherever a small farm plot might be cultivated, a ruined concrete cottage stood. Stone towers, of uncertain purpose but dedicated to that temporary god Mussolini, lined the road at instructive intervals; the Senussi, in their pride, merely ignored them. A few Italians still lived in Barce and from one we bought some luscious sweet oranges which he had grown himself. Thinking of the fertile fields that lay neglected along the road I had mixed reactions; it was a pity that all the Italian farmers had been driven out; surely their crops would add income to the very poor purse of the country. Yet, Graziani, Italy's cruel colonizer marshal had driven out the Senussi with great brutality in the early days of colonizing and the colonizers had done little for the people of the country besides building roads.

Ruins of the ancient Greek port of Cyrene near Barce Africa

I wondered about the earliest colonizers, the Greeks, and what they had done for the local people. Just like the Italians, they established coastal cities to relieve pressures of population during the seventh century BC. Just before Barce we had stopped, all too briefly, at the shady grove which shelters the Greek ruins of Cyrene. Scattered on different levels of a prow-like cliff which juts into the sea, the ruins retain their nobility and grace. We inspected some of the ruins closely, the agora and a temple to Zeus, but mostly we just breathed the atmosphere of this ancient city. Even in the mid-afternoon the hill-top was cool and winds gently swayed the olives and pines.

We relaxed in the serenity of the place ignoring the munching sheep and goats with their urchin tenders. Several women, swathed in bulky dark sheets, stared at me from a discrete distance but fled as I took out my camera. It would have been an ideal place to camp for several days, but we had no time to spare. At length, reluctantly, we drove on. Along this *jebel*, or mountain range, rains are frequent, so when we stopped for the night in a grassy pasture some distance beyond Barce we made the effort to rearrange the car and sleep, warm and dry, inside. I had always thought of this coast of Africa as being one vast sand dune; concern over rain and dew was not something I had anticipated. Another excellent argument for travel: seeing is believing.

DESPITE THE PLEASANT NIGHT, the next day started out as one of those days in which everything went wrong. We had buried our trash, then left the shovel behind. The ammeter began to act up and the carburetor complained. When we arrived in Anghagi about nine o'clock we found that since British influence continued paramount in Cyrenaica: the day was a holiday in honor of the coronation of Queen Elizabeth. With all the shops closed we could not have the car repaired or even change money. We simply had to continue driving.

It was mid-afternoon by the time we arrived in Benghazi, the capital of Cyrenaica, which alternates with Tripoli for the honor of being capital of the United Kingdom of Libya; King Idris, called the emir, changes his residence every two years. But as we circled the town, it looked only like a bedraggled port, not like the capital of anything. Rubble from war damage lay where it had been dumped; squatters' shanties abounded in open areas. Even pukka buildings were unpainted and musty. We passed one building less dreary than most; it was the American consulate and, joy, it was still open, so we went in to ask about changing travelers checks. The vice-consul, a taciturn young man named Mr. Mason, gave us an I-can't-be-bothered look and sent us down the street with an airy "just change it anywhere" reply. In fact we found the rate good and the moneychangers still open. With our wallets full, we bought more oranges in the market, filled up with petrol and water, and prepared to get out of town as fast as possible.

But hardly had we headed the car south than a slow sizzle started: a flat tire. Great gloom. Mil did not dare to drive the miles of desert from Benghazi to Tripoli with no usable spare tire; we would have to wait until the next day for a garage to open. Mil was sweating out the changing of the tire when frosty Mr. Mason walked up somewhat thawed, perhaps by all the heat of activity, but more likely by the reassurance he felt having found Mil's name in the US Foreign Service Directory. I suggested returning to the consulate to ask the administrative assistant whether he knew of a garage that was still open. I stayed with Mason at the office to wash off some of the grime while Mil and the assistant went off across town. Then, since the consulate was closing, I decided to walk to the garage. Mason offered to accompany me, but hardly had we set out than Mil came trudging up saying that the repair would take an hour so that meanwhile he too would like to wash. Mason and I stood amicably talking on the front steps until Mil returned whereupon Mason turned with an abrupt good-by and departed, leaving us gaping after him.

Mil and I had hardly recovered from our surprise when Mason, thinking better of this abrupt dismissal, came back to ask us to his apartment for a cooling drink. His small but comfortable bachelor's flat was full of books, many in Arabic which he was learning, of classical music records and tapes, and of art. If outwardly this son of Maine was frosty, he let his heart soar in the privacy of his own flat. He was still enigmatic toward us, furnishing us one drink with the polish of a professional, then pointedly ignoring the empty glasses. His attitude toward the Foreign Service was equally ambivalent, criticizing bitterly all the protocol and rigidity of the department, yet pleased with the language program. Perhaps the glare of the sun on the desert set against the dark shadows, the heat and the cold, permeates the mind after a time and makes all thoughts and opinions extremes.

AGAIN WE TURNED THE car south and followed the border of eucalyptus trees out of town past clusters of Senussi tents into the desert again. Our map called the road dangerous, and for a time Mil held down the speed for we knew this was the oldest section of the road, built by the Italians in 1937. But just as the surface was becoming badly cracked we came on a smooth and glorious newly built section of asphalted highway which cut bravely across the yellow, tufted dunes where the old road had been content to meander around, up and down and through the soft sand. Half-covered by the shifting sands lay all manner of discarded implements of war: wheels, chassis, tanks, kerosene tins, junk. Further south the dunes became hills, the sand stretched as vast and rolling as the distant sea, and the road roller-coasted along. Except for an occasional sand drift across the road, we speeded unchecked on our private highway. At each depression the glare of the sun would catch the tracks of the older road winding and turning; Mil said he felt that same superior relief that he had from the train between Atbara and Wadi Halfa in seeing what we didn't have to go through!

Sometimes, too, in the troughs of the sand waves would be an oasis, slender date-palms sheltering the humpy tents of the nomads and their scraggly animals. The camels seemed smaller than those in the Sudan, with odd tufts on their humps; one, I swear, had a wispy beard. Even the donkeys and dogs, which these Senussi kept despite their reported allegiance to all things Koranic, were shaggy against the desert wind. The tribesmen, their Arab stock only minutely diluted with Berber, had shortened the flowing Arab robes and wound their legs against the pelting sandstorms blown up from the vast waste of the Libyan desert. Their turbans were no mere decoration, but rather a shield against the sand and sun that could be pulled down to cover the face as well. Thus the men as well as the women assumed anonymous shapes with only color to distinguish sex: white for men and brown-black for the women.

The towns shown on the map consisted merely of several huts constructed of rusting kerosene tins set on their sides like bricks and perhaps a battered adobe house or two. At Agedabia, a metropolis of a dozen adobe dwellings, we passed the police check point for Cyrenaica. Innocently I asked the police officer why there were such checks between two states of the same federation. Even in his halting English his reply was clear: "We Senussi do not want union with Tripolitania and Fezzan but first the Italians, I spit on them, forced us; now the United Nations forced us. Those men from Tripoli," he muttered, contempt in his voice, "we do not trust them." Then he grinned slyly, "but they are all under our emir, Mohammed Idris Al Mahdi Al Senussi, he is king of Libya." Clearly the United Kingdom of Libya has yet to feel or act united, a fact which was uncomfortably stressed for us when we tried to leave the country.

AFTER AGEDABIA THE ROAD turned southwest, then west, as we rounded the Bay of Sirte. The road was no longer new, but the sand waves had somewhat subsided so that the road was flatter, if more treacherous from pot-holes and sand-drifts. At El Agheila we were checked through yet another control. Here, too, the single telegraph line that had played chase with the road all the way from Benghazi at last gave up its meandering. Not far beyond this cluster of huts, a stone wall and tower proclaim our entrance into Tripolitania. The late afternoon sun threw elongated shadows across the road making the driving more difficult. But for all the desolation, the asphalted road gave the desert an air of civilization.

In the odd, flat, light I thought I saw a pyramid ahead. Then this huge shape became a crouching dog, a stylized Chinese porcelain with paws out, ears erect, mouth wide open. Only as we were close to approaching it did the shape become itself: Mussolini's Triumphal Arch, monument to his dreams of an African empire, a latter-day Temple of Mars. It has been left standing as a valuable navigational aid for airplanes and is irreverently known to the British pilots as the desert's Marble Arch even though it is not of marble and does not resemble in shape London's own Marble Arch. We stopped at the base of this towering structure and pulled up in the shade to have a closer look. The entire inside of the arch was solid with carved relief scenes: a native in flowing dress learning to use the wheel; a road gang of nomads, their skirts put aside, pounding rocks under vigilant eye of Italian soldiers and the sour stares of their own camel.

The people eyed us curiously as we clambered around the arch, but showed no interest at all in the arch itself. They were drinking hot mint tea which meant that there was a source of water nearby. Just north of the arch we noticed a collection of low shanties and drove toward them looking for the well. It was nearly dark and the map showed nothing but sand for several hundred more miles. Any sort of structure would help shelter the car from the wind; any sort of water would be welcome. I shuddered every time I thought of the careless American couple Mr. Mason told us about who had merrily driven from Tripoli to Benghazi as though they were still in Texas. They carried not a drop of water, but happened fortuitously to have nearly a case of Coca Cola. Both we and Bublee had consumed much water just between Benghazi and the Marble Arch. I wondered how well a car would be cooled with Coke.

WE FOUND NO OBVIOUS source of water and no one around to ask about it so we simply stopped behind a low crumbling stone wall and began to cook our dinner, assuming that the shanties had long since been deserted. Almost immediately a young Arab in Western trousers and shirt appeared out of the night to ask us our purpose. He proudly used his limited English vocabulary to say he was a guard of the emergency airfield which the British maintained here. When we told him we merely wished to spend the night here he said there was a rest house some thirty kilometers along. By that time we had already settled in for the night and, being somewhat skeptical about the correctness of his information, we decided to stay where we were.

Later on an older man came over, more regal in his flowing gown. We greeted him in our best Arabic and Mil gave him a cigarette whereupon he abruptly disappeared, returning in a few moments with two glasses of steaming hot tea. Eeking out a conversation in Italian, he told us he had been a guard at the airport since the Italians built it. In fact I got the feeling that he considered himself sheikh of the airfield and all of its workers; once there had been so many men under him that he was considered a big man. Now, unhappily, only a few guards were left. Their duties were to keep the packed runways free from drifting sand and to protect the petrol stores which were held for emergency use. He left with many good wishes and promised to warn the night guard to keep watch over us too!

All night the wind beat on the sand making miniature whirlwinds and dust storms. Protected as we were between the stone wall and the car, we lay out of the worst of the blast.

In the morning we found we had run out of kerosene so we stopped at the Arab shanty by the Arch for tea to go with our crackers and cheese. Then we were off across a slightly pink desert, an expanse utterly unrelieved except by the refuse of war: burned-out tanks, rusting trucks, chunks of engines, kerosene tins, wheels, pipes, even ghosted decaying barracks. Soon we came upon the *ristorante*-bar which the young guard had mentioned. It was a tiny place, hardly larger than a diner, but it may have had one room for guests. The dark-skinned owner came out at the sound of our motor and stood looking forlorn and lonely. It was much too early to stop again, even for coffee, so we merely waved, and pushed steadily on.

IT WAS DREARY GOING, alone in nothingness. I wrote until there was nothing more to say about the desert and its pervasive emptiness. I balanced books and figured budgets until I had practically memorized the figures. I had run out of historical notes to read. We tried playing word games, but the piercing sun seemed to interfere with any mental process, however simple. I even drove while Mil dozed, and tried to doze in turn, but my straw bonnet which I had tied like Little Bo-Peep to shield my eyes from the glare kept bumping against the seat and the window. Then, as if it were not hot enough, the wind shifted and blew off the desert, hot and gusty and filled with sand. In this stuporous atmosphere I apparently kept up a running commentary of non-sequiturs until Mil began to threaten to call me, like the hot wind, *ghibbi*. I had been "Shanti Rao" in Kenya: Shanti means peace in Hindi, Irene means peace in Greek. Rao was a cruel reference to my ambitions to be a writer like Santa Rama Rao. Mil started calling my "weary-ful" during the last few days, because of my exhaustion. Now Mil added all my various names

497

together: Shanti Ghibbi Rao Weariful Tinker Walker. That name, perhaps, gives you some idea of our punchiness.

Sirte was a small harbor town hugging the shore, a few trees, several whitewashed houses, another restaurant. Too quickly we were back in the monotonous desert again, for miles and miles and dreary miles. Only when the road again hit the coast at Gidda did we officially enter Tripolitania although we had driven some three hundred miles in the state. We nearly drove past the police check post and had to back up half a block. The official in charge merely looked at our passports and waved us on; this seemed a bit strange to us since we had stamps showing that we had entered and left Cyrenaica, but none to show we were now in Tripolitania. We could only think that these Tripolitanian officials were less provincial than those of Cyrenaica. Later, the absence of a duty stamp was to lead to much trouble.

Now signs of habitation began appear: first aid stations lined the road at distant intervals and a telegraph line paralleled the road. The square colonizer houses began once more to dot the fertile fields. Here, unlike Cyrenaica, many to the houses were still occupied and we saw Italian farmers working in their fields. Scattered among the Italian farms were plots tilled by natives. In Tripolitania, the Berber stock is nearly pure and apparently Berbers are more inclined toward farming than the Arabs are. These native farmers seemed to rely on wells rather than on irrigation ditches as the foreign farmers did. The well supports, looking like a set of whitewashed steps up into nowhere, were connected by a piece of wood on which was slung a long wooden handle with a skin bucket on one end. Dip and slop, dip and slop. At least there was water in the wells; the irrigation ditches, neglected during the war, were often choked dry with reeds and rubble.

AT HOMS WE TURNED off the road to look over another of Mussolini's projects: the excavation of Leptis Magna. Several acquaintances along the route had urged us not to miss this ancient Roman town which was being reclaimed from the sand dunes, but we had not been prepared for the glory and the grandeur which is there. Here again the quietude, the complete absence of intruding guides, gave us the sense of discovery, of exploration. We sat high in the nearly perfect amphitheater gazing across the stage, beyond the graceful columns which rise tier on magnificent tier, and out on the rippling blue Mediterranean. The soft red light of late afternoon lent emotion to the white marble statues which rim the amphitheater making them come alive with fluid grace. We wandered through the deserted streets looking over the baths, the market, a basilica, and other public buildings. Only as the light grew too dim for photographs or even for seeing did we reluctantly continue toward Tripoli.

By now we were driving through settled agricultural land. Petrol pumps and restaurants could be found in even the tiniest settlement. It was getting late and we were hungry so we stopped at a small Italian inn for food. There we also inquired about hotels in Tripoli and were told there were only two: the older, more expensive colonial edifice and the former officer's club.

In a mixture of Italian and English I was taking down directions to the latter when another customer in the restaurant, an Italian, said that he was also on his way to Tripoli and if we would care to follow his jeep he would show us the club. Gratefully we accepted his offer, for finding your way about a strange city at night is never easy, and Tripoli, with its 800,000 inhabitants is indeed a large city.

IT WAS AFTER ELEVEN when we finally checked in to former

club and were shown a tiny cubicle with double bunks, rather more like a shipboard tourist cabin than a proper hotel room. But the beds looked soft and the room clean, and after our four non-stop, non-bath days of driving fourteen hundred desert miles we were dead tired. We rushed our baths, and in moments were in bed. Hardly had we begun to doze when we began to hear loud noises from the lobby and bar. At first it was just loud talking, then drunken songs, then nasty, pitched argument, then softer but penetrating alcoholic whining. After several hours of this, I became furious, the more so because it was clear that the voices were American, undoubtedly pilots from the American air base near Tripoli. Over and over we rang for the room boy and told him to do something about the noise. This, of course, was futile. At length I trailed out, fire in my eye, and gave those sots a tongue lashing, all the more effective because I had forgotten my glasses and the whole party looked as blurred to me as I am certain I must have looked to them. This did the trick for at least ten minutes; then they were at it again, worse than ever. Mil went off to the manager; but why should he stop such a lucrative party for two transient guests? Mil asked for a room further from the bar but the manager insisted that the hotel was full. Then, as if the noise and the heat of the airless inside room were not enough, we both suddenly developed mild cases of dysentery. It was a horrible night; we thought of the empty open desert with nostalgia.

Eventually, I suppose we slept. When we awoke, we both had miserable headaches as if we ourselves had been roaring drunk. My temper was as vile as possible. I chewed out the management and demanded a room in the corner furthest from the bar into which we promptly moved. Then, still grumbling, we went out to attend to the usual chores. The car needed checking, checks needed cashing. At the Embassy we met empathy in the person of Wally Thompson. A sensitive man, interested in novel writing, he found the Foreign Service protocol only put barriers between officials and the people of the country; he too was leaving the service as soon as his tour was over. We had lunch with Wally and his wife Ruth at the American swimming club: authentic American hot-dogs. The hot-dogs, and most of the members, came from the Wheelus Air Force Base just outside the town where nearly ten thousand Americans, pilots with their wives and children, lived their suburban lives. We started a rather desultory discussion among the men eating at the large family-style table, but the weather was hot and the sea inviting. Wally took his children up the beach where the coral bottom attracted tiny fish and you could drift for hours, watching them through a face mask. Then Ruth took the children off to lessons while we tried their masks. Relaxed and refreshed by our swim in the tepid, glinting sea, our interest in the future of Libya revived.

Over beer we learned that the air force base contributed heavily to the economy of Tripolitania for America not only pays an annual rent of four million dollars but it also provides direct employment for two thousand men not to mention the house servants, vendors, merchants. "But more important," stressed a man from the Embassy technical assistance section, "the existence of the base gives America a stake in the country. Did you know that Libya receives more per capita aid from the United States than any other country in the world?" he asked. "Of course Libya is sparsely populated. It has only one and a quarter million people in an area a fifth the size of United States; still the various grants and aid and assistance come to twenty or thirty million dollars a year."

I scribbled in my notebook as an American from FAO put in a word about the aid other countries were also giving

Libya, directly and through the United Nations. "WHO, UNESCO, FAO, we all have projects here. I'm involved with advising several irrigation schemes meant to provide larger, more constant water supplies for agriculture. But really, a little water won't help much. The real key to solvency here lies in the discovery of oil. So eager is Libya to find the liquid treasure that eleven different companies have been licensed to search the vast hinterland."

Listening to the talk, it almost seemed like Somalia all over again, except that politically the Libyans appear to have evolved even less than the Somalis, perhaps because their independence was handed to them, thrust upon them, before they had even decided to ask for it. "The three parts of the country have no feeling of unity. The UN just put three eggs in one basket, not even the same kind of eggs," complained a vice-consul. "I wonder what will happen when they hatch. Everything will be subject to the same sort of rivalry that happens now over the capital. Darned expensive, this business of moving the capital city every two years between Benghazi and here. Worse is the waste of money by the old emir to build yet another capital at Beida in the Green Mountains near Cyrene. One day Fezzan will want a capital, too. Ridiculous, the whole country."

Everyone could list the problems; no one had the answers. "They have to help themselves," cried one. "We cannot go on subsidizing laziness and backwardness forever," spat out the air force colonel. "If we don't, the USSR will," countered the information officer. "Serve the Russians right, being saddled with this country," retorted the colonel. "It's the UN's baby," declared another. "Bottom's up." We toasted that, there seemed little else to say.

In the late afternoon our Italian guide and friend of the night before took us for a quick tour of the amazing jumble of cultures that is Tripoli. Not only is the city old and new, it is ancient Roman, antique Hebrew, ageless Arab, unimaginatively modern, rococo Italian-colonial, functional army. There was no war damage, as in Benghazi, for the town had been spared bombing. The only real change caused by the war, said the Italian, was that the British Army opened up the ghetto. Still the various races, particularly the Jews, tended to live their own lives in their own areas. He showed us the different quarters, but our weary minds and heavy eyelids could absorb little more than the kaleidoscopic patterns though I remember, as in a dream, seeing the carved top of a Roman marble column holding up an ordinary plaster house! After a delicious Italian meal at the city's best restaurant, courtesy of our Italian merchant, we returned to our bunks and to a blessedly quiet night.

FAR FROM RESTED, BUT at least awake, we checked out of the hotel about nine. The bill presented was for one night only and, still furious about the noisy night, I did not bother to correct the mistake. Instead, with great glee, I used that carefully budgeted money, one Libyan pound, for a dozen oranges and for a dainty pair of silver filigree earrings I had admired but resisted the day before. In a gamin mood we headed for the border.

The speedometer had clocked ninety-one miles from Tripoli when we came up to the small town of Zuara, control of post for leaving Libya. A collection of adobe offices clustered around a square and we found the customs man with no difficulty. He accepted the letters which we had brought from the customs officer in Um Saad with gracious thanks and quickly filled in and stamped our carnet. Relations could not have been more cordial until the passport officer came in. He was a younger man than the customs official,

but evidently outranked him. Immediately he picked up our
carnet and checked the entries, a sneer on his face. Then
he spied the letters from Um Saad and suspiciously read
through them all, cross-examining us as to the reason we had
them and reprimanding the customs officer for not having
brought them to him at once. Still flaunting his power, this
arrogant man demanded to see our passports. Slowly he
devoured the information therein; then with obvious pleasure he announced that we had no exit visa and so could not
leave the country. When we had checked in Tripoli, we had
been told that for persons in transit, staying in Libya less
than two weeks, an exit visa was unnecessary.

When we commented on this, the man accepted our
point with a shrug saying that in any case our passports
were out of order; we had no stamp showing our entry into
Tripolitania. We would have to go back to Gidda for that,
or at least get a clearance in Tripoli. I demanded to know
whether it wasn't true that Libya was a United Kingdom.
We clearly had entered Libya at Um Saad and intended to
leave at Zuara; surely the intermediate points were unimportant. That observation, said with considerable heat, drew
a fiery retort about the backwardness of the Senussi and how
modern Tripolitanians had been saddled with the Senussi's
feudal emir. I tartly remarked that at least the backward
Senussis knew to stamp the passport while the Tripolitanian
in Gidda had either forgotten or been too lazy to do it.

That tactless comment bristled the officer who causti-
cally noted that besides our lack of entry stamp our Libyan
visa itself was out of order because it had been issued in
Cairo by the Iraqi Embassy. It so happened that at that time
the Iraqi government was fulfilling diplomatic functions for
Libya wherever that young kingdom lacked its own representation. No one else had questioned the visas, and we

had passed four other check points. I said as much, getting more and more annoyed, particularly because I badly needed to get out to the desert again as my diarrhea had returned. Worse, I also needed to change my tampax. Gleefully the man pointed to the visa in my passport and showed that the ordinary Iraqi visa had had the word Libya written on it but in Mil's passport there was only the stamped visa which must therefore only be good for Iraq, not for Libya. It was obvious, of course, that this was a clerical error, but the passport officer, a satisfied grin on his face, reiterated that we could not leave Libya until we had returned to Tripoli and had the passport put in order.

The fact that we had diplomatic status made no impression on him even when I foolishly threatened to make trouble for him if he remained adamant, which he did, growing in arrogance as we argued. He was obviously enjoying his superiority to these foreign infidels. Back to Tripoli, was all he would say. It happened to be Friday, Muslim day of prayer; government offices all shut by 10:30 am and did not open again until Saturday. Going back to Tripoli would mean wasting a whole day of the precious time and money that we had left. I blew, I stormed, I called the man a bloody so-and-so, an epithet he unfortunately knew in the stronger, British sense. It was all I could do to keep from slapping his sneering face. If we had not entry stamp into Libya, then we needed no exit stamp, I declared, and reaching for our passports, tried to leave.

Mil had been mad enough at the passport official; now he was furious with me. Peremptorily he ordered me back to the car and warned me not to interfere again. As I sulked out I could hear the passport official telephoning ahead to the further customs check telling them not to let through a green

Austin with two Americans just in case we did try to leave before he was ready to let us go.

BROODING IN THE CAR I saw Mil and the official come out of the customs office and walk across the hot barren square to a larger office, that of the District Official. Still in a temper, I backed the car round, and raced to follow the men, almost running a man down and not caring a bit. Mil wisely ignored me, so I parked under some low evergreen trees, livid, practically in tears from a mixture of shame and complete exasperation, and in great physical discomfort. I finished a cigarette, and still the men did not come out of the office.

Desperate for something to take my mind off the situation, I took a camera over to the tiny market place where, surprisingly, everyone was eager to pose. Most of the men wore loose pajama pants under long open shirts, their dull dark clothes brightened by striped multi-colored vests and gaudy sashes. The boys often lacked one piece of the combination and wore just a shirt or a vest and short pants. All the males had the tiny skull cap on, ready for the mosque. The women also posed, face uncovered, but head and body swathed in two lengths of rough cloth, the one piece worn toga-like over a blouse, the other wrapped and draped as a large shawl. A few men wore the same burlap cloth as an extra toga over their other clothes.

I was rapidly recovering my humor when Mil called sharply across the square, saying to come at once. When I reached the car he said abruptly, "get in," and we drove off without another word. Only after we had passed the last Libyan check post did Mil thaw enough to tell me what happened. The District Officer had quickly sized up the situation as one of face for the troublesome passport official. After calmly listening to the man he had made a phone call, but

Mil had noticed that the phone was not connected! Apparently this was all for show. Then he instructed the passport official to give us the proper exit stamps because we were diplomatic. Obstinate to the end, the official kept muttering at Mil: your wife insulted me. Mil finally gave him two packs of cigarettes and an apology, noting I was always temperamental when I had my monthly illness. Still his hand was out for more. Probably that is all that he wanted in the first place.

A *ghibbi* blew up, appropriate to my temper, Mil said, and started calling me Ghibbi Rao. With his teasing, I knew I had been forgiven. Even so, the day had lost much of its charm; it is hard to recapture gaiety, especially in the midst of a sand storm. At least we were out of Libya, across the desert. Ahead lay only the well-kept roads of French North Africa. We had finished with Arab-Berber Africa; Tunisia, more than anything, is a European suburb.

CHAPTER 34

# *Tunisia reflects many centuries of colonizers*

THE *GHIBBI* BLEW ON TOWARD THE SEA, SWIRLING THE SAND
from the great interior erg and mixing it with sand
dunes on the coast. Beyond the storm we came upon a collection of neat white adobe buildings, bright with blue shutters: the Tunisian border control of Ben Gardane. The Tunisian officials, with their snappy uniforms and smooth French
accent, were politeness itself to Mil; I kept carefully in the
background. To prove that this was still Africa, the ragged,
unkempt soldiers at the barrier still begged for cigarettes and
Mil donated the rest of his pack.

AS WE DROVE ON across pebbly waste the road turned inland,
then split several times, each branch carefully sign-posted in
French, Arabic, and English. Sand still occasionally swirled

across the asphalt, but stone villages began to crown the hill-tops and look down over yellow grass fields. Women walking barefoot along the road still wound rough cloth into skirts, but the cloth was shades of red or orange, and draped to reveal most of the long sleeved blouses they wore beneath. Mil stopped the car and I bounded out to photograph one attractive female whose earth-red skirt was caught up with a fiery red bandana; her blouse was of bright green, patterned with what looked like printed coins of gold and silver. Her head was covered with a hive-like cap of deep red which covered her ears and made her large silver earrings flap out. She wore bracelets on her arms and ankles and walked with her head held high. When she saw me she stopped with a nod and posed as she was, calmly certain of her beauty.

As a brief holiday to cut our continuous driving, we turned right toward the sea in order to visit the island of Djerba. Near the coast olive trees and date palms sprouted form the sandy ground. Across the shallow bay we could see the island which since Roman times   when it was known as the Land of the Lotus-Eaters – has been connected to the mainland by a causeway. Camels were the only other traffic on the gravel road though locals fishing for sponge as well as fish used the way as a pier for their boats. As we crossed the flat island to the main market on the opposite side we passed women in yet another costume: deep blue woolen blankets with red borders swirled about them tied, it seemed, rather like an Indian sari with one end around the waist and the other drawn up and over the head. Their faces were bare until I tried to photograph them, then they held the loose ends modestly across their faces.

Closer to the town, however, the women let the blue covering fall from their shoulders and instead, like many of the men, worn white towels as head coverings. Thus we could study their features. And what a range of features there was! Djerba has long been a sort of backwash for the peoples of the mainland. Whenever a new conqueror overran Tunisia a few more refugees fled to the island. Carthaginians came there fleeing the Romans; early Jewish and Christian colonies fled the onslaught of Islam. For a time Normans from Sicily controlled the island and left a few strains of their blood. Then came Berbers and Spanish, and finally the Turks under whose suzerainty the whole coast of Tunisia became a pirates' paradise. In the nineteenth century Britain, France, and Italy all stepped in to control this piracy, so that modern European influence on the country and the island is also profound. Eventually, in 1881, the French established a protectorate over the area which was still in force when we were driving through.

Blood from all these races seems to have mingled there in Djerba; its culture was also a conglomeration of foods, dress, and architecture. We stayed at a small French inn which once had been an Arab mansion. The room boy claimed to be pure Berber, but his dark skin, shinny black against his loose white shirt, revealed a mixture of African blood. He took me to see his wife, a blue-clad figure with much stylish dark blue tattooing on her brown face. In the streets we dodged camels loaded with bundles of burlap, their nomadic owners fresh from the desert. The many bicycles were ridden by youth whose bare legs ranged in tint from pinky white to ebony. Most amazing were the donkeys: their Jewish riders seemed straight out of Biblical times with their flowing robes and white caps. Indeed this Jewish community on Djerba has lived there, unmolested since the days of Herod. Their synagogues contain relics which are the subject of pilgrimage for the newer Jewish groups in the coastal cities from Tripoli

Djerba: many religions, many modes of transportation

to Tunis. Most of the old group are content in their age-old ways but a few have emigrated to Israel where they are considered hopelessly old-fashioned. Nor has the Tunisian government pressured its Jewish citizens to leave, whether the antiquated Djerba Jews or the sophisticates of Tunis.

On Djerba, the Muslims favored red hats, shorter than fezzes and with no tassel, but the peasants merely covered their heads with towels or cloth or straw hats. All manner of things from straw were for sale in the market, some aimed specifically at the tourist trade. But the commodity for which Djerba is famous is blankets, subtly striped woolen blankets made soft with silk threads. The Bedouins use the blankets for their burnooses so the sizes are extra large. We chose a green, brown, and white combination that is so pretty we seldom cover it with a bedspread.

WE RELAXED THAT WEEKEND. Djerba seemed not only un-African, but positively European. The fact that the Tunisian nationalist party was agitating, sometimes with riots, for independence, did not detract at all from our sense of accomplishment. Now we knew we had finished the grueling challenge of our African adventure. We also knew that both of us were frazzled from the experience and badly in need of rest. We were not only tired and temperamental; we both still had annoying, if not serious, cases of dysentery. Once again we sat down with a calendar: we had two weeks left. Let's enjoy it the easiest possible way, we decided, slowly, by the most direct route.

I knew I would have no time to interview either the nationalist or French administrators and I doubted my French would have been good enough, anyhow. I did learn from the newspapers that the leader of the Neo Destour party, Habib Bourguiba, was once again in prison; party members were conducting a low level guerilla war to urge the French to leave. The guide book said that since 1881 the French had controlled international affairs for the country while state affairs were under the Bey. "Well, not all state concerns," I remarked to Mil. "Just like Shanghai, the French were judged in French courts but the locals appeared before an Islamic court. Not clear if we would be able to use the French courts if we were arrested, though, not like the Mixed Courts in Cairo." In 1935, the British had granted India control of domestic affairs so their leaders had many years experience running the country internally. In contrast, Bourguiba had spent nearly 20 years in French prisons while the traditional rulers had minimal control in Tunisia. And while the British introduced their civil law in India, their courts could be were used by all Indian citizens. Trying to compare these two forms of colonialism, I fell asleep.

We were slow enough getting off Djerba. After a lazy start we stopped several times to examine the glazed pottery which is also a specialty of the island. One little man was so eager to show us his small shop that we, in our new relaxed mood, spent an hour pumping his turn wheel, sipping tea, and buying several pretty little flower vases. Leaving Djerba on the west meant taking a ferry. Passengers crowded into small sailing dhows. Whenever an auto needed to cross, the owner simply laid tracks of wood across the seats! We shared our dhow with two camels and a donkey plus various owners and riders, all taking dates and vegetables to the mainland. The day was clear and calm, and the bay so shallow that you could almost walk across it. Still, we were not anxious for Bublee to take a swim: the car looked quite precarious sitting crosswise high above the bulwark amidships. Of course there were blocks under the tires, but any real rocking would have upset it.

SAFELY ON THE MAINLAND, we crossed over the main asphalted road going north to Tunis and drove inland toward the rocky hills toward Matmata. Once again I had been captivated by a note in the guide book which mentioned troglodytes. Mil was happy enough to take a detour just so long as we did not have to walk; no more Cleopatra's Temples for him! We passed more stone villages set, for protection, on the tops of the rolling hills. As the hills became steeper we came upon some fascinating villages whose brown adobe houses looked more like dozens of loaves of bread laid side by side than anything else I could think of. Perhaps these were the prototype of the Quonset hut! Further on, surrounding an elegant mosque, were houses of the same rounded construction, but two and three stories high. Clearly these Berber villagers were not the troglodytes we were seeking.

Only as the road wound up into the low mountains and the ground became too rugged for dry farming did we begin to see signs of the cave dwellers. Even these people were not the gnomes of my imagination. If their main home was a cave, each cave was fronted with a cottage of stone no more primitive looking than, say, an Irish cot, and some of them were a good deal fancier. There were no men to be seen; perhaps they tend sheep higher up the mountain side. The women all wore the blue Berber garb, but they also covered their entire face with a transparent veil so that their tattooing looked rather like decoration on the veil instead of on their face. They did not seem at all shy of me or my camera, and one young woman changes positions to show off the intricate tattoo on her hand which would have been the envy of many a sailor. Remembering the history of piracy in Tunisia I wondered whether the men did not cover themselves with impressive tattoos as well. And what better place for these pirates to hide than in mountainside caves? Unhappily, I could not communicate with any of the women; even my Arabic phrases made no impression. So I nodded my thanks and departed. Mil, in fine spirits, decided I needed a new name and began to chant the whole mouthful: Irene Shanti Ghibbi Rao Weariful Troglodyte Tinker-Walker.

Nearer the sea, on either side of the highway, were olive plantations looking well-tended and prosperous. Due to our snail's progress, it was already late afternoon: yet we could hardly camp in an olive grove We turned down a side road toward the sea, thinking that a tepid swim would be in concert with the mood of the day. Squatting on the beach like a discarded toy was an octagonal concrete pill box, used as a gun emplacement during the war. We promptly explored its empty dank interior, then set up camp in the lee of its walls.

From pill box to Tunis was a mere hundred miles; once again we dawdled. After a morning swim we rejoined the main road just outside of Sfax. The vast olive groves spread out on both sides of this ancient port, giving a clear idea of the source of the wealth of Tunisia. Then, as the road cut slightly inland, the groves changed to the more brilliant yellow-green of citrus trees. The whole scene was such a change from the desolate landscapes through which we had been driving the past months. No wonder that this area has been colonized and fought over by all the Mediterranean powers ever since Phoenician times. Add to the prosperity of the country its strategic geographical position astride the sea lanes, and much of the history of the area writes itself.

The marketplace in El Djem encompasses and ancient Roman coliseum El Djem

I was reading aloud from one of our books about the four hundred years of Roman rule when Mil interrupted with, "Ghibbi, look!" Directly ahead, dominating the horizon, was a tremendous coliseum which, from our distance, looked almost completely whole. As we drove closer we could see the brown village of El Djem clustered around this ancient monument looking like a visual extension of the granite structure. Only the rounded dome of the whitewashed mosque had any individuality in face of this overwhelming amphitheater. It seemed strange indeed to drive through the thronged marketplace right up to the walls of the coliseum. Being so incorporated into a town gave a sort of living quality to the place; here was not a ruin isolated with museum-like reverence as in Rome. I was not at all surprised to learn that the grounds inside were still used occasionally for political meetings. Unfortunately a sort of sunken runway in the center of the playing area made the amphitheater useless for sports; instead I had visions of tigers or lions being loosed on helpless prisoners.

At Sousse we neared the sea for a time. Here evidences of the most recent colonizers were everywhere. Modern apartment buildings dominated the outskirts of the city and French automobiles clogged the streets. Citroen seemed to have done particularly well, its V-shaped radiator symbol on its big and larger models outnumbered all other kinds, but there were also many of Renault's bug-like Quartre Cheveaux and occasionally one of those Citroen minimum cars that look like slices of tiny Quonset huts. Along the beaches to the north were tented swimming spas while roadside restaurants and cafés increased in frequency. The whole holiday area was thronged with French families making merry use of this vacation day; it was a saint's day, the garage attendant informed us, but whether Catholic or Muslim I was not able to find out.

Drawn by the thought of a leisurely French dinner, we stopped at one restaurant set on a hilltop overlooking the blue sea below. Unfortunately the meal was anything but restful; indeed we were frazzled by the chaos long before we were even served. Every French family seemed to have one child at each age group from one to ten, and all were crying and yelling at once. Perhaps it was merely European exuberance that was so startling, or the seeing of so many families at one time in a public place. You would not see Arabs or Africans or Indians in such circumstances; taking the family out for a holiday celebration is a Western phenomenon.

WE FLED FROM THE holidayers as soon as we could. Tunis was just a short ride up over a low mountain pass; cradled by the sea lay this glittering white city. The *medina* or native section of the city appeared more Oriental that Cairo in its atmosphere and buildings, perhaps because it is less contrived. The narrow, walled lanes were brightened by the blue tiles of the mosques with their square Moorish towers or the more usual rounded Arabic ones. In the *souk* I was fascinated by the metal craftsmen inlaying silver into bronze, gold into silver, bronze into copper. The large eating trays were lovely to look at but finances forced me to be content with one small ashtray. With a Tunisian student as guide, we toured the simple airy house of the old Bey whom the French had removed after the war as a collaborator but who now had become a hero. Since his death his home was opened to visitors as a sort of nationalist shrine.

That house and the student were as close as we came to meeting nationalist leaders. The French were obviously fighting a losing battle for granting Tunisia independence, and soon. Important nationalists found it prudent to remain in exile, knowing that jail cells had been reserved for them should they return. We had tried to visit Tunisian and Algerian leaders in Cairo, but though our contacts were good, we had been told that the important men were out of the country. I contented myself with a visit to the French department of information and came away with several glossy books boosting the glories of French colonialism and the French Union. Every Frenchmen we met concluded his arguments for the continuation of French government in Tunisia with the footnote that of course we knew that the most influential nationalist leader, Habib Bourguiba, had a French wife. Somehow this fact was supposed to clinch the positive values of the French assimilationist policies.

It was certainly true that the Tunisians we met were very French in their attitudes and mannerisms; Tunis, outside the *medina,* was very much a French suburb. In some respects the whole of Tunisia seemed a suburb of Europe. Perhaps that is why we could not get too excited over the independence movement: it was so civilized, so organized, and so certain of victory. One had few fears over the future of an independent Tunisia; we saved our emotional support for more the risky ventures we had encountered earlier on our road trip.

Mil was still very uncomfortable with his dysentery and spent several days resting in the hotel room, making all the arrangements for our ferry departure by phone. From Tunis boats that ordinarily carry cars go as far as Rome or Marseilles. We decided on the shortest and least expensive route, an overnight ferry to Palermo, Sicily, figuring that once we were back in Europe, we would no longer be seen as wealthy colonials and thus could go third class.

Getting out of Tunisia proved more difficult than getting in. The customs official at the ferry dock, proper in a grey woolen suit, demanded that we take everything off the roof and out of the car. His assistant, informally dressed in a loose red sports shirt, nodded in agreement. "Pas possible," I told them in lousy French which got worse as I became agitated at the idea of unpacking Bublee. But they began to laugh at my choice of words and decided, after Mil took down the trunk from the roof for inspection, that we could leave the empty jerry cans where they were and not pull out all the loose cans of food from the nooks and crannies of the boot. Still we had to pay 600 francs departure fee that we had not expected.

At last, the car repacked, we were free to go. As the ferry pulled out of the harbor we saw again the hill of old Carthage. So well had the Romans destroyed the city that only bits and pieces of columns mark the spot, dumped like so many gravestones between brilliant red and white flowers. Across the bay the scenic Cape Bon reached out into the Mediterranean, guarding the harbor. "Out of Africa" I thought, gazing with some nostalgia at the quickly receding city. Yet we had really been out of real Africa for some time though precisely when we left is hard to say. On the Nile River boat between Sudan and Egypt? Still those two countries meld into each other and had very nearly formed a federation. When we left Ethiopia? But Khartoum is more African than Addis Ababa.

Almost as if to prove the uselessness of such speculation, Sicily seemed hardly more European than Tunisia as we drove around the north rim of the island to catch another ferry from Messina to Reggio di Calabria on the mainland. Indeed, the French suburbs of Tunis exhibited the most modern Western buildings we saw until we got to Naples. The only real difference in the countryside scenes between North Africa and Sicily or southern Italy was in the skin color of the farmers, the laborers on the road, or the herdsmen. After two years of living and traveling in Asia and Africa, seeing European menials was something of a visual shock; imagine what a revelation it must be to the Indian or Kenyan who had been schooled in the White Sahib concept! How false such sights make any claims to racial superiority.

WE MADE OUR LEISURELY way up Italy's boot from its picturesque and pastoral south to its raucous industrial north. The twisting mountain roads in Calabria made our pace slow, but gave us ample time to absorb the lovely scenery, feudal castles on the rims of hills, colorful villages clinging to the steep cliffs. We saw few peasants in traditional dress: one sheep herder even wore a shiny old pinstripe suit. Yet in one tiny village the priests were carrying their local saint in a procession that wound through the town. Young girls in their white communion dresses followed the priests and would assist in changing the robes of the saint. The country people had dressed in their gayest clothes for the celebration. Not unlike Hindu processions in India.

We spent one night in Lauria at an inn unchanged for centuries; Richard the Lionhearted could have walked in for dinner and I would have not been surprised. In Pompeii we viewed the dead ruins of an even earlier era, nor did we miss the spectacular Amalfi Drive and a swim in the Gulf of Naples. By this time we were unrepentant tourists, if a second or third class type. We had both been Rome before; I even found the same cheap little students' restaurant off the Spanish Stairs where it was possible to eat well on nothing at all; we thoroughly enjoyed our four course meal and wine for 55 cents each. Who should just be leaving the restaurant as we arrived than the hotel manager from Wadi Halfa, Mr. Haylor, who morosely informed us that he still had not heard from the borrowing couple in the Bentley. We cheered him with coffee, and he cheered us with brandy at a near-by cellar.

After Rome, we drove on through Siena to Florence. Mil had developed a nasty infected boil under his arm and we had to look for a doctor. It was quickly treated, and we spent a happy two days in my favorite Italian town. In Zurich we celebrated Mil's birthday by taking two longtime friends, an American couple studying in the university there, to a delightful fondue dinner. That was Friday night, the 19th of June. Saturday we swam in the Lake of Zurich. Then, after another night on the floor of our friends' apartment, we drove through France toward the Channel, stopping to taste pleasant products of a winery and again to view the lovely cathedral at Rheims.

WE HAD PAID IN advance for the ferry across the Channel: I had five one pound notes from the exchange in Zurich to use for a room in London and to give us time to collect expected funds at the American Express office. Mil had exactly 1200 francs left after filling the tank for the last time. It had been raining most of the day so that the thought of sleeping out was not inviting. No longer embarrassed by our impecunity I went into a tiny pension in a small town near Calais and asked to proprietress what sort of dinner and room we could have for our remaining francs which I placed on the counter. Looking at us kindly, she fed us a hearty soup and provided us with a bed that was clean and dry.

Next morning we used Mil's warm shaving water to make up the last of our Nescafe for breakfast, then headed, with longing, for Calais. At the dock our tickets waited; the passage could not have been more routine to the officials. They knew nothing of our months of adventure, our efforts to reach this particular ferry on this particular day. They could not know my elation at seeing the White Cliffs of Dover, or of driving across Waterloo Bridge once more; Bublee's speedometer recorded our road trip from Mombasa as 12918 miles.

Two years before, in a Ford Anglia, I had driven across the Waterloo Bridge and away from London. In those two years I had crossed the Middle East and Africa by car, studied the elections in India, and found myself a most wonderful spouse. What a long, and short, two years it had been.

# Endnote

ONE YEAR LATER, ALMOST TO THE DAY, MIL AND I AND BUBLEE again crossed the Waterloo Bridge and headed for the Dover. In the intervening months our adventures had largely been of mind rather than body. Mil had returned to Washington. More disillusioned that ever about the morale and working conditions within the State Department, Mil resigned his job to return to academic life. Back in London, he studied Chinese at the School of Oriental and African Studies while I labored over my doctoral dissertation for the London School of Economics. It was an enchanting year, living in a charming one-room apartment on Highgate West Hill that in more gracious days had been the mansion's kitchen. We went to the theater or ballet or symphony nearly every week because tickets to these were cheaper than to movies. Student friends, especially those from Africa and Asia, thronged to our enormous open houses until they filled our converted kitchen and spread onto the grassy backyard. Insisting on equality, I would pressure these young men into kitchen duty, washing and drying dishes – tasks they had never done in their own homes.

It was an intense year: meeting politicians, scholars, and writers; absorbing, thinking, living. It was a successful year, but exhausting. In the backwash of achievement I lost my interest in coffee while the taste of cigarettes made me ill. Still the excessive smoking and drinking had spurred on the writing. The thesis was in and in my physical exhaustion my spirit danced: I had reached my goal –

I was a doctor of philosophy.

Determined to complete at least part of our tour of North Africa, we took the ferry to Europe and headed through France and Spain for Morocco. After Paris and Chartres, it was new ground for both of us so we progressed slowly, savoring the atmosphere, buying wines and cheeses in the village markets to make our picnic lunches almost party affairs. Nights we sought out three star hotels from Guide Michelin and reveled in the gastronomic fare. Thus we drifted through the lovely Loire Valley, admiring the chateaux and the prehistoric Lascaux Caves at Perigueux. We climbed the Pyrenees to Andorra then drove into a Spain still under the authoritarian dictatorship of Francisco Franco. Soldiers in olive drab were everywhere, but they waved at us as we drove toward the Costa Brava for a swim in the Mediterranean. Next day we drove to Barcelona. Here the soldiers were outnumbers by the police in dark green uniforms and triangular hats with a flap in back to protect their necks from the sun.

A Spanish graduate student at LSE had asked if we would deliver a letter and some money to his mother. He had been blacklisted by Franco and did not dare return home. Following his careful instructions, we navigated the lower middle class area of Barcelona and found the rundown apartment house where his mother lived. Suspicious at first about these strangers knocking on her door at duck, she immediately embraced me once she read the letter. Nothing would do but that we must stay for dinner. Clearly they were poor and the money from their son would keep the family for many months. She laboriously cooked omelets over a primus stove, one egg at a time, and served them cold with bread. We were no longer carrying tins of food and could not contribute to the meal. But watching her I did learn how to make a superb omelet.

The route from Barcelona to Gibraltar provided a tour of Spanish history with its Catholic and Arab influences. Visitors who have never seen real Arabic lands are often captivated by the oriental feeling of many buildings. Arabs, perhaps, find these rather European. We thought them an inferior mixture of the two. The tiny dressed statue of the Virgin in the ungainly railroad station of a church in Saragosa was to us as pagan as any Hindu temple. After the voluptuous angels in many of the cathedrals, the dignified calm of the old mosque in Seville was a distinct relief. Franco's grandiose mausoleum enshrined only his ego, to the country's sorrow. Still, the Prado Museum was an artistic experience: eating langoustine in drafty cellars was fun, and in one Madrid restaurant we went wild over paella, that ambrosial mixture of seafood and rice. All in all, we were not sorry to leave Spain. Except in small doses, tourist-ing is a poor substitute for studying a country.

From Algeciras we ferried to the International Zone of Tangier which was integrated into Morocco in 1956. We drove to Ceuta, a remnant of Spanish rule which remains an autonomous city under Spain. In 2005, Africans, seeking work in Europe, have descended on this one piece of Europe that has a land border with any African country and has turned the town into a fortress surrounded by barbwire. When we stopped the night, Ceuta was a charming hilly town overlooking the Mediterranean.

In 1954, Morocco was experiencing unrest from nationalists demanding an end to the French Protectorate. The French had exiled Sultan Mohammed V and outlawed the Istiqlal Party, but riots and violence continued to occur in the old walled sections of major cities. Only in Fez was I able to enter the *medina*, and that was by subterfuge. We were in a museum whose back gardens bordered on the carpenters' *souk*. A student I had been interviewing agreed to take me through the gate into the area forbidden to foreigners. We explored the covered markets for about a half hour before he suddenly pulled on my arm and rushed me out an exit: he had seen some men exchanging ominous glances.

After visiting Meknes we drove into the Atlas mountains before dropping down to Marrakech with its marvelous *souk* before continuing to Casablanca. Everywhere we stopped we talked to students and administrators, newsmen and Embassy staff. Our minds were filled with information, but the time was too short to do more than observe and listen about the nationalist movement. Nonetheless these experiences have added depth to our African road trip and our subsequent teaching.

Independence was granted to Morocco only two years later, in 1956. Taking the title of King, Mohammed exerted his own powers rather than let Istiqlal leaders to run the government. Currently Morocco is seen as a progressive constitutional monarchy with greater rights for women than other Islamic countries.

In Casablanca, we sent Bublee off on a cargo ship. Mil and I took the train and ferry to Gibraltar, which remains a British overseas territory, and embarked on a passenger ship to New York where we arrive long before the car did. After seeing our families in New York and Delaware, we drove Bublee to Berkeley, California. Mil enrolled at the University of California while I took up a research job with the Modern India Project. That winter, on a ski trip to the Sierras, Bublee collapsed.

Since then we have owned many more cars, visited many more countries, raised three amazing children, and taught in many universities. Our courses have been informed by our understanding of colonial practices we experienced in Africa and the nationalists we met on our 1953 road trip. Roots of many contemporary conflicts may easily be traced to problems we encountered during our road trip. My increasing outrage at the treatment of women that I observed laid the foundation for my passionate involvement in the global women's movement that has ameliorated women's lives around the world.

TODAY, AFRICA IS IN the news in print and on the internet. Debates center on which countries are failed states, where the UN Peacekeeping forces should be sent, and how to end the famine that continues to plague the region. As I read, I think back on the colonial attitudes and administration that we observed, the differing views of Africans themselves on how to prepare for independence, and how the actions of European and Asian settlers influenced the politics in the countries. In order of our visit, I list below some of current issues persisting in the countries through which we drove over fifty years ago.

~~~KENYA: AFTER INDEPENDENCE WAS granted in 1962, Kenyatta served as president for fifteen years. In 2007, riots broke out in Nairobi and the Rift Valley following elections for president. The Luo candidate Raila Odiga was leading in the polls until the incumbent president Mwai Kibaki, a Kikuyu, manipulated the results. Underlying causes of the riots were two: tribal rivalry for the spoils from control of the government, and land grabs by Kikuyu in land in the Rift Valley. Mediation by former UN Secretary-General Kofi Anna led to a power-sharing agreement whereby Odinga is Prime Minister and Kibaki is President. Note that Tom Mboya, the young Luo leader we met in 1953, was assassinated in 1969 by a Kikuyu.

~~~UGANDA: FOLLOWING INDEPENDENCE IN 1962, rivalries among the tribal groups and efforts to centralize the government provoked two bloody dictatorships by Milton Obote and Idi Amin. In 1972, Idi Ami expelled the Indians. The current president, Yoweni Museveni, has introduced "non-party" elections but tends to govern as a dictator. His tribal allegiances aggravated the dissention in the north of the country where the Lords Resistance Army continues to fight central rule, often recruiting children as sex slaves and soldiers after killing their parents. In 2008 the Kabaka was once again contesting his powers within Uganda. In March 2010 the old palace/tomb was burned to the ground.

~~~RUANDA-URUNDI WAS DIVIDED INTO Rwanda and Burundi when the two tiny countries became independent in 1962. Rwanda voted to abolish the Tutsi monarchy encouraging many Tutsi to migrate to Tanzania, the new name for Tanganyika when that country was united with Zanzibar and granted independence in 1964. A constitutional monarchy

was continued in Burundi which caused many Hutu to move to Uganda. Continued rivalry between the two ethnic groups in Rwanda led to the 1994 genocide. Currently the Tutsi guerilla groups continue to terrorize eastern Congo.

~~~CONGO HAS SUFFERED FROM the lack of educated leaders, the absence of trained Congolese administrators, and from the history of violence perpetrated by King Leopold. Mobutu Sese Seko seized power in 1965 and ruled as a corrupt dictator until 1997. He supported the Hutu in Rwanda and tried to force the refugee Tutsi fighters out of Congo. Uganda, Burundi, and Rwanda combined to force Mobutu out. Eastern Congo continues as a site of ferocious warfare. Meanwhile, countries surrounding Congo have coveted its mineral resource and supported provincial strong men.

~~~SOMALIA, ALSO LACKING EDUCATED leaders and experienced administrators, has become a scene of tribal wars, UN peace keeping efforts, and Islamic revival. Former British Somaliland has split off from the rest of the country and calls itself Puntland, a state unrecognized internationally.

~~~ETHIOPIA HAS ALSO SUFFERED under a series of army strong men ever since the Emperor was overthrown in 1974. Agriculture has withered and a series of major famines have ravaged the country. Attempts to dominate Eritrea led to a war between the two countries from 1961-1991. Skirmishes between the two countries continue, undercutting economic development in either.

~~~SUDAN GAINED INDEPENDENCE IN 1956 but had since been plagued by secessionist movements in south. The colonial

policy of keeping Arabs out of southern Sudan has made any united government difficult. The discovery of oil means that the north will never allow a separate state in the south. In the west, fighting in Darfur revolves around land issues between nomads and settled agriculturists.

~~~EGYPT IS STILL CONTROLLED by the military which holds sham elections periodically. US pours large amounts of money into the country in hopes President Hosni Mubarak will provide a moderating force between the Muslim Middle East and Israel that the US also funds.

~~~LIBYA'S POVERTY WAS ENDED with the discovery of oil in 1959. The corruption of the emir and his family led to the revolt in 1969 when a young Group Captain, Omar Gaddifi, seized control. His strong man rule has somewhat moderated in recent years as he seeks readmission to the international community.

~~~TUNISIA CONTINUES TO PROSPER as a country. The gradualism of Bourguiba allowed continued good relationships with France. Algeria, by contrast, was the scene of lengthy war because France considered that country a province of France, not a protectorate. The result has been a flood of Algerian French, and more recently Algerian Muslims, into France.